Mona Lisa

Contemporary Italy:
Politics, Economy and Society Since 1945
One Hundred Years of Socialism

Mona Lisa

THE HISTORY OF
THE WORLD'S
MOST FAMOUS PAINTING

DONALD SASSOON

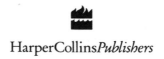

HarperCollins*Publishers*

HarperCollins*Publishers*
77–85 Fulham Palace Road,
Hammersmith, London w6 8jb

The HarperCollins website address is:
www.**fire**and**water**.com

Published by HarperCollins*Publishers* 2001
1 3 5 7 9 8 6 4 2

A catalogue record for this book is
available from the British Library

ISBN 0 00 710614 9

Set in Postscript Linotype Minion with Photina display
Typeset by Rowland Phototypesetting Ltd,
Bury St Edmunds, Suffolk

Printed and bound in Great Britain by
Clays Ltd, St Ives plc

To Anna and her smile

CONTENTS

ILLUSTRATIONS

27. *Self-portrait* (?), Leonardo da Vinci (1512–13? Biblioteca Reale, Turin). *Photograph © The Bridgeman Art Library*
28. The Countess of Castiglione (Musée d'Unterlinden, Colmar). *Photograph © Christian Kempf*
29. *Nana* by Edouard Manet (1877, Kunsthalle, Hamburg). *© Kunsthalle, Hamburg*
30. *La Jeune fille à l'oeillet* by Hippolyte-Jean Flandrin (1858).
31. Franz Hals, *La Bohémienne* (c.1630, Louvre). *© Gérard Blot/ Photo RMN*
32. *Bocca Baciata* by Dante Gabriel Rossetti (1859, Museum of Fine Arts, Boston). *Gift of James Lawrence, 1980.261. Courtesy, Museum of Fine Arts, Boston. Reproduced with permission. © 2000 Museum of Fine Arts, Boston. All rights reserved*
33. *Lise with a Parasol* by Auguste Renoir (1867, Folkwang Museum, Essen). *Photograph © The Bridgeman Art Library*
34. *La Vierge du chancelier Rolin* by Jan Van Eyck (c.1436, Louvre). *© C. Jean/Photo RMN*
35. *Mona Lisa with a Pipe* by Sapeck (Eugène Bataille) (1887, Jane Voorhees Zimmerli Art Museum, Rutgers, The State University of New Jersey). *Acquired with the Herbert D. and Ruth Schimmel Museum Library Fund. Photograph by Jack Abraham*
36. *L.H.O.O.Q.* by Marcel Duchamp. (1919, Philadelphia Museum of Art). *Photograph © Giraudon. © Succession Marcel Duchamp/ ADAGP, Paris and DACS, London 2001*
37. *Composition with Mona Lisa* by Kasimir Malevich (1914, State Russian Museum, St Petersburg). *Photograph © The Bridgeman Art Library*
38. *La Joconde aux clefs* by Fernand Léger (1930, Musée National Léger, Biot, Alpes Maritimes). *Photograph © Gérard Blot/ Photo RMN. © ADAGP, Paris and DACS, London 2001*
39. *Excelsior* announces the theft of the *Mona Lisa*, 23 August 1911. *Courtesy of Archivio Leonardismi del Museo Ideale Leonardo da Vinci, Vinci, Firenze, Italy*
40. *Domenica del Corriere*'s 'reconstruction' of the theft.

ACKNOWLEDGEMENTS

The ideas contained in this book were discussed at a pre-Christmas dinner in 1998 at the home of my friends Hilary Bowker and Bassem Abdallah. Initially, I had in mind a television documentary. Anna Coote suggested I turned the idea into a book. She was right, as usual. I also thank her for reading the first draft with understanding and firmness, and for her many valuable suggestions.

The outline of the book was 'tested' in the form of a lecture to the Italian Cultural Institute in London in September 1999. I am grateful to its director, Benedetta Bini, for organising the event and to the *History Workshop Journal* for publishing the lecture. The original idea of examining how a product of 'high culture' became an object of popular consumption occurred to me in 1997–98 while researching the history of cultural markets thanks to a Nuffield Social Science Fellowship.

I wish to thank the following friends and relatives for keeping me supplied with newspaper clippings, postcards and other documentation. I hope I have not forgotten anyone: Bill Birtles, Ruby Coote (for bringing to my attention the song 'Smooth'), Annie Davies, Beatrice de Gerloni, Ilaria Favretto, Jill Forbes (for help with Swinburne), Sara Galletti, Jamila Gavin, Natasha Gowman (for a Mona Lisa mandarin), Pia Locatelli, Silvana Seidel Menchi, Toby Mundy, Anne Showstack Sassoon, Joe and Doris Sassoon, Tanya Sassoon (for supplying a Mona Lisa fridge magnet and a tin for tobacco or similar substance decorated with a cannabis-smoking Mona Lisa), Valentina Tandelli, Sarah Tasker, Monica Threlfall (and for help with Ortega y Gasset), Gabriella Turnaturi, Laura Voghera.

I wish to thank my old friend Renato Mannheimer, Italy's

leading psephologist, for conducting on my behalf a survey on Italian perceptions of famous paintings; Deirdre Toomey for bringing to my attention some interesting literary references to the *Mona Lisa*; the Maison des Sciences de l'Homme and its Director, Maurice Aymard, as well as the staff of the Maison Suger (Paris) for their hospitality in July 1999 and July 2000; Madeleine Korn for helping me with slides, picture research and bibliographical information; the late Francis Haskell for bibliographical advice; my agent, Giles Gordon; my publisher, Richard Johnson, and editor, Robert Lacey, at HarperCollins; the ever-so helpful and courteous staff of the Bibliothèque Nationale of France, in particular those working in the audiovisual department; the staff of the British Library; the staff of the University of London Library; Eilis Rafferty, the Arts Librarian at Queen Mary, University of London; Brian, Jay and François of the computing advisory staff of the Faculty of Humanities at Queen Mary, University of London; the Faculty of Letters of the University of Trento, where I was a visiting professor in the first semester of the academic year 1999–2000 and where a considerable part of this book was written; Alessandro Vezzosi, the Director of the Museo Ideale Leonardiano at Vinci, and his staff for allowing me such generous access to their facilities.

I would not have been able to write this book without the facilities provided to researchers by the Louvre, above all by its excellent Service d'Étude et Documentation du Départment des Peintures. I wish to thank its Director, Jacques Foucart, and, in particular, Madame Marie-Thérèse Genin, whose efficiency and kindness were remarkable. I also wish to thank the staff of the Bibliothèques et Archives des Musées Nationaux, Musée du Louvre; Cécile Scailliérez, the curator responsible for the paintings of the Italian Renaissance (and hence of the *Mona Lisa*) at the Département des Peintures of the Louvre and Anne Krebs of the Service Culturel Études et Développement des Publics (Louvre), who have, with great courtesy and kindness, assisted me with their time and knowledge.

Acknowledgements

I am grateful to the following for permission to reproduce song lyrics: Warner Chappell Ltd for 'You're the Top' by Cole Porter, 'You and the Mona Lisa' by Shawn Colvin, 'Smooth' by Carlos Santana, and 'Wrap her Up' and 'Mad Hatters and Mona Lisa Part Two' by Elton John; BMG Music Publishing International Ltd for 'Mona Lisa' by Jay Livingston and Ray Evans; Peermusic for '3D Mona Lisa' written by Robert Charles Voice, © Peermusic (UK) Ltd. Every effort has been made to trace holders of copyright material, but I apologise for any omissions, which I will happily rectify in any future edition.

Finally I wish to thank the various *jocondologues* and collectors, above all Jean Margat, for keeping the Louvre archives so well supplied, greatly facilitating the task of scholars.

DONALD SASSOON
London, November 2000

CHAPTER ONE

Mona Lisa, the Smile and Lisa

A young woman is seated, her right hand upon her wrist, her left hand on the wooden arm of the chair, gripping its edge. The arm of the chair is parallel to the picture plane, as is the unseen lower part of her body. If she sat straight, we would see only her profile. But she turns towards us, presenting three-quarters of her upper torso. Her white visage faces us almost directly. Her brown eyes glance towards the right. Her missing eyebrows enhance her broad forehead. Her cheeks are full. Her hair, shoulder-length, is wrapped in a translucent veil. She wears a sober, dark dress. Her left shoulder is adorned by a thickly pleated mantle. Her neckline reveals the inception of her breasts.

She wears no jewels.

She smiles.

The loggia or balcony supporting her appears to be suspended on the edge of a chasm. Immediately behind her, at the back of the parapet surges a complex, strange and distant landscape: rocky formations, mountain peaks, hills and valleys; on the left a lake and a winding path; on the right a river crossed by a bridge, the forlorn sign of human existence in a barren landscape.

This is what is represented by means of oil paint on a piece of poplar wood. It is small: seventy-seven centimetres high and fifty-three centimetres wide. The Louvre identifies it by the inventory number 779, one of the six thousand paintings it currently holds. Only this one, however, is in a special container, set in concrete and protected by two sheets of bulletproof triple-laminated glass, separated from each other by twenty-five centimetres. The painting has been in this box since 1974.

It is inspected annually; the silica gel used to maintain the temperature is changed; the wood is checked to establish whether it has contracted or expanded.[1]

In 2003, in time for its presumed five hundredth anniversary, painting number 779 will have a room of its own. Until then it will be kept with the Venetian paintings, which comprise ten Titians, eight Veroneses including his gigantic *Marriage at Cana*, and five Tintorettos. Just outside, along the walls of the Grande Galerie, reputedly the longest corridor in Europe, are five paintings by Leonardo da Vinci, various Raphaels, Bronzinos, Correggios, Fra Angelicos and a marvellous Caravaggio. Further along, visitors can find Velázquez, Dürer, Van Eyck, Vermeer – not to speak of Rubens, Poussin, Rembrandt and Goya.

These works – among the most celebrated of Western art – can all be contemplated at leisure, even in the summer months when the season is at its peak, by any of the five and a half million people who visit the Louvre every year. All except number 779, known in France as *La Joconde*, in Italy as *La Gioconda* and everywhere else as the *Mona Lisa*. This is, allegedly, the portrait of a Florentine lady, Lisa Gherardini, the wife of Francesco del Giocondo, a wealthy merchant. She would have been addressed as 'Monna' Lisa, Monna being a contraction for Madonna (*mia donna*), or my lady. The spelling 'Mona' is erroneous, but has become established in English and I shall use it throughout.

The obstacle to anything remotely resembling a contemplative viewing of this portrait is the constantly shifting crowd (fifty and more during the summer) trying to catch a glimpse of it, and to photograph it. The reflection from the flashes of the cameras bouncing continually from the glass makes an examination of the work even more difficult. The unprepared visitor, upon entering the room and seeing the crowd, may well assume that the object of such commotion is not a painting at all, but some celebrity, a renowned personality from the world of the cinema, television, fashion or music, or a member a major royal household. The museum rule that there should be no more than thirty people before a single painting is disregarded. For other paintings, it is hardly necessary. Tourists, who are otherwise well-behaved and somewhat in awe of the museum, also disregard the prohibition to use flash photography. It is almost as if taking a picture of the *Mona Lisa* was one of the main purposes of their visit to Paris. This makes them prepared to defy the guards, who in most instances have given up trying to stop them.

No other painting receives this treatment. No other artefact in the Louvre is subject to such adoration and curiosity, not even the Greek statues known as the Venus de Milo and the Victory of Samothrace – though these share with the *Mona Lisa* the privilege, if that is the word, of having their position identified on all tourists' maps of the museum and being signposted throughout. No other major museum in the world possesses an exhibit that so overwhelms in popularity all others. Even Botticelli's *Birth of Venus* at the Uffizi in Florence, Rembrandt's *Night Watch* at the Rijkmuseum in Amsterdam, or Velázquez's *Las Meninas* at the Prado in Madrid do not have such status. Even the vault of the Sistine Chapel in the Vatican, Michelangelo's complex and grandiose work depicting the Creation, the Great Flood and the Last Judgement, does not outdo in the popular imagination the portrait of this soberly dressed and unknown woman.

Why is the *Mona Lisa* the best-known painting in the entire world? A simple glimpse at even some of her features – her silhouette, her eyes, perhaps just her hands, brings instant recognition even to those who have no taste or passion for painting. Its commercial use in advertising far exceeds that of any other work of art.

Art historians, poets and admirers have tried to explain the commanding place that the *Mona Lisa* has in our cultural life with reference to criteria intrinsic to the work. There is something, they argue, *inside* the painting that speaks to us all, that unleashes feelings, emotions and recognition. This idea originated with the Romantics at the beginning of the nineteenth century, though it had precedents. It is still the position of many modern and even 'post-modern' art critics.

The art historian Kenneth Clark, writing in 1973, could not accept that the *Mona Lisa* was famous for reasons other than its inner qualities. There are millions of people, he explained, who know the name of only one picture – the *Mona Lisa*. This, he argued, is not simply due to an accident of accumulated publicity. It means that this strange image strikes at the subconscious with a force that is extremely rare in an individual work of art. Ancient symbols come from the subconscious and continue to touch it. *Mona Lisa* is a comparatively recent creation that has the magical power of a very ancient one.[2]

Clark's conception of art history is now regarded as somewhat old-fashioned. This is not the case with the 'post-modern' Paul Barolsky, who in 1994, seeking to explain what it is about the *Mona Lisa* that 'holds us in thrall', pointed to Leonardo's remark-able technique, which creates a sense of texture and depth.[3] The painter, he added, rendered the 'inwardness of the sitter, the sense . . . of her mind or soul, her *animus*'. This was achieved by the power of her smile and her glance. Her serene smile places her in a position superior to that of the viewer. We look up to her. Her superiority is intensified by her position with respect to the landscape. Although the hills and the mountains are much larger than she is, Mona Lisa appears to be in a commanding position. Though small, it is, as has often been remarked, a monumental picture. For Barolsky, as for many nineteenth-century commen-tators, 'her gaze is as intense as that of a divine personage. No wonder the *Mona Lisa* has on occasion been called a secular *Madonna*.'[4] The dominant position of this particular painting in our culture is thus explained in a simple yet highly suggestive way: Mona Lisa is dominant because she dominates the viewer. She gazes at us more than we gaze at her. We are more the subject of her attention than she is of ours.

Anyone who has spent several hours looking at the crowd looking at the *Mona Lisa* might be tempted to agree. Inside her box, protected by glass and bodyguards, she appears to have a serenely ironic detachment from the strange behaviour of her visitors, and their scrambling for a better viewing position.

I think one should avoid succumbing to the charm of a myth, to the idea that inside every masterpiece that has remained alive for centuries something imponderable speaks to us as it has spoken to the previous generations. It is of course intensely pleasurable to imagine that, as we face the products of Leonardo, Raphael and other great artists of bygone ages, armed with nothing but our 'innate' artistic sensibility, or as we sit in a concert hall, alone though in a crowd, and listen to the notes of the 'divine' Mozart, a mysterious yet almost palpable contact is established. The dead Master is alive, and speaks to us, to me, directly, unmediated, his greatness confirmed once again because I, so different, so distant, separated by class, race, language, and above all by time, communicate directly with this great creator.

However, many of those who stand before the *Mona Lisa* or other famous artefacts are left a little disconcerted. By the conventions of the twentieth century, she is neither beautiful nor sexy. The painting is not grandiose, or politically inspiring, like Delacroix's *Liberté guidant le peuple*, for example. There is no gore, no violence. It does not tell a story. Just a plain woman smiling, perhaps.

The remarks one hears by observing, over a period of weeks, those who observe her (or it) reveal a deep frustration. While they accept that a special skill has been deployed to produce the famous portrait of the Florentine lady, denied the intellectual and cultural means of contextualising it, deprived of reference points that would make the experience more interesting, they may wonder, 'Why her?' Why should such an incredible fuss be made over such a comparatively tiny painting.

There are works of art that appear to be universal, in the sense that they are still loved, enjoyed, and consumed centuries after their conception. They awake instant recognition in millions throughout the world. They speak not only to their own time – the relatively small audience for whom they were originally conceived – but to worlds beyond, to future generations, to a mass society connected by international communications that their creators could not suspect would ever come into being.

It is precisely because such universal appeal cannot be separated from the system that amplifies great works and gives them resonance that one should question the idea that the success of artistic works lies only, or mainly, within the work itself. The Western origin of so many masterpieces suggests that they need, for their global development, appropriate political, ideological and technological support.

These views are unexceptional. Mozart was, we know, revered not only in Vienna, but also in Paris, London and Prague. He would not be as widely known as he is today without the invention of recording equipment, film music, advertising jingles, and plays and films about his life. Mozart would not be 'Mozart', the great universal artist, without adequate technical and marketing support.

Resistance to the idea that masterpieces need marketing is understandable. The word, unpleasant as it is, suggests a kind of conspiracy. It conjures up a group of individuals who, for financial or political gain, decide to make products or persons better known and admired than they would otherwise have been. It suggests that people can be manipulated, their taste determined, and that the most banal artefact can be transformed into a world masterpiece.

I don't believe it. Marketing people take what is already famous, and may make it more famous still. They consolidate, but seldom innovate. Like most historians, I start with the assumption that the renown of masterpieces rests on a complex, historically determined sequence of events, the participation of various historical agencies (people, institutions, processes) working in a largely unplanned or unconscious manner for different ends. I propose to explain how such forces have turned the *Mona Lisa* into the best-known painting in the world. This book tries to answer the question of how one work wins the competition for artistic fame.

Whether the *Mona Lisa* 'deserves' this position is a judgement I happily leave to the reader. My task is to explain why certain things occur, and others don't. It is not my business to establish whether some things are better than others, and why.

By the nineteenth century, the *Mona Lisa* was already part of an artistic canon established by a cultural elite. In the twentieth century what had been known and seen by a few became the property of millions. The development of the mass media, magazines, cinema, radio, television, and the concomitant expansion of the advertising industry have diffused to an unprecedented extent this high culture – and, in so doing, have changed it. The cinema and television have relentlessly plundered the repertoire of fiction – especially nineteenth-century fiction – either directly, by adapting Victor Hugo and Balzac, Jane Austen and Charles Dickens, Manzoni and Melville, Tolstoy and Goethe, or by borrowing their plots and narrative structures.

Advertising provided a new audience for many of the great masterpieces of the Renaissance, the impressionists and the post-impressionists, modern art from Picasso to Dali and Warhol, and, duly transformed into advertising jingles, snatches from Mozart, Bach, Verdi, Rossini and Beethoven.

The worldwide renown of the *Mona Lisa* makes it part of popular culture. Yet it is, unquestionably, the product of high culture: painted by one of the great masters of the Renaissance, bought by the King of France, held in the most famous museum in the world in one of the great cities of the world.

It has stood the test of time. In 1568 it was regarded as a masterpiece by Leonardo's near contemporary, the painter and historian Giorgio Vasari: 'Looking at this face, anyone who wanted to know how far nature can be imitated by art would understand immediately ... all will acknowledge that the execution of this painting is enough to make the strongest artist tremble with fear.'[5] Four and half centuries later it was hailed by the art historian Ernst Gombrich: 'Like a living being she seems to change before our eyes and to look a little different every time we come back to her . . . All this sounds rather mysterious, and so it is; that is so often the effect of a great work of art.'[6]

Those who bewail the forthcoming end of civilisation and high culture should take some comfort here. A work of art with impeccable cultural credentials winds up also being the most popular. For it is the most popular. A survey conducted in Italy for this book by the Istituto per gli Studi sulla Pubblica Opinione in February 2000 revealed an even higher degree of popularity than anticipated – and in a population surrounded by some of the greatest and best-known works of art in the world.[7] To the 'open', i.e. unprompted, question 'What do you think is the best-known painting in the world?', a staggering 85.8 per cent of those who answered (i.e. excluding the don't knows) said the *Mona Lisa*. Second, with 3.6 per cent, was Van Gogh's *Sunflowers*; third Botticelli's *Spring* (2.1 per cent); fourth Munch's *Scream* (2.01 per cent).

A survey conducted among art students in France in 1974 asked them to choose 'the best' out of ten selected paintings. The *Mona Lisa* had been excluded to avoid distorting the response. This time, without Leonardo, Van Gogh made it to the top, followed by Picasso and Goya.[8]

In 1984 the magazine *Paris-Match* asked its readers to select their favourite Louvre painting from a list prepared by the personnel of the museum. The *Joconde* topped it, followed by Raphael's *Baldissare Castiglione* (whose pose was inspired by that of the *Mona Lisa*).[9] In 1989 the Hamburg daily the *Hamburger Abendblatt* commissioned a survey of people's favourite painting: 32 per cent of respondents put the *Mona Lisa* first, followed by Carl Spitzweg's *Der arme Poet* (The Poor Poet, 1839), a funny picture of a man in bed with an umbrella protecting him from a leak in the ceiling (27 per cent) and Dürer's *Feldhase* (The Hare, 1502).[10]

'Where is the *Joconde*?' is the most frequently asked question at the information desks of the Louvre, according to a survey conducted on 6 February 2000. The question was asked seventy-six times. It was followed by the existential 'Where am I?' (fifty-three times). 'Where is the Venus de Milo?' was asked once. No other enquiries were received for a specific painting or sculpture.

The renown of the *Mona Lisa* has brought great prestige to a museum that already has enormous status. This global craze – whose origins and development I will map out – confers upon the Louvre some advantages, but also poses some problems. The advantages are obvious. The fame of the *Mona Lisa* attracts to the Louvre people who would otherwise never go to a museum. Once inside, having paid the substantial entrance fee, the hope is that they will look at other exhibits.

The problem for the Louvre is that the transformation of the *Mona Lisa* into an icon of popular culture forces the museum to devise appropriate strategies and responses. To have a painting whose fame outstrips all the others to such an extent vexes the professionalism of curators. While they may think that some works are better than others, they do not like the idea that there is such a thing as the 'best' painting, as if art history were a tournament like the World Cup. What also irks them is that they have lost control of the *Mona Lisa*. Modern museums, usually heavily subsidised institutions, are accountable to politicians. In practice, the politicians are quite happy to delegate this kind of power to experts; they do not interfere with decisions on where to hang a Vermeer or a Rubens, or how to spend money on new acquisitions. But when it comes to the *Mona Lisa*, things are different. The painting, though extremely fragile, was sent, for political reasons, to the United States in 1963 and to Japan in 1974, against the wishes of all the Louvre's experts. The French government won the day only on the condition that it would never be taken away again (there is also an international agreement not to send abroad works painted on wood). But what can be done can be undone. The *Mona Lisa* may have been around for five hundred years, but democratic politics is short-termist.

The *Mona Lisa* cannot be treated like a 'normal' masterpiece. It is exhibited in a special box. All the normal maintenance work which is carried out on a painting must be done, in this case, in such a way as never to remove it from public view. Tuesday is the Louvre's closing day, so any work on the *Mona Lisa* has to be carried out between Monday evening and early on Wednesday morning. The risk of upsetting tourists who have come to see it from distant places is too great.

The *Mona Lisa* cannot be restored. It looks as if it cannot even be cleaned. It is actually quite dirty, partly due to age and partly to the darkening of a varnish applied in the sixteenth century. In 1988 the art critic Federico Zeri urged a thorough cleaning of the painting. The enigma of the *Mona Lisa*, he claimed, was due to its dark tints. With the colours restored, the enigma would dissolve.[11] However, no curator – so far – has wanted to run the risk of ending up in history as the person who wiped the smile off the Mona Lisa's face.[12]

The crowds are such that it has become necessary for the *Mona Lisa* to have her own room. Those curators who wanted the painting to be placed alongside the other works of the Italian Renaissance as if it were a 'normal' masterpiece lost out, as have those who had hoped for a Leonardo room. Lisa's room has been funded by the Japanese network Nippon Television (NTV), sponsor of the 1982–85 restoration of the Sistine Chapel, to the tune of £2.5 million: a further sign, should one be required, that the charms of the *Mona Lisa* are truly global.

The idea is not new. On 29 December 1938, during a parliamentary debate on the French arts budget, Senator Jean Bosch suggested that the *Mona Lisa* should have its own separate room. He pointed out that the painting attracted foreigners like a magnet, and that all the Cook's tours took them to see it. The idea was examined again after 1991. The scheme that finally prevailed was to reduce the size of the Salle des États, leave there the Venetian works and create a new room behind Veronese's *The Marriage at Cana*. Visitors will be able to proceed from the lifts to Lisa and back again without ever walking down the Grande Galerie, or ever seeing the five other Leonardos.

The Louvre and the French Ministry of Culture have played an integral role in the development of the *Mona Lisa* industry. The excellent database of all paintings in state museums is called *Joconde*; as is the Louvre's magazine. On the museum's website the icon you are asked to double click for information on the picture galleries' collections is an effigy of the *Mona Lisa*. Even the Café Muffin, under the Louvre Pyramid, has a poster of Mona Lisa holding a muffin.

The visitors who jostle before the painting know that they are there because it is the most famous work of art in the world. Few of them know why. Many think it has something to do with the mystery of the *Mona Lisa*'s smile.

This 'mystery' originated in the nineteenth century. Previously, the almost imperceptible smile attracted little attention. It was not regarded as enigmatic or mysterious. Giorgio Vasari, author of the first commentary on the *Mona Lisa* (in *Le Vite de' più eccellenti Architetti, Pittori, et Scultori Italiani*, 1550), noticed it, but provided a prosaic explanation in the form of a much-quoted anecdote: musicians, clowns and other performers had entertained the sitter while Leonardo painted her.[13] Lisa smiled because she was amused. In any case, smiles are not infrequent in Renaissance paintings, and they also abound in Greek statues. The works of Leonardo's own teacher, Verrocchio, often represent smiling faces of great subtlety. Donatello produced such smiles decades before Leonardo,[14] and Antonello da Messina, who allegedly introduced the Italians to the use of oil, painted a beautiful portrait of a smiling man who looks directly towards the spectator (see plate 2).

We do not know the origin of his mischievous smile, and few appear to care. Is this because da Messina is not as renowned as Leonardo? Is it because (usually male) commentators are not intrigued by a man's smile? Is it because the portrait of the 'unknown man' hangs at the Museo Mandralisca in Cefalù, in far-away and peripheral Sicily, and not in the heart of Paris? And if artist and place are determinant, why has attention not been directed towards other Leonardesque smiles? These are far from rare. At the Louvre, Leonardo's *La Belle Ferronnière* may be unsmiling, but his *Bacchus*, his *St John* and his St Anne glow happily a few feet away from the *Mona Lisa*, and the portrait of Cecilia Gallerani (a mistress of Leonardo's patron Lodovico Sforza) smiles from the Czartoryski Museum in Cracow).

What is really unusual in Renaissance paintings is a sad face. Leonardo did paint one of those: the *Ginevra de' Benci* (c.1475, see plate 7), whose dejected face can be seen in Washington. Yet what saddens the beautiful Ginevra has not generated a fraction of the interest that there has been in Lisa's smile.

By the very artifice of its origin, the mystery of the smile is open-ended. There is no way of satisfactorily resolving it. It may endure for as long as there is interest in the painting. Smiling, after all, is a mundane way of presenting oneself to the world. We smile when we meet someone, when we wave at somebody we know. We smile to our children, friends and loved ones. Politicians smile when campaigning, singers when singing. Variety dancers grin broadly, as do television presenters. Smiles are virtually mandatory whenever a snapshot is taken.

Any visual representation of an emotion necessarily leaves open the question of its cause, unless it is included in the representation. There is no mystery in the countenance of a woman in tears if the artist represents her holding a dead child. But, almost by definition, the illustration of an emotion separated from its cause enables the viewers, if they so desire, to speculate freely. It is what is called an 'open' work, that is a painting (or a text, or a piece of music) that allows the recipient/interpreter (the viewer, reader or listener) to determine its meaning.[15] Although viewers have considerable leeway in deciding what is being represented, this freedom can be restricted by the author's contextualisation of the work. In other words, no work is ever totally open (or totally closed). A painting called – say – *Portrait of an Unknown Mother* is far more 'open' than one labelled *Virgin Mary with Child*. Viewers aware of a work's symbolic and iconographic contents will find their interpretative freedom restricted: they would not be able to avoid accepting that what is being represented is not just any woman with her child, but the mother of the incarnation of the Christian God. Western art has moved away from such relatively closed texts towards so-called 'polysemic' works, works open to a plurality of meanings. A Jackson Pollock, for example, gives us more freedom of interpretation than does the Annigoni portrait of Queen Elizabeth II. The *Mona Lisa* can be regarded as one stage in the development of Western art towards the emancipation of the artist – and hence of the viewer.

Viewers facing a relatively open text confront two possibilities. They can utilise to the full their freedom to decide their own interpretations. Alternatively, if faced with too great a range of possible meanings, or simply unwilling or unable to make the effort, they can abdicate their freedom of decision in favour of a meaning established by a recognised elite of decoders (or art critics) who do the work for them.

The *Mona Lisa* 'smile' is produced by barely raising the left corner of the mouth. Leonardo himself, in his *Treatise on Painting*, says that the 'person who laughs raises the corners of his mouth' – as every child who has drawn a beaming face knows.[16] Laughs – as opposed to smiles – are rare in Renaissance paintings, and are never used when depicting the aristocracy and the upper classes. Mona Lisa does not laugh; she exercises restraint and decorum. A smile can be regarded as an understated laugh, as the French word, *sou-rire* – 'under-laugh' – and its Latin etymological root, *subridere*, suggest. In the highly codified world of fifteenth-century Italian court life, smiles were not left to personal initiative. Numerous books were available for those who wished to be instructed in the proper code of behaviour. The most significant was Baldassare Castiglione's *Il Cortigiano* (The Courtier), published in 1528 and – as Italian manners were regarded as a universal model to be followed – later translated into English (1561). Castiglione advised his readers to steer away from

> affectation at all costs, as if it were a jagged and danger-
> ous reef, and to practise in all things a certain – to use
> a novel expression – *sprezzatura* in order to conceal all
> artistry and make what one says or does seem uncon-
> trived and effortless.[17]

Sprezzatura means, literally, disdain and detachment. It is the art of refraining from the appearance of trying to present oneself in a particular way. In reality, of course, tremendous exertion went into pretending not to bother or care. Such celebration of the understated did not last long (it reappeared much later, and briefly, too briefly, among the English bourgeoisie), but it was still being promoted in the middle of the sixteenth century by the Italian writer Agnolo Firenzuola (1493–1553). His treatise on feminine beauty and behaviour, *Della perfetta bellezza d'una donna* (On the Perfect Beauty of Woman, 1541), was well known even three centuries later: the Swiss historian Jacob Burckhardt, whose *The Civilization of the Renaissance in Italy* (1860) provided the decisive interpretation of that period, devoted more space to Firenzuola than to Leonardo or Michelangelo.[18] Firenzuola suggested that the art of restraint and understatement should include smiles. One should never display, he wrote, more than six upper teeth (which should allow for a fairly broad smile).[19] Ladies should close the right side of the mouth while suavely and briskly opening the left, as if smiling secretly. This is so close to what the *Mona Lisa* appears to be doing that it is possible that Firenzuola had this portrait in mind when he proffered his advice.[20]

The *Mona Lisa*'s smile is now so famous that it is almost impossible not to see it. As Ernst Gombrich wrote, 'descriptions can be adhesive. Once we have read and remembered them, we cannot help finding the picture subtly changed.'[21]

Twentieth-century art historians, in spite of the continuing popular interest in the matter, left the business of the Mona Lisa's smile to amateurs and concentrated on the pose, which produces the idea of movement; on the technique, which provides a sense of depth; on the history of the painting; and, in particular, on the identity of the sitter. The smile, though the most remarked and famous feature of the *Mona Lisa*, is never seriously discussed by art historians today.

The first serious analysis of the smile, as opposed to a simple signalling of its presence (Vasari) or a definition of it as enigmatic, is a 1933 study by Raymond Bayer, *Léonard de Vinci: La Grâce*. A smile, Bayer points out, can light up a whole face. It is a play of cheeks, chin, eyes. It is a question of light.[22] The smile of the *Mona Lisa* is a half-smile, *un sourire attenué*. Cover the top of the face, suggests Bayer, and the smile of the mouth is more in evidence. Cover everything except the eyes and the smile is present in them, but only by taking the eyes as a whole. The pupils do not smile. The look has no spark. It is mournful, meditative. Concentrating on individual parts of the face, he points out that the lower lip protrudes a little, taking the light, while the mouth remains closed; hence the hint of disdain. Thus, he suggests, a multiplicity of readings is made available, perhaps the basis for the painting's success with posterity.[23]

The mystery of the smile is a manufactured one. Other mysteries are not. When and where did Leonardo paint the *Mona Lisa*? Who is she? Who commissioned it? Why did Leonardo keep the painting? How did it end up in the collection of the French king, François I – and hence of the French state?

It is equally perplexing that among the thousands of preparatory sketches, studies and drawings Leonardo left behind, there is not a single study for the *Mona Lisa* – though the ever-hopeful pretend to discern in a drawing of a pair of feminine hands in the Windsor collection of Leonardo's drawings those of the *Mona Lisa*.[24]

This uncertainty contributes to the enigma and the magic surrounding the *Mona Lisa*, and hence to its popularity. Since the development of art history and art appreciation as distinctive fields of study – that is, since the nineteenth century – scholars and writers have tried to find answers to questions surrounding the *Mona Lisa*. In the twentieth century, when the celebrity of the *Mona Lisa* reached global dimensions, novel hypotheses concerning the history of the painting (including old, forgotten ideas recycled as new) received a greater share of media coverage than similar historical debates over other important Renaissance paintings. Each 'solution', widely reported, encouraged others to join the fray. Mysteries sell. Yet those pertaining to the *Mona Lisa* are far from unique or unusual. A considerable number of Renaissance paintings have equally recondite origins. At least, in the case of the *Mona Lisa*, it has never been seriously doubted that the Louvre portrait was painted by Leonardo. This is hardly the case with the other Leonardos of the Louvre. The Baedeker guide to Paris of 1914, reflecting conventional views of the time, thought that the *St Anne with Virgin and Child* (plate 5) and the *St John* (plate 4) were painted with the help of pupils, that the *Belle Ferronnière* (plate 9) may have been by Boltraffio, and that the *Bacchus* (plate 3) was a copy of a lost painting.[25] The *Mona Lisa* alone has always received an uncontested attribution.

The identity of the sitter did not perturb nineteenth-century writers. They assumed that Giorgio Vasari's account was correct. He identified her as Lisa, daughter of Antonmaria di Noldo Gherardini and wife of Francesco di Bartolomeo di Zanobi del Giocondo, hence the designation of '*Gioconda*' ('*Joconde*' in French). This account came under question only in the twentieth century. One of the first to challenge it was André-Charles Coppier, a distinguished engraver of the *Joconde* (his print is still being sold at the Louvre) who thought the sitter could not be an ordinary Florentine wife, but was in fact an idealised person.[26]

The identity of a sitter matters to art historians in so far as the reconstruction of the history of any work of art is central to their discipline. From the point of view of aesthetic appreciation it matters very little. A new identification has no impact on the beauty of the *Mona Lisa*, the originality of its setting, the ingenuity of the technique used, the innovative pose, the intriguing connection between the human figure and the landscape behind. Public interest would not be modified significantly if it were to be discovered that Lisa Gherardini was not the model for *Mona Lisa*, though the persistence of the quest for the 'real' Gioconda helps to keep the painting in the public eye.

The more we probe into the past, particularly the distant past, the less we can be certain about questions of identity and attribution. The *Mona Lisa* is no exception. When the sitter for a portrait is a powerful person – a sovereign, an aristocrat or a wealthy patron – identification is relatively easy. Besides, painters were usually hired for a particular purpose. Contracts were signed, archives were preserved, records kept. Those who commissioned the painting retained the finished product. It became part of the family possessions, recorded, listed in wills and, when sold, the subject of written contracts. In most instances it is perfectly possible to produce an account of the vicissitudes of artistic products: when they were painted, by whom and for whom. Problems of identification occur when the sitter is not well known and, above all, when the artist keeps the portrait – which is what Leonardo did with the *Mona Lisa*, thus unwittingly facilitating the development of a mystery.

It was unusual for a painter to keep a portrait, but then Leonardo was an unusual painter. While he drew a great deal, he painted very little, and kept for himself a disproportionate amount of his own production, unlike his Renaissance rivals Raphael and Michelangelo.

Much of what was known about Leonardo in the nineteenth century was based on the main source on the life of Renaissance painters and artists, Vasari's *Le Vite de' più eccellenti Architetti, Pittori, et Scultori Italiani* (1550; a larger edition was published in 1568). Born in 1511, Vasari was eight when Leonardo died, and started his *magnum opus* around 1540. This monumental work, 800,000 words long, is the most important book on the history of art ever written, providing a biographical account of the lives of some 160 artists. Vasari gave pride of place to his Tuscan countrymen. Beginning with the 'childhood of Italian art' (Cimabue and Giotto), he proceeded to cover the fifteenth century (Brunelleschi, Donatello, Masaccio and Piero della Francesca) before reaching what he regarded as the apogee, the era of Leonardo, of Raphael and, above all, of the 'divine' Michelangelo, 'he who ranks above all the living and all the dead and transcends and surpasses them all'.[27] Accordingly, Michelangelo is dealt with in seventy-five-pages, Raphael twenty-two, and Giotto fourteen. Leonardo ranked fourth, with ten pages.

Vasari's description of the *Mona Lisa* was probably written in 1547.[28] Leonardo had been dead for twenty-eight years, Francesco il Giocondo for eight. Lisa Gherardini was still alive. Vasari lived in Florence on and off between 1524 and 1550 and stayed at the Medici palace, not far from the home of Francesco and Lisa. It is possible that he knew them both, and that they were the source of some of his information.[29] Given the paucity of solid evidence concerning the identity of the painting's sitter, Vasari's version is the least unreliable. This short passage is almost the entire body of sixteenth-century evidence we have on the *Mona Lisa*. Here it is, in full:

> Lionardo undertook to paint the portrait of the wife of Francesco del Giocondo, Monna Lisa. He worked on this for four years, but did not finish it. The work is now at Fontanableò with King Francesco of France. Looking at this face, anyone who wanted to know how far nature can be imitated by art would understand immediately, for here even tiny details were reproduced with artistic subtlety. The eyes were sparkling and moist as they always are in real life. Around them were reddish specks and hairs that could only be depicted with immense subtlety. The brows could not be more natural: the hair grows thickly in one place and lightly in another following the pores of the skin. The nose and

its beautiful pinkish and tender nostrils seem alive. The mouth, united to the flesh-coloured tints of the face by the red of the parting lips, seems of real flesh and not paint. Examining very intensively the hollow of the throat, you can feel its pulsation. All will acknowledge that the execution of this painting is enough to make the strongest artist tremble with fear. He also used an ingenious expedient: while he was painting Monna Lisa, who was a very beautiful woman, he had her constantly entertained by singers, musicians and jesters so that she would be merry and not look melancholic as portraits often do. As a result, in this painting of Lionardo's there was a smile so enchanting that it was more divine than human; and those who saw it marvelled to find it so similar to that of the living original.[30]

This description is fairly accurate, considering that Vasari had never seen the painting, but there are mistakes and omissions. He did not mention two features which were unusual at the time: the strange landscape in the background; and the hands, seldom used in portraiture. He describes the eyebrows, although they are clearly missing – perhaps removed by subsequent restoration – and states firmly that the painting was unfinished. These errors have led some historians to question the rest of Vasari's account. He may have seen only an unfinished copy of the portrait or, more plausibly, have obtained his description from an informant who had either seen it unfinished or who reported it as unfinished. Vasari also provides us with information on the date of the composition, claiming that Leonardo had started working on it after his return to Florence from Milan (1500) and that it took him four years to complete.

Leonardo had originally left Florence in 1481 to work in Milan under the patronage of Lodovico Sforza, Duke of Milan, known as 'Il Moro'. After the French had defeated Lodovico in December 1499, Leonardo returned to Florence. Between 1506 and 1513 he was frequently travelling between Florence and Milan (by then under French control). In 1513 he went to Rome and placed himself under the patronage of the Florentine Giuliano de' Medici, brother of the new Pope Leo X. When Giuliano died (March 1516), Leonardo left Italy and went to Amboise (on the Loire) at the Court of the King of France, François I, where he died in 1519.

Leonardo went to Amboise because he was unable to find patrons worthy of his stature in Italy, which had not yet been supplanted by France as Europe's major artistic centre. The competition was overwhelming. In Venice, then the richest and most vibrant commercial city in Europe, Titian ruled supreme. In Rome, the Pope found Leonardo unreliable because he did not finish any paintings, and preferred Raphael who, at the age of thirty, was the rising star. After the feat of the Sistine Chapel Michelangelo, now forty, was widely regarded as the supreme artist in Italy, unparalleled in both sculpture and painting. In other words, Leonardo went to France because, after the death of his protector Giuliano de' Medici, François I's was the best offer he could get. It was a generous one: an ample annuity and a comfortable manor house, Clos-Lucé, linked to the royal residency, the castle of Amboise, by a narrow passage. There the now elderly man basked in the admiration of a powerful king besotted with all things Italian, and had the peace and quiet he required for his research and writings. He became a court decoration for the greater glory of François, organising parties, drawing, and devising mechanical toys, and lost interest in painting. He had no French assistants, left no French followers, and had little impact on the subsequent course of French painting. Perhaps Leonardo too was the best François could get, having tried unsuccessfully to convince the very prolific and active Titian and Michelangelo to come to France. Neither king nor artist could have been aware that their association would provide the *Mona Lisa* with the best possible setting for its global success five centuries later, and the Louvre with the jewel in its crown.

When did Leonardo actually paint the *Mona Lisa*? The claim by Vasari that it was painted during his second Florentine stay (i.e. between 1500 and 1506) has been largely vindicated by the most meticulous and evidence-based account we have – that of Frank Zöllner in 1993 – which proposes March 1503 as the most likely starting date for the work.[31] Completion would have occurred around June 1506, when Leonardo left Florence for his second Milanese period (although he might of course have continued working on the *Mona Lisa* later). Zöllner's dating is unavoidably circumstantial, but it rests on more than speculation.

In the spring and summer of 1503 Leonardo was earning little or nothing at all. He was withdrawing money from his bank account and nothing was coming in. He must thus have been available for work. He could not have started the *Mona Lisa* before 1500, because he was still in Milan, and we know everything he did there.

After short stays in Mantua and Venice he returned to Florence in April 1500. He could not have accepted a commission to portray the *Mona Lisa* before June 1502, because he had plenty of work. There are detailed accounts of Leonardo's work in progress in 1501, but none mentions the *Mona Lisa*.

For most of 1502 until March 1503 he was the architect and engineer-in-chief of Cesare Borgia, the famous – or infamous – son of Pope Alexander VI. His military work for Cesare took him to Urbino, Pesaro, Cesena and Porto Cesenatico. He was thus far too busy to start painting the portrait of a Florentine lady.

It is unlikely he would have started it after October 1503, because by then he had been offered an important government commission (and money): painting a mural representing *The Battle of Anghiari* (soon completely ruined because Leonardo had used unsuitable materials).

This leaves a blank: the period between March and October 1503, and this is the most likely starting date. There is some corroborating evidence: various works by Raphael clearly allude to the *Mona Lisa* (see pages 39–40).[32] Raphael must have seen the portrait, probably not yet finished. Vasari may have been right after all.

There is, however, no consensus. In 1939 Kenneth Clark had accepted 1503 as the start date, but by 1973 he had become convinced that Leonardo drew Lisa Gherardini in 1504 and painted the portrait later, between 1506 and 1510, idealising it in the process.[33] It is perfectly possible that during the composition, as Leonardo was becoming increasingly involved with it, he altered the original traits of Lisa, and that the result turned out quite dissimilar to the original drawing, and hence no longer a portrait. This would also explain why he could not give it to Francesco il Giocondo; and it leaves open the possibility that Leonardo painted most of the picture in 1503–06 and continued to work at it, sporadically, well after that.[34]

The idea that the *Mona Lisa* may have started life as the portrait of Lisa and ended as someone else's opens up further possibilities. There is a 'two Lisas' hypothesis: Leonardo first painted Lisa and handed the portrait over to her husband, and this is the portrait described by Vasari; but he had made a copy, then altered its features, idealising them, and took that with him to France. The first portrait was lost. The second survives and is the one we know and love.[35] There is no real evidence for any of this, but the theory has its charm: perhaps the first portrait was not irretrievably lost, in which case it could be anywhere, perhaps in someone's attic. When we are not sure of something, anything is possible.

Who was Lisa Gherardini? The registry of the Battistero di San Giovanni confirms she was born in Florence, on Tuesday, 15 June 1479. Her family, though not rich, belonged to the petty nobility. Her father Antonmaria, legally required like all residents to declare the amount of her eventual dowry, replied that she had none. At sixteen Lisa was married to a man nineteen years older and twice widowed: Francesco di Bartolomeo di Zanobi del Giocondo, a Florentine notable. By then her father had managed to assemble a reasonable dowry, 170 florins. This was only one-eighth that of Maddalena Strozzi Doni (celebrated in a similar pose by Raphael in 1506) – but Maddalena came from one of the richest families in Florence, the Strozzi, and was marrying into an equally grand family, the Doni. Lisa's dowry, then, was probably average for one of her social standing. By the time Leonardo had started painting her she had already had three children, one of whom, a girl, had died in 1499.

In 1503 Francesco del Giocondo moved with his young family into a new house. As Zöllner points out, a prosperous merchant would have taken this opportunity to ask a leading artist to portray his young wife. Lisa had already given him two male children, the second just born (December 1502), thus providing a further cause of celebration.[36] Then as now, the upwardly mobile *nouveaux riches* took their lead on how to behave from those of more established wealth. Buying art from prominent local painters was the done thing, and Francesco could afford to pay the going rate. So why should not Lisa smile? She had a wealthy and loving husband, two boys, and a bright new home. Had Leonardo delivered the finished portrait, Francesco and Lisa would have hung it on the wall, and the *Mona Lisa* might not be in the Louvre.

In our democratic age, it may be somewhat appealing that the countenance of the daughter of the middle-class Gherardinis, the loyal (I presume) wife of an ordinary merchant, the devoted (ditto) mother of Piero and Andrea, should have become the best-known icon in the world, used in advertising, on mugs, ashtrays, calendars, folders, T-shirts and computer mousepads. In so far as we can ascertain, Lisa did nothing exceptional during her entire life except sitting still while Leonardo drew her. Andy Warhol famously wrote that in the future everyone will be famous for fifteen minutes. Lisa has been famous for five centuries, without having done anything at all.

There is, perhaps, an unconscious wish on the part of some commentators to establish that the sitter was of nobler birth, or at least of a standing proportionate to that of her painter. It may be baffling to some that Leonardo never painted a king, a queen, a pope, irksome that his patron, Duke Lodovico Sforza, who had Leonardo with him for nearly twenty years, never asked him to paint his portrait. Indeed, some have claimed that the real sitter was one of the outstanding women of the Renaissance, the rich and powerful Isabella d'Este, Marquise of Mantua, who it is known implored Leonardo to paint her portrait. In fact, in February 1500 he had gone to Mantua and drawn her portrait, now in the Louvre (see plate 8).[37]

Isabella d'Este would have been eminently suitable as a subject for Leonardo. In 1899 Eugène Müntz, one of Leonardo's first biographers, hugely praised her: she was a wonderful wife, a 'tender yet firm mother', the most accomplished woman of the Renaissance, and a lady of great taste and exceptional moral qualities.[38]

There is no doubt that Isabella wanted Leonardo to paint her portrait. In 1498 she had written to Cecilia Gallerani asking to be shown the portrait Leonardo had made of her – the one we know as *Lady with an Ermine*. Cecilia complied, pointing out that the picture no longer looked like her – not because of any faults of the painter, 'a master who has no equal', but because she was no longer as young.[39] Isabella pursued Leonardo for nearly eight years, receiving only vague promises from him, and he did not go further than the drawing of 1500. Unless, of course, the *Mona Lisa* is really Isabella d'Este, as claimed in 1946 by Raymond Stites and, more recently, by Hidemichi Tanaka.[40]

But there are other distinguished candidates. In the late nineteenth century, writers such as Séailles, Dmitri Merezhkovsky and Tristan Klingsor claimed that the real Lisa was a Neapolitan aristocrat, Costanza d'Avalos, Duchess of Francavilla. This hypothesis was popular in Italy in the first half of the twentieth century. It was advanced by Adolfo Venturi, supported by Benedetto Croce and enshrined in the entry for Leonardo in the 1933 *Enciclopedia italiana*.[41] Costanza was an aristocrat, wife of Federico del Balzo, who attempted to regain Naples from the French at the end of the fifteenth century. To Italian patriots, she was a better choice than Lisa del Giocondo. There is a problem: Costanza was forty at the time the portrait was painted, too old to be the Gioconda.

Carlo Vecce, author of a recent biography of Leonardo, has claimed that 'Lisa' was Isabella Gualanda, a Neapolitan lady, friend of the famous poetess Vittoria Colonna. His theory is that Leonardo started the portrait of Lisa Gherardini in 1504, worked on it for four years, but never finished it – as Vasari had claimed.[42] When Leonardo was in Rome (1513–16) as part of the entourage of Giuliano de' Medici, he was asked to paint the portrait of Isabella Gualanda. He had to agree, and simply recycled the unfinished portrait he had brought with him, providing it with the features of Isabella.[43] When Vecce first suggested this hypothesis, it was reported thus in the *Birmingham Express & Star* (1 February 1991): 'Mona Lisa was a highly-paid tart, says Professor Carlo Vecce of Naples University. He says she was a beauty who took the Vatican by storm.' The story is of course appealing, but there is no contemporary record of Leonardo painting anything of note in Rome. Indeed, as Vasari reported, Pope Leo X (Giuliano's brother) complained that Leonardo never finished anything because he thought too much about the end product.[44] In an earlier article, Vecce declared that 'we can only be sure that the *Mona Lisa* is not the portrait of Monna Lisa.'[45] But human beings don't like uncertainty: in his Leonardo biography (1998) Vecce says he is sure that it is Isabella Gualanda's portrait that hangs in the Louvre.[46] The leading Italian Leonardo scholar Carlo Pedretti concurred.[47] The catalogue of the exhibition *Leonardo scomparso e ritrovato*, held in Florence between 28 July and 15 October 1988, is equally categorical: the *Mona Lisa* is described as *Ritratto di Isabella Gualanda detto Monna Lisa*, and dated 1513–15, the period when Leonardo was in Rome. In 1956, however, Pedretti thought it possible that the lady in question might have been Pacifica Brandano, Giuliano's mistress.[48] And in 1953 he was reported as being convinced that she was not the mistress but the wife of Giuliano, Filiberta di Savoia.[49] Though a minority view among art historians, Pedretti's and Vecce's dating has been incorporated, unquestioningly, into the cultural database of RAI, Italy's state television.[50]

All those arguing against the identification of the *Mona Lisa* with Lisa Gherardini base their theories on the only available source that *may* have seen the *Mona Lisa* in Leonardo's lifetime. This is not Vasari, who as we know never saw the portrait or met Leonardo, and who thought the painting had never been completed. Perhaps Vasari's informant had seen the incomplete painting, with the background barely sketched (which would explain why Vasari did not mention it). Perhaps – and this seems to me the most likely explanation – Leonardo, never satisfied, regarded it himself as unfinished, as was hinted, perceptively, by Stendhal in his *Histoire de la peinture en Italie* (1817).[51]

The only contemporary of Leonardo's who actually claimed to have seen the *Mona Lisa* and who left a document was Antonio de Beatis, the faithful secretary of Cardinal Luigi d'Aragona, a Neapolitan prince related to both Lucrezia Borgia and Isabella d'Este. D'Aragona, a keen traveller, had instructed de Beatis to keep a detailed diary of their journeys,[52] and the pair were probably the first 'tourists' to see the *Mona Lisa*. They left Italy in May 1517, and visited the Tyrol, Switzerland, Bavaria, Cologne and Holland. By August they had reached Calais, intending to visit Henry VIII in England. Dissuaded by the news, possibly false, that an epidemic was devastating London, they proceeded towards Rouen to pay homage to François I, the 'Most Christian King', then went on to Amboise, by the banks of the Loire, to visit their famous countryman Leonardo.[53]

In what became subsequently a much-commented-upon and debated account, de Beatis wrote that Leonardo, the 'most famous painter of our time', and seventy years old (in fact he was sixty-five), no longer painted because he could not use his right arm (he was, in fact, left-handed).[54] They were shown three paintings – '*tucti perfectissimi*'. One was a young St John, the other the *St Anne with Virgin and Child* – both now at the Louvre. The third painting, reported de Beatis, was the portrait of a 'Florentine lady' commissioned by the late Giuliano dei Medici. If de Beatis had written simply 'a Florentine lady', then it could only have been Lisa Gherardini, the *Mona Lisa*. But 'commissioned by Giuliano'? Giuliano would not have commissioned Lisa's portrait. Was it Isabella Gualanda? Or Costanza d'Avalos? But neither was from Florence. Perhaps it was the so-called 'Colombine' *Gioconda*, now hanging at the Hermitage in St Petersburg. This, now attributed to Leonardo's pupil Francesco Melzi, would have been regarded by Leonardo as his, and hence worthy to be shown to the Cardinal of Aragon.[55] Perhaps de Beatis misunderstood what Leonardo was saying, and in so doing started an endless debate.

To complicate matters for historians, de Beatis wrote that on the day after the meeting with Leonardo, the Cardinal, visiting the nearby Château de Blois, stopped by a portrait of a woman and noted that she 'was not as pretty as the Lady Gualanda'. Isabella Gualanda had not been mentioned in the account. Was she the 'Florentine lady' whose portrait had been seen the previous day? But how could that be? She was not from Florence . . .

It is possible that Leonardo failed to deliver the portrait of Lisa del Giocondo to her husband, but it is scarcely credible that he would have kept for himself a portrait commissioned by a powerful man like Giuliano de Medici, his protector and brother to the Pope.

The balance of probabilities is that the portrait Leonardo showed Beatis and the Cardinal d'Aragon was indeed that of Lisa Gherardini, who could adequately be described as a Florentine lady. This assumption is strengthened by another much-cited source, Cassiano del Pozzo, who visited Fontainebleau in 1625. He clearly described the painting that now hangs in the Louvre, which he found highly damaged because the varnish had altered the colours. Nevertheless, Cassiano, an admirer of Leonardo and a patron of the arts, was impressed, calling it '*la più compiuta opera che di quest'autore si veda, perché dalla parola in poi altro non gli manca* ('the best-known work of this painter, because she lacks only the power of speech').[56] Cassiano referred to this painting as '*la Gioconda*', and described it so: a woman in her mid-twenties, the face a little puffy, simply dressed, the hands beautifully drawn and the eyebrows missing. Of course, he may have simply read his Vasari, but his mention of the 'beautiful' hands and the missing eyebrows, not remarked upon by Vasari, suggest otherwise. Finally, Pierre Dan, the Father Superior of the monastery of Fontainebleau, in his *Le Trésor des merveilles de la maison royale de Fontainebleau*, wrote that he had seen there in 1642 the portrait of a virtuous Italian lady, whose name was 'Mona Lissa' (sic), commonly known as '*La Joconde*'.[57] This may be significant, because it firmly connects 'Mona Lissa' to the '*Gioconda*'.

The evidence around which these portentous debates centre is extremely slim. This is why they could go on indefinitely. All we have is a paragraph from Vasari (who never saw the portrait), a few lines from the diary of a traveller reporting on a few of Leonardo's words and the mutterings of the Cardinal. The rest is hearsay. The prudent course of action for historians is to admit that, though the weight of evidence suggests that the *Mona Lisa* is the portrait of Mona Lisa, it is rather light. No wonder the art historian Martin Kemp cautiously decided in 1981 to call the picture *Portrait of a Lady on a Balcony*.[58]

In 1991 two scholars, Janice Shell and Grazioso Sironi, advanced a new hypothesis based on their discovery of the inventory of Andrea Salaì (whose real name was Gian Giacomo Caprotti), Leonardo's assistant, adoptive son, perhaps lover. They claim that this find confirms the identification of the *Mona Lisa* with Lisa Gherardini and the date of its creation. They suggest that the *Mona Lisa* did not remain in France after Leonardo's death, but returned to Italy and was subsequently brought back to France.[59] This scholarly essay, like most things concerned with the *Mona Lisa*, made press headlines, including one in the *Observer* of 27 January 1991: 'Smile on, Gioconda it really was you'. As the two authors point out, what happened to the *Mona Lisa* after Leo-

nardo's death is uncertain. It was assumed that Francesco Melzi
had inherited it. According to Leonardo's will (of which we only
have a nineteenth-century transcription), Melzi was to be Leonardo's executor and receive his books and effects.[60] Salaì, who
had subsequently married, was killed by French soldiers in Milan
on 19 January 1524, perhaps after a brawl. He left no will, so an
inventory of his personal effects was made on 21 April 1525 when
a dispute arose over the property. The inventory included a surprisingly large number of pictures: a Leda with Swan, a St Jerome,
a St Anne, a Virgin with Child, a '*Joconda*' and many others.
Were these Leonardo's works? Leonardo was not mentioned, but
the generous values given to the paintings suggest that perhaps
they were not thought to be mere copies: the Leda was estimated
to be worth 1,010 lire, nearly as much as Salaì's house; the
'*Joconda*' was worth 505 lire, as was the St Anne. It could be a
precious clutch of Leonardos. Perhaps Leonardo had given them
to Salaì before his death.[61]

If Shell and Sironi are right, and the '*Joconda*' mentioned in
the inventory is in fact the *Mona Lisa*, it could mean that the
portrait was taken back to Italy by Salaì and was later bought by
agents sent by François to scour Italy in the 1530s and 1540s for
artwork to buy. Of course, it is equally possible that Salaì made
copies of paintings by Leonardo, and that these were taken to be
authentic by those who made the inventory in Milan.

The first implication is that, contrary to general opinion, François I may not have bought the *Mona Lisa* from Melzi or from
Leonardo. Later accounts simply say that the King paid a considerable sum for it.[62] The second is that the term '*Gioconda*' was
already used to designate the portrait of a woman in what was
becoming a classic pose. Does the inventory confirm Vasari's
account? Not unequivocally, but it seems more likely that the
portrait described as '*Joconda*' was that of the wife of Francesco
del Gioconda than Isabella d'Este or Isabella Gualanda. It shows
that a painting called '*Gioconda*' was associated with Leonardo
and with the other works that became part of the French royal

collection. This is the comforting implication Louvre experts like Sylvie Béguin have drawn, because it appears to confirm the identity of their famous exhibit.[63]

The paucity of the evidence available, though, keeps the experts divided and, as a consequence, leaves the door open for others, with fewer scholarly qualifications or professional expertise, to intervene with unsubstantiated claims. The revelation that the 'real' Mona Lisa is X and not Y never fails to attract press attention.

There is nothing extraordinary about uncertainties regarding attributions, particularly of Renaissance paintings. The records are sparse. Titles were not given. Works were rarely signed. As a consequence much traditional art history deals less with the aesthetics of the works examined than with identifying who painted them, when and where. The scholarship devoted to the problem of the *Mona Lisa* is a result of its popularity. Far less time has been spent on another equally 'mysterious' portrait, also by Leonardo, that of a beautiful and slightly brooding woman – 'charming and cruel', to use the words of one of Leonardo's first biographers, Gabriel Séailles, in 1892.[64] In the seventeenth century it was erroneously identified as *La Belle Ferronnière*, the mistress of François I. It was actually painted in Milan, probably in 1490. The sitter was a lady of the Milanese court, probably Lucrezia Crivelli, a mistress of Lodovico il Moro. Some have identified her as Beatrice d'Este, others as Isabella of Aragon, wife of the Duke of Milan, Gian Galeazzo Sforza (ousted by his brother Lodovico).[65]

The mysteries surrounding the *Mona Lisa* do not by themselves explain the popularity of the painting, but they play an important role in the creation of the *Mona Lisa* story, and reinforce the view that the *Mona Lisa* is a special kind of painting. A 'secret' smile holds a secret story. Why does she smile, and who is she? As in all quests, there is a prize. For historians, it is the celebrity bestowed on those who resolve famous mysteries about famous paintings. A competitive field is established, and with it a mechanism of continual reinforcement. Each 'solution' is contested, thus augmenting the interest generated.

Does the *Mona Lisa* possess intrinsic qualities as a work of art, qualities necessary to its subsequent transformation into a global icon? In Leonardo's own lifetime the painting was regarded as a masterpiece because of the originality of the technique used, the innovative pose adopted by the sitter, and because it was 'true to life' (Vasari). It was a revolutionary painting.

CHAPTER TWO

A Revolutionary Painting

The *Mona Lisa*, one of the few surviving works by Leonardo, is complete and undamaged. Small though it may be, it is Leonardo's largest portrait. It is also his latest surviving work.

Only four of Leonardo's female portraits survive. The *Mona Lisa*, the *Ginevra de' Benci*, the *Lady with an Ermine* (Cecilia Gallerani) and *La Belle Ferronnière* (Lucrezia Crivelli). The *Ginevra de' Benci* (c.1475), Leonardo's earliest surviving portrait, had been originally commissioned by Bernardo Bembo, Venice's ambassador to Florence – unrequitedly in love with Ginevra. A large portion of the lower section was cut off, reducing the painting by one-third, presumably because Leonardo had not finished painting the hands.[1] In 1967 the Liechensteins of Vienna sold it to the National Gallery in Washington DC; it thus became the only Leonardo outside Europe.

The portrait of Cecilia Gallerani, the *Lady with an Ermine*, once in the possession of the Polish art collector Prince Czartoryski, has been at the Czartoryski Gallery of Cracow since the 1870s. Thus, only the portraits of Lisa Gherardini and Lucrezia Crivelli, which belonged to the French crown, have been continuously available to the public – at the Louvre – since the beginning of the nineteenth century.

The *Mona Lisa* we see at the Louvre is not quite the same as that painted by Leonardo. As with other Renaissance paintings, the colours are not as bright as they were. The gradual yellowing of the varnish makes the portrait even darker.[2] The first X-ray examination of the painting, in 1952, noted an old attempt at restoration.[3] The eyebrows, lovingly described by Vasari, either vanished on the first cleaning or were never there, plucked by Lisa Gherardini herself, following the fashion in early-sixteenth-century Florence. Stendhal thought it odd that 'such a pretty woman should have no eyebrows'.[4]

Considering that we are dealing with a piece of wood some five centuries old, the painting appears to be in a good state – at least according to the Louvre. In 1997 the curator, after the yearly inspection of the *Mona Lisa*, declared himself 'astonished' at the 'exceptional state' of the painting, which 'never seems to deteriorate . . . or grow old because the old wood is in a perfect state, which is very unusual for an old master'.[5] Even in our secular age, it is difficult to resist the temptation to treat the *Mona Lisa* as if it possessed some miraculous qualities

It is not impossible, however, to establish just how good a painting the *Mona Lisa* is without being unduly influenced by its celebrity. The *Mona Lisa* could not have acquired its present position as a global icon unless it had been previously regarded as a major painting. Almost all famous works of art – those known by non-specialists – have first had to pass the test of the professionals and the self-appointed experts, the main gatekeepers of the realm of the aesthetic.

The popularity of the *Mona Lisa* is not just modern hype. This is an innovative and revolutionary painting. Even in comparison with earlier masterpieces of portraiture such as Piero della Francesca's Montefeltro diptych, 'its astonishing novelty becomes . . . truly apparent', opined Martin Kemp.[6] Taken one by one, few of the innovations deployed in the *Mona Lisa* were originally devised by Leonardo. As in other fields (literature, philosophy, cinema) there is a difference between being the first to produce a novelty and being the first to understand fully its implications and able to use them in a masterly fashion. The pose of the *Mona Lisa* was one such significant innovation. She sits presenting a three-quarter view, while the face looks in a different direction – the so-called *contrapposto* position. She looks directly at the viewer, another innovation. Leonardo had broken his own rules, for he had written that women should be painted in a demure position, 'their heads lowered and inclined to one side'.[7] Titian and others often painted women with downcast eyes, as if they avoided the insolence of the male gaze.[8] Mona Lisa looks back, defiantly.

The translucent veils add depth to the painting. The numerous ripples of the garments, the rivulets of drapery falling from her shoulders and the spiral folds of the mantle across the left breast highlight the close spatial relationship between the sitter and the landscape in a way that was very unusual.[9] The barely perceptible columns at either side frame the portrait. The background is asymmetrical, the right side being a little higher than the left.

In traditional Renaissance portraiture, the main function of a landscape was to contribute additional elements for the identification of the sitter – for instance, the Tuscan countryside, or an urban setting. The landscape background of the *Mona Lisa* is not easily identifiable. Behind the balcony on which the woman is sitting are rocks, lakes, streams, but no trees or plants. The sole human structure is a bridge on the right-hand side. Some Tuscan scholars, keen to identify their own countryside, think the bridge is the Ponte a Buriano, which crosses the Arno in the Val di Chiana near Arezzo.[10] The landscape is constructed vertically, the depth being obtained by 'reading' it from top to bottom, like a Chinese painting where the base is foregrounded.

Some paintings representing the Virgin Mary, painted before the *Mona Lisa*, had hills and winding streams in the background. Leonardo's own *St Anne with Virgin and Child* also has a strange and not clearly identifiable landscape of scraggy hills. In portraits, such completely imaginary backgrounds are rare.

The result of the complex system of asymmetric relations is to produce the idea of movement, the great challenge that dominates Leonardo's work. *The Last Supper* was an attempt to freeze a particular moment of a narrative, the reaction of the disciples to Jesus's announcement that one of them will betray him. This almost fuses two chronologically distinct moments (the announcement and the reaction) into one. We 'see' the reaction, but we deduce from it the chronologically preceding moment. A similar effect is at work in the *Mona Lisa*, but in a far more purely visual way, because we are not helped by a known narrative, as we are with *The Last Supper*.

We can imagine Lisa sitting straight on the chair in the loggia just before she is 'captured' by the eye of the painter – almost like the lens of a camera. At that unrepresented moment, only her left-facing profile would have been visible. Then – as if we called her, attracting her attention – her face turns completely until she comes to face us. Her bust remains halfway through the movement. It is the *contrapposto* position. The unseen lower part of her body remains in the original position, facing left. 'She reacts to us, and we cannot but react to her,' in the words of Martin Kemp.[11]

The pose had been employed in sculpture, notably by the Greeks, and was used to great effect by Michelangelo in his *David* (which was nearly finished by the time Leonardo started the *Mona Lisa*). The *Mona Lisa* constitutes a major development in the use of the *contrapposto* technique in paintings. The *contrapposto* was an attempt to solve a riddle that had baffled painters for a long time: how to represent on two dimensions (the flat surface) the three-dimensional conception of movement. By definition, a pose is static: the sitter remains still in order to enable the painter to draw. To represent the idea of movement, the static pose of the sitter must constitute a single moment in a sequence – like a photograph of an object in motion. By having the visage of the sitter facing a point different from that facing the torso, the entire body appears to be in motion. This structure had been used in complex works with several figures, but seldom in one with a single sitter, as is the case with Mona Lisa. She is now a person in motion. In our age, the *contrapposto* position is regularly used by ordinary photographers, who tell their sitters to look away from the direction in which the body is facing so as to avoid the rigidity and stillness of body and face looking symmetrically towards the camera.

Leonardo had used the *contrapposto* previously, notably in the *Lady with an Ermine* (Cecilia Gallerani), where not only the sitter but also the furry animal is 'in movement'. But Cecilia looks away from us, and the background is dark and neutral. Even the profile drawing of Isabella d'Este can be regarded as part of Leonardo's lengthy experimentation with the *contrapposto*: Isabella is viewed in profile but her bust is turned towards us. The *Mona Lisa* was his solution to a series of technical experimentation he had been working on for decades, the culmination of a lengthy artistic itinerary.[12]

The technique used to give the impression of movement was impressive. But Leonardo used other innovations. He was an early convert to the use of oil paint in place of the quick-drying tempera – the technique of using egg yolk to bind the paint together. Oil paint, slower to dry, appealed to perfectionists. It enhanced the luminosity of the painting and permitted a more detailed and accurate representation. It was first used in northern Europe, and reached Venice and then the rest of Italy in the first half of the fifteenth century.

The northern European connection, though very important, was not one-way. Albrecht Dürer sojourned in Venice repeatedly to learn the techniques of the Italians, who in turn were dazzled by the inventiveness of his prints. Antonello da Messina was supposed to have studied in Bruges with the Van Eyck brothers and brought back to Venice the innovative use of oil paint. Indeed Vasari attributes to 'Giovanni da Bruggia' (John of Bruges, i.e. Jan Van Eyck) the invention of oil paint.[13] This is unlikely, but the story illustrates the considerable cultural interchange in fifteenth-century Europe.[14] Antonello had preceded Leonardo in Milan by some ten years and had used both the *contrapposto* and the direct look.

Hands were often represented in Flemish portraits, but seldom so fully displayed as in the *Mona Lisa*, where they are crucial for framing the lower edge of the picture. Prior to Leonardo, conventional portraits represented people only well above the waist, upward from the shoulders or the neck. It was not possible to say whether the model was sitting or standing. The *Mona Lisa* is represented from above the hips, sitting down. Here too there are precedents in northern Europe. Jan Van Eyck had experimented with half-length or head-and-shoulder portraits. Flemish portrait painters – Hans Memling and Roger Van der Weyden, as well as Van Eyck – had started to represent their sitters in a three-quarter position, their hands joined together and their faces looking towards the viewer. The two barely visible columns on either side of the *Mona Lisa* are reminiscent of Van Eyck's *The Virgin of the Chancellor Rolin* (also at the Louvre, see plate 34). Memling's 1487 *Benedetto di Tommasi Portinari* (at the Uffizi) and his c.1470–75 *Portrait of an Old Woman* (Louvre) are set in loggias with a landscape background, like the *Mona Lisa*. Columns as a framing device were rare in Italy at the time. Flemish painters, especially Van Eyck, had used them first, but usually in an enclosed space.[15] The abrupt juxtaposition of a figure against a distant landscape, an arrangement particularly striking in the case of the *Mona Lisa*, however, had often been used in Italy during the preceding century.[16]

When Italian Renaissance painters included the sitter's hands in a portrait they usually had a function: they held a symbolic object that provided a clue to the identity of the sitter, as is evident in Botticelli's *Young Man Holding a Medal of Cosimo il Vecchio* (which also uses the *contrapposto*), or Perugino's *Francesco delle Opere* holding a scroll (both at the Uffizi). Leonardo himself had identification clues in his *Lady with an Ermine, Ginevra de' Benci* and *Portrait of a Musician* (c.1495, at the Pinacoteca Ambrosiana in Milan). The ermine was a symbol of Lodovico il Moro (a member of the Order of the Ermine), and its Greek name was '*gallè*' – two clues which suggest that the lady depicted is Cecilia Gallerani, Lodovico's young mistress. Ginevra de' Benci is painted against a juniper tree ('*ginepro*' is the Italian for juniper). The musician's craft is identifiable from the document he holds.

Mona Lisa's hands hold nothing. They have no obvious function. They do not suggest fear, or prayer, or pain.[17]

Many Renaissance paintings are full of objects and consumer goods: rugs, cushions, chests, jewels.[18] The *Mona Lisa* has nothing.

The *Mona Lisa* was painted on poplar wood, as was still the practice at the time. The technique used by Leonardo required many layers, hence the length of time taken to finish the portrait, because it was preferable to wait each time for the paint to dry. Leonardo also took an inordinate amount of time to complete it not only because of his perfectionism and the demands his other projects made on his time, but because he deliberately used extremely thin brushes – so thin that X-rays have not been able to identify the brush-strokes.[19] There is no question of Leonardo being driven by artistic fury, as may happen in the composition of some contemporary art.

The *sfumato* (literally 'smoky') technique Leonardo pioneered consisted in building up layers of paint from dark to light, letting the previous one come through, thus achieving, through a play of shadows and lights, the optical illusion of a relief.[20] As he wrote: 'Shadows and lights are the most certain means by which the shape of any body comes to be known, because a body of equal lightness or darkness will not display any relief but gives the effect of a flat surface.'[21] Hegel – as Karl Jaspers noted in 1965 – called it a magic of coloured illusions in which objects evaporate. Even the deepest shadows diffuse some glow and are imperceptibly transformed into the brightest radiance.[22]

Leonardo's contemporaries were impressed by the *sfumato*. It appeared to have solved the problem of moving from one colour or one gradation of light into another. This was useful for representing distant objects. As Leonardo explained:

Although at a long distance the definition of the boundaries is lost, [the painter] should not on this account neglect to observe that a smoky finish is to be seen, and not boundaries and profiles which are sharp and harsh.[23]

This enabled him to achieve the effect so desired at the time: to provide a depth that could not be achieved with a clearer and neater break between zones of colours. With Leonardo we lose any impression of a painting as a drawing which has been coloured, as is the case in early Italian art.

As Gombrich noted, the *sfumato* technique was applied to the *Mona Lisa* to great effect. The corners of the eyes and mouth (the main identification points of a facial expression) were blurred, thus adding to the uncertainty surrounding the expression of the face. It is not quite clear whether she is sad or happy, whether she is smiling or not, or what kind of smile she has.[24] This tone of mystery would add considerably to the charm of the picture in the nineteenth century, when paintings came to be regarded as harbouring an essence to be interpreted.

Finally, Leonardo also perfected the usage of the 'pyramidal' composition, where the sitter's hands provide the base of a pyramid, with her head at the apex. This structure gives the painting a monumental appearance. Mona Lisa seems to tower over the mountain peaks behind her.[25] Such complex structure had been used in works with several figures, but never before in one with a single sitter.[26] There is also a fantastic element in the composition. If the woman is sitting on a balcony, it would have to be very high to explain the view we have of the landscape behind her.[27]

Leonardo's contemporaries, above all Raphael, appreciated the innovations of the *Mona Lisa*. Though he may have seen only Leonardo's preliminary drawing of the *Mona Lisa*, Raphael was captivated by it.[28] His debt to Leonardo is manifest in his drawing *Young Woman in a Loggia* (see plate 10), where exactly the same pose as that of the *Mona Lisa* is used. This was probably a study for the portrait of Maddalena Doni, but the sitter represented is not Maddalena Doni (see page 23). Could it be the authentic Lisa Gherardini? The actual finished *Maddalena Doni* uses the same pose as Mona Lisa, though Raphael framed it between two highly visible columns, and ignores the landscape, locating the sitter in a conventional, recognisable Florentine urban background (see plate 11).

Raphael returned again and again to Leonardo's work for inspiration, for example in his *Lady with a Unicorn* (1506, Galleria Borghese, Rome), *La Muta* (1507, Galleria Nazionale delle Marche, Urbino), *Donna Velata* (c.1516, Palazzo Pitti, Florence), his portrait of Giuliano de Medici and his famous portrait of Baldissare Castiglione (see plate 12) which, before it was cut, revealed the sitter's hands.[29]

Raphael used Leonardo's technique of pyramidal composition to depict individuals. In so doing, as the art historian Luba Freedman points out, an individual would be represented 'with the majesty and monumentality ordinarily reserved for religious paintings'.[30] The lack of distinguishing clues helped to transform the *Mona Lisa* into a portrait in general – no longer the conventional portrait of a particular individual (by definition a portrait is the visual representation of a specific person). Raphael's *Maddalena Doni*, on the other hand, is definitely that of the historical Maddalena, wife of Agnolo Doni: the Florentine background, the jewellery she wears, the blemishes on her face identify her. Raphael had done his duty by the Doni family. Instructed to paint a real person, he produced a specific portrait using the lessons he had learned from Leonardo, the painter of the individual in general.

We know that Leonardo was widely admired during his lifetime because of the number of copies made of his works. In an age when information about a painting could travel only through written comments and the production of copies, the activities of Leonardo's followers, mainly in northern Italy, functioned as an information system which contributed to the expansion of his fame. Copies could be made of copies. When Henri IV decided to restore the Appartement des Bains in Fontainebleau (1594–1600), the pictures were removed and copied on canvas. This is when Ambroise Bosschaert, known as Dubois (1543–1614), copied the *Mona Lisa*. Charles Simon again copied it, in 1624.[31]

In the sixteenth century a variety of women were portrayed in what was becoming known as the '*Gioconda*' pose. Nearly sixty copies, imitations and derivations were painted before the end of the eighteenth century. In the twentieth century, when the painting had become widely known, various owners of copies claimed to own the 'real' *Mona Lisa*. *Giocondas* were also sometimes painted or drawn in the nude in the classic *contrapposto* position with the now traditional folded hands. There is one at the Musée Condé in Chantilly (*Monna Vanna*, 1513, see plate 13), drawn in black chalk, and one in Nuremberg, at the Germanisches Nationalmuseum, painted in the sixteenth century by Barthel Bruyn and called the *Nude Gioconda*.

In Bergamo, at the Accademia Carrara, there is a seventeenth-century oil painting based on the Chantilly chalk drawing once thought to be of Flemish origin, but now attributed to the brothers Carlo Antonio and Giuliano Cesare Procaccini. In 1535 Joos Van Cleve painted a *Gioconda*, now at the Musée de Valenciennes. In Tours, at the Musée des Beaux-Arts, there is a seventeenth-century *Gioconda with Bodice* attributed to Jean Ducayer. At Hampton Court, near London, there is a sixteenth-century *Gioconda*-like painting known as *Flora* attributed to Bernardino Luini, one of Leonardo's most distinguished followers. The Alte Pinakothek of Munich also has 'its' *Gioconda*, painted in oil in the seventeenth century. Other seventeenth-century copies can be found in Japan, Épinal and Oslo. The Prado of Madrid has an anonymous sixteenth-century copy of the *Mona Lisa*. At the Hermitage in St Petersburg there is a *Gioconda* with her left breast exposed, body and face turned towards the left, and with an object in her hand, known as 'Colombina' and attributed to

Francesco Melzi (see plate 14). There are sixteenth- or seventeenth-century copies of the *Mona Lisa* in various European and American museums, some probably commissioned by ladies who wished to be portrayed in the pose of the *Mona Lisa*.

What all this suggests was that the term '*Joconde*' or '*Gioconda*' had come to stand for any female portrait using a pose vaguely similar to that of Leonardo's famous original. For instance, the term '*une Joconde*' (without attribution) was used to describe a painting in a French inventory of 1629.[32] A handwritten note in the inventory of Jean-Baptiste de Champaigne (1681) recorded the presence of '*une Joconde daprés Leonard Davency* [sic]'.[33] In 1701 the inventory made of the estate of Marie Boncot, wife of Jacques Benoist, counsellor at the Cour des monnaies, contained an entry stating simply '*une Joconde*'.[34] The *Catalogue* of the auction of the estate of Louis-Jean Gaignat, who died in 1768, described one of his paintings as '*Une Joconde*', adding that it is 'the famous work by Leonardo da Vinci that belonged to King François I'. No one was fooled: the painting went for 950 livres, while a Rembrandt was sold for 5,420.[35]

Prior to the development of techniques for reproducing colour and, above all, prior to the invention of photography, the fame of a painting had to rely on the proliferation of imitations and replicas. These also provided younger artists with the necessary examples to use in order to learn the techniques of the established classics. Every imitation or copy is also a direct tribute to the original.[36]

Copies were highly valued. Their disparagement is a modern impulse connected to a search for authenticity more marked in a society where art can be reproduced easily. In Lombardy – where Leonardo had many followers – in the fifteenth and sixteenth centuries, imitators abounded. Without constant copying and imitation, variations and distinctions, there could be no artistic development at all. Correggio, for instance, derived considerable stimulus from his encounter with the works of Leonardo.[37]

Thus in 1821 the Royal Academy purchased a copy of *The Last*

Supper and preserved it among its treasures, something which few major institutions would now consider doing.[38] As copies proliferated – some commissioned by the French crown – the *Mona Lisa* remained in the royal collection. It was mentioned by Rascas de Bagarris (1567–1620) in his list of *les plus rares peintures de Fontainebleau* (1608–10), by Cassiano del Pozzo in his diary (1625) and by Pierre Dan in his 1642 inventory of *Le Trésor des merveilles de la maison royale de Fontainebleau*.[39]

Louis XIII, who became king of France in 1610, was not an art lover. Cassiano's diary tells us that in 1625 the Duke of Buckingham, sent by Charles I of England (who was a patron of the arts) to take Louis's sister Henrietta-Maria back to marry him, had proposed a swap. The French should give him the *Mona Lisa*, and would receive in return Holbein's *Erasmus* and a Holy Family by Titian. Louis was tempted to accept, but his courtiers intervened. The *Mona Lisa* was, they protested, one of his best pictures. It should not leave France. Louis accepted their advice and instead gave Leonardo's *St John* to the deeply disappointed Duke.[40] Later the banker Everhard Jabach bought back the *St John* at the sale of Charles I's collection after his execution and sold it to Louis XIV for the same sum he had paid: 140 pounds.[41]

The *Mona Lisa* remained in France, somewhat neglected. Roger de Piles, who classified paintings in 1691, ranked Leonardo eleventh (with a poor grade – four out of twenty – for the use of colour), well below French painters such as Charles Lebrun.[42] By 1695 the *Mona Lisa* was in the Petite Galerie du Roi at Versailles, visible only to hurried courtiers, though even then it was not without its admirers. For instance, Lépicié, in his 1752 *Catalogue des tableaux du Roy*, described it as 'one of the most perfect of Leonardo's paintings'.[43] By 1760, however, it had been relegated to the office of the Directeur des Bâtiments (the keeper of the royal buildings). At the Luxembourg Palace in Paris on 14 October 1750 the best 110 items of the Royal Collection were shown to the public (a highly selected public). The *Mona Lisa* was not among them.

Then came the Revolution. There was no longer a Royal Collection. Its contents would be accessible to its new owners, the citizens of France. A commission was appointed with the task of preparing the list of the paintings to be moved from Versailles to a new museum which would be created inside the palace of the Louvre. At its eighteenth meeting, on 13 July 1797, the final list was ready. The *Mona Lisa* was included in the core of the Royal Collection. 'Citizen Fragonard' – as the minutes recorded – was entrusted with the transportation and duly signed the receipt.[44] There is something poignant in this, for Citizen Fragonard was Jean-Honoré Fragonard (1732–1806), the highly celebrated court artist of Louis XVI, a painter of historical subjects and later of light-headed slightly erotic themes, and of whatever pleased the court at Versailles. The Revolution had executed Fragonard's patrons and swept away the artistic genre he had been associated with. The new regime much preferred Jacques-Louis David's virtuous and high-minded neo-classical art, already acclaimed in the final years of Louis XVI. David embraced the Revolution with fervour, and acquired almost complete control of the state's artistic policies. Though he voted for the execution of the king, he did not extend his zeal to the persecution of fellow artists fallen on hard times, and procured the down-and-out Fragonard a job at the Musée. This is how Fragonard ended up overseeing the transportation of the Versailles collection – including the *Mona Lisa* – to the new museum. He would have been comforted to know that several of his own paintings now decorate the walls of the Louvre.

From this moment onward, the history of the *Mona Lisa* is inextricably linked to that of the Louvre.

CHAPTER THREE

Lisa Enters the Louvre

The Revolution enhanced the development of artistic life in France. It established the Louvre, the Bibliothèque Nationale, the Musée des Arts et Métiers, the École des Beaux-arts and the annual Salon, where painters could exhibit their works and compete for prizes.

Some of these developments would have occurred even without the Revolution. The *ancien régime*, under the inspiration of Enlightenment philosophers, Diderot in particular, had plans for a museum in the Louvre.[1] The Grande Galerie should have been opened to the public in 1787, but financial difficulties forced the government to delay the project.

In some countries, steps towards the public exhibition of artistic treasures had been taken earlier. Oxford University established, in 1683, the Ashmolean Museum. In 1734 the Capitoline Museum was opened in the Vatican, in 1743 it was the turn of the Uffizi in Florence, and a year later Dresden acquired its public picture gallery. The British Museum opened in 1753. The idea that the state should defend the nation's artistic patrimony was pervading the whole of Europe.

France, however, had been instrumental in reorganising art in the countries it had occupied during the revolutionary and Napoleonic wars. In northern Italy between 1803 and 1807, the French invaders – with the help of local supporters – created picture galleries in Milan, Bologna, Genoa, Venice and Mantua. In Holland, in 1808, Louis Napoleon, a brother of the emperor, established the Koninklijk Museum in Amsterdam, later the Rijks-museum. Another brother, Joseph, conceived in 1809 the Prado in Madrid (established in 1819).

In the course of the nineteenth century the trend accelerated: in 1824 the National Gallery was inaugurated in London, while in Berlin an entire set of museums was created. St Petersburg saw the opening of the Hermitage in the 1840s. The South Kensington Museum (later renamed the Victoria and Albert Museum) was launched in 1852, the Neue Pinakothek of Munich in 1853, the Metropolitan Museum in New York and the Museum of Fine Arts in Boston in 1870, the Art Institute of Chicago in 1879 and the Tate Gallery in London in 1897. Thus the *Mona Lisa* was one of many thousands of paintings which had become accessible to the public.

The Louvre, big and half-empty, had been the obvious choice for a major museum in Paris. This fortress, built by King Philippe Auguste in 1190, had been turned in 1546 into a proper Renaissance palace by François I. The Grande Galerie was added by Henri IV in the early seventeenth century to link the Tuileries Palace with the Louvre.

In handing over to the people artefacts hitherto in the hands of a narrow elite, the Louvre provided a 'transparent metaphor for the triumph of the new order' and sought to impress the world with the intellectual achievements of the young republic.[2]

As often happens in French history, culture was becoming an extension of politics, to an extent unparalleled in Britain, where access was equally 'democratic'. Jean-Marie Roland, the Interior Minister, in a letter to the painter Jacques-Louis David, then a member of the National Convention, explained:

> The idea is to transform the Louvre galleries into a museum; this is what the decree says. As Minister of the Interior, I am its executor and its overseer. I must account to the Nation: this is the spirit and the letter of the law. This Museum must cultivate the great wealth

of drawings, paintings, sculptures and other artistic works owned by the nation. My view is that it should attract foreigners and become a focus of their attention. It must nourish a taste for the arts, train art lovers, and serve artists. It must be open to all. Everyone must be able to set their easel before any painting or statue, draw them, paint them, or model them, as they think fit. This museum will be a national monument. It will not be reserved for the pleasure of any one individual . . . Like Greece, France must expand her glory to all times and to all peoples; the National Museum will be admired by the whole world . . . Such great ideas are worthy of a free people who wish to dominate only through wisdom, and who accept no dictate but that of reason . . . The museum will so impress the spirits, lift the souls, and warm the hearts that it will become one of the most powerful symbols of the French Republic.[3]

This was on 17 October 1792, in Year One of the French Republic, and these have remained the defining objectives of the Louvre. As recently as 1963 the Curator of Paintings, Germain Bazin, concluded his introduction to the Louvre catalogue by declaring that the museum's dual role was *exprimer le sens de l'universel, exalter les valeurs françaises*, 'to represent the essence of universalism, and to celebrate French values'.[4]

On 10 August 1793, exactly a year after the abolition of the monarchy, the Louvre was inaugurated, but it was not until 1797 that the *Mona Lisa* and the remainder of the Versailles collection were transferred to the new museum. The catalogue included a description of the *Mona Lisa*, drawing attention to the smile and adding, '*Madame Lise ditte la Joconde . . . célèbre par sa beauté*'.[5]

Napoleon must have appreciated the beauty of 'Madame Lise', because in 1800 he had the portrait removed from the museum and placed in his bedroom in the Tuileries. It was returned to the Louvre in 1804 when he was crowned emperor.

Originally called the Musée Central des Arts, the Louvre became the Musée Napoléon in 1803 and the Musée Royal after the Restoration of 1815. The defeat of Napoleon and the return of the monarchic order ensured, paradoxically, that the *Mona Lisa* could no longer be removed from the public gaze for the personal delectation of a sovereign or a dictator. The Restoration had not restored the absolute power of the sovereign, and no future charismatic leader of the stature of Napoleon could hope to appropriate a national treasure. The *Mona Lisa* now belonged to a collectivity, ill-defined perhaps, but a collectivity nonetheless.

The revolutionary armies Napoleon had led to the conquest of Europe in the 1790s had returned laden with artworks. In Britain, what amounted to sanctioned looting would have been left to the private initiative of aristocrats such as Lord Elgin. In France it occurred under the twin banners of universalism and nationalism. After Waterloo France was compelled to return the stolen masterpieces, usually to newly created museums, not to their original owners. Thus the Revolution had accomplished one of its tasks, the export of modern values.[6] The Italians magnanimously allowed the French to keep works by painters not highly regarded at the time, including Cimabue, Giotto and Fra Angelico. The removal of artistic masterpieces had caused a stir even in countries – such as Prussia and England – which had done their own share of similar pilferage. The most popular English woman poet of her time, Felicia Dorothea Hemans (*neé* Browne, 1793–1835), dedicated to their return to their rightful homes a long poem: 'The Restoration of the Works of Art to Italy' (1816).[7] She prefaced it with a quote from a well-known travel book:

> The French, who in every invasion have been the scourge of Italy, and have rivalled or rather surpassed the rapacity of the Goths and Vandals, laid their sacrilegious hands on the unparalleled collection of the Vatican, tore its Masterpieces from their pedestals, and

dragging them to Paris, consigned them to the dull
sullen halls, or rather stables, of the Louvre.[8]

In spite of the loss of so many paintings, these 'dull stables'
were rapidly becoming a major artistic centre, attracting artists
and copyists as well as its first foreign 'tourists' – mainly from
Britain.[9] Previously, painters who wished to have access to major
works of art had had to ingratiate themselves with the owners or
rely on copies. Now they were able to develop their artistic education directly at the Louvre. It had become 'their' museum. In
the new ten-day revolutionary week, the artists had the Louvre
all to themselves for five days, two were reserved for cleaning
and only three to the general public.[10] Deference towards these
hallowed works did not prevent the students and copyists removing them from the walls, putting them on easels dangerously
close to the heating stoves, and using chalk to draw lines directly
on the paintings.

Access to such bounty of artistic wealth made art more self-
referential. Those who copied to sell tried to be as faithful as
possible; those who copied to learn introduced variations or produced new work inspired or influenced by what they had copied.
British painters arrived in Paris with innovative ideas. They made
copies directly in oil on canvas, or in watercolour on paper,
working fast, changing the colours, and studying the interplay of
night and day. Turner, along with many other artists, had gone
to Paris in 1802 to see the pictures looted by Napoleon and the
permanent collection. He was particularly impressed by Poussin
and Titian. Delacroix (and, later, Cézanne) copied Rubens, Ingres
drew Raphael and Poussin. Others copied Velázquez and Murillo.
Everyone was inspired by the Venetians, by the Flemish and
German painters and, above all, by Vermeer, Pieter de Hooch,
Frans Hals and Rembrandt. Poussin was copied throughout the
nineteenth century by most major French artists – from Ingres
and Géricault to Degas, Rodin, Seurat and Cézanne. As Cézanne
wrote in a letter, '*Le Louvre est un livre où nous apprenons à lire*'

('The Louvre is a book wherein we learn to read').[11] Delacroix – who wrote in his diary *on commence toujours par imiter* ('one always begins by imitating') – copied Rembrandt, Rubens, Raphael and Correggio.[12] He was in turn copied by Cézanne, Picasso, Manet, Odilon Redon, Gauguin, Matisse, Guttuso and many others.[13]

And the *Mona Lisa*? A portrait which inspired Raphael failed to excite nineteenth-century painters. They all admired the great Florentine artists, but few copied Leonardo.[14] Delacroix, for instance, though he included Leonardo in his list of the seven greatest painters (the others were Raphael, Michelangelo, Titian, Correggio, Rubens and Rembrandt), did not copy any of the Louvre Leonardos – although he admired his drawings.[15] Cézanne, a keen student of Michelangelo drawings, did not draw any Leonardo. There were, however, major exceptions, such as Camille Corot, who painted Berthe Goldschmidt – the famous *La Femme à la perle* – in the Mona Lisa pose in 1869 (see plate 15), and Degas, who drew the Gioconda's hands and face in 1854 (now at the Louvre in the Department of Graphic Art) and a study of Leonardo's *Adoration* (1869, now at the Elmer Belt Library of Vinciana, UCLA). Jean-François Millet painted in 1841–42 the *Portrait of Pauline-Virginie Ono* in the three-quarter pose, hands folded, looking directly at the viewer, but standing, not sitting. It now hangs at the Prefectural Museum of Yamamashi, at Kôfu in Japan. His *Madame Eugène Canoville* (1845) has her hands in her lap *à la* Mona Lisa. Others who were similarly inspired are less well-known: the prolific Jean-Baptiste Carpeaux (1827–75), the principal sculptor of his day; Gustave Le Gray (1820–82), painter and photographer; and the Swiss-French painter Félix Edouard Vallotton (1865–1925).[16]

Odilon Redon, a great admirer of Leonardo, painted in or around 1908 a *Hommage à Léonard de Vinci*, but used the head of the Virgin from the St Anne painting.[17] Ingres drew *La Belle Ferronnière*; later he was inspired by the Mona Lisa pose and landscape for his famous *Portrait de Madame Rivière* (1805). However, most of the artists working in the Louvre were just professional copyists. Until the 1855 Universal Exhibition in Paris, the public, and hence the copyists' potential customers, were allowed access only at weekends (Napoleon had reverted to the seven-day week in 1802). After 1855 the museum was opened to everyone every day. The change was welcomed by the painters themselves, now able to sell their copies more easily.[18]

Most of the copyists were women, engaged in work deemed ideally suited to them. In 1860 the writer Léon Lagrange felt that women would find painting morally preferable to drama or music. When they did not copy, they could paint at home while looking after the children and the household. Though constitutionally unable to paint works of genius, he claimed, they could still paint the portrait of a loved child, or pictures of flowers and religious images, or decorate books, or make copies to be sent to the provinces. This, Lagrange continued, would provide women with a profitable career 'without perils for their moral dignity', and might encourage men to return to more manly pursuits.[19]

Lagrange's optimism – he was a champion of the right of women to work – may have been misplaced. The museum was warm and frequented by the well-to-do. This attracted prostitutes. It was also used as a pick-up place for artists. The novelist Champfleury (Jules Husson, 1821–89) provided unimaginative young male artists with handy tips: spot an enticing female copyist at work, settle down to paint the painting next to hers, refrain from chatting her up until near closing time so that the conversation can continue outside the museum.[20]

By the beginning of the twentieth century there were numerous complaints that *clochards* (dossers), taking advantage of the free entry, were sleeping in the galleries of the Louvre. The abolition of free entry in 1902 (except on Thursdays and Sundays) reduced the problem. Teachers, artists, critics and schoolchildren (if accompanied by an accredited artist) were still granted free access.[21]

At first, there were only 538 paintings on display and the museum comprised only the Grande Galerie and the Salon Carré. After 1850 the museum was enriched by important legacies, such as that of Dr Louis La Caze in 1869. Many of the masterpieces which attract visitors to the Louvre today come from the collection of Dr La Caze, whose villa in Paris was stripped of furniture to make room for over eight hundred paintings, including works by Ribera, Frans Hals, Rembrandt, Rubens, Watteau and Fragonard. By the 1880s the Louvre held the richest collection of paintings in the world.

Until 1848 the annual exhibition of new paintings took place in the Salon Carré of the Louvre, hence its name ('the Salon'). It was a huge and growing success. In the 1830s more than a thousand artists displayed two thousand works. In 1846 it was visited by 1,200,000 people – more than the entire population of Paris.[22] Foreign visitors, such as William Thackeray, were astonished by the French love of painting. The taste of the aristocracy was still dominant, but the patrician art establishment had to open its doors to dealers, intellectuals, *nouveaux riches* and high-level bureaucrats. The French press devoted increasing space to the arts. The first art critics, usually writers and essayists, emerged. Balzac, George Sand, Alfred de Musset and Théophile Gautier wrote in influential art magazines such as *l'Artiste*. The more academic *Gazette des Beaux-Arts* had, by 1880, some two thousand subscribers.

A substantial market for engravings developed for the new middle classes. Painters were enthusiastic. Their work, once engraved, could be sold over and over again, like that of playwrights and novelists. A further advantage was that they could become known to a wider circle of people – as did the engravings of Old Masters.

The visitors, then as now, were relatively well educated. The Parisian *nouvelle bourgeoisie* were curious to see for themselves what the aristocracy had deemed of great value. On Sundays they had little to do, even in Paris, and, after a stroll in the Gardens of the Tuileries they could take their children to visit the Louvre.[23] The Louvre was on its way to becoming a popular museum. Though mass attendance was yet to come, the timid 'new' visitors attracted the supercilious comments of the real connoisseur. These new middle classes were regarded, justifiably so, as terribly conventional. The bourgeoisie, it turned out, had bourgeois taste. Zola described, with barely suppressed contempt, a crowd of visitors in 1867:

> Ten people of normal intelligence facing a new and original picture are transformed into one big child: they elbow each other and comment on the painting in the most comic way.[24]

Ten years later, in 1877, this vignette found a place in one of Zola's great novels, *l'Assommoir*. Here the visitors are not middle-class philistines but the working-class guests at Gervaise and Coupeau's wedding who decide to visit the Louvre. Intimidated by the gold-braided uniforms of the porters, more intrigued by the copyists at work than by the originals, they end up in the Salon Carré. 'Coupeau paused by the Joconde. She looked like an aunt of his, he remarked. Boche and Bibi-la-Grillade chuckled while glancing at the nudes.'[25]

None of this should have been surprising. It was only towards the end of the nineteenth century that museums became 'modern' by making available some basic information about their exhibits: title, artist, period, and sometimes the school.[26] Even now the Louvre is largely francophone, though 70 per cent of its visitors are foreigners.

The middle classes, however, provided jobs for artists: they bought copies of their favourite paintings. Between 1851 and 1880 (when photography became widespread) Murillo's *Immaculate Conception* was copied 197 times, Correggio's *St Catherine* 186 times, Veronese's *Marriage at Cana* 167 times, and Titian's *Entombment* 130. The *Mona Lisa* was copied seventy-one times, a remarkable achievement, but it was easily outdone by popular

French paintings such as Jean-Baptiste Greuze's *Cruche cassée* (138 copies) and Pierre Paul Prud'hon's *L'Assomption de la Vierge* (130 copies).[27]

The best-selling copies were mainly of religious inspiration. Popular piety was not the only explanation. Then as now the state influenced, through patronage, the organisation of the arts. The Second Empire (1852–70) commissioned copies to send to provincial museums, town halls and churches. At least half of the two thousand works commissioned by the state were of religious subjects.[28]

Thus the *Mona Lisa* found itself at the centre of a thriving artistic life, surrounded by visitors, copyists and artists. In the early nineteenth century it was not the centre of attraction. It was regarded as an important work, painted by a famous Old Master, but there was no cult, no adoring crowds surrounded it. Samuel Morse's *The Gallery of the Louvre* (see plate 16) depicted paintings in the Salon Carré for Americans unable to see the originals. Morse's painting was not a faithful reproduction – he had included only his favourites: Poussin, Titian, Van Dyck, Rubens, Rembrandt, Guido Reni, Murillo as well as the *Mona Lisa*.[29] However, it is missing from John Scarlett Davis's *The Salon Carré and the Grande Galerie of the Louvre* (1831, see plate 19). Even *l'Artiste*, the review directed by Arsène Houssaye, a great admirer of Leonardo, whose best-known contributor was Théophile Gautier (who exalted the *Mona Lisa* as the outstanding portrait of the Renaissance), failed in 1849 to mention the *Joconde* in its lead article dedicated to a survey of the paintings in the museum.[30]

The painting was little known even among art lovers. In 1843 a French court was asked to adjudicate on a complaint made by a Monsieur Lambert, a diplomat. Lambert told the tribunal that he had been defrauded by Monsieur Bruslé, an art dealer: 'He had a painting for sale which immediately seduced me: it was Leonardo's *Joconde*. I paid 24,500 francs for it.' Unfortunately for Lambert, the tribunal found there was no evidence that the art dealer had claimed the picture was the authentic *Joconde*, and the complainant was forced to pay the costs of the hearing.[31]

The *Mona Lisa* was less highly valued than other well-established Renaissance masterpieces, as can be seen by examining the official Louvre catalogues listing the paintings held. A commission of experts chosen by the Louvre was asked to provide a market valuation of each painting – that is, how much it would fetch at auction. The 1849 edition, edited by Frédéric Villot, is a useful indicator of the standing of the *Mona Lisa*. The market value of what was then Inventory Number 300 – *Le Portrait de Mona Lisa connue sous le nom de la Joconde* – was set at 90,000 francs, an appreciation of 10,000 over its 1815–21 valuation.[32] This was a considerable valuation, though modest by the standard of today's international art market: at the time a comfortable middle-class house in a good district of Paris could be had for 50,000 francs. In 1852, when the museum's acquisition budget was only 100,000 francs, it used it to buy, among others, Perugino's *Virgin, Two Saints and Two Angels* for 53,302 francs and Memling's *St John and St Magdalen* for 11,728 francs.[33] Estimated at 90,000 francs, *Mona Lisa* was doing well, but not as well as Leonardo's own *Virgin of the Rocks* (150,000 francs), although much better than *St Anne with Virgin and Child* (30,000 francs), the authenticity of which was contested at the time.[34]

Mona Lisa was easily outdistanced by Titian's *Les Pélerins d'Emmaüs* (150,000 francs), and dwarfed by Raphael's *La Vierge, l'Enfant Jesus et Saint Jean* (known as *La Belle jardinière*) (400,000 francs, up 100,000 since 1821) and *Sainte Famille* (600,000 francs).

Only around the middle of the century did the *Mona Lisa* start attracting greater interest, but it was still just one of many celebrated paintings. For instance, Joseph Castiglione in his painting *Vue du Salon Carré au Musée du Louvre* (1861, see plate 20) showed visitors contemplating the great hall where the most important paintings were hanging. The large Veroneses can be easily seen, but only with some effort is it possible to discern the tiny *Mona Lisa*, partially hidden by the turbans of two Moorish visitors. For a painting to edge its way towards the status of popular masterpiece, more than a mere presence is required. To be in the Louvre at all was already a sign of high status, but such glory was shared with hundreds of other pictures. Museums, wrote André Malraux, do not simply exhibit masterpieces, they create them. This is partly true. It is also necessary for paintings to be talked and written about. This is where the art critics came in. Museums provided them with the raw materials. Visitors, faced with a vast display of artefacts, were open to suggestions about what to think.

In the sixteenth century Vasari had started a trend when his *Le Vite de' più eccellenti pittori, scultori e architetti* was clearly aimed at providing a league table of painters, sculptors and architects. Excellence was defined as the ability to display special skills – grandiose buildings with complex decorations for architects, and representing life as it really is for painters and sculptors. But later artists and art critics could not be content with the mere imitation of nature, or with marvelling at skills and techniques. They found a new role: to point out to the naive spectator what *at first sight* was not apparent.

This became all the more necessary in the twentieth century, as artists sought increasingly to represent ideas, moods, feelings and concepts in an increasingly elliptical way. Ordinary viewers were often reduced to baffled reactions, such as 'What is this all about?' and 'Even a child could do that,' thus revealing at once that they did not belong to the community of art connoisseurs.

No one looking at the *Mona Lisa* would say that a child could do it, but most would be able to give the kind of description given by Vasari, essentially a list of superlatives. Later art critics moved beyond this. In the nineteenth century, the self-appointed decoders of visual art were poets and writers, not yet academics and professional experts. What was at stake was the power to decide the meaning of a work of art. In France more than elsewhere, leading men and women of letters wrote extensively on the arts: Stendhal, Théophile Gautier,

Charles Baudelaire, George Sand and Émile Zola.

A century later, the growth of universities and the professionalisation of art criticism enabled academics to win their battle against the *littérateurs* and transform art history into an academic discipline. To reinforce their advantage the academics were led, in this as in other fields, to develop a specialised technical language. The prose-poetry used by Gautier and others in France, and by Walter Pater and John Ruskin in England, was replaced by a less purple, and less pleasurable, style. The heritage of the *littérateurs*, however, remained strong. They had established a wide audience many modern experts wanted to keep. Kenneth Clark, Director of the National Gallery in London in 1933 when he was not yet thirty, was deeply influenced by the style and mode of thought of Pater and Ruskin. This enabled him to communicate to a wider public. Years later, the broad interest in visual art and its obvious appeal to television programmers transformed him – thanks to the TV series *Civilization* – into an international celebrity.

Art history and expertise also became inevitably linked to a market dominated by speculators, merchants and collectors who required experts able to guarantee authenticity and to advise on acquisitions. Proficiency in assigning a specific picture to a particular painter on the basis of its similarity to other works by the same painter, the skill of attribution, enabled its most prominent practitioners – such as Bernard Berenson, Roberto Longhi and Federico Zeri – to become wealthy and to mix with moneyed elites out of the reach of specialists in other historical fields.

In the nineteenth century, however, neither academics nor attributionists held sway. An elite of writers, poets and essayists – all exercising a kind of high-level cultural journalism, formed taste. They did not classify painters into schools, and paid little attention to attribution or to the reciprocal influence that painters may have had on each other. These writers and their audience shared a common knowledge of the principal Greek and Roman myths, of the Bible and of the rough outlines of European history since the fall of the Roman Empire. They all knew that Zeus had changed himself into a swan in order to seduce Leda, and that Jesus had told his disciples that one of them would betray him. Usually, this kind of knowledge was all that was required to decode the most common symbols used by Renaissance artists. The decipherment of more recondite codes and complex allusions would have to wait until the next century. What the literary *amateurs* did was to provide texts that would capture the resonant mood of a painting, drawing attention to its connections – real or imagined – with other cultural expressions, with poetry and music, and to state these with utter self-assurance. This was all that mattered; perhaps all that matters even today.

'At the age of nine or ten' – wrote Kenneth Clark in his memoirs in the mid-1970s – 'I said with perfect confidence "This is a good picture, that is a bad one" … This almost insane self-confidence lasted till a few years ago, and the odd thing is how many people have accepted my judgements. My whole life might be described as a long, harmless confidence trick.'[35]

Well before Clark, the men of letters had sought to capture the 'inner meaning' of the work of art and convey it to a public which had already been persuaded that works of art did have an inner meaning, and that all that was required to unlock it was to possess the key. This apparent elitism went hand in hand with an ability to speak directly to the common sense of those who went to contemplate works of art or who were able to buy them. Nineteenth-century art critics paid little attention to the details of a painting. A comprehensive glance aimed at the overall cognisance of the work as a totality was a distinctive characteristic of this tradition: the *coup d'oeuil*, the first impression, which, in the case of many hurried visitors, is also the last.

This was a further step towards the 'democratisation' of the understanding of art. At first the paintings themselves (or many of them) had been snatched from the preceding aristocratic elites. Now the formation of taste was becoming the property of middle-class intellectuals. The new age was one where talent was becoming more important than birth, though the latter remained a strong determinant of the former. Taste is the outcome of a complex negotiation in which what is at stake is the power to define, to provide meanings, to influence opinion. We find it difficult, when observing a painting, to cast out of our mind information previously received, such as the identity and intention of its artist, an anecdote about it, the putative intention of the artist, the opinion of a respected critic. This is also true of novels, plays, poems and musical works, but the consumption of these cultural products never has the rapidity of visual appreciation. The time taken to listen to a symphony or read a novel allays the impact of dominant meanings. To be authoritatively informed that Cimabue and Giotto are the founders of modern Western art, that Manet's *Déjeuner sur l'herbe* was at first regarded as disgraceful and offensive, that *Guernica* is an anti-fascist work denouncing the aerial bombing of a Basque town, contributes considerably to how we will view the work in question. The same is true when we are told that a particular smile is enigmatic or mysterious.

The frame of mind with which we approach a painting is never entirely divorced from its artist (whether an individual such as Raphael or Picasso, or a collective noun like 'the Ancient Greeks'). The painting is approached with greater reverence when its creator is generally regarded as a great painter. It follows that the task of the arbiters of taste was not limited to endowing a painting with meanings and signification, but to establishing its ranking. To put it crudely, one of the many prerequisites required by the *Mona Lisa* to become *the Mona Lisa* was not only maximum visibility but also its association with a very special creator. Being in the Louvre was only one of the many contributory factors to the fortune of the *Mona Lisa*. Being painted by Leonardo was another, but that too was not sufficient. Charles Clément, the biographer of the three great artists of the Renaissance, and former Deputy Keeper at the Louvre, enthused about the *Mona Lisa* in 1861, but dedicated only three pages to it; he was far more obsessed with the androgynous St John – which he regarded as the representation of the Eternal Feminine – than with the *Joconde*.[36] Etienne Delécluze, in his 1841 essay on Leonardo, rapidly and cursorily mentioned the *Mona Lisa* along with the Ginevra de' Benci portrait before moving on to other, more important, aspects of the painter.[37]

Yet Mona Lisa needed Leonardo. The development of the *Mona Lisa* myth required the construction of the myth of Leonardo.

CHAPTER FOUR

The Cult of Leonardo

Imagine the throng of tourists in a large museum, feet aching, bewildered at the prospect of 'doing' hundreds of paintings in a couple of hours. They pause briefly, furtively glancing at the names of the artists. Then, a look of recognition: it's a Botticelli, or a Monet, or a Caravaggio. The pause lengthens slightly; the glance changes into a respectful look. Brand names and designer labels operate in high culture, where paintings must compete for attention and admiration. Here the renown of the artist is a major factor. To be the work of an exemplary Renaissance genius is an unparalleled advantage. It was an essential ingredient in the rise to fame of the *Mona Lisa*.

Modern intellectuals found Leonardo da Vinci alluring. To them he is 'one of us'. No other painter, not even Michelangelo, has so captivated the attention of individuals of the calibre of Goethe, Walter Pater, Paul Valéry and Sigmund Freud.[1]

The cult of Leonardo started in the nineteenth century, when the Italian Renaissance was 'discovered' and a knowledge of its art was becoming almost compulsory for the educated. Previously only a small circle of upper-class travellers and intellectuals with easy access to aristocratic homes had delighted in Italian art. Throughout the eighteenth century numerous Italian artists – painters, singers, composers, architects – unable to find patronage at home sought and gained work and fame from Russia to Portugal.[2] But Rabelais and Montaigne, who travelled to Italy in the sixteenth century and who wrote of their Italian experiences, seldom referred to famous Renaissance artists. What fascinated these early tourists was the glory of Rome and Greece. Greek sculptors, such as Lysippos and Pheidias, and painters such as Apelles, were held in awe. Their fame was entirely derivative: only some Roman copies of their works existed. In establishing renown, direct experience is seldom necessary; one defers to authority. Greek poetry, Greek drama and Greek philosophy had not been bettered in over two thousand years. Who could doubt that Greek art, had it reached us in a pristine state, would have offered further unsurpassable models of perfection? Rome and its antiquities, rather than Florence or Venice, was the real destination of early travellers to Italy.

By the middle of the nineteenth century, the Renaissance came to be seen as on a par with the ancient world. As Charles Clément put it in 1861, with typical nineteenth-century disdain for the Middle Ages, centuries of darkness and ignorance had left 'nothing but ruins', until, out of this morass, the 'slow dawn', the 'summer day' of the Renaissance erupted and 'in a single flash Dante and Giotto revived poetry and painting'.[3]

As the fascination with the Renaissance grew, so did the admiration for Tuscany, enhanced by the renown of Vasari, who had praised, in his *Le Vite de' più eccellenti pittori, scultori e architetti*, the Florentine artists at the expense of the Venetians. In the eighteenth century (and for most of the nineteenth) the best-known and certainly the most admired Italian artist was Michelangelo, Vasari's own favourite. Unlike Leonardo, Michelangelo had been prolific and his great works could be seen by all. During his lifetime, his supremacy was so unprecedented that he could 'forgo all public honours, titles and distinctions'.[4] His funeral in 1564 was the most elaborate yet given to an artist.[5]

Thus the eighteenth and nineteenth centuries, in celebrating Michelangelo above all others, were reproducing a consensus largely established in the sixteenth. Leonardo, even though he had died in France as an honoured guest of a great king, was seldom discussed prior to 1800.[6] By then, of course, Leonardo,

Raphael and Michelangelo were regarded as Old Masters. The nineteenth century recruited Botticelli, Piero della Francesca, Giotto, Vermeer, El Greco and many others to their ranks. In the twentieth century very few new names were added to this exclusive club.

Count Francesco Algarotti's influential *Saggio sopra la pittura*, published in 1762 and almost immediately translated into French, English and German, declared that 'Raphael is now universally allowed to have attained that degree of perfection, beyond which it is scarcely lawful for mortals to aspire.'[7] William Hazlitt in his 1817 essay 'On the Fine Arts' (written for the *Encyclopaedia Britannica*) regarded Leonardo as a man of learning who 'vitiated his pictures with too much science', and whose women have an expression equally characteristic of the mistress or the saint.[8]

Horace Vernet's famous painting *Raphael au Vatican* (1832, see plate 21) placed Raphael firmly centre stage – he is, after all, its principal subject. Raphael is represented as young and handsome – as he always was, having died at the age of thirty-seven. He is seen surrounded by friends and admirers in the act of drawing, almost surreptitiously, a young mother holding her baby who was there by chance. In the foreground, on the left, lurks Michelangelo, his arms laden with papers, plans and a small replica of one of his statues, his attention captivated by an old woman, a possible model. On a platform, Pope Julius II is busy examining future projects. Leonardo is also there, but on the distant right-hand side, partially seen, looking wistfully (or perhaps indifferently) at the busy scene near him.

In an earlier painting, Anicet Lemonnier's *François I recevant dans la salle des suisses a Fontainebleau la Grande Sainte Famille de Raphael* (1814, see plate 22), the king is shown surrounded by his entire court, including various painters and writers – among them Thomas More, Rabelais and Primaticcio – admiring Raphael's *Holy Family*, just acquired by François I. The king appears to invite Leonardo – on the right – to share in the general admiration, but the old man – after the king the main subject of the picture – seems visibly unenthusiastic and a little resentful.

In 1796 Hubert Robert, the Louvre's Chief Curator of Pictures, produced a vast canvas in which he imagined how the Grande Galerie would look once it had become a vibrant museum (see plate 23). In the foreground, in pride of place, Raphael's *Holy Family* is being devoutly copied by various artists. Nearby are paintings by Guido Reni and Titian (his *Entombment*). On the floor, other copyists are at work. Of Leonardo and Mona Lisa there is no trace.

Nowadays, to leave out the *Mona Lisa* from a selection of representative paintings from the Louvre would be a deliberate act of iconoclasm. Yet, though the *Mona Lisa* has become the best-known painting in the world, Leonardo has never become acknowledged as the greatest painter. In art history he has probably been outdistanced, in terms of the volume of work dedicated to his paintings, by Michelangelo, Raphael, Picasso and Rembrandt – each of whose output was far greater than his. There is no doubt that the number of studies on Leonardo's works is enormous, but many of them are dedicated to his scientific works and to his drawings. The *Bibliografia Italiana di Storia della Scienza* records some 379 essays on Leonardo and science since 1979 alone. A keyword search of the holdings of the US Library of Congress produced 1,219 'hits', one at the New York Public Library 411. Even so, Leonardo is outdistanced by Michelangelo (1,635 and 602 respectively) and above all by Picasso (1,804 and 935).[9]

What contributed to the construction of the cult of Leonardo was that he was regarded not only as a major painter but also as a great scientist. Here too the French were instrumental. In 1796 Napoleon, having conquered most of Italy, had taken back some of Leonardo's scientific manuscripts.[10] A year later Giovanni Battista Venturi, an Italian diplomat and scholar, gave an important lecture on the 'Physical-mathematical Works of Leonardo da Vinci', which was immediately published with extracts from the manuscripts. Later Friedrich von Humboldt, in his five-volume *Kosmos* (1845–62), and David Brewster in his *Life of Sir Isaac*

Newton (1831) described Leonardo as the scientific Columbus.[11]

In fact, contrary to common perception, Leonardo's role in the history of science and technology is marginal. Unlike Galileo Galilei or Isaac Newton, he never made a major scientific breakthrough. In engineering and technology he examined a multitude of cases, especially in hydraulics, but never discovered a scientific law. His contribution to the philosophy or methodology of science is very modest if one compares him to Bacon, Leibnitz or Hume. The most that could be said about his engineering drawings is that they presaged future technological developments; but he never actually invented anything of note. His works in hydraulic technology and military machines were commonplace at the time. He built, like all engineers, on the works of his predecessors, people like the Sienese Mariano Taccola, and Francesco di Giorgio Martini, whose *Treatise on Architecture* Leonardo had studied thoroughly but did not surpass.[12] In Milan, at Lodovico's court he worked mainly as an engineer, but others such as Bramante were in charge, and were regarded as Leonardo's superiors and teachers. There is very little evidence that Leonardo ever had the 'slightest professional engagement' with architecture.[13] As Bertrand Gille observed in 1978, the notebooks Leonardo kept when working for Cesare Borgia resemble the diaries of a visiting scholar preparing to draft a report, not the notes of the chief engineer.[14]

The manor house of Clos-Lucé, where Leonardo lived the last years of his life, is now a museum. The basement is dedicated to his machines, carefully constructed from his drawings under the sponsorship of IBM. Similar machines could have been constructed on the basis of the drawings of Leonardo's contemporaries or predecessors. But they did not paint the *Mona Lisa*.

In Leonardo's native town of Vinci, in Tuscany, the small Museo Leonardiano exhibits some fifty-five machines and models built on the basis of his drawings. These include the famous multi-barrelled gun, a tank, a bridge canal with sluice gates, and even a sketch of a bicycle, reconstructed from Leonardo's Madrid

Codex (discovered in 1966) with a note defending its highly dubious authenticity. The Vinci Museum has however, to its credit, set Leonardo's achievements as an engineer in their proper context by showing similar drawings by Giovanni Fontana, Francesco di Giorgio and various anonymous draughtsmen. The explanatory leaflet informs the visitor that Leonardo 'perfected the machines and mechanisms handed down in the technical literature of the fifteenth century', and admits that some of the 'inventions' are more the result of the imagination of those reconstructing the drawings than of Leonardo's intentions. Visitors, however, marvel at Leonardo's prescience. A rival museum in Vinci, the Museo Ideale Leonardo, is even more explicit in debunking the exaggerated claims made on behalf of Leonardo, but it too, unavoidably, exhibits the famous machines. Thus the contemporary popular image of Leonardo as a great scientist who also painted the *Mona Lisa* and *The Last Supper* is similar to that produced by some of the intelligentsia of the nineteenth century. And as scholars are not as secluded from what matters to the wider public as is sometimes believed, the scholarly work devoted to Leonardo's contribution to science far exceeds that on his equally or more talented contemporaries.

In fact, it may be near the truth to admit that Leonardo was a little 'technologically challenged'. His one great attempt at a major sculpture, a gigantic equestrian statue – seven metres high – in memory of Francesco Sforza, known as '*il Cavallo*' and aimed at rivalling his teacher Verrocchio's *Bartolomeo Colleoni* in Venice, was never made because the Milanese needed the bronze to cast cannon to defend themselves against the French. But it is unlikely that it could ever have been cast: the surviving drawings had not resolved the technical problems involved in holding in the desired position such a monumental sculpture.[15] Indeed, Lodovico himself doubted Leonardo's ability to deliver, and wrote to Lorenzo il Magnifico asking him whether there was anyone else in Florence with the required skills.[16]

Leonardo's *Treatise on Painting* contains rules that he himself never used. Gombrich noted that the contrast 'between his practice as a painter and his observations in the *Trattato*' are 'astonishing'.[17]

His plans to change the course of the Arno and to dig a canal between Florence and Pisa were abandoned. His *Last Supper* began to deteriorate almost as soon as he had finished it because he used oil mixed with tempera instead of the quick-drying fresco. *The Battle of Anghiari* – the most important work he had ever been commissioned to produce (1504) – was left unfinished, and the parts he did complete deteriorated immediately because Leonardo, once again, had used an inappropriate paint mix. It was eventually painted over by Vasari, who expressed his puzzlement at Leonardo's *modi stranissimi nel cercare olii per dipingere e vernice per mantenere l'opere fatte* ('rather bizarre method of making oil for painting and varnish for preserving the works').[18]

Leonardo's notebooks are full of references to projects that existed only in his mind. They are written in a fragmentary form, probably because he was unable or unwilling to draft ideas in a coherent and consistent way. Vasari's famous comment that Leonardo 'started many things and never finished them' was a view widely shared by his contemporaries.[19] Centuries later this trait was regarded as praiseworthy, a sign of true genius. Leonardo's slow workmanship came to be seen as perfectionism. He took four years or so to paint the *Mona Lisa*, all 77 × 53 centimetres of it. In the same span of time Michelangelo painted the entire ceiling of the Sistine Chapel.[20]

Admirers regard Leonardo as prefiguring technological developments. Yet, with the possible exception of the parachute, not one of the great breakthroughs in hydraulics or aviation owes anything to his insights.[21] The famous drawing of the bicycle led some to imagine that Leonardo had invented this contraption. One does not have to be a Renaissance genius to realise that with pedals longer than the wheels, no movement would have been possible. The drawing even shows a chain, an innovation that would not come until the end of the nineteenth century.[22]

Leonardo's famous drawing of a helicopter resembles that of a toy popular around 1460 (when he was a child), in which tiny windmill wings were propelled by a rapidly unwinding piece of string. And Leonardo failed to understand that the muscular structure of human beings could never release the energy sufficient to reproduce the flying capacity of birds. His obsession with flapping-wing aircraft was 'peculiarly fruitless'.[23] The idea of flying machines had of course preceded Leonardo. In any case, to imagine a future discovery is a far cry from contributing to its invention – Jules Verne conceived of a rocket flying to the moon, but was never regarded as a man of science.

The popular image of Leonardo as a major scientist has remained alive to the present day. This is hardly surprising: much of twentieth-century popular culture had its origins in nineteenth-century 'bourgeois' culture, which in turn owes much to the preceding 'folk' culture. Leonardo's stature as a painter and draftsman is unassailable, but few scholars now claim that he was a major scientist or a great engineer, though a stream of popular books in the nineteenth-century mould continues to be produced, extolling his contribution to science. Every year, articles and books add to the tally. Mario De Micheli's introduction to a selection of Leonardo's writings, originally published in 1952 (for the fifth centenary of his birth), revised in 1982 and reprinted in 1991, calls him a path-breaker who 'opened the way for discoveries and inventions made centuries later'.[24] The introduction by distinguished art historians to a book published in 1981 identified Leonardo, rather fashionably, as the forebear of the modern ecological movement because he had foreseen the trend towards deforestation.[25] When in 1902 Marcelin Berthelot, a politician and scientist, tired of hearing Leonardo praised by his colleagues at the Académie des sciences, suggested that his scientific work was of limited value, he was regarded as eccentric.[26]

Genius is an odd category. Being a genius, like being a celebrity, consists in being regarded as one by others. The implication of the term is that however much effort is expended, what really makes these individuals outstanding are some inner qualities, or a gift from God or its modern equivalent: having the right genes. Nineteenth-century descriptions of Leonardo emphasise the fact that he manifested his genius from childhood (like Mozart, etc.). In mathematics he quickly outwitted his teachers; his father showed one of Leonardo's drawings to Verrocchio, who was astonished.[27] One becomes a genius by being born one, not just by working hard – a consolation to the rest of us who do not make the grade.

The powerful myth of Leonardo amounts to this: he is a genius *tout court*; a genius at everything – really universal. It makes no difference that he did not actually invent anything. On the contrary, if he did not make anything it is because he had the misfortune to have been born in what was, technologically and scientifically, the 'wrong' century. In spite of this handicap he prefigured what was yet to come. And that is, narcissistically, our own age of modern rationalism. We understand him. They didn't. He is *one of us*.

The assumption that there is such a thing as a scientific 'prefiguration' is a nineteenth-century view of how history and science proceed: every aspect of the future is contained in the past, the present is the unfolding of what has preceded us. Hence the search, whenever we are faced by an oak tree, for the inevitable acorn. This is still a common view. The genius is always 'ahead of his time', and is thus misunderstood. We, who come so much later, can finally put right history's wrongs, make amends for the mistakes of the past, and recognise true genius.

This is how Leonardo was and is still seen. Alienated from his own times, he speaks to us directly, for we have a superior sensibility. We can understand the great men of the past better than their relatively ignorant and superstitious contemporaries. Living in a garret, writing, composing or painting, the great artist had to be a driven man. Alienated from society, he was able to keep going because, deep inside, he knew that future generations would appreciate him: the case of Beethoven's late string quartets, labelled 'For a Future Age', is an illustration of this Romantic myth. In fact, there are very few major artists – notwithstanding famous exceptions such as Van Gogh – who suffered this predicament. The norm, for great talent, is to be successful and appreciated in one's own time: Shakespeare, Goethe, Voltaire, Mozart, Beethoven and Verdi as well as Michelangelo, Titian, Raphael and, of course, Leonardo, who was revered by many and who worked for the great patrons of his time. Not all celebrities are remembered by posterity, but it is helpful to be known when one is alive: that way one's works are protected and preserved and have a good chance of surviving.

It is thus remarkable, and not inevitable, that in the nineteenth century Leonardo should have become the object of a cult. His drawings were not widely available, his grandiose works were unrealised, his notes were scattered everywhere, his paintings were damaged or largely unfinished. There is no doubt that what fascinated his admirers was the idea of an inquisitive mind at work, both scientist and artist, constantly shifting interest from one field to another, never satisfied, steadily searching for the new. As such he fulfilled the nineteenth-century idea of true genius.

The Russian Renaissance scholar Leonid M. Batkin pointed out in 1988 that Leonardo was really *of his time*, a time when it was far more acceptable than it is today not to deliver immediate and practical results, but to produce instead a mass of disconnected observations on natural phenomena, technology and the properties of things.[28] This is fair enough. The pursuit of blind alleys is a necessary precondition for scientific progress. Such 'useful' failures are seldom recognised. We remember Marie and Pierre Curie, not those scientists who paved their way, such as Wilhelm Roentgen, who discovered radium, and Antoine Henri Becquerel, who shared their Nobel Prize. Jean-Baptiste Lamarck and Alfred Wallace are not household names, Darwin is.

The construction of the cult of Leonardo the Great Scientist was the work of non-scientists, of men of letters and assorted intellectuals. It was with admiration that major nineteenth-century writers such as Stendhal, who knew nothing about science, unhesitatingly claimed that 'one hundred years before Francis Bacon, Leonardo had reached the conclusions which made Bacon great. His fault was to have left them unpublished.'[29] He praised Leonardo's achievements as an engineer extravagantly:

> Under this scorching sun, he made sure that water could reach all corners of the Milanese countryside. Travellers owe him this wonderful landscape where the fertility of vast green spaces is matched by the strange shapes of snow-covered mountains, forming, a few miles away, a dream horizon and a feast to the eye.[30]

By the twentieth century Leonardo had become the archetypal 'folk' scientist, the prolific inventor, full of ideas, churning out schemes and projects from the solitude of his laboratory. In his time, however, the conventional separation between disciplines had not yet developed. Universalism was an attribute common to all gifted men of the Renaissance, not a unique trait of Leonardo's.[31]

The conception of art which prevailed during the Renaissance required a knowledge of science. The invention of perspective – the great achievement of Western art – was more than simply a way of representing shapes in the right proportion. It consisted in applying the Euclidean geometric principle of proportional triangles to painting before applying it to other fields such as architecture, as Brunelleschi had done.[32] Leonardo wrote: 'Perspective is a rational demonstration by which experience confirms that all things send their semblances to the eye by pyramidal lines.'[33]

Leonardo moved easily from science to art and back again. Only in a culture in which there were no rigid boundaries between the two could this take place. Like many of his contemporaries, he believed that painting was a scientific activity that used the principles of arithmetic and geometry.[34] There were also practical considerations. During the Renaissance it was advisable to be competent in a variety of fields because, as Lisa Jardine has explained, 'The artists most highly in demand with noble employers . . . were those with drafting, engineering and architectural talents as well as creative and aesthetic flair.'[35]

When, in 1482, Leonardo wrote to Lodovico offering his good services – a letter cited in virtually all studies of Leonardo – he emphasised his skills as a military engineer. This is usually seen as reflecting Lodovico's own priorities, but there is no evidence that they were not Leonardo's too. Of the ten areas listed in which he claimed to excel – revealing his own self-assurance rather than any real achievements – nine were directly concerned with war. 'I can,' he boasted, 'build bridges and battering rams, secret passages, covered wagons behind which soldiers can hide.' Only the tenth and last item of expertise concerned peacetime activities: 'I can carry out sculptures in marble, bronze, or clay, and *also I can do in painting whatever may be done, as well as any other, be he who he may*' (my emphasis).

The modern admiration of universalism as a sign of genius is part of a Romantic longing for a pre-industrial golden age, when knowledge had not yet become compartmentalised. Leonardo did not reject specialisation; it is just that the concept had not yet been invented. He was breaking the conventions of the nineteenth century, not those of his own times.

He was in good company. Machiavelli not only wrote his famous treatise on politics (*The Prince*), but also history and a play (*La Mandragola*) still frequently performed. Albrecht Dürer studied mathematics and geometry, wrote a treatise on measurement in 1525 and on military engineering in 1527, and was a supreme master of woodcut and copper engraving as well as a major painter. Michelangelo, unlike Leonardo, managed to excel in four distinct fields: architecture, painting, sculpture and poetry. Yet as these are all 'artistic' activities he is regarded as a great artist, not a universal genius. Until recently he was not even regarded as a significant poet. Had Michelangelo not been an artist, the quality of his poetic output – some three hundred poems and fragments, not published until 1863[36] – would have won him recognition as one of the most talented poets of the sixteenth century. But the artist overwhelmed the poet.

Nineteenth- and twentieth-century admirers were dismayed to find out that Leonardo organised parties for Lodovico il Moro and had a mechanical lion built for François I. This was taken as further proof of the low esteem in which he was held by his contemporaries. A Renaissance genius made to organise parties! The man who might have invented the flying machine forced to make mechanical toys! Yet there is no evidence that these tasks were regarded as undignified. Vasari, to whom we owe these anecdotes, far from depicting them as demeaning, used them to illustrate Leonardo's range.[37] There is no evidence that Leonardo himself felt humiliated by them. François I had not wanted him to be his engineer. He had plenty of excellent Italian engineers busy building fortresses along the country's borders and great towers to defend Le Havre and Toulon. Leonardo was not expected to build bridges or dig canals. He was at court to be a *savant*, a man of learning and wisdom, whose wit and brilliant conversation would enhance the intellectual prestige of the French king.[38] He was there as a great Italian: the French court was then in thrall to all things Italian. This is hardly surprising. In 1500 Italy had wealth, science, technology and the best financial system in the world. Italians were the best engineers, the best painters, sculptors and architects, the best bankers, the best artisans.

This day passed, and by the end of the eighteenth century the literary perception of Italy – thanks to Gothic novels by Anne Radcliffe and others – was as a land of bandits and scheming priests, conspiracies and plots, the birthplace of sinister characters such as Machiavelli and Cesare Borgia. By the second half of the nineteenth century this image had changed considerably. Italy had become the site of a glorious artistic past, a dazzling country inspired by the spirit of beauty, the birthplace of modernity and individualism: 'The Italian . . . was the firstborn among the sons of modern Europe,' wrote the historian Jacob Burckhardt in 1960.[39] It was the birthplace of the 'all-sided man – *l'uomo universale* – who belonged to Italy alone'.[40]

Throughout most of the nineteenth century liberal intellectuals regarded the struggle for Italian unification, the Risorgimento, as a major progressive cause. It would rescue Italy from the double oppression of clerical obscurantism and Austrian despotism. In Britain even conservatives had sympathy for Italian national aspirations. In France it was one of the issues uniting progressive republicanism against Catholic monarchism. The cult of Leonardo as the paragon of progressive and modern thinking was part of this political and ideological project. Its main proponents were the 'progressive' anti-clerical historians Jules Michelet, in his multi-volume *History of France* (of which the Italian Renaissance is an integral part), and Edgar Quinet in his *Revolutions in Italy* (1848–52). Hippolyte Taine, whose *Voyage en Italie* (1865) exalted Leonardo as the hero of the modern age, further enhanced this image. Nineteenth-century intellectuals travelled to Italy to find confirmation of what they already believed.

They regarded Leonardo as someone who had left behind all religious dogmas. He was not afraid to dissect corpses; he did not paint halos on his religious figures – thus 'uncrowning the Middle Ages' (Quinet). Unlike Raphael and Michelangelo, he was never the servant of popes. He put Man at the centre of creation.[41]

Michelet exhorted his readers:

> Go to the Louvre, in the Grande Galerie. On your left you will find the old world; on the right the new. On one side the lethargic images of Fra Angelico, still at the feet of the medieval Virgin; with their ailing sight, moribund ... Opposite this archaic mysticism shines, through the paintings of Leonardo da Vinci, the genius of the Renaissance ... they are of the same epoch as Angelico's, yet a thousand years separate them.[42]

Michelet and Quinet regarded themselves as the voice of progressive France, fighting against the obscurantism of religious piety, and as the disciples, in their historical works, of the project of the Renaissance and its greatest spirit, Leonardo. Thus the entire Renaissance, and Leonardo in particular, was conscripted into the service of the Enlightenment and the ideals of the French Revolution. Michelet dismissed the Middle Ages as a 'bizarre and monstrous era . . . whose only achievement was its length and an obstinate resistance to nature'.[43] The only true scientists of the Middle Ages, he claimed, were Arabs and Jews.[44]

Michelet's nationalism and pride in his country had that peculiar French characteristic of regarding itself as universal. The young George Eliot castigated such 'ridiculous excess of *amour de patrie*'. France, she wrote, had become a kind of lay religion and the French people 'a sort of second chosen race, who alone have the mission to propagate, by pen and by sword, the truth which is to regenerate the nations'.[45] This ideology enabled the French to turn Leonardo into Léonard de Vinci – an honorary Frenchman – and his *Joconde* into a product of French culture.

Leonardo became a *français manqué*, adopted by the country which – it was claimed – understood him better than his native Italy. France, declared the best-selling novelist, Leonardophile and director of the Théâtre-Français Arsène Houssaye in 1869, was the only nation which could build on the heritage of Leonardo: in Italy nothing was left of art since the end of the Renaissance, in Germany nothing since Dürer, in Spain nothing since Velázquez and Murillo, in Holland nothing since Rubens and Van Dyck. As for the English, concluded Houssaye, they could paint nothing but scenes of steeplechase.[46] 'It is Léonard de Vinci' – wrote the critic François-Anatole Gruyer in 1891 in his *Voyage autour du salon carré au musée du Louvre* – 'who gives our national museum its unique value and incomparable originality.'[47] This was not lost on the English-language Baedeker guide to Paris in 1900: 'Leonardo da Vinci, whom the French are inclined to claim as one of their own artists'.[48]

A cult usually needs a body to worship or a place of pilgrimage, but Leonardo's birthplace was relatively distant, and his body could never be found: in 1863 Arsène Houssaye, determined to find it, dug up round the site of the church of Saint-Florentin in Amboise (destroyed in 1808) and found several skulls. Having selected a particularly appropriate-seeming one, he hailed it as the remains of the great man, but was discomfited to discover that he had been looking in the wrong place.[49] The body of the Renaissance genius, the anatomist who had performed over thirty autopsies, remains undiscovered to this day, though tourists to Amboise are still entreated to visit his burial place.

The Catholics weighed in. Though some attacked the Renaissance and all its works, others – for instance Alexis Rio in his 1855 *Léonard de Vinci et son école* – attempted to depict Leonardo as a good Catholic. Charles Clément took issue with Vasari's hint that Leonardo was irreligious.[50] Had not Leonardo left in his will detailed instructions for a strictly religious funeral? This act (prudence, or genuine conversion?) had embarrassed freethinkers such as Gabriel Séailles.[51] Stendhal had no doubts: 'Leonardo was too intelligent to submit to the religion of his century.'[52] It was this latter view which prevailed. Intellectual heroes had to be consistent and coherent. The ideal scientist was the Galileo figure, persecuted by the Church, compelled to recant to save his works from destruction. Isaac Newton's fervent and genuine religiosity was forgotten or regarded as anachronistic and aberrant. Michelet's son-in-law Alfred Dumesnil hailed Leonardo as the precursor of Galileo as the man who had set for himself tasks which 'three hundred years have not sufficed to resolve'.[53]

In the 1850s and 1860s, during the Second Empire, the liberal admirers of Leonardo were in opposition. Michelet had been forced into exile. But he lived long enough (he died in 1874) to find himself lionised by the Third Republic. Later, his books became required reading in schools, and an army of teachers dutifully relayed his interpretation of the past to new generations. As anti-clericalism developed, Michelet's secular themes were echoed with increasing fervour. By 1908 René Bonnamen was praising Leonardo *because* he was a 'free spirit' who had rejected Catholicism (or so Bonnamen assumed). He was hailed as the precursor of the great scientists of the nineteenth century, from Claude Bernard to Louis Pasteur, from Jean-Baptiste Lamarck to Charles Darwin, a connection previously made by Michelet himself.[54]

A hundred years after Michelet, anti-clerical writers including Marxists such as Mario De Micheli still hailed Leonardo as a tenacious pursuer of the truth, 'the real reason why he is a true contemporary of ours', emancipated from theological preju-dices.[55] The Communists – as heirs to the Enlightenment – had long celebrated Leonardo as a pioneer of modern thought. In 1952, on the occasion of the fifth centenary of Leonardo's birth, the French Communist paper *Avant-garde* intoned:

> The peoples of the world celebrate a great son of the Italian people, one of the high points of the struggle against reaction and obscurantism, a materialist thinker. The USSR, in changing the course of great rivers to transform Siberia into happy and fertile regions, has continued the work of Leonardo. This was aimed at the improvement of the people, of all those who, through their labour created the wealth and the beauties of the world. Why did he go to France? Because she was already a relatively free nation, fighting against obscurantism.[56]

Later, capitalists admired Leonardo too. They were prepared to bid enormous sums for his autograph manuscripts. One of these, the so-called Leicester Codex (bought by Lord Leicester in 1715) fetched $5 million when it was sold in 1980 to the Armand Hammer Foundation, who promptly renamed it the Hammer Codex. In 1994 it was sold for $31 million to Bill Gates, who *did not* rename it the Gates Codex or Microsoft Codex.

In the nineteenth century, the Individual was celebrated as the

maker of his own destiny. History had long been the history of
Great Men, but the idea of the heroic was acquiring a new dimen-
sion, celebrated by Carlyle in his *On Heroes, Hero-Worship and
the Heroic in History* (1841). The new modern heroes were no
longer soldiers but men of culture, fearless interpreters of modern
ideas.[57] Leonardo was not the only beneficiary of this fashion.
The new reading public became fascinated by biographies.

There are, of course, precedents: Plutarch's *Lives* had been the
model for Vasari's own lives of artists and for Shakespeare's
Roman plays. Boswell's popular *Life of Johnson* started a new
genre: the recording of conversations between a Great Man (e.g.
Goethe) and his adoring and respectful interlocutor (Johann
Peter Eckermann) – the forerunner of the modern interview.
Autobiographies too became more fashionable. At first they were
contrite accounts of one's life – Jean-Jacques Rousseau's *Confessions*, with St Augustine as his great antecedent[58] – but they
soon became less penitent, if not triumphalist: Goethe's *Aus
meinem Leben: Dichtung und Wahrheit* (1809–14, 1830), Thomas
De Quincey's *Confessions of an English Opium-Eater* (1821), Silvio
Pellico's *Le mie prigioni* (1832), Stendhal's *Vie de Henry Brulard*
(1836), George Sand's *Histoire de ma vie* (1854), John Stuart Mill's
Autobiography (1873) and many others.

By the mid-1850s the biographical genre had become well established, particularly in France and Britain. The multi-volume
French publication of Vasari's *Lives* started in 1839, the English
edition in 1850. There was an expanding market for the 'Lives of
Great Men' (and, occasionally, of Great Women). Publishers
began series like 'English Men of Letters', 'American Statesmen',
'Les Grands écrivains français'.[59]

It is from this wider perspective that the burgeoning cult of
Leonardo and other Renaissance artists should be viewed. During
the Renaissance itself 'real' artists had started to distinguish themselves from mere artisans. The work of art was becoming the
unique and unrepeatable product of a 'genius' working in iso-
lation. Leonardo himself was a defender of this emergent status,

insisting that painting was superior to sculpture (a skill at which he did not excel). He claimed that painting was an intellectual activity, like science, because it aimed at bringing the three-dimensionality of nature into a different, 'flat', world. Sculpture was physical, hence a craft, hence inferior:

> The truth of this is evident in that the sculptor when making his work uses the strength of his arm in hammering . . . This is an extremely mechanical operation, generally accompanied by great sweat mingling with dust and turning into mud. His face becomes plastered and powdered all over with marble powder, which makes him look like a baker . . .
>
> The painter, on the other hand, is a real gentleman. He sits before his work at the greatest of ease, well dressed . . . His residence is clean and adorned with delightful pictures, and he often enjoys the accompaniment of music or the company of the authors of various fine works.[60]

The discipline of art history, barely extant in the nineteenth century, dealt with the work of art within the context of a wider narrative, that of the artist and his work or 'life-and-work'. This could not be done with the works of antiquity, whose creators were untraceable. Had art history been based on the works of antiquity, it would have been far more centred on the works themselves. Had it been based on medieval art, it would have been centred largely on the co-operative activities of workshops and centres of production. The choice of the Renaissance as the main core of the discipline, at least initially, brought about a development of the study of the creator and his work.

This was paralleled by the development of the idea of the uniqueness of the work of art itself, and hence of the artist. The importance of attributing works of art to specific artists is a relatively recent and largely Western practice.[61] Industrialisation had made the reproduction of identical objects on a vast scale commonplace, thus making the original work itself far more valuable.[62] The unique work of art is, by definition, in a position of monopoly. There is, after all, only one *Mona Lisa*; there will never be another one. In a world dominated by reproducible commodities whose value plummets as technology lowers production costs and makes them available to an ever expanding mass of consumers, to be the 'one and only' becomes a major selling point. For this to happen, it is necessary that the producer should be exceptional; better still, a certified artistic genius. A painting by an unaccredited artist, an amateur, someone not previously authenticated, is of little or no value. Past masters have the advantage over their contemporary rivals of having had their fame repeatedly endorsed by a succession of arbiters of taste. Such fame will be well defended by those who regard themselves as the authorities on these matters. A body of specialists, museum curators, art historians, experts certified by other experts, vouch for the authenticity, singularity and uniqueness of works of art. They declare whether it was painted by a particular Old Master, whether others aided him, whether it was the first of a series, and how the work and the artist rank with respect to others. The terminology used always has financial as well as qualitative implications: an 'early' or 'derivative' work, a 'minor' artist, 'school of', 'a pupil of', tend to mean 'not worth as much as' and 'not as good as'.

It is, of course, a tautological circle. A museum masterpiece can only have been painted by an established master; an established master is one whose works are to be found in a major museum. After the Renaissance, that is when works of art became routinely associated with a particular creator, the artistic value of art turned out to depend largely on the identity of the artist.

One can envisage multiple objections to this. We do not know the identities of the creators of the Rosetta Stone, or the Elgin marbles, or, to stick to Louvre artefacts, the Venus de Milo or the Winged Victory of Samothrace. Nevertheless, they are as 'priceless' as the *Mona Lisa*.

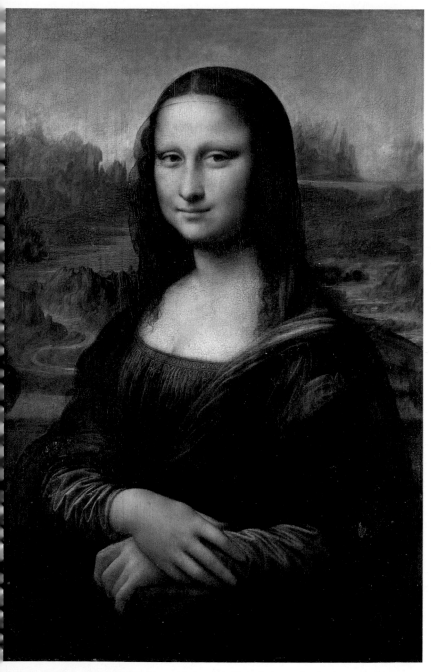

1. *Mona Lisa* by Leonardo da Vinci (1503-6?, Louvre). Though the attribution has never been questioned, everything else has. Is it really the portrait of Monna (= m'lady) Lisa Gherardini, wife of Francesco del Giocondo, born in Florence on 15 June 1479? Leonardo's contemporaries thought it was a masterpiece. The smile, however, became 'enigmatic' only in the middle of the nineteenth century.

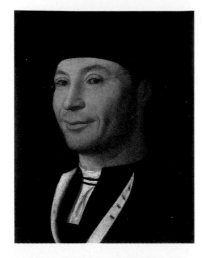

2. LEFT *Portrait of an Unknown Man* by
Antonello da Messina (1470, Museo
Mandralisca, Cefalù, Sicily). Few wonder
why this handsome man is smiling or
who was the sitter. The portrait is
regarded as outstanding, but men are
more intrigued by the smiles of women,
particularly if they hang in Paris and not
in distant Sicily.

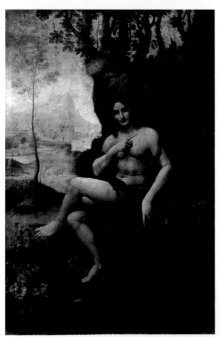

3. *Bacchus* by Leonardo (1513?, Louvre).
Arguably this was Leonardo's last painting.
He started painting it in Rome and took it
with him, unfinished, to France along with
the *Mona Lisa*.

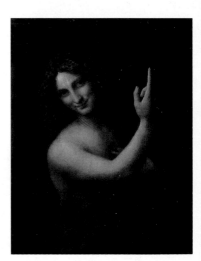

4. *St John the Baptist* by Leonardo
(1508-13, Louvre). In the depiction of
this smiling adolescent Leonardo
displays all the techniques at work in
the *Mona Lisa*: the internal movement
known as *contrapposto*, the play of
shadows (*chiaroscuro*), the blurry
smoky look (*sfumato*), and a strong
suggestion of androgyny.

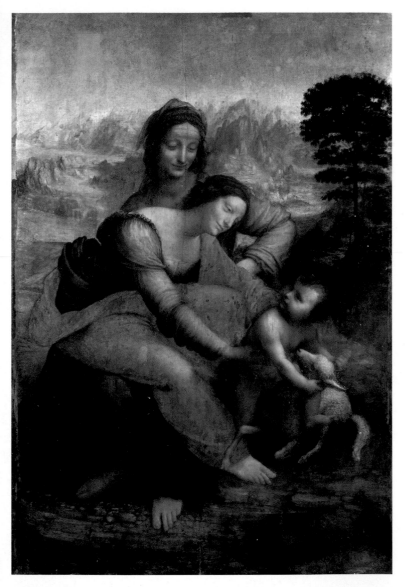

5. *St Anne with Virgin and Child* by Leonardo (date uncertain, probably between 1508 and 1510, Louvre). A complex composition which has the Virgin sitting on the lap of her mother, St Anne, calmly restraining Jesus who is playing with a lamb. Everyone smiles most unmysteriously. The strange rocky landscape is reminiscent of the background to the *Mona Lisa*.

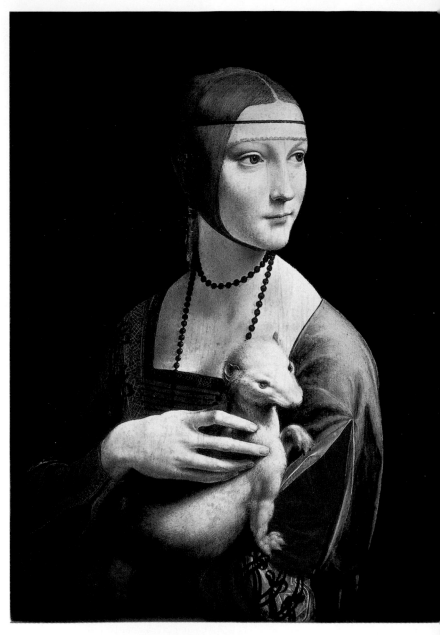

6. *Lady with an Ermine* by Leonardo (1488-90, Czartoryski Museum, Cracow). The portrait of Cecilia Gallerani, the mistress of Leonardo's patron Lodovico il Moro. Cecilia's smile could be regarded as ironic and inscrutable, her looking away seductive, her hand caressing a furry animal rich in Freudian implications. But she hangs in Cracow and not in Paris.

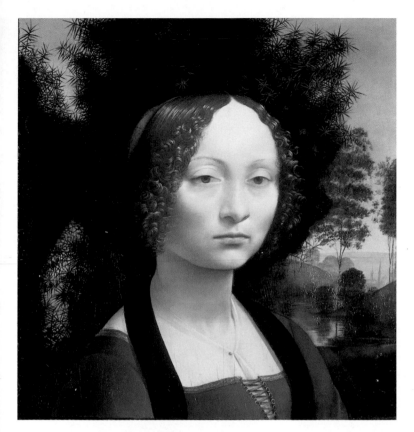

7. *Ginevra de' Benci* by Leonardo (*c.*1475, National Gallery, Washington D.C.). An early Leonardo and the only one now outside Europe. What saddens the beautiful Ginevra, an aristocratic Florentine lady, has not generated a fraction of the interest of Lisa's smile, yet 'sad' expressions were rare in Renaissance portraits.

8. *Portrait of Isabella d'Este* by Leonardo (1500, chalk on paper, Louvre, Department of Graphic Arts). The rich and powerful Isabella d'Este, Marquise of Mantua, had beseeched Leonardo to paint her portrait. Leonardo never went further than this drawing, but it can be regarded as part of his lengthy experimentation with the *contrapposto*: Isabella is viewed in profile (unusually for Leonardo), but her bust is turned towards us in the three-quarter view of his other major portraits.

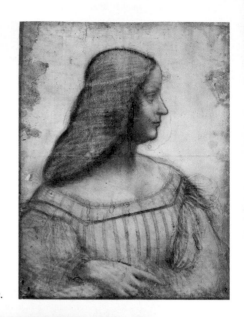

9. *La Belle Ferronnière* by Leonardo (1495-99, Louvre). Long thought to be the mistress of François I (hence the name), this is in fact the portrait of Lucrezia Crivelli, a mistress of Leonardo's patron Lodovico il Moro. A case could be made that her expression is as mysterious as that of the *Mona Lisa*.

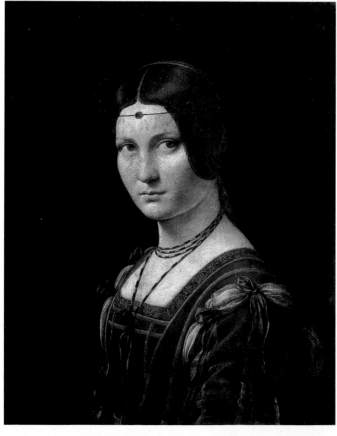

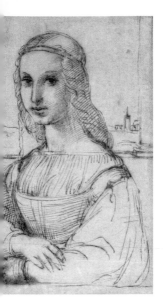

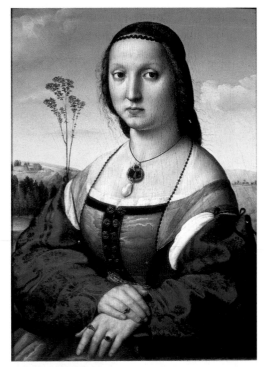

ABOVE *Young Woman in a Loggia* by Raphael (1504, Louvre, Department of Graphic Arts). This was probably a study for the portrait of Maddalena Doni, but the sitter represented is not Maddalena. Could it be the authentic Lisa Gherardini, drawn by Raphael after seeing Leonardo working on the *Mona Lisa*?

ABOVE RIGHT *Portrait of Maddalena Doni* by Raphael (1505, Palazzo Pitti, Florence). The sitter has the pose of the *Mona Lisa*, but the Florentine background, the jewellery she wears and the blemishes on her face identify her as the historical Maddalena Strozzi, wife of Agnolo Doni. The Strozzi and Doni families were among the most powerful in Renaissance Florence.

RIGHT *Portrait of Baldissare Castiglione* by Raphael (1514-15, Louvre) Another example of Raphael's use of the *Mona Lisa* pose. Castiglione, a close friend of the painter and author of the celebrated treatise *The Courtier*, urged courtesans to refrain from affectation at all costs, and to pretend that everything they did was uncontrived and effortless.

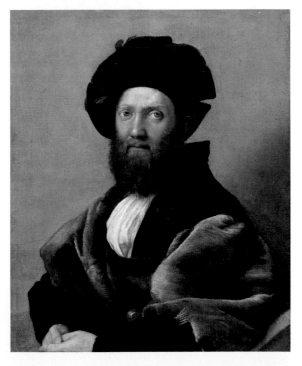

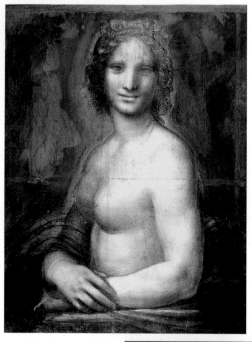

13. LEFT *Monna Vanna*, after Leonardo (*c*.1513, Musée Condé, Chantilly). Also known as *The Naked Gioconda*, this drawing in black chalk was probably inspired by a similar painting or drawing by Leonardo. In the sixteenth century there were many 'Giocondas' painted or drawn in the nude in the *contrapposto* position with the hands folded.

14. BELOW *Portrait of Colombina*, attributed to Francesco Melzi (Hermitage, St Petersburg). Melzi, a pupil of Leonardo's, inherited his tools and notebooks. Her left breast exposed, and body and face turned towards the left, this 'Gioconda' – attributed by some to Leonardo – has a visage strongly reminiscent of the smiling face of the Virgin in *St Anne with Virgin and Child*.

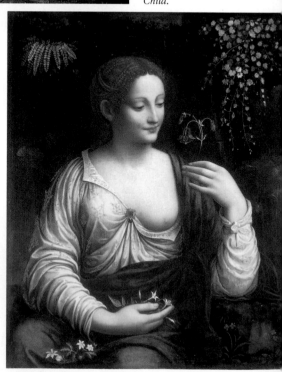

What happens is that where, as is the case with the art of antiquity, authorship cannot be traced, artistic value is determined on the basis of other criteria, such as age, ownership and location. Otherwise it is the renown of the artist which – generally speaking – determines modern concepts of artistic rarity and value. There are, of course, exceptions: Munch's *The Scream* must be one of the few modern works of art which is better known than its creator. But the *Mona Lisa* acquired its special status because of its association with Leonardo, not the other way round.

The primacy of the creator in the determination of artistic value is quite evident when we think of the reactions of owners and museums when the Rembrandt Research Project (which started in 1968) found that many of their 'Rembrandts' were not by Rembrandt at all, but by his pupils. Such discoveries, which could have had no effect on the paintings' aesthetic value, were regarded as the equivalent of 'demoting' hundred of pictures. In 1820 the recently opened Dulwich Art Gallery exhibited Rembrandt's *Jacob's Dream*, then regarded as a supreme masterpiece. The painting is still there, but it is now attributed to Aert de Gelder, and consequently is much less highly esteemed. Rembrandt's *Saskia as Minerva* was sold in Munich in 1931 for £6,700, and in London in 1965 it reached £125,300. Then Dutch experts raised doubts about its attribution, and in 1975 it fetched only £2,500.[63] The paintings had remained the same, but not the 'signature'.[64] We insist, absolutely, that art be the expression of its maker.[65]

The identity of the painter is the most important determinant of the value of a work of art, but other things count too: possession by a prestigious owner such as a king, a great lord or a celebrity contributes to enhancing the painting. Fame rubs off on fame.

The initial 'marketing' of Leonardo in the nineteenth century had been largely a French affair. There were practical reasons for this. Leonardo was better known in France than in Italy. He had lived and died in France. The collection of Leonardos at the

Louvre was, by far, the most important in the world and was easily accessible. As late as 1979 it was still claimed that Leonardo's 'message is part and parcel of the normal intellectual and artistic heritage of the French . . . because its main elements are in accord with the French genius'.[66]

As Leonardo's cult developed, the historical account of his final years in France – his 'true home', where his genius was finally recognised – obtained great prominence. Michelet gave a somewhat exaggerated account of the importance of Leonardo at the court of François I. He wrote that although Leonardo was eighty (he was actually sixty-four when he arrived), he deeply influenced fashion, and his hair and beard style, his clothes and even his Italian accent were imitated by courtiers.[67]

In the nineteenth century the death of Leonardo was often represented in painting. Vasari had vividly described the event in a vignette retold countless times. The artist had been ill; the king, concerned, had gone to his bedside; Leonardo sat up, confessing his past faults; the effort caused him a paroxysm of impending death; the king held his head to comfort him; Leonardo, as if acknowledging that he could hope for no greater honour, expired in the arms of François I. It is almost as if he had timed the hour and organised the manner of his death to maximum effect. This account has, of course, often been challenged: it seems that the king could not have been in Amboise on that day. The story is nevertheless quite appealing, and was repeated, without qualms, as recently as 1991.[68]

Artists and intellectuals liked this sort of anecdote, and kings and princes relished them too. The former felt flattered by the idea of powerful men deferring to, even humbling themselves before, art and intellect. The latter fancied the role of a Renaissance prince: magnificent, cultured, generous and wise. Such stories were already fashionable in Vasari's time, and had multiplied since: from the tale of Charles V bending down to pick up a brush dropped by the ailing Titian to Francesco de' Medici deferentially rising to embrace Michelangelo.[69]

The vogue for historically based works of art played its part in such myth-making. The first known pictorial representation of Leonardo dying in the arms of the king was by Angelica Kauffmann (1741–1807), a Swiss painter who lived in London, Rome and Venice, and who worked indefatigably to meet the enormous demand for Italian paintings brought about by the increasingly popular Grand Tour. The British, then the most prominent tourists, were the main collectors of Italian art. In the early eighteenth century they had made the fortunes of Canaletto and other painters (and their British imitators) who represented Venice, Rome and assorted antique ruins.

Kauffmann was extremely popular. Stendhal referred to her as *la célèbre peintre*.[70] When Goethe stayed in Rome she was his regular companion and a dear friend, and introduced him to the great works of the Renaissance. Goethe described her as a talented and financially successful artist, growing increasingly tired of commissions but entreated to persevere by her husband, who thought it 'wonderful that so much money should roll in for what is often easy work'.[71] A founding member of the Royal Academy, she produced more than five hundred paintings. Her *Leonardo's Death in the Arms of François I* – now lost, and presumably painted in Venice – was exhibited at the Royal Academy in 1778.[72]

In 1781, three years after Angelica Kauffmann's painting was shown, the French artist François-Guillaume Ménageot exhibited his own version of Leonardo's death at the Salon (it is now at the Musée de l'Hôtel de Ville, Amboise).[73] An engraving and a Gobelin tapestry helped propagate both this work and the scene. At about the same time (1783–85) Giuseppe Cades, an Italian of French origins, produced a set of pastel drawings on the subject (now at the Ashmolean Museum, Oxford). In c.1815 Richard Cosway painted a watercolour of the dying Leonardo with François. The deathbed scene was also painted in Italy in 1811 by Santi Soldaini (the watercolour is now at the Brera, Milan) and by Cesare Mussini in 1828. In some later lithographs, such as Gigoux's *Derniers moments de Léonard de Vinci* (c.1835), the king is absent. The best-known of these death scenes was painted in 1818 by Ingres (see plate 24), and later engraved by Claude-Marie Dien.

By the early nineteenth century, in the midst of the post-Napoleonic restoration, these representations had a political subtext. The depiction of Leonardo, in the arms of the king, about to receive the last sacraments (and hence images of crosses, priests, cardinals, bibles, etc.) had an unmistakable whiff of royalist Catholicism.[74] This provided a balance for the liberal attempt to recruit Leonardo as an anti-clerical *ante litteram*.

Deathbed scenes were only one of the historical themes available to the cult of Leonardo. In Italy, the revival of science and the technological achievements of Italian scientists encouraged painters to celebrate Leonardo the scientist. Thus in 1843 Nicola Cianfanelli painted Leonardo being introduced to Lodovico il Moro by his friend the mathematician Luca Pacioli, author of the celebrated *De Divina Proportione* (1508) – for which Leonardo had provided some sixty or so illustrations. Cherubino Cornienti showed him explaining to Lodovico his plans for the '*naviglio*' or canal of Milan (1858–59). Cornienti also painted distinguished visitors observing Leonardo working on *The Last Supper* in Santa Maria delle Grazie (1857), while another Italian, Francesco Podesti, showed Leonardo discussing the same work with Lodovico (1846). The statue of Leonardo which faces La Scala in Milan, erected only in 1872, is surrounded by those of four artists and followers, all with tools in their hands. But Leonardo holds nothing. He touches his beard and thinks. The inscription reads: '*Al rinnovatore delle arti e delle scienze*' (To the renovator of the arts and the sciences).

Leonardo as the painter of the *Mona Lisa* was not a frequent subject of other artists. It was not even represented in Cesare Mussini and Ménageot's deathbed scenes, though they showed *St Anne with Virgin and Child*. The first to depict Leonardo painting *Mona Lisa* was Aimée Pagès (1803–66), who exhibited it at the Salon in 1845. Only the engraving by Paul-Prosper Allais now survives (see plate 25). Though the picture is entitled 'Raphael being introduced to Leonardo', Aimée Pagès positioned the famous portrait at the centre. Lisa Gherardini, full size, sits smiling on the right, facing the viewer with, at her back, the musicians mentioned by Vasari. Leonardo proudly shows the portrait to the younger Raphael, who looks on with admiration.

By then Mona Lisa was just beginning to be the subject of a literary cult. In 1863 it was well under way, and Cesare Maccari provided a full pictorial representation in his *Leonardo che ritrae la Gioconda* ('Leonardo painting the *Gioconda*'; see plate 26). The centre is held by the musicians. Leonardo sits on the right, by the portrait. Lisa is opposite him on the far left. Maccari chose this theme for the competition of the Istituto per le Belle Arti di Siena. He won the first prize, and the Istituto kept the painting. As Maccari was a protégé of the director it is possible that he was informed that such a theme would have a good chance of winning.

In these paintings Leonardo is almost always represented as he appears in the famous red-chalk drawing, allegedly a self-portrait (see plate 27). By the end of the nineteenth century it had become the archetypal image of Leonardo, and it has remained so ever since.[75] It was actually not found until the 1840s, though various engravings of it circulated beforehand.[76] The drawing is a highly stylised portrait of a wise old man, who is yet strong and manly. The subject looks like Moses or God the Father, with long white hair and beard, the quintessence of the sage. This stereotype may have a basis in reality: Raphael's *School of Athens* (1509–10, Vatican Museum), representing famous philosophers – Aristotle, Socrates, Zeno, Xenophon, etc. – depicted Plato with the appearance of Leonardo, with long hair and beard. In 1590 (just over seventy years after Leonardo's death) Gianpaolo Lomazzo, a painter who turned writer when he became blind, described him thus: 'he wore his hair and beard so long that he incarnated the true nobility of learning.'[77]

In a popular narrative it is always useful if physical appearance conforms to the expected type: the hero and heroine should be handsome, the wicked man ugly, hypocrites should look lean and mean and have tiny eyes. As many pictures tell a story, this stereotyping is also useful to artists, for it provides the spectator with essential information. The Leonardo of the 'self-portrait' looks like a prophet, a magician or a wise man, not like a painter or an artist as the nineteenth century thought an artist or painter should look: obsessed, driven, erratic, slightly manic – like Michelangelo. The Leonardo of the 'self-portrait' is calm and controlled. His long hair is carefully combed, not dishevelled like that of the stereotypical 'mad' scientist or absent-minded professor of the twentieth century, presumably inspired by the famous Einstein photograph.

The use of an engraving of this image by Giuseppe Bossi in one of the earliest books on Leonardo, *Del cenacolo di Leonardo da Vinci, libri quattro* (Milan 1810), helped to make it known. With his book Bossi, a painter himself, contributed to the celebrity not only of the portrait but also of *The Last Supper*, undoubtedly the best-known of all Leonardo's works well into the nineteenth century.

The fame of *The Last Supper* spread rapidly after it was engraved by Raphael Morghen in 1800. Produced in an edition of five hundred, it became the most prominent of all nineteenth-century prints of the renowned but very damaged mural.[78] The painting, however, had been famous from its creation. Louis XII, having occupied Milan in 1499, had become so enamoured of it that he proposed to detach it from the wall of the refectory of Santa Maria delle Grazie and cart it off to France. The Cardinal of Amboise had a copy made for his residence. François I had it copied as a tapestry for Pope Clement VII. Rubens engraved it.[79] Later the spread of tourism further enhanced its reputation. Clutching Francis Palgrave's *Handbook for Travellers to North Italy*, one of the most successful travel guides, published by the enterprising John Murray in 1842, Charles Dickens stopped by the famous mural in November 1844.

In the old refectory of the dilapidated Convent of Santa
Maria delle Grazie, is the work of art, perhaps, better
known than any other in the world: the Last Supper,
by Leonardo da Vinci – with a door cut through it
by the intelligent Dominican friars, to facilitate their
operations at dinner time.[80]

Algernon Swinburne, asked by his sister Alice in 1863 what she
should see in Milan, provided a helpful list, adding: 'I don't need
to remind you that the supreme crown and glory of Milan is
Leonardo's Last Supper . . . To it of course you will be carried
off at once.'[81]

At this time Leonardo was the great Renaissance scientist who
had painted *The Last Supper*, not the creator of the *Mona Lisa*.
Goethe, who had seen *The Last Supper* in Milan in May 1788,
declared it was 'a real keystone in the vault of one's notion of
art'.[82] But he held this view even before seeing the original: in
Rome in January 1787 he had seen a copy of it and had been so
impressed that he wrote: 'I am trying to make arrangements to
have an etching made, either of this copy or of another. It would
be the greatest blessing if a faithful reproduction could become
available to a wide public.'[83]

When Goethe reviewed Bossi's book some twenty years later,
he had become Europe's Grand Man of Letters. His review was
translated into English and French, thus contributing to the
further success of Bossi's book and Morghen's work.[84] This led
to further engravings of *The Last Supper*, notably by Giovanni
Folo in 1831. In 1864 Morghen received what must be the
engraver's supreme accolade: he was engraved engraving Leonardo's *Last Supper* (G. Castagnola, *Raffaello Morghen che incide
il Cenacolo di Leonardo*). Decades later, Marcel Proust still found
Morghen's print deeply moving.[85]

Twentieth-century art historians, though far from unanimous,
have also praised *The Last Supper*. Kenneth Clark endorsed
Goethe's view: it was 'the keystone of European art'.[86] Leonid

Batkin declared it 'the most accomplished, most exemplary and most perfect achievement of Leonardo'.[87] One of the founders of modern sociology, George Simmel, writing in 1905, claimed that *The Last Supper* had visually solved the problem of life in modern society, namely 'how to bring together different individuals into one organic unity'.[88]

Stendhal introduced his account of *The Last Supper* in his *Histoire de la peinture en Italie* with the words: 'It is impossible you should not know this painting, it is the original of Morghen's beautiful engraving.'[89] He barely mentioned *la Joconde*, a painting he was surely well acquainted with, having been entrusted between 1810 and 1811 with the task of overseeing the cataloguing of works requisitioned by Napoleon, and therefore being in constant touch with the Director of the Musée Napoléon (i.e. the Louvre), Dominique Vivant Denon. Thus when Stendhal began his first Italian trip in August 1811 he had already acquired a considerable understanding of Italian art in particular. In Italy he also read the third edition of Luigi Lanzi's *Istoria pittorica dell'Italia* (1809, first edition 1792), as well as Vasari's *Vite* and Bossi's book on Leonardo.[90] He started dictating his *Histoire de la peinture en Italie* in Paris in December 1811. But Stendhal was easily bored and found more exciting things to do, such as joining Napoleon in his disastrous Russian campaign. There marauding Cossacks stole his luggage, including his manuscripts. Back in Paris in 1813 and short of cash, Stendhal returned to his *Histoire*, but was unable to complete it until 1817.

It is a disorganised work, full of digressions, relying heavily on English and Italian published works, but it was the first popular history of painting published in France. Though Michelangelo and Raphael are the stars of the book, one-tenth of it is devoted to Leonardo, and most of that to a discussion of *The Last Supper*, mainly culled from Bossi.[91] The 'Monna Lisa' is mentioned only twice, almost incidentally: 'Leonardo started painting pretty society women: Ginevra de' Benci ... Monna Lisa ...' Of the

Mona Lisa he simply says, 'It is odd that such a pretty woman should have no eyebrows.'[92]

For Stendhal, Leonardo's three great works were *The Last Supper*, *The Battle of Anghiari* and the statue of the *Cavallo*.[93] The first was severely damaged; the other two were lost. This may well have been part of the charm of Leonardo for the Romantics: a tragic genius who leaves after him only the idea of his greatness. The primacy of the literary construction of the past is here revealed in the admiration for the man, abstracted from his works. The paintings hanging in the Louvre – in Stendhal's neighbourhood, so to speak – remain in the background.

The *Histoire de la peinture* was not an immediate success in spite of Stendhal's efforts to market it. Eventually he managed to place a favourable review, almost an advertisement, in *Le Moniteur universel* of 23 September 1817.[94] Six months later, on 6 March 1818, another favourable review appeared in the conservative *Journal des débats*.[95] The book, the reviewer wrote, had filled a gap: Vasari was far too long, the English books assumed too much knowledge, the Italians were too verbose. Here, finally, was something readable: 'It would not be the first time that a Frenchman would explain to foreigners their own glorious past.' Stendhal's assessment of Leonardo 'makes a happy contrast to that of the truculent Michelangelo'.[96] It was the latter who got the lion's share of the commentary. The *Journal de Paris* of 12 November 1818 also praised Stendhal for his succinct style, found the episodes describing Leonardo's life amusing, and discussed Michelangelo at great length.[97] The first Italian review, in *Biblioteca italiana* (April, May and June 1819), was mainly negative, peeved at the indictment of Italian art historians as too prolix.[98]

The *Edinburgh Review* (October 1819) was favourable. Stendhal had produced 'one of the most entertaining books that have appeared for some time', though he had lifted passages from other books and used an 'extremely offensive tone' towards religion. But what else could one expect from a 'follower of Buonaparte; a soldier who has passed his life ... between making war [and] making love'. The *Edinburgh Review*'s opinion of Leonardo was that he was inferior to Michelangelo in the fine arts, but otherwise excelled in 'almost every pursuit, from the abstract sciences, to the ordinary amusements and occupations of life'. His achievements in optics and mechanics were praised, and Stendhal's ranking of Leonardo with Francis Bacon quoted approvingly. Leonardo's best painting was the ruined *Last Supper*, but fortunately – continued the *Review* – we still had Morghen's 'justly famous print'.[99]

Other reviews followed, including one in *Galignani's Magazine and Paris Monthly Review* (May 1823), an English-language magazine printed in Paris. It was ecstatic in its praise – not surprisingly, as Stendhal had written it himself: 'We cannot therefore but feel grateful to Mr Beyle [Stendhal]' for ploughing through all those verbose and unreadable Italian art historians.[100] Stendhal himself singled out as 'the most interesting' part of his work the sections on Leonardo, evidently 'written *con amore*'.[101]

Though Stendhal's *Histoire* never made its author serious money, it became influential in artistic and literary circles after being reprinted in 1825.[102] The special praise granted to *The Last Supper* has stood the test of time. The painting is still Milan's prime tourist site. Santa Maria delle Grazie is constantly besieged by tourists, and the recent restoration of the fresco (1999) has further enhanced its renown. It is also appreciated in rather distant places. On Gau, an island in central Fiji, tapestries reproducing *The Last Supper* hang on the walls of most of the village churches and homes. They were brought back from the Lebanon by villagers serving there as members of the United Nations Interim Forces after 1978.[103]

A year after Stendhal's book was reviewed in the *Edinburgh Review*, Wordsworth included in his *Memorials of a Tour on the Continent* (1820) a poem called 'The Last Supper by Leonardo da Vinci, in the Refectory of the Convent of Maria della Grazia – Milan'. Although upset by the state of the mural ('Though searching damps and many an envious flaw/Have marred this Work . . .'), Wordsworth said that 'the copy exhibited in London some years ago, and the engraving by Morghen, are both admirable; but in the original is a power which neither of those works has attained, or even approached.'

Lesser poets followed him in the admiration of Leonardo. Charles Lamb (1775–1834) produced a rather maudlin poem on Leonardo's *Virgin of the Rocks*, celebrating not so much the painting as the event it depicted. Mary looks on as the child Jesus plays with the future St John, unaware

> . . . as yet the full event
> Of those so low beginnings,
> From whence we date our winnings.[104]

W.C. Bennett's 'Sonnet at Milan in the Convent of the Madonna delle Grazie' (1862) intoned:

> Oh how fine
> Was thy great genius, Leonardo! . . .
> O mightiest master, as our Raphael dear

Aubrey De Vere echoed these feelings in his 'Leonardo's Last Supper at Milan' (1884).

And our *Mona Lisa*? No one seemed particularly inspired by it, though, as usual, there were noteworthy exceptions. Thomas Moore, once regarded as the Irish national poet, in his *Rhymes on the Road* (1819), written while travelling in Italy, accepted the general view of Leonardo as 'a bearded sage' who dabbled in geometry and mathematics and traced 'upon the dusky earth/Strange learned figures with his wand'. But he was also the painter of Italian Renaissance women whose beauty could still be found unaltered, says Moore, in the features of present-day young Florentines, 'Arno's dark-ey'd maids', who recalled to him 'Mona Lisa, on whose eyes/A painter for whole years might gaze'.

Years later, Moore returned to the *Mona Lisa* in 'Summer Fête'

(1831).[105] This lengthy satirical poem describes a fancy-dress party on the banks of the Thames, attended by all those of 'beauty, rank and power',

> From the young spinster, just come out,
> To the old Premier, too long in.

Amidst the revellers was a lute singer

> with voice that, like a ray
> Of southern sunshine, seem'd to float.

> A dark-ey'd nymph, array'd
> Like her, whom Art hath deathless made,
> Bright Mona Lisa – with that braid
> Of hair across the brow, and one
> Small gem that in the centre shone
> – With face, too, in its form resembling
> Da Vinci's Beauties . . .

The description does not match the Louvre painting. Perhaps Moore had only seen a copy. Felicia Dorothea Hemans may have had Mona Lisa in mind when she wrote in her poem 'The Maremma', published posthumously: 'Fair as that daughter of the south, whose form/Still breathes and charms, in Vinci's colour warm'. An (un)helpful footnote – probably by her sister, Harriet Hughes – tells us that this is an allusion to Mona Lisa, Leonardo's wife (sic), whose portrait was 'supposed to be the most perfect imitation of Nature ever exhibited in painting'.[105]

These early literary mentions of Mona Lisa treated her as representing a distinctive Italian beauty. The now almost obligatory smile is unmentioned. She has not yet been transformed into the archetypal enigmatic *femme fatale*. This was the work of French Romantic writers. When, in the footsteps of Stendhal, Théophile Gautier undertook his own Italian tour in 1850, he stopped, like everyone, at the Church of Santa Maria delle Grazie, and marvelled, like everyone, before the ruined *Last Supper*. Unlike his predecessor, he was not put off by the deterioration of the fresco;

on the contrary, the damage suited Leonardo, he claimed, 'the painter of the mysterious, the ineffable, the crepuscular'.[106] But he had not yet applied these terms to the *Mona Lisa*.

As the fame of Leonardo became more established, the literary representation of the portrait of Lisa Gherardini acquired a new meaning. The Romantics, for whom science was a kind of magic, redefined Leonardo the scientist as the painter of the Eternal Feminine. This reflected one of their own central preoccupations, the representation of women. The renown of the first Leonardo fed the success of the second. Leonardo was not an accidental choice. No other Renaissance artist could assume both roles so perfectly. Only a magician could have painted a magical woman's magical smile. Only a universal genius could have painted the Universal Woman.

CHAPTER FIVE

Mona Lisa Becomes Mysterious

Vasari had praised the *Mona Lisa*, it had inspired Raphael, it had been widely copied and imitated; but it had to wait until the second half of the nineteenth century to become famous. Charles Blanc, editor and founder of the *Gazette des Beaux-Arts* and later Director of the École des Beaux-Arts, claimed in 1859 that only his own century could understand the *Mona Lisa*. The eighteenth century – 'noisy, brilliant and ironic' – had lacked the indispensable contemplative spirit.[1]

Be that as it may, one of the chief obstacles to the wider diffusion of the *Mona Lisa* was the lack of accessible prints. To be widely copied augmented a painting's renown, but to become really famous among the rising middle classes it was necessary to be printed, for prints were far cheaper and more easily available. *The Last Supper* owed much of its popularity to Morghen's engraving and its subsequent diffusion in a print run of five hundred. But none of the great engravers of the past – Jean Morin, Edelinck, François de Poilly or Gérard Audran – had attempted to reproduce the *Mona Lisa*. It was not an easy painting to engrave. Even a talented engraver could not easily convey the sensation of depth produced by the elaborate and delicate *sfumato*. Raphael's work presented fewer problems, hence the frequency with which his works had appeared in print format.[2] The task of engraving the *Mona Lisa* had finally been accomplished, announced Blanc, by the great Italian engraver Luigi Calamatta (1801–69) in Paris in 1857. In reality it had been engraved several times previously: anonymously (head only) around 1820 (printed by Engelmann), then by d'Aubry-Lecomte in 1824, by Jean-Baptiste Massard in the 1830s, by Hermann Eichens in 1840, and many others. Calamatta himself had attempted an earlier engraving in 1838.[3]

So it had taken Calamatta twenty years to engrave an image painted by Leonardo in four. Blanc explained: there are some works on which an artist can work only on 'the good days'. Leonardo, the supreme perfectionist, had worked at the painting without ever being completely satisfied. Calamatta had followed his lead.

In celebrating the new engraving, Blanc, a former pupil of Calamatta's, was perhaps paying homage to his teacher. He recollected, with nostalgia, Calamatta's crowded studio and the throng of visiting intellectuals: one could see George Sand with Chopin, 'muttering in a strong Polish accent', Ingres and other celebrities. Entering the studio, one immediately faced a drawing of the *Mona Lisa*, positioned between Calamatta's worktop and that of his principal assistant. It exercised a fascination on all visitors:

> Shrouded in the mystery of the half-tint, this charming head, serene and proud, emanated a barely contained provocation, her delicate smile sporadically veering towards the satanic; it beguiled us by her timeless and voluptuous gaze.[4]

The *Mona Lisa* magic was already in the air. It was treated as an unfathomable painting, and Blanc's words were part of the linguistic arsenal used by Romantic writers in their descriptions of it. This was the beginning of the transmutation of Lisa Gherardini from a cheerful housewife into a mysterious, iconic woman. This required a new context for the representation of women: the invention of the *femme fatale*.[5]

Before the nineteenth century, the *femme fatale* was fairly rare. It had not yet become a type. In medieval courtly literature and fairy tales women were often represented as inaccessible beings on whose behalf men attempted great deeds to obtain their favours, though occasionally they were seen as insidious temptresses whose object was to seduce men.[6]

But these beautiful ladies were seldom *fatales*. To the dismay of the knights, they usually remained chaste and hard to get. Occasionally the lady was heartless, or far away, or unreachable. The myth of the woman who is both desirable and intrinsically dangerous had not yet materialised except as an expression of the Devil. Thus Jean Cousin's painting *Eva prima Pandora* (c.1540, Louvre) represents an expressionless yet idealised woman along with a death's head, an apple branch, Pandora's vase (rather than box) and a serpent.[7]

In Romantic literature the *femme fatale*, if spurned, often turned into a castrating female, the reincarnation of a mythological or biblical figure. She became Medea, the Sphinx, or Delilah, who seduces and ruins Samson; and, above all, Salomé, the woman who had John the Baptist decapitated because he resisted her. She inspired the painter Gustave Moreau (*Salomé dansant devant Hérode*, 1876); Gustave Flaubert's story 'Hérodias', one of the *Trois Contes* of 1877, where the *femme fatale* is the mother rather than the daughter; Oscar Wilde's poetic one-act play *Salomé* (written in French in 1896) and its operatic adaptation by Richard Strauss (1905). Other favourite historical or mythological models were Helen of Troy; Cleopatra, whose charms provoked a civil war in Rome; Messalina, the sex-crazed murderess wife of the Emperor Claudius; and Lucrezia Borgia, who poisoned her lovers.

The new *femme fatale*, unlike some of the wicked female monsters of the past, such as the Gorgons, was not an ugly demon, or one sent by the devil to bring discord, to destroy cities and brew deadly poisons, as in the Middle Ages.[8] The *femme fatale* was beautiful, and perfidiously used her beauty to ensnare hapless men. These unfortunates, once in love, were enticed towards inescapable perdition, folly and ruin.

That love could make men mad had long been known. Ludovico Ariosto, Leonardo's contemporary, had celebrated in his *L'Orlando Furioso* (1516–32) the folly of men in love. He had done so somewhat ironically – an indication that the genre was well established. But the women loved by Ariosto's heroes were innocent. Men's madness was due to misplaced jealousy; his Angelica was as blameless as Othello's Desdemona. In literature the obstacles to a happy union were usually other men: jealous husbands, stern fathers, cruel kings, selfish guardians, or the dastardly plots of evil rivals. Once the obstacles were overcome and love had conquered all, a happy ending was assured. The beautiful lady inflicted no pain on the man she loved. She waited, more or less meekly, to be rescued.

Most fictional women were either whores or saints. But there were women of power and influence, wise women, educated women, sexy women, religious and saintly women, practical châtelaines who looked after the affairs of the domain while the husband was away on the crusade, heroines (Joan of Arc, Boadicea), voracious sexual beings, choleric and melancholic women, temptresses.[9]

Between 1500 and 1800 literature provided a stream of heroine prostitutes who thoroughly enjoyed sex. None of them, however, was terribly evil, just immoral: *La Celestina* of Fernando de Rojas (1519), Grimmelshausen's *Courasche* (1670, adapted by Bertholt Brecht as *Mother Courage* in 1939), Defoe's *Moll Flanders* (1722), the Abbé Prévost's *Manon Lescaut* (1731) and John Cleland's *Fanny Hill* (1749).[10]

Jacobean drama was full of scheming and nasty women who – alongside even nastier men – killed and poisoned others. The Gothic novel, that great English speciality, regularly featured vicious women, often Italian or Oriental – hardly ever English – and teeming with deadly lust.

Some of these were precursors of the nineteenth-century *femme fatale*, but they did not yet constitute an established type.[11] In literature a few *femmes fatales* are not sufficient to cast the cliché. This requires constant repetition and imitation, until a critical mass is reached. Only after the accumulation of its haunting apparitions in a sequence of narratives, of novel after novel, play after play, does the *femme fatale* become entrenched in the collective memory of the public. Then she can be recognised at once, the moment we encounter her in fiction. But it takes time for such literary conventions to become established. The word 'seductress' entered the English language only in the nineteenth century, while the male term 'seducer' was used by Shakespeare.

Nineteenth-century popular fiction was replete with virtuous, or weak or frustrated, men in conflict with ghoulish, vampiric and sexually threatening women. By the middle of the century, in certain circles, the type was truly cast. Edmond and Jules de Goncourt, in the entry for 11 March 1860 of their celebrated *Journal*, tell of their visit to the salon of Adolphe Dennery, and describe his mistress Gisette thus:

> All women are enigmas, but she is the most mysterious
> of them all . . . like a sixteenth-century courtesan, she
> is all instinct and no rules, and wears, like an enchanted
> mask, the smile full of night of the Gioconda.

One never knew, they added with some discomfiture, whether she wanted to sleep with you or make fun of you.[12] But then, these famous brothers were mortally afraid of all women, even of their devoted chambermaid.[13] The same could be said of the great literary critic Sainte-Beuve, who divided women, unoriginally, into the angelic and the diabolic. Of the latter he wrote in his novel *Volupté* (1834):

> I learned in my lascivious pursuits to find, pursue, fear
> and desire a kind of beauty I regard as a lethal and
> mortal snare . . . I have also learned that this beauty is
> not true, that it is the enemy of the soul, that it kills,
> crushes . . .[14]

The success of the *femme fatale* stereotype owes much to its general appeal. It attracted men because it blamed professional seductresses for men's occasional 'moment of madness'. Virtuous women used it to exhort men to cling to their wives and spurn predatory women. Finally, the seductress appealed to not-so-virtuous women, who regarded it as a role model for how to wield power over men – or who simply liked sex.

The *femme fatale* was depicted as a 'deviant' case, as fictional characters often are. Real women are expected to behave normally, and hence as unfatally as possible. Throughout the nineteenth century, as in previous centuries, women were asked to be the essence of unearthly purity and self-sacrifice. They should turn the home, to quote Ruskin, into 'a sacred place, a vestal temple, a temple of the hearth watched over by household gods'.[15]

Not many novels, however, especially in France, had as their heroines dutiful daughters, devoted wives or exemplary mothers. French poets appeared haunted by sexually devouring women. The most obsessed of them all, Charles Baudelaire, was regarded in Britain as the perpetrator of shocking excesses. This made him all the more attractive to those, like Algernon Swinburne, who regarded the Victorian world as unbearably puritanical.

Baudelaire's representation of women was a mixture of misogynist sadism, envy of their alleged power, abject humility before their redemptive capacity, and submissiveness mixed with idolatry. As he wrote in 1856, his ideal of Beauty was

> a seductive and beautiful head, a woman's head, a head which can make one dream of lust and sorrow; involving the sensation of melancholia, weariness and even of satiety, with its opposite: vigour, and the desire to live.[16]

In the poem 'l'Idéal' he rejected

> those figurine beauties, spoiled products of a lethargic century . . . Let Gavarni, the poet of anaemic women, keep his grazing flock of hospital *belles* . . . What I need for my heart, deep as an abyss, is you, Lady Macbeth, soul devoted to crime . . .

In his 'Je t'adore à l'égal de la voûte nocturne', he tells his mocking mistress 'I cherish, o implacable and cruel beast, even *cette froideur par où tu m'es plus belle!*' (this cold disdain which makes you, for me, even more beautiful). The theme of self-abasement is carried out consistently throughout his *Les Fleurs du mal*. In the sexually impotent Baudelaire, the devouring *femme fatale* found a poet of astonishing power. His poem 'Les Phares' ('The Beacons', 25 June 1857, in *Les Fleurs du mal*), dedicated to the great painters of the past, hints at the *Mona Lisa*. In the passage on Leonardo, Baudelaire describes a sweet and yet mysterious smile against a strange landscape:

> *Léonard de Vinci, miroir profond et sombre,*
> *Où des anges charmants, avec un doux souris*
> *Tout chargé de mystère, apparaissent à l'ombre*
> *Des glaciers et des pins qui ferment leur pays*

> Leonardo da Vinci, deep and sombre mirror,
> Where charming angels, whose sweet smile
> Is suffused with mystery, appear in the shade
> Of glaciers and pines enveloping their domain

Linking mystery and beauty was fairly common. Théophile Gautier's 1852 poem 'Caeruli Oculi' was typical of the genre:

> *Une femme mystérieuse,*
> *Dont la beauté trouble mes sens,*
> *Se tient debout, silencieuse,*
> *Au bord des flots retentissants*

> A mysterious woman,
> Whose beauty disconcerts my senses,
> Stands, silently,
> By the crashing waves.[17]

These were common fantasies of men, particularly young men. Flaubert, in *Novembre*, an early work (1842), describes a sex-troubled adolescent who fantasises about running away with Cleopatra on an old galley. The mere mention of the word '*mai-*

tresse' 'conjured up a satanic being, the name threw me into ecstasy'.[18]

By the end of the century the *femme fatale* stereotype had become so well established that it was not unusual – claims the great Italian literary critic Mario Praz – to observe in some salons women affecting enigmatic smiles and audacious clothes.[19] Men too appeared to follow the trend. In 1898 the novelist Jules Renard, author of the bestseller of suffering childhood *Poil de Carote*, made fun in his diary of the writer Hugues Rebell for trying too hard to smile like the *Joconde*: 'Leonardo, they say, worked on it for four years. Rebell spent a lifetime.'[20]

Arsène Houssaye, in his memoirs, described the enigmatic smile of the Princess Belgiojoso as 'a pure masterpiece of unsatiated Gioconda'.[21] The Countess of Castiglione, another of these *Jocondes manquées*, had over four hundred photographs of herself taken in 1856–65 and 1895–98 in a variety of extravagant clothes: a deliberate presentation of her own person as a highly desirable sexual object (see plate 28).[22]

As the uses of the *femme fatale* image expanded, the range of variations became wider and were used by writers, painters and, in the twentieth century, film-makers. Jules Barbey d'Aurevilly, in his short stories, appropriately entitled *Les Diaboliques* (1874), supplied a miscellaneous collection of devilish women: 'Not one here,' he wrote in the preface, 'who is pure, virtuous and innocent.'[23] In Zola's *Nana* (1880) the eponymous heroine, though neither enigmatic nor mysterious, inflamed men's passion and caused their undoing. Nana came to epitomise the end of an era, dying of the smallpox as the Franco–Prussian war was about to break out (see plate 29). Zola, for all his naturalism, transformed Nana into the great Temptress, a 'golden fly' emerging from the slums to avenge the downtrodden by bringing devastation to the bourgeoisie with her irresistible sexuality, a true *mangeuse d'homme*. No different was Frank Wedekind's Lulu in the two plays in which she appears, *Erdgeist* ('The Spirit of the Earth', written in 1893, staged in 1902) and *Die Büchse der Pandora* ('Pandora's Box', written in 1894, staged in 1904, turned into a film by G.W. Pabst in 1928 and into an opera by Alban Berg in 1937). Hundreds of similar stories have followed, depicting the lubricity and carnality of women. The stereotype survived even the passing of literary fashion. In 1884 Joris-Karl Huysmans broke with naturalism, to Zola's great chagrin, with his novel *À Rebours*. But he did not break with the *femme fatale*. His anti-hero, the seriously neurotic des Esseintes, finds in Gustave Moreau's painting of Salomé the

> symbolic deity of indestructible Lust, the goddess of immortal Hysteria, the accursed Beauty . . . the monstrous Beast, indifferent, irresponsible, insensitive, who pollutes, as did the Helen of antiquity, everything near her, everything that contemplates her, everything she touches.[24]

That style, those ideas had been pioneered by one the most influential exponents of the myth of the *femme fatale*: Théophile Gautier (1811–72). And Gautier was also the chief maker of the *Mona Lisa* as a mysterious woman with a strange smile. Thus repositioned – one might almost say 're-branded' – the fame of the *Mona Lisa*, enhanced by its association with Gautier, flourished. Eventually the juxtaposition of 'smile' and *Mona Lisa* was so deeply ingrained that it became impossible to separate the two. Today, when people comment on the enigmatic and mysterious smile of the *Mona Lisa*, they echo the mid-nineteenth-century views of Gautier and his circle: when the young Elizabeth II visited the Louvre in 1956 she paused by the *Mona Lisa* and, after, a long silence, murmured 'rather enigmatic'.[25]

There was nothing inevitable about the transformation of *Mona Lisa* into a *femme fatale*. Gustave Planche, critic of the *Revue des deux mondes*, enthused in 1850 about the beautiful and graceful features of the *Mona Lisa* without any fantasies about devouring females.[26] But they were, so to speak, in the air, even if they had not yet converged on the portrait of Lisa Gherardini. There were other candidates. Planche's favourite was Leonardo's *Medusa* at the Uffizi – in fact a seventeenth-century Flemish work erroneously attributed to Leonardo. Planche was building on Shelley's 1819 poem 'On the Medusa by Leonardo da Vinci in the Florentine Gallery', which he had helped to popularise in France.

The *Mona Lisa* needed a prominent writer, someone like Gautier. He was the author of successful novels (*Mademoiselle de Maupin*, 1835–36, *Le Capitaine Fracasse*, 1853), travel books, libretti for ballets (*Giselle*, *La Péri*) and poetry. The repute of his poems was enhanced by the numerous composers – Berlioz, Offenbach, Bizet and Massenet – who set them to music. The Lovenjoul catalogue (1899) lists no fewer than 476 *chansons* based on his poems.

Baudelaire dedicated his *Fleurs du mal* to Gautier: 'the impeccable poet, the perfect magician of French literature'. In 1873, a year after Gautier's death, a commemorative volume, *Le Tombeau de Théophile Gautier*, was published with celebratory poems by Victor Hugo, Mallarmé and Swinburne.

Gautier was also – by far – the most popular and respected art critic active in Paris in the middle of the nineteenth century. He had studied the fine arts, originally intending to become an artist. Though he soon turned to literature, his writings maintained a strong sense of the visual. In 1856 he became editor of *l'Artiste*, the art magazine founded by Arsène Houssaye, a committed Leonardo admirer. Gautier's commentaries on the annual exhibition of paintings, the Salon, were enormously influential: 'His praise is sufficient to sell a work of art ... There is no painter, sculptor, actor, vaudeville writer, acrobat' – wrote his first biographer Maxime Du Camp – 'who does not write to him to solicit his support.'[27] Between 1836 and 1855 Gautier wrote over a thousand articles, often on the arts, for Émile Girardin's *La Presse*, one of the first large-circulation dailies. The literary elite read them with admiration.[28] Gautier was at the epicentre of Parisian, and hence European, artistic life. He was thus suitably positioned to influence the taste of the *nouveaux riches* (often newly ennobled), the notables and the younger writers. Now he is almost forgotten as an art critic, unlike Baudelaire, but he was so popular in his lifetime that one of his articles praising Ingres ('Une visite a Monsieur Ingres', 1847) caused no fewer than three thousand visitors to descend on the artist's *atelier*.[29]

Gautier was the leading proponent of the idea of art for art's sake which he outlined in the controversial preface to *Mademoiselle de Maupin* (1835–36), his novel on androgyny and sexual ambiguity. His fiction as well as his poetry made constant reference to painters and paintings. His descriptions of landscape and people were intensely pictorial, obsessed by the visually beautiful, the exotic and the voluptuous. Like other nineteenth-century art critics, notably Walter Pater, Gautier was mainly concerned with the impression a painting made on him and how it allowed his imagination to run freely. His views were not unlike those of the 'naive' and uneducated viewer (hence his popularity), though with a stylistic virtuosity that impressed his readers and with the cultural references of an intellectual.

Gautier regarded portrait painting as an elevated form of art, though it was also how 'art enters bourgeois life'.[30] At its highest, however, it revealed the thoughts behind the features, the inner person behind the appearance.[31] Leonardo had held a similar view when he wrote that 'The good painter has to paint two principal things, that is to say, man and the intention of his mind. The first is easy and the second difficult.'[32]

Gautier did not regard his art criticism as a different genre from his fictional and poetic works. Writers, he believed, were the best art critics. Their task was to discover the still-invisible, the yet unknown, the hitherto unmasterable. This view was common currency in the nineteenth century. Later, art criticism turned into a serious academic discipline, largely thanks to German-speaking intellectuals. But in Gautier's days, as Anita Brookner put it in 1971, with perhaps excessive youthful emphasis, the genre was 'a career open to all the talents', not 'the rigid toadying exercise that it has become today'.[33] The writer, although using words instead of colours, shared the same project as the artist: the revelation of the truth, once the prerogative of religion, was the function of Art. The task of understanding art and explaining it to others could only be done by artists, that is by men of passion, not by desiccated academics. Understandably, this view, though widely held, is distinctly unfashionable in universities.

Théophile Gautier regarded himself as being endowed with the sensitivity and insight required to probe deeply into the famous portrait of Mona Lisa. In it, perhaps one should say in *her*, he discovered the images and fantasies haunting his own psyche. In his fiction Gautier had frequently used the trope of the disquieting, threatening, devouring and exotic woman – the *femme fatale*, the *belle dame sans merci*, the kind of woman with whom it is dangerous to fall in love. Gautier, as was the convention, borrowed his feminine images from antiquity – Cleopatra, Helen of Troy, and other dark, mysterious women.[34] His devouring women usually came from the South: Italians, gypsies, Jewesses or Orientals. The *femme fatale* was part of another well-known cliché: the contrast between the icy, cold and probably frigid blonde maiden of the North and the sensual, sexy, lustful dark beauty of the Mediterranean.

Gautier's obsessions could be found not only, as one would expect, in his novels and short stories, but also in his essays and reviews. In May 1851, much impressed by the Spanish ballerina Petra Camara's performance at the Théâtre Gymnase, he wrote an enthusiastic review declaring that Camara was reincarnating Inès de la Sierras, the eponymous protagonist of a novel by Charles Nodier (1780–1844), who had popularised stories dealing with the supernatural, eroticism and madness. *Inès de la Sierras* was the tale of the spirit of a dancer, dead for three hundred years, who reappears to haunt her murderer and former lover. A year later Gautier dedicated his poem 'Inès de la Sierras' to the dancer.[35] The theme of the dead woman whose love and passion wanders through the centuries recurs throughout his fiction and poetry.

In some of his stories – particularly in the so-called *Récits fantastiques* inspired by the German Romantic writer and music critic E.T.A. Hoffmann – the main male character often falls in love with the representation of a woman as a statue, or a painting. In *Le Roman de la momie* (1858), an English aristocrat, Lord Evandale, falls desperately in love with a beautifully preserved three-thousand-year-old mummy, victim of what Gautier calls 'retrospective desire' – a passion 'inspired by the sight of a statue or a painting representing a woman of the past', the ultimate in impossible love.[36] In the short story 'Le Pied de la momie' (1840), the object of lust is the embalmed foot of an Egyptian princess, who reconstitutes herself for the gratification of the hero. In *Arria Marcella: Souvenir de Pompéi* (1852), the lava-preserved shape of a pair of beautiful female breasts found in Pompeii drives the handsome Octavien to paroxysms of desire: the eruption had conserved 'the contours of a breast throughout the centuries while so many empires had left no trace'.[37] His desire brings Marcella to life: 'One is truly dead,' she explains, 'only when one is no longer loved.' Alas, by bewitching Octavien with her pagan wiles she has broken the rule set by her puritanical father, a Christian convert, and is reduced to dust.

In *La Morte amoureuse* (1836), Romuald, about to be ordained into the priesthood, glances at a woman during the service. He is seduced at once: 'This woman has completely overwhelmed me. One glance sufficed to breathe her will in me. I no longer lived for myself but for her and through her.'[38] Some time later, Romuald, now a priest, arrives – too late – at the bedside of a dying young noblewoman. The dead woman was a famous Italian courtesan, the beautiful and mysterious Clarimonde, the very same whose piercing eyes had troubled his ordination. She had died, he is told, after a protracted orgy – eight days and nights of frenzied pleasure. It was rumoured that her lovers all died in mysterious circumstances. The desire of the young priest is so intense that Clarimonde revives. Romuald offers no resistance. Indisputably in control, she takes him to Venice – the classic city of sin and intrigue. There they live in ostentatious luxury in a marble palazzo overlooking the Grand Canal. Two Titians, 'among the best', hang in their bedroom, looking on while the couple indulge their irrepressible lust. Soon Clarimonde's health deteriorates and she grows pale and cold, recovering only after licking Romuald's bleeding finger, which he has inadvertently grazed. Clarimonde is a vampire – one of the earliest female vampires in literature. Eventually persuaded that his soul is in grave danger, Romuald opens the grave where Clarimonde had originally been buried. And there she is, lying under the marble stone, beautiful as ever, cold, a drop of blood glistening red as a rose on the corner of her mouth. Holy water is cast, and Clarimonde instantly reverts to dust. Romuald concludes with a message of warning: 'Never glance at a woman. Walk with eyes steadfastly on the ground. However chaste and serene you might be, an instant is enough to make you forfeit eternal salvation.'

Clarimonde has a little of the Cleopatra in her. And Cleopatra, throughout the nineteenth century, represented the classic *femme fatale*. In Gautier's *Mademoiselle de Maupin* she is remembered with admiration by the eponymous heroine – in control of her destiny throughout – as a woman who killed in the morning the lovers with whom she had spent the night: '*Grande voluptueuse, comme tu connaissais la nature humaine, et qu'il a de profondeur dans cette barbarie!*' ('Oh woman of awesome sensuality, how well you understood human nature, and what wisdom in your savagery!')[39] In the short story 'Une nuit de Cléopatre' (1845) the bored queen kills the loved male. In all these narratives an optimistic ending is emphatically ruled out. One never lives happily ever after with a *femme fatale*.

The idea of falling in love with the image of a woman (and hence with an idealised woman) was hardly Gautier's invention: the theme can be found in mythology and fairy tales. Falling in love with one's own work was a classical motif at least since Ovid told the story, in his *Metamorphoses*, of the Greek sculptor Pygmalion falling in love with a statue he had made, later turned into the living Galatea by Aphrodite. Or the story – told by Pliny and turned into a play by John Lyly (1584) – of the Greek painter Apelles' love for Alexander the Great's mistress Pancaspe, whose portrait he was painting; this too had a happy ending: the generous emperor donated the girl to the painter.

Leonardo too thought it was possible to fall in love with a painting. In his defence of the art of painting he explained that such is

> the power of a painting over a man's mind that he may be enchanted and enraptured by a painting that does not represent any living woman. It previously happened to me that I made a picture representing a holy subject, which was bought by someone who loved it and who wished to remove the attributes of its divinity in order that he might kiss it without guilt. But finally his conscience overcame his sighs and lust, and he was forced to banish it from his house.[40]

By the end of the nineteenth century the idea that the created image had special powers had become common. Oscar Wilde's Dorian Gray (1891) does not grow old, but his portrait – the depiction of his soul – does. In Offenbach's opera *The Tales of Hoffmann* (1881), the mechanical doll Olympia – with whom Hoffmann falls in love – takes on a life of her own. In Vernon Lee's *Amour Dure* (1887), Spiridion Trepka, a young, Faust-like scholar, becomes obsessed with the story of the infamous Medea da Carpi, who had brought to a violent end five of her lovers and whose husband had her strangled in a convent. Fearing that her extraordinary charms would seduce her killers, he resorted to using female executioners. Eventually Spiridion, who is looking for a non-earthly love, finds a portrait of Medea: 'And such a portrait! – Bronzino never painted a grander one ... She looks out of the frame with a cold level glance; yet the lips smile.' Medea eventually materialises and requests that he perform a demonic deed; her love will be his recompense. Spiridion complies, but dies tragically, stabbed in the heart.[41]

Gautier had been a modern pioneer in this genre. In his *La Cafetière* (1831) portraits come alive at night, including that of Angela, a beautiful woman, '*mystérieuse et fantastique*', with whom the hero makes love until dawn. Then she vanishes, leaving him desolate.[42] In *Omphale* (1834), the charming feminine image is a picture on a tapestry. In the novel *Spirite* (1865), the hero and Gautier's *alter ego*, Guy de Malivert, sees the image of the beautiful Spirite in a mirror: her 'smile in the manner of Leonardo da Vinci, yet more tender and less ironic, gave her lips an adorable sinuosity'.[43]

For Gautier paintings and images have a secret power: they preserve the past. His stories often allude to the mysterious and alluring ages of Rome, Greece and Egypt, in which interest had recently been enhanced by Napoleon's expedition and the large number of artefacts seized there. This led to a fascination with Ancient Egypt not only in Paris but also in London, Rome, Berlin and Turin – cities which became the repositories of the world's main collections of Egyptian antiquities.

Italy, however, remained a favoured destination of French, English and German writers, and an ideal setting for stories. It had the advantages of being nearer and less dangerous than Greece and Egypt. It combined in one country two major historical epochs: Ancient Rome and the Renaissance. It had been the favourite setting for the late-eighteenth-century English Gothic novels (after Italy became less mysterious, it was the turn of Transylvania) – when he visited Venice in 1850, Gautier wrote: 'We felt we were travelling in a novel by ... Anne Radcliff [sic] illustrated by Goya, Piranesi and Rembrandt ... The old histories of the Three Inquisitors, the Council of Ten ... masked spies. A cold terror, damp and black all around us, had taken possession of us.'[44]

Gautier saw images of mysterious and disturbing women everywhere. For instance, when he discussed *La Jeune fille à l'oeillet* by Hippolyte-Jean Flandrin, exhibited at the Salon of 1859 (see plate 30), he declared:

In her beauty there is something strange, mysterious, and disturbing, the eyes have a sphinx-like malice, her severe mouth betrays an imperceptible smile. What are her thoughts? And whom does she mock? In front of this figure as with certain of Leonardo da Vinci's canvases, you feel a little ill at ease; she seems to belong in another sphere. Yet she is enchanting.[45]

'With Mona Lisa,' he added, 'Madame Devauçay and El Greco's daughter, this is one of the most eternally alive portraits ever.' Other contemporary critics too noted the connection with Leonardo, for instance Maurice Aubert, who also declared Flandrin's painting 'one of the most "eternally alive" portraits'.[46]

Madame Devauçay was painted by Ingres and exhibited at the Salon of 1833. Discussing it in 1855, Gautier deployed his *Mona Lisa* language:

> I have never been able to observe the portrait of Madame D. without being deeply troubled. Ingres reached here a frightening intensity . . . these black eyes . . . enter my soul like two streams of fire. They follow you everywhere. They observe you . . . The imperceptible smile which hangs over her thin lips appears to mock your impossible love. Ingres did not paint a woman, but the portrait of the Chimera of old in modern dress. Only one portrait produces in me a similar effect, that of the daughter of El Greco as painted by her father, who was in love with her and, his work completed, became insane.[47]

No mention of Mona Lisa! As for El Greco's 'daughter' — probably the portrait of his mistress, Jerónima de las Cuevas — Gautier had described it in 1850 as a painting that 'follows you everywhere, like Leonardo's *Mona Lisa*'.[48] The portraits mentioned by Gautier — the El Greco, the Ingres, the Flandrin — are all of young women, portrayed in a three-quarter position, facing the viewer directly, their hands on their laps — just like the *Mona*

Lisa. It was as if he had decided what kind of gaze his *femmes fatales* should have. Indeed, he often found the *Mona Lisa*'s ironic and mocking smile in contemporary art, for example in Eugène Faure's *l'Education de l'Amour* and Adolphe de Bouguereau's *l'Amour blessé*, both exhibited at the Salon of 1859.[49] Even Leonardo's Virgin of the Rocks is attributed with an enigmatic and vague smile (though neither mocking nor seductive).[50]

Gautier's fiction is dominated by a haunting obsession with beauty. The lips are always shining, inviting, tempting. The body is always white as ivory, the breasts full. A glance is enough to make one fall passionately in love. One may acquire virtue, renounce or indulge in vice, but beauty is a divine gift, beyond the reach of those who have not got it. There is an extraordinarily material sensuality in Gautier's descriptions of the female form. Occasionally he included in his stories uncommonly handsome men, but, as if to emphasise that beauty is a prerogative of women, he usually added that they were 'too beautiful', almost feminine. Androgyny is another recurrent theme of Gautier's fiction. He does not like 'real' men. He found Michelangelo's *David* too grand, too stout, with monstrous biceps, 'a powerful porter waiting to load a sack on his back'.[51]

Authors' intentions are, ultimately, unknowable, but in Gautier's case his descriptions suggest a genuine absorption with the idea of the Beautiful. His fiction carries enormous descriptive weight (the plots are flimsy), while his art criticism is so strongly framed into a narrative (portraits speak to us, summon us, etc.) that the difference between the two genres is minimal.

Gautier had so deeply internalised the conception of the eternal feminine to whom men must utterly surrender that he exhibited it in his own personal life. On and off for almost thirty years he unsuccessfully pursued Carlotta Grisi, one of the great ballerinas of her time. Her rejection fed a fantasy dominated by the theme of the impossible love. Carlotta was the first to dance *Giselle* (in June 1841), for which Gautier had provided the libretto, based on Heine's *Reisebilder* (1826–31), about the ghosts of girls who die before their weddings, and Gautier fell in love with her after seeing her dance.[52] This did not prevent him from having a long relationship with her sister, the opera singer Ernesta Grisi, by whom he had two daughters. Though rejecting Gautier's advances, Carlotta was manifestly fond of him. Her letters, written in middle age, amply demonstrate her deep friendship and her concern for Gautier, by then in poor health, and their correspondence intensified after 1865, when her liaison with Prince Radziwill ended. Gautier often visited Carlotta at her villa in Geneva, wrote *Spirite* there and sent her a unique, specially printed copy – which she lost. In a letter written to her on 11 January 1868, when the poet was fifty-six and Carlotta approaching fifty, Gautier almost impersonates one of his characters, asking Carlotta to play the role of the *femme fatale*. The letter was written after a visit to Carlotta, and Gautier laments that only his body 'has returned ... my soul is with you and follows you everywhere'. He complains that she was, with him, too often

> so reserved, so impenetrable, so enveloped by veils of reticence that I find it sometimes difficult to see what is in your mind . . .
>
> . . . you are my life, my soul, my eternal desire . . . you hold in your hands my happiness and my misery. You can be certain of this, o wicked, o cruel, o unjust! Why make me wait so long after having allowed me to hope . . . What do I have to do to gain your heart? Do not wait until my death to have pity on me . . .
>
> . . . let me imagine that I hold you in my arms, close to my heart, that I breathe your soul upon your lips and that you do not refuse mine.
>
> Yours, indestructibly, obstinately and passionately. Your slave, Théophile Gautier.[53]

There is no record of Carlotta's reply, but her letter of 27 January is as friendly as ever – perhaps too friendly. To the poet who had announced his indestructible passion she asks what should be done with six pairs of socks knitted for him at fifteen francs for ten pairs. Should they be sent to him in Paris? Did this upset Gautier? Perhaps he consoled himself with the thought that enquiring about socks was the ultimate ploy of the true *femme fatale*.

It is evident that Gautier frequently transformed desirable women, whether in fiction or in life, into dominant *femmes fatales*. It is thus not surprising that the *Mona Lisa* was eventually subjected to this treatment. The first fuller reflection appeared in a review he wrote in 1855 of a play called *La Joconde*, by Paul Foucher and Régnier.[54] It is the banal story of a well-born young woman, an orphan called Joconde, who is all alone in the world. She is courted by a rich old prince but marries a poor young nobleman. Gautier started the review in the outraged mode:

> *La Joconde*! This name makes me think immediately of this sphinx of beauty who smiles so mysteriously in Leonardo da Vinci's painting, and who seems to pose a yet unresolved riddle to the admiring centuries. It is dangerous to conjure up such a ghost. Who has not contemplated for hours this head bathed in half-tints, enveloped in translucent veils . . . ? Her gaze intimating unknown pleasures, her gaze so divinely ironic. We feel perturbed in her presence by her aura of superiority.

Her deep eyes hide forbidden secrets, her 'mocking lips' are those of 'all-knowing gods who despise the vulgarity of human beings'. Never had the 'feminine ideal' been represented in a more ineluctably seducing form. Had Don Juan met her he would have renounced the three thousand women on his famous list. The unfortunate authors of the play had not realised the expectation they raised by using this 'formidable name'. They should have 'spent a day at the Louvre before doing so. One would need Shakespeare, Goethe and Byron rolled together to meet the challenge.'

Gautier recycled these thoughts over and over again, sometimes using exactly the same words. In an article published in 1857 in *l'Artiste* on Leonardo's caricatures he described the smiles of the contorted faces as 'mysterious, deep, penetrating, wise. They cause disquiet and fascination, they bring about love as well as fear.' Then, discussing the smile of Mona Lisa, he added that 'the arc of her lips appears to be about to erupt into divine sarcasm, heavenly irony, angelic derision; some inner pleasure whose secret we cannot fathom makes these lips turn into an inexplicable curve.'[55]

By 1867 Gautier had added the final touches to what could be considered his literary reconstruction of Mona Lisa. In his *Guide de l'Amateur au musée du Louvre* he transformed himself into a guide taking us into the Salon Carré of the great museum, the holy of holies where are kept, he wrote, 'the most glorious assembly of painters in the world'. As if taking us by the hand, Gautier, doing what so many guides were to do after him, points to the *Mona Lisa*, 'that miracle of painting, that work which, in our view, has come closest to perfection'.[56] His love for 'Monna Lisa del Giocondo', he wrote, was not recent: 'my passion for some living beings has not lasted as long' – forgetting, presumably, Carlotta Grisi. He then unearthed the passages from his 1855 review before adding:

> I have seen her frequently, since then, this adorable Joconde. She is always there smiling with sensuality, mocking her numerous lovers. She has the serene countenance of a woman sure that she will remain beautiful for ever and certain to be greater than the ideal of poets and artists.[57]

In the same year Gautier contributed a long essay on Leonardo to the collection *Les Dieux et les demi-dieux de la peinture* (it was illustrated by Calamatta).[58] He returned to the *Mona Lisa*: her singular charm could not be attributed simply to her beauty. Some of Raphael's women were finer. She was 'no longer young, but at least thirty years old'. Her dress, now discoloured, has become almost that of a widow. What was irresistible and exhilarating, however, was the smile, 'wise, deep, velvety, full of promises':

> ... the sinuous, serpentine mouth, turned up at the corners in a violet penumbra, mocks the viewer with such sweetness, grace and superiority that we feel timid, like schoolboys in the presence of a duchess. So the head, with its violet shadows, half-perceived as through a black gauze, makes you dream for hours, and pursues you in memory like the motif of a symphony. Under the form expressed is felt a vague, indefinite, inexpressible concept like a musical thought. One is moved and troubled. Previously seen images pass before one's gaze, confused and soft, smiling familiarly, and whispering languorous confidences in your ear. Repressed desire and desperate hopes struggle painfully through a luminous shadow. And you discover that your melancholy springs from the fact that the Joconde received, three centuries ago, the confession of your love with the same mocking smile she still wears today.[59]

Gautier was certainly obsessed with women, but not with the *Mona Lisa*. There are no direct references to her in his fiction, which are full of allusions to paintings and painters. What he did was to turn Mona Lisa into an archetype, a beauty not historically circumscribed but eternal, because she reaches towards us from the depth of a mysterious past (Egypt, Greece, Rome); hence the contempt she has for us, poor earthly creatures. We (this is an unmistakably masculine 'we') desire her, yet she is distant and unreachable. We fail to possess her not because she belongs to another man or to a higher class, or because she is demure, chaste and pure, and belongs to God and religion. She is unreachable because that is her wish. She knows she is desired, relishes the thought and is aware that she will be desired as long as she remains distant. She is amused by the dismay she causes in men, hence the mockery, the irony. That is why she is so dangerous and so irresistible.

Gautier thought that 'normal' women could never satisfy men. 'A real woman, who eats and drinks, gets up in the morning and goes to bed at night,' muses the Chevalier d'Albert, the protagonist of his *Mademoiselle de Maupin*, 'can hardly bear comparison to women represented by the sculptors of Ancient Greece and the painters of the Renaissance.'[60] Thus libertine behaviour, perhaps with misogynist connotations, is made acceptable by the worship of the Eternal Woman. The serial seduction of ordinary women was the inevitable consequence of the impossibility of touching the heart of the unreachable Great Enchantress.

In the nineteenth century the idealised woman acquired a new role. She is no longer dominated, but dominant. A subtle strategy, perhaps, whereby literary men, from the vantage point of their privileged position as the definers of identities, are directly engaged in the construction of the modern woman, even to the extent of regarding her as the harbinger of modernity. Thus Edgar Quinet, with Jules Michelet the main progressive French nationalist historian, interpreted in 1849 the smile of the *Mona Lisa* as a *demi-ironique sourire* of the human soul gazing upon a world finally liberated from ancient terrors and superstitions.[61] The political programme of the Enlightenment was read into the smile. Here there was no room for Gautier's fantasies about the *femme fatale*.

Gautier's theme, however, turned out to be more universal, and hence more dominant. And more modern, too: the Byronic Don Juan, the Casanova who drives women mad with passion causing them to abandon husband, children, honour and family, belonged in reality to the eighteenth century. He now yielded the centre ground to the dangerous woman.[62] Exit *l'homme fatal*, enter *la femme fatale*.

The theme of falling in love with an image had become so common that many found the idea of Mona Lisa enchanting Leonardo almost irresistible. By the nineteenth century the typical sitter for a portrait was a woman, and the nude was almost invariably a female. Older women were seldom represented. It was widely assumed that models who sat naked had affairs with those who painted them.[63] When describing the *Mona Lisa* Joseph Lavallée, in his catalogue of the Galerie du Musée Napoléon (1804–15) – as the Louvre was then – allowed his fancy to prevail over every known historical fact:

> If only this seductive woman could speak! What secrets and confidential stories she would tell! What conquests she would relate! And Leonardo so handsome, elegant in body in spirit, as amiable as a gallant knight as he is as an artist . . . was Leonardo really only Mona Lisa's painter? I don't know, but one can see the genius of love and seduction cannot go much further than that.[64]

The young Jules Verne probably liked this idea. In 1851, at the age of twenty-three, well before producing his string of formidable bestsellers, he wrote a play in verse (in the style of Alfred de Musset), originally entitled *Léonard de Vinci*. Then, in 1855, he decided to call it *Joconde*, then opted for *Monna Lisa*. It was eventually read before the Academie of Amiens in 1874 but it has never been performed, nor does it deserve to be. It was published only in 1995.[65] Monna Lisa, who loves Leonardo, is the wife of Joconde, an elegant Florentine gentleman. She is sure her love is reciprocated – otherwise why would Leonardo take such a long time to finish the portrait? Of course she is right, but she has forgotten she is dealing with a genius, and that geniuses have higher calls. As soon as Leonardo is told that a despicable-looking model for the Judas of his *Last Supper* has been found in Milan, he departs.

The idea that Leonardo and Mona Lisa had fallen in love with each other proved alluring to many, in spite of the lack of evidence. Hippolyte Taine dismissed such fantasies, frequently recycled in later popular fiction, in his 1865 lecture on Leonardo, but the story was too good to drop.[66] Charles Clément assured his readers that Leonardo was in love with Mona Lisa.[67] Gruyer echoed this: Lisa was irresistible, and knew it – 'Mona Lisa had taken possession of Leonardo.' The artist had put into this portrait 'his whole science, genius, passion, and heart', and all his subsequent works preserved traces of this.[68] Dmitri Mereshkovsky in his fictionalised account of Leonardo's life (*The Resurrection of the Gods*, 1900) has him fall in love with the portrait and its haunting smile.[69] Arsène Houssaye was quite certain that Lisa's smile was one of mockery addressed to her husband, who was not as young and handsome as Leonardo.[70] In fact Francesco il Giocondo was eight years younger than Leonardo, and we have no idea what he looked like. Mereshkovsky too makes Francesco older than Leonardo and unattractive – as husbands often are (in novels).

Gabriel Séailles's variant (1892) was that Lisa was a lovely, impulsive woman who fell in love with a complex and brooding genius: she belonged not to her husband but to Leonardo, who had waited for her, felt her beauty, anticipated it, and had 'recognised her' when he saw her.

> She went towards him without haste, yielding to the charm of this genius for whom she was no stranger. There was between them a *je ne sais quoi*, a mysterious link uniting the thought and the object. Their love was not the ecstatic folly of the spring of life ... Impulsive, not knowing her own soul, the woman fell in love with a man whose complex spirit remained impenetrable to her. His lucid intelligence decoded the secrets of her unconscious. Leonardo loved in her the boundlessness of nature when nature is not aware of itself; he appropriated her body and her soul and then provided us with the means of finding for ourselves the mystery that had inflamed his passion.[71]

In the nineteenth century, Leonardo's supposed homosexuality was unmentioned. The presumption rests on his trial for sodomy in 1476 (when he was twenty-four), although he was acquitted. There is also no trace of any involvement with a woman in his life.[72] Later, when the issue could be discussed openly, new interpretations were produced. Thus, in 1973, Kenneth Clark decided that Leonardo's sexual preferences were a key to understanding his work, and that the artist 'gladly allowed his homosexuality to penetrate to the depth of his being'. Leonardo understood, explained Clark, that

> the creative process ... was predominantly a female process. The male part of procreation was short, easy and beyond his powers of analysis. The female part was long, complex and a possible subject for investigation.[73]

Thus sexuality remained present in any twentieth-century discussion of Leonardo and Mona Lisa. The origin of this lies firmly in the nineteenth century, when images of women multiplied exponentially and women were discussed – usually but not exclusively by men – with an unprecedented intensity.[74]

An early path-breaker had been Goethe, who concluded his *Faust, Part Two* (completed in 1831) with a celebration of the superiority (and redeeming quality) of a still idealised woman: '*Das Ewig Weissliche/Zieth uns hinan*' (Eternal Womanhood/Leads us above). Women – hitherto whores or saints or just 'normal' – had become complex beings, less encumbered by conventions than men, more 'natural', more real and, as we would say nowadays, 'more in touch with their feelings'. Throughout the second half of the nineteenth century major writers positioned women at the centre of their narratives: Prosper Mérimée with *Carmen* (1852, inspired by Gautier's *Voyage en Espagne*, 1843), Gustave Flaubert with *Madame Bovary* (1857), Leo Tolstoy with *Anna Karenina* (1873–77), August Strindberg with *Miss Julie* (1888), Thomas Hardy with *Tess of the d'Urbervilles* (1891) and Theodor Fontane with *Effi Briest* (1895). These heroines all die tragically, surrounded by men unable to express their emotions or devoid of them, or trapped by stultifying conventions. Women's authentic feelings empower them to soar above the misery of established rules and customs. They become free spirits, the embodiment of the Modern. Marie Duplessis, the heroine of Alexandre Dumas's 1848 novel *La Dame aux camélias*, the Violetta of Verdi's great operatic adaptation (*La Traviata*), starts as a courtesan and dies a saint. But either condition – which she freely entered – set her apart from the narrow bourgeois world of conventional morality represented by her lover and his father. In 1879 Nora slams the door and escapes from Henrik Ibsen's *Doll's House*. Henry James's Isabel Archer, the heroine of *Portrait of a Lady* (1881), decides – and decides freely, if after much anguish – to remain trapped in an unloving marriage.

In the nineteenth century women were often represented as a source of power. Nations, in that age of nationalism, were female, helped, no doubt, by the grammatical rule that makes most countries feminine in gendered language. Russia – as well as martyred Poland – was represented as a Mother. The insurgent Italy of the Risorgimento was depicted as a young woman. Marianne became the symbol of France. The cult of Joan of Arc became established. The Motherland, *la madrepatria*, *la mère-patrie*, *die Mutterland*, was invoked more often than the fatherland.

The Roman Catholic Church participated in such feminisation. On 8 December 1854 the pope, after centuries of debates, promulgated the dogma of the Immaculate Conception (*Ineffabilis Deus*): the Mother of God had been conceived without original sin. New shrines such as Lourdes in France and Marpingen in Germany attracted massive pilgrimages.

The educated elite regarded the cult of the Virgin as peculiar to the uneducated masses blinded by a plebeian religiosity. They were probably blind to their own cult of fatal femininity. Gautier, for instance, identified naive worship with Leonardo's *St Anne with Virgin and Child*, for which he had sentimental words tinged by a condescending paternalism.[75] Faced with female symbols of religion, appropriately desexualised, he was untroubled by dark thoughts or enigmatic smiles. St Anne and the Virgin Mary, he explained, exuded celestial delicacy and a charming familiarity. Above all they were, reassuringly, mothers. St Anne's daughter, Mary, sat on her mother's lap, sweetly and tenderly extending her arms to her son, who played with a lamb (the sacrificial animal allegorically signifying the Passion). Mary's smile, far from enigmatic, is infused with a secret joy. Gautier found St Anne charming: 'seldom has an old woman been more amiably painted by an artist . . . Her beautiful wrinkles are full of grace.'[76] This is far from surprising: St Anne, following the pictorial convention of the fifteenth century, is represented as being of the same age as her daughter, the Virgin Mary, which is why she has neither grey hair nor wrinkles and looks barely over thirty. The scene is untroubling, comforting and reassuring. It induces a serene feeling of male superiority.

Mona Lisa, the dangerous seductress, was a different matter, at least in Gautier's perception. He admitted that when faced with the *Mona Lisa* he felt like a schoolboy before a duchess. Yet such unleashing of male masochism was relatively safe. To be dominated by an idealised woman could be exciting while remaining harmless. It was a well-established Romantic trope, at least ever since Rousseau had written in his *Confessions* in 1781:

> To fall on my knees before a masterful mistress, to
> obey her commands, to have to beg for her forgiveness,
> have been to me the most delicate of pleasures; and
> the more my vivid imagination heated my blood the
> more like a spellbound lover I looked.[77]

Every male required a woman to worship. Catholics had the Virgin Mary, Republicans had Marianne, and now intellectuals could use, if they so wished, the masterpieces of Renaissance geniuses. These paintings, of course, provided ample opportunities. They depicted, alongside an endless vista of virgins and saints, an array of proud noblewomen. The problem with these was that they belonged to someone: they were the wives and mistresses of powerful men. Above all they could be easily identified. There was no mystery. The *Mona Lisa* was a different matter. The utterly unknown wife of Francesco Giocondo could be the Unknown Woman. She had no history behind her. The real Lisa, mother and wife, could quietly disappear under the weight of male fantasies. In her place an elaborate structure of images could be erected which no historical research could ever demolish. An indeterminate portrait became the terrain for infinite variations on the same theme.

Gautier, by refashioning the *Mona Lisa* to suit his visions, almost separated Leonardo from his own work. Professional artists would find this early 'death of the author' unacceptable. Thus Odilon Redon, the great Symbolist painter, though impressed by the *Mona Lisa*, wrote in his diary that it was not the smile which had led to four centuries of praise by painters, but Leonardo's mastery in reproducing on a flat surface, thanks to the *chiaroscuro*, the depth of a face and the radiance of its spirit.[78] But for Gautier the Louvre *Mona Lisa* was an improvement on Leonardo's: the patina of time and its progressive darkening had improved the picture, rendering it more mysterious. And Séailles wrote in 1892 that though Mona Lisa had lost her colours, she was the most alive of Leonardo's works: 'She is not an image, she is a person, we know her, we speak of her, she has her enemies and her worshippers.'[79]

This is how a work of art becomes, conspicuously, the result of multiple interventions: by the original artist, by the passage of time, and by its viewers, their wishes and desires.

Gautier's construction of the meaning of the *Mona Lisa* became the dominant one, not because he was the first to deal with the portrait in such a way, but because he was the most important, the most influential and the most talented. Above all he was in the right place at the right time. A Europe-wide myth could only develop in a country with global cultural pretensions, and in a capital city that was at the centre of major intellectual commerce. Besides, Gautier's poetry and fiction required an icon representing his *femme fatale*.

I am not suggesting that Gautier made a conscious selection. Such things are seldom planned, and when they are, are seldom planned well. But let us assume Gautier deliberately set out to choose the portrait that would best fit his purpose. Why pick the *Mona Lisa*?

Firstly, the *femme fatale* could not be a virgin, let alone the Virgin Mary. The writer and French Minister of Culture André Malraux had a point when he told President de Gaulle – incredible as it may seem, they were discussing the Eternally Feminine – 'The turning point in art is when a painter discovers the Eternally Feminine *against* the Virgin.'[80]

Secondly, modern portraits – of which Gautier was a champion – were not suitable either. The man who lusted after Egyptian mummies and Roman statues needed something with a sense of the past, a status only the patina of time could bestow. The women of Ingres, David, Delacroix and Courbet, and even Goya's haughty Spanish ladies, were too modern. The Flemish and German women of Hans Memling, Van Eyck and Vermeer were too severe and dour, too sullen and cold, too strait-laced and simple and, above all, too Nordic. Frans Hals's bourgeois women were too bourgeois. In 1869 (a little late for Gautier) the Louvre obtained a portrait of Hals's bohemian girl (see plate 31), but her smile is too inviting and unambiguous.

In the same year the museum also acquired Rembrandt's *Bathsheba*, one of the rare full nudes painted by the artist. The model, Hendrickje Stoffels, once the servant of the painter and later his mistress and favourite sitter, is too sensually earthy and too naked. To be '*fatale*' a *femme* must have her clothes on. As Gabriel Séailles says, an undressed Mona Lisa would efface the mystery, the dream; Lisa would become a Carmen.[81] Rubens's, Boucher's and Fragonard's ladies were far too fleshy, far too pink; Cranach's too thin, too sickly.

A major feminine icon does not have to be a painting. It could be a statue. Indeed, since 1821 the Louvre has possessed Mona Lisa's main rival, the Venus de Milo. Her nose was fixed shortly after her arrival, but not the missing arms. More beautiful – to modern taste – than Mona Lisa, equipped with the necessary barely perceptible smile, half-naked, she is now ogled by hordes of tourists who have had to trek half the Louvre from the *Mona Lisa*. In 1878 the Baedeker guide to Paris declared it 'the most celebrated of the treasures of the Louvre', and granted it more space than the *Mona Lisa*.[82] It held on to this view in its 1900 edition,[83] but by 1911 it had become only the best-known *statue* of the Louvre.[84] It has, unquestionably, remained one of the best-known statues in the world, instantly recognisable thanks to the missing arms.

The Venus was surrounded by more mysteries than Mona Lisa. We are not even sure it is a Venus. Who was the sculptor? Was it part of a group of statues? And, above all, what was she doing with the missing arms? She too has been the subject of contrasting interpretations. Is she a coquette? Is she chaste? She too was celebrated by nineteenth-century poets, from Théodore de Banville (1842) to Armand Silvestre (1882) via Leconte de Lisle.[85] Even Gautier did not let the opportunity slip by, announcing: 'There is a statue all the museums of Europe envy us. It is regarded, and rightly so, as the most accomplished representation of beauty, the most perfect realisation of the *Eternal Feminine*. Everyone knows I am speaking of the Venus de Milo.'[86]

One cannot resist adding that evidently he said that to all the girls.

There is another Leonardo which, in principle, might have filled the role taken by Mona Lisa. This is *Lady with an Ermine*, the portrait of the beautiful Cecilia Gallerani (1473–1536), mistress of Lodovico il Moro, Leonardo's patron. The painting can provide enough uncertainties to keep art historians busy with mystery stories. Is it really Cecilia? As late as 1933 the *Enciclopedia italiana* doubted it.[87] Was she really Lodovico's mistress? When was it painted? Why is she holding an ermine? Is it really an ermine? Was she a rival to Lucrezia Crivelli, the presumed sitter of the other Leonardo portrait in the Louvre (*La Belle Ferronnière*) and reputedly also Lodovico's mistress? What happened to it between the time it was painted and the eighteenth century, when it came to be owned by a Polish prince, Adam Czartoryski?[88]

As noted in Chapter 2, the animal she holds in her hands could constitute a wordplay on Gallerani's name (the Greek for ermine is '*gallé*') or be a reference to Lodovico, who became a member of the Order of the Ermine in 1488. The ermine is also a symbol of purity (in mythology it is supposed to prefer death to sullying its coat). The furry animal, ambiguously caressed by Cecilia, could lead to a variety of complex Freudian interpretations. Cecilia's smile could be deemed ironic and inscrutable. Her looking away could be seen as seductive, withholding herself while enticing. It is true that this portrait, masterful though it is, is not as innovative as the *Mona Lisa*. It lacks depth. The technique of the *sfumato* is not as mature. The landscape is not interesting. It did not inspire other painters, though, unlike *Mona Lisa*, it was celebrated by a court poet of the time. Bernardo Bellincioni's sonnet 'Sopra il retracto de Madona Cicilia qual fece maestro Leonardo' ('On the portrait of Milady Cecilia as painted by Master Leonardo') praises the true-to-nature pictorial skill of Leonardo:

> *Di che te adiri, a chi invidia hai, natura?*
> *Al Vinci che ha ritratto una tua stella . . .*

(O Nature, what incenses you, who provokes your envy?
Vinci it is for he portrayed one of your stars . . .)

However, the portrait of Cecilia Gallerani was not bought by a French king, did not end up in the Louvre, and Leonardo's authorship was established only in the twentieth century. The painting was actually in Paris in 1830 with the Czartoryski family, and remained there until about 1876, when it was taken to Cracow, to the museum founded by Wladislaw Czartoryski. It remains there to this day. Thus the *Lady with an Ermine* was in Paris throughout the crucial years when the myth of the *Mona Lisa* was being developed. But Gautier does not appear to have even known of its existence. No art historian, no connoisseur, no engraver, no writer appears to have mentioned *Lady with an Ermine*. The art press remained silent. Walter Pater believed it had been lost.[89] Arsène Houssaye, writer, member of Gautier's bohemian circle during the July monarchy and ardent Leonardo admirer, knew nothing about it. Almost certainly, along with the majority, he ignored it, assuming that it was not a Leonardo. In 1899 Eugène Müntz, Leonardo's first major biographer, wrote that it just was not good enough to be by Leonardo.[90] By then, of course, it was in out-of-the-way Cracow, beyond the reach of the tourists and artists who visited Paris. In any case the belief that it was not by Leonardo persisted for a long time. Both Francesco Malaguzzi-Valeri, the Italian author of a book on the court of Lodovico (1917), and Osvald Siren, the Swedish author of a biography of Leonardo (1911), refused to recognise Leonardo's hand.[91] A Renaissance painting whose attribution is in doubt was unlikely to be a match for the *Mona Lisa*.

Were there other candidates for the role of the *femme fatale*? As we have seen, Gautier had also lusted after portraits by Ingres and Flandrin, but these were too contemporary, and the El Greco he mentioned was not in the Louvre. Further south there was a profusion of beauties, but how could the demure Virgin Marys and Mary Magdalenes and all the saintly Catherines and Cecilias and Annes depicted by Raphael and others be transmuted into mocking and sexy *femmes fatales*? Perhaps some of the sexually desirable women of the Bible might be more amenable, like Tintoretto's *Susanna at the Bath*? Or one of the goddesses of mythology such as Botticelli's Venus or Flora in his *Spring*? Beautiful though they may be, they are too blatantly so, too open, too available. It may be amusing to stroll through the Louvre scouting for possible *femmes fatales*. One may pause by Titian's *Jeune femme à sa toilette*, or Raphael's *Jeanne d'Aragon*, or Veronese's *La Contessa Nani*. Tastes may differ, but clearly *Mona Lisa* did not have many competitors. Gautier's supply was limited.

At more or less the same time that Gautier was erecting

his image of a dangerous and seductive Mona Lisa, others had come up with similar thoughts. These may have been jointly fashioned by chattering artists in cafés. Appealing ideas, like clever inventions, have a way of emerging at the same time – when there is a public ready to buy them. Gautier was not the only propagandist for Lisa *la fatale*. The critic Alfred Dumesnil, in an essay written in 1854, claimed that the darkening of the *Mona Lisa*

> brings out well her deceitful sweetness . . . the smile is suffused with attraction, but it is the perfidious attraction of a diseased soul which makes others ill. This sweet gaze, yet voracious like the sea, is a devouring smile.[92]

The image of the *Mona Lisa* as a kind of irresistible vampire was further elaborated by Charles Clément who, when he turned to discuss it, unleashed a prose he did not employ for any of the works of Michelangelo or Raphael:

> The seduction and enchantment of Mona Lisa has survived for over three hundred years. Thousands of men, of all ages, speaking different languages, have crowded round this narrow frame. They have been inflamed by these limpid and burning eyes. They have listened to words of deception from these perfidious lips. They have carried this poisoned dart into their hearts and taken it to the four corners of the world. As long as some vestiges of this fabulous and fatal beauty endure, all those who seek to decipher the mysteries of the soul on the traits of a face will journey towards this ageless sphinx to demand the solution of the eternal enigma. Lovers, poets, dreamers, go and die at her feet! Neither your desperation nor your death will erase from her mocking mouth the enchanting smile, the implacable smile that promises rapture and denies happiness.[93]

Such intoxicating prose was common currency. Jules Michelet had resorted to it not only for the *Mona Lisa* but for two of the other Louvre Leonardos, *St John* and *Bacchus*. As you look at these three pictures, he wrote, 'they' look at you and

> you are fascinated and troubled as if by a strange mag-
> netism . . . masters of the depths of the world, of the
> unknown abyss of the ages – speak, what do you want
> of me? This canvas attracts me, revolts me, consumes
> me; and I go to her in spite of myself, as the bird to
> the snake.[94]

Note the transition: a discussion of three paintings converges on one, 'they' turns into 'her', the *Mona Lisa*. The plural *'vous'* in 'you are fascinated' turns into the personal pronoun 'I': 'I go to her in spite of myself'.

Leonardo himself, Michelet went on, became the prey of his own work, fascinated as if it had been produced by something outside himself: 'For years he laboured without being able to extricate himself from this fluid, shifting, ever-changing labyrinth he had painted . . .'[95]

When Michelet wrote this, around 1852, he was already the best-known historian in France – 'the presiding genius of the Romantic school of historiography'.[96] He had just recovered from a mid-life depression following his political disappointment at the failure of the 1848 revolution, the forfeiture of his chair at the Collège de France and his exile. In 1849, at fifty-one, he met and married his second wife, Athénaïs Mialaret, twenty-eight years younger. Recovery ensued. Michelet hailed Athénaïs as his saviour, his Joan of Arc. It was no ephemeral passion; years later he wrote in his diary: 'I have an advantage over my friends. I am very much in love with my wife.'[97] A new 'feminine' phase in his life had begun. He decided to write books women would want to read, books that would go beyond political history and deal with nature and society. In 1856 he wrote *l'Oiseau*, then, in quick succession, *l'Insecte* (1858), *l'Amour* (1859), *La Femme* (1860) and, in 1862, a history of women called *la Sorcière*, in which he defended witches as unjustly persecuted by the Church for attempting to penetrate the secrets of nature.

He had, however, to finish his massive history of the French Revolution (seven volumes, 1847–53) and return to his interrupted *Histoire de France*. The first six volumes of this had appeared prior to 1844 and contained a sympathetic account of the Middle Ages. By the 1850s, Michelet had changed his views. The Middle Ages had become dark and crawling with priests. The Renaissance heralded the dawn of humanity. It was in the seventh volume that Leonardo was hailed as the first modern man and the *Mona Lisa* described in such purple prose.

Michelet's rhetoric puzzled even some of his admirers. Hippolyte Taine, reviewing the volume on the Renaissance in *Revue de l'instruction publique* (February 1855), thought the author had been intoxicated by his own prose. Michelet's scholarship and erudition were not in dispute, but Taine felt that the power of his prose almost compelled the reader to accept on trust all his interpretations. However, admonished Taine, when the language of prophets and preachers displaces the dispassionate style of the historian, one must part company from Michelet: 'History is an art, yes, but it is also a science; it demands from the writer inspiration but also reflection ... Michelet has allowed himself to be overcome by poetic imagination.'[98]

The line 'This canvas attracts me, revolts me ...' was singled out as a case of 'mental hallucination'. Purple prose, however, can be catchy. When Taine later visited Italy, assuming that a *Modesty and Vanity* in the Palazzo Sciarra in Rome was by Leonardo, he turned enthusiastic, declaring it more beautiful than the *Mona Lisa*, her smile even more mysterious. In Florence, visiting the Pitti, he found yet another 'Leonardo' (wrong again): a nun. He proceeded to enthuse about her white veil, and called her Mona Lisa's sister because she was equally complex, equally unfathomable. Was she a nun, a princess, or a courtesan?[99] However, when lecturing on Leonardo at the Beaux-Arts in 1865 he spared his students such conjectures and simply referred to the *Mona Lisa*'s 'charming and delicate smile'.[100]

Taine's criticism was fairly conventional. Historians should stick to a style appropriate to their craft and not use that of the poet. Michelet could have argued, quite legitimately, that if historians want to be listened to outside the profession, they must use a language appropriate to their subject, not to their discipline. There are times when they must write like Gautier. Michelet treated history as Gautier treated paintings: what mattered was to convey the impression received. For Michelet history was like a person one loves. To understand it one must relive it oneself, as to understand a piece of music one must re-compose it in one's head.

Perhaps Michelet had come up with his conception of the *Mona Lisa* independently of Gautier. But intellectuals, especially in mid-nineteenth-century Paris, do not exchange ideas simply by publishing them. The earliest identification of the *Mona Lisa* as a Romantic icon may well have occurred in a café in the Quartier Latin. After all, far from being inaccessible, it was available to all in the Louvre just across the Seine.

In the formation of a public view on questions of taste, four factors are paramount: what is being said, who says it, how it is said, and where it is said. During the nineteenth century, when taste was a major element in the self-identification of the emergent middle classes, rich and somewhat exhilarating language was imperative. Taste-formers and opinion-makers established their claim to authority on questions of taste by using an uncommon and flowery discourse. What may now appear as unnecessarily bombastic and 'over-the-top' was then a condition for the establishment of one's credentials as an authority. Brevity of expression, simple, immediate language devoid of nuances, the authoritative listing of items (first, second, third! one, two, three!) and other rhetorical devices belong essentially to the twentieth century, to the era of mass communication, popular newspapers, advertising, radio and television. The power of the image is multiplied when enhanced by an authoritative interpretation.

A cursory review of some of Gautier's contemporaries confirms not only the importance of the rhetorical mode of presentation but the systematic use of a set of keywords whenever the *Mona Lisa* is discussed. Here is Houssaye, friend of Gautier's, admirer of Leonardo's:

> In this frighteningly seductive painting, lies a mystery ... It is true to life yet cannot be contemplated as if it were mere matter. As we stand before it, we feel as if alone on a mountain top with, at our feet, a dizzying abyss into which we are about to fall, into which we do fall. It is the infinite abyss of a dream.[101]

It continues thus for three pages:

> ... this young charmer ... this divinity of the chiaroscuro whose brown gaze holds chained at her feet all the generations of men ... Sweet-named Monna Lisa ... dominated, chaste, triumphant, naive, sensually ineffable, do not ask who she is, ask who she is not ... so perfidiously and deliciously womanly with six thousand years of experience behind her ... What did she think when Leonardo painted her ... ? Perhaps she could see her future as a *femme dominatrice*, eternally adored ...[102]

Pierre Marcy, in his 1867 *Guide populaire dans les musées du Louvre*, called the *Mona Lisa* 'one of the most precious jewels of the Louvre'. He was 'astonished by the power of expression of this figure', and wrote that her 'melancholic look and her divine smile, exercise some kind of fascination or charm on us'. He concluded by appealing to literary authority, citing George Sand, as many have done since:

> What is disquieting about this image is the soul shining through, appearing to contemplate yours, with lofty

serenity reading into your eyes while you vainly try to read into hers.[103]

The citation selected reinforced the dominant view. George Sand's original text was more complex, one of the rare nineteenth-century literary comments on the *Mona Lisa* by a woman. Published in 1858 in the popular daily *La Presse*, the essay was intended to promote Calamatta's engraving of the painting.[104] Sand began, daringly, to say what many have since thought – Lisa is not a beautiful woman: she has no eyebrows, her cheeks are too full, her hair too thin, her forehead too broad, her eyes do not sparkle, she is plump. But she is a *laide séduisante*, seductively plain (like George Sand herself). Nevertheless, she continued, there is an undertone of cold malice in her smile, a riddle in her expression difficult to forget. The real secret lies not in the painting but in the painter: how he achieved an idealised portrait; how he instilled his powers of expression into it. What we see in the painting is the genius of the painter, the soul of a master, the hopes of a superior man. This attempt to discuss the work in terms of its creator was not successful. Sand's conclusions – 'Whoever looked at her for an instant cannot forget her' – were frequently quoted, the rest of her essay forgotten.[105]

Hyperbolic descriptions continued. Seldom have men, at least in the nineteenth century, openly expressed the view that Mona Lisa did not fit any of the prevailing criteria for aesthetic beauty. Women have been less reluctant. For instance the art critic Jeanne de Flandreysy, writing in 1903, while falling in with the majority view that the lady portrayed possessed 'an irresistible attraction', prefaced this with a blunt 'She is not beautiful, her cheeks are full, her eyes puffy.'[106]

Towards the end of the nineteenth century Leonardo's biographer Gabriel Séailles attempted to calm things down: the *Mona Lisa* was, after all, the product of a meticulous analytical mind.[107] It was necessary to examine it 'intellectually'. But Séailles realised that it was getting difficult to say anything new: 'To speak of her is now so banal that I lack the courage.'[108] Nevertheless he found it, and though clearly unable to control the purple prose, pleaded

> to leave aside clichés on the Eternal Feminine and the mystery of its incarnation in this woman whose sensibility is but the surface ... of a sea without shores which pervades her unceasingly.[109]

A century later, such a way of describing the *Mona Lisa* had become so commonplace and popular that the few intellectuals still interested in the portrait emphasised spirituality rather than wanton sexuality. Thus, in the 1950s, the philosopher Karl Jaspers wrote about the *Mona Lisa* in these terms:

> The open eyes under the high forehead, the barely suggested smile, the quietness of her attitude, the aristocratic negligence of the folded hands have made spirituality visible in the corporeal figure of this woman.

Mona Lisa was no longer the devouring temptress, the castrating terror of men:

> In her there is no coquetry, no seduction, no social mask, but the serene aloofness of the soul ... Leonardo saw the dignity of woman, of which her sexuality is only one component.[110]

This was probably one of the last philosophical reflections on the *Mona Lisa*, as the painting's rise to global stardom made it less interesting to intellectuals. But at the close of the nineteenth century, when Lisa was still under-explored and under-hyped, her portrait still excited intellectuals – and not just the French; the British too joined the fray. Thus Mona Lisa found herself promoted by the two most globally influential cultures of the time.

The high-flown language used in France was not peculiar to the French. The leading British art critics of the second half of the nineteenth century deployed it with relish, obeying the same rules followed on the other side of the Channel. The construction of the *Mona Lisa* as a representative icon of the Eternal Feminine continued, following the pattern established in France, but with variations. Intellectuals in the rest of mainland Europe – in Italy and Spain, Poland and Russia – took their cultural fashion and trends mainly from France, particularly on all matters of art. And they took it directly, in French, their second language. There was no need for any local cultural mediation. In Victorian Britain, however, the indigenous intellectual elites were directly in charge of matters of taste. They themselves determined what should be imported from France, and how it should be altered to make it conform to local taste.

In the nineteenth century, France and Britain were practically in charge of the validation of high culture throughout most of Europe. Their intellectual elites were concentrated in single centres, Paris and London (with Oxford acting as its academic extension). Berlin, Brussels and Vienna would match them only towards the end of the century. Before then Vienna functioned as an artistic counterpart and rival to Berlin, decreasing the latter's potential strength, as did Frankfurt, Dresden, Leipzig, Munich and Hamburg. The German-speaking world was not culturally centralised – a major handicap never wholly compensated by Germany's strengths: a unified language, an exceptionally high rate of literacy, the largest reading public in Europe and a formidable book-distribution system. These, in fact, enabled foreign cultural products to penetrate Germany much faster than elsewhere. As for Italy, it was in no position even remotely to resume the pre-eminent cultural leadership it had enjoyed in the sixteenth century. Only recently united as a state, it had no dominant cultural centre. The new capital, Rome, had long been cut off from mainstream European culture and trailed well behind Naples, Florence, Milan and Turin, none of which could compete with Berlin and Vienna, let alone with Paris or London.

There were fields, such as music, where Britain was absent, at least as a producer, and France not supreme, for primacy here belonged to Germany and – for opera only – to Italy. Even in opera, however, European validation required a Parisian success, as both Rossini and later Verdi had fully realised.

When it came to contemporary art, Paris had no rivals. It was the natural home for artists from other countries, as the repository of much ancient and Renaissance art but also as the leading centre for the interpretation of art. Britain, however, had its own critics, such as John Ruskin and Walter Pater. But their international impact was limited. While the French tended to be free-thinking progressives, Ruskin was a reactionary bent upon the recovery of heroic and feudal ideas, and though he championed innovative and revolutionary artists like Turner, he was also a great supporter of Gothic architecture and of the pre-Raphaelites. Pater was the foremost British exponent of the principles of art for art's sake, pioneered by Gautier. Both were recognised masters of a highly emotional style of English prose. But while Ruskin disdained the Renaissance, Pater was its most influential British proponent. This led him to Leonardo, and hence to Mona Lisa. It was he who made her famous outside France, and his fame grew with hers.

CHAPTER SIX

Mona Lisa as a Visual Zeitgeist

In 1936, in his idiosyncratic introduction to his *Oxford Book of Modern Verse 1892–1935*, W.B. Yeats reprinted part of Walter Pater's famous prose passage on the *Mona Lisa* as free verse to underline its 'revolutionary importance':[1]

> She is older than the rocks among which she sits;
> Like the vampire,
> She has been dead many times,
> And learned the secrets of the grave;
> And has been a diver in the deep seas,
> And keeps their fallen day about her;
> And trafficked for strange webs with Eastern
>   merchants:
> And, as Leda,
> Was the mother of Helen of Troy,
> And, as Saint Anne,
> The mother of Mary;
> And all this has been to her but as the sound of lyres
>   and flutes,
> And lives
> Only in the delicacy
> With which it has moulded the changing lineaments,
> And tinged the eyelids and hands.

It is no accident that Yeats was so taken by these lines. Though he never referred to the *Mona Lisa* in his poetry, his own idealised lady, Maud Gonne, had inspired many of his poems and had been at the centre of his thoughts about womanhood.[2]

By 1936 Pater's single lengthy prose sentence, and the wider text in which it appeared, had become famous. Kenneth Clark, in 1973, said: 'Fifty years ago we all knew it by heart.'[3] Mario Praz, though well aware of French precedents, wrote that it was Walter Pater 'who made the great discovery: reading the history of the femme fatale in the famous smile of the Gioconda'.[4]

Yet there is no mention of a smile in Pater's passage. The smile was already so well known that it could be subliminally subsumed as an integral part of the *Mona Lisa*. Admittedly, in the preceding page Pater mentioned an 'unfathomable smile, always with a touch of something sinister in it' – but added that such smiles were common to Verrocchio, Leonardo's teacher.

The full passage, which must be cited in its entirety, is as follows:

> The presence that rose thus so strangely beside the waters, is expressive of what in the ways of a thousand years men had come to desire. Hers is the head upon which all 'the ends of the world are come,' and the eyelids are a little weary. It is a beauty wrought out from within upon the flesh, the deposit, little cell by cell, of strange thoughts and fantastic reveries and exquisite passions. Set it for a moment beside one of those white Greek goddesses or beautiful women of antiquity, and how would they be troubled by this beauty, into which the soul with all its maladies has passed! All the thoughts and experience of the world have etched and moulded there, in that which they have of power to refine and make expressive the outward form, the animalism of Greece, the lust of Rome, the mysticism of the middle age with its spiritual ambition and imaginative loves, the return of the Pagan world, the sins of the Borgias. She is older than the rocks among which she sits; like the vampire, she has been dead many

times, and learned the secrets of the grave; and has been a diver in deep seas, and keeps their fallen day about her; and trafficked for strange webs with Eastern merchants: and, as Leda, was the mother of Helen of Troy, and, as Saint Anne, the mother of Mary; and all this has been to her but as the sound of lyres and flutes, and lives only in the delicacy with which it has moulded the changing lineaments, and tinged the eyelids and hands. The fancy of a perpetual life, sweeping together ten thousand experiences, is an old one; and modern philosophy has conceived the idea of humanity as wrought upon by, and summing up in itself, all modes of thought and life. Certainly Lady Lisa might stand as the embodiment of the old fancy, the symbol of the modern idea.[5]

Walter Pater was thirty when he wrote this. The essay on Leonardo – of which this passage is a small segment – was published in the *Fortnightly Review* in November 1869, and republished with other essays in 1873 as *Studies in the History of the Renaissance*. Leonardo, of course, was already an established icon in the wider British culture. In 1880 the Royal Academy would acquire a copy of the *Virgin of the Rocks*, and in the same year Leonardo's manuscripts were published in English by Jean Paul Richter.[6] The interest in his scientific works was growing. But Pater had no interest in Leonardo's science, or experiments, or thoughts, or inventions. His Leonardo was, exclusively, a painter.

The success of Pater's text was due to the beauty of the prose and to the literary and visual associations it conjured: a 'strange presence', the weight of the past ('a thousand years'), 'fantastic reveries and exquisite passions', beautiful Greek goddesses, the 'animalism of Greece', the 'lust of Rome', medieval mysticism, paganism, the Borgias, vampirism and ghosts ('she has been dead many times'), the Orient (trafficking with 'Eastern merchants'), Leda and Helen of Troy. All the usual suspects were there.

It is striking that Flaubert's *La Tentation de saint Antoine*, published in the same period, used similar words: a woman called Helen offers herself, unsuccessfully, as one of St Anthony's temptations:

> She has been the Helen of the Trojans . . . she has been Lucretia, the patrician raped by kings. She has been Delilah who cut Samson's hair. She has prostituted herself to every nation. She has sung at every crossroads. She has kissed every face.[7]

There is no question of reciprocal plagiarism, not even influence. Flaubert had finished his story in 1872, having started it some twenty years previously, and it was not published until 1874.

The popularity of a text depends on its ability to resonate inside a pre-existing consciousness, rather than on its novelty. The theme of the beautiful woman who brings doom to her men was a great connecting element between the popular 'shocker' Gothic novels of the end of the eighteenth century, the French Romantics, British and French Decadentism and Symbolism, the pre-Raphaelite movement and the birth of modernism.

The quality of Pater's prose, though it encountered some criticisms, acted as an amplifier of themes already existing in the culture. We have seen how French intellectuals made connections similar to Pater's. The linking of antiquity with modernity by using feminine images occurred frequently, though it was not yet focused on any particular visual representation such as the *Mona Lisa*. Dante Gabriel Rossetti had painted specific women, such as Goethe's Marguerite (from *Faust*) and Dante's Beatrice, as 'an object of ambiguous attraction, part temptress, part priestess, both corrupting and innocent'.[8] But neither Rossetti nor John Everett Millais, nor Edward Burne-Jones nor George Frederic Watts – to mention only the British painters who shared the same female-centred project – ever succeeded in establishing a powerful recognisable icon. None of the representations of women they painted ever acquired renown outside the world of art connoisseurs: not even Rossetti's *Bocca Baciata* (1859, 'The

Kissed Mouth' – the title originates in a sonnet by Boccaccio; see plate 32), much admired by the young Swinburne and widely imitated in the 1860s, nor his Helen of Troy (1863), his Aurelia (1863), his Lilith (1864–68), his Medea (1866–68), nor Frederic Sandys's Mary Magdalene (1859), nor Edward Burne-Jones's Sidonia von Bork (1860–61), nor George Frederic Watts's Eve Trilogy (*She Shall Be Called Woman*, c.1888–92).[9]

Similarly, the French Symbolist artists did not produce a particular representation of the *femme fatale* sufficiently powerful to establish itself as the archetype – not Gustave Moreau, many of whose women display a Gioconda's smile, or Odilon Redon, who admired Leonardo's *sfumato* technique.[10] Along with the Symbolists in France and Belgium (Fernand Khnopff), and the *Sezession* group in Germany and Austria (Gustav Klimt), the pre-Raphaelites frequently painted women leaning on parapets, gazing wistfully into their own souls or at the viewer, combing their hair. These artists were obsessed by the same themes that had obsessed Gautier, Baudelaire and Swinburne: pleasure and pain, love and death. They were captivated by images of exotic women; women in Antiquity; sensual, mystical, moody women; disdainful women; women absorbed in thought; women with melancholic expressions.

Women had become the hub of artistic fixation. It was as if 'the Feminine' was a distant and mysterious land, just sighted by apprehensive explorers who, afraid to conquer it, let alone understand it, contented themselves with describing it from afar, magnifying its danger, exaggerating its mystery, embellishing their own predicament. This ideal woman had – as yet – no fixed visage, but multifarious expressions and poses.

Pater's great achievement was to devise resonant words with which to capture this strange *Zeitgeist* and link them to a specific painting representing an unknown woman, already mythologised, painted against a landscape equally mysterious and unknown. This achievement conferred great fame on Pater. He was the first to benefit directly from his association with Mona Lisa. Gautier or Michelet had not become better-known because of what they wrote on the *Mona Lisa* – they were already acclaimed, and their fame rubbed off on the portrait. But Mona Lisa helped Pater to establish his own fame, while he in turn inscribed her in the decadent literature of the *fin-de-siècle*. Even today, if Pater is remembered at all by non-specialists, it is chiefly as the author of the *Mona Lisa* passage.

With Pater, a kind of symbiotic relationship was established between the painting and its various champions. By attracting attention to the *Mona Lisa*, they attracted attention to themselves. Pater's name became indissolubly linked to a particular interpretation of Leonardo's painting at a time when the Leonardo cult was intensifying in Britain.

Pater understood, in spite of all the references he made to the past, that his way of looking at the *Mona Lisa* was dramatically modern. The Lady Lisa, he had written, might be 'the embodiment of the old fancy' – the fancy of 'sweeping together ten thousand experiences' – but she was also 'the symbol of the modern idea'. This Oxford aesthete, in love with the past, was at one with the *Zeitgeist*.

Pater's debt to the French is glaring, as any juxtaposition of his text with those quoted in previous chapters makes clear. The historical evidence for such a debt is also fairly substantial. He cultivated his French throughout 1863, visited Paris in 1864 and read Quinet and Michelet – both of whom are explicitly mentioned in his Leonardo essay. Pater was, of course, indifferent to their progressive ideological and political agenda, and adopted *in toto* the idea of art for art's sake propounded by Gautier and Swinburne. The theme of reincarnation – the essence of womanhood resurfacing throughout the ages in new embodiments – was common to both Gautier and Pater.[11]

Pater was familiar with all of Gautier's *Contes fantastique* as well as his *Mademoiselle de Maupin*.[12] He had read the *Histoire de Léonard de Vinci* by Arsène Houssaye, Gautier's friend and admirer, and must have been struck by the purple passages on the *Mona Lisa* where Houssaye fantasised about the love between Leonardo and Lisa.[13] In fact, some passages of Pater's essay on Leonardo originated in a review he had written of Houssaye's biography. Subsequently he removed all references to Houssaye, perhaps because the book had been badly received in England.[14] Pater had also read Gautier's essay on Leonardo in *Les Dieux et les semidieux de la peinture* (1864).[15]

Pater's main direct source – after Vasari – was Charles Clément's book on the three great Renaissance figures (*Michel-Ange, Léonard de Vinci, Raphael*, 1861), in particular Clément's remarks on the *Mona Lisa* (quoted more extensively on page 127):

> Lovers, poets, dreamers, go and die at her feet! Neither your desperation nor your death will erase from her mocking mouth the enchanting smile, the implacable smile that promises rapture and denies happiness.[16]

This is the theme of the scornful woman. Women are dangerous tricksters. They promise and then deny. It is also the Medusa theme – the hub of Pater's interpretation of the *Mona Lisa*. She glances at the hapless man, and before he is aware of it he is hers, petrified. It is no wonder that Pater unquestioningly accepted that the painting of the Medusa at the Uffizi was by Leonardo: 'the fascination of corruption penetrates in every touch its exquisitely finished beauty.'[17] His source, Clément, had warned that the attribution was doubtful. Clément was right: a seventeenth-century Flemish painter was the creator of the Uffizi Medusa. Nevertheless, Medusa was too obvious a mythic representation of the *femme fatale* to be left out of the Leonardo canon. Shelley's famous 1819 poem 'On the Medusa of Leonardo da Vinci in the Florentine Gallery' highlighted the mix of attraction and danger:

> 'Tis the tempestuous loveliness of terror;
> . . . and ever-shifting mirror
> Of all the beauty and the terror there –
> A woman's countenance, with serpent-locks,
> Gazing in death on Heaven from those wet rocks.[18]

George Sand had explicitly linked the Medusa to the *Mona Lisa*: she found both frightening.[19] Such a connection has remained part of the collective subconscious, and was even gently parodied by Umberto Eco in his 1988 novel *Foucault's Pendulum*, where one of the protagonists, finding himself alone at night in a museum, reassures himself: 'no one has ever been devoured by the Gioconda – an androgynous monster, a Medusa only for the aesthetes.'[20] Such irony belongs firmly to the 1980s, not to the 1890s, when Eugene Lee-Hamilton's sonnet 'On Leonardo's Head of Medusa' opened with the lines: 'The livid and unutterable head,/Fresh cut, lies welt'ring in its mane of snakes.'[21]

So strong was the belief that the painter of the *Mona Lisa* had also painted the Uffizi Medusa that the entry for 'Medusa' in Brewer's 1894 *Dictionary of Phrase and Fable* declared: 'The most famous painting of the Medusa is by Leonardo da Vinci; it is called his *chef d'oeuvre*.'[22]

Pater forced Leonardo the painter to the attention of the British public. Before him, British visitors to the Louvre, armed with Pilkington's *Dictionary of Painters*, would be told that Leonardo was not as great as Raphael or Michelangelo because they had painted more.[23] Had they relied on Bayle St. John's 1850 *The Louvre: or Biography of a Museum*, they would have been told that Leonardo stood the comparison with Titian 'well', and that the *Mona Lisa* was a 'magnificent portrait',

> so profound, and pushed to the very last limits and extreme delicacies of Art ... quoted by Vasari as an instance of the inconsistency and changeableness of Leonardo, whom he accuses of not having finished it!

However, wrote St. John, the better picture was next to it: Jan Van Eyck's *Vierge au Donateur* (known as *La Vierge du chancelier Rolin*, c.1436; see plate 34). This 'braves all comparisons, and compels attention by its brilliancy and wonderful state of preservation'.[24] This perceptive judgement was due to the hanging strategy of the mid-nineteenth-century curator: the museum put what it regarded as its greatest masterpieces together in one room, the Salon Carré, where one could find Perugino, Poussin, two Titians, two Leonardos (the *Mona Lisa* and *St Anne with Virgin and Child*) and four Raphaels.[25] Thus Van Eyck's painting, with its Virgin sitting down, in three-quarter view and with landscape in the background, found itself near the *Mona Lisa*. It belongs to a tradition that influenced Leonardo's revolutionary portrait. Nowadays, when pictures are grouped by 'nationality', such comparisons are harder to make. Van Eyck's Virgin is with the Flemish paintings, a very long way from the Italians.

In England, Anna Jameson had been the first art critic to attribute to Leonardo the status he achieved later. In her *Memoirs of the Earlier Italian Painters* (1845), she wrote that Leonardo represented a '*résumé* of all the characteristics of the age in which he lived'.[26] At the time this was far from being the consensus. John Ruskin, who was regarded as Britain's leading art critic (he was Pater's older rival at Oxford, though the two, incredibly enough, never met) did not rate Leonardo highly:

> Because Leonardo made models of machines, dug canals, built fortifications, and dissipated half his artpower in capricious ingenuities, we have many anecdotes of him – but no picture of importance on canvas and a few withered stains of one upon a wall. But because his pupil, or reputed pupil, Luini, laboured in constant and successful simplicity, we have no anecdotes of him; – only hundreds of noble works . . . He is a man ten times greater than Leonardo.[27]

Bernardino Luini Ruskin regarded as a 'mighty colourist', while Leonardo was only 'a fine draughtsman in black'. Time alters perception, and Ruskin's views now seem eccentric. Luini just about makes the 1968 *Penguin Dictionary of Art and Artists*, where he is described as 'one of the most popular Milanese painters in the early sixteenth century, principally because he succeeded in vulgarising the style of Leonardo'. Ruskin championed Luini because he was a secondary master he could claim to have discovered himself. Championing Leonardo or Michelangelo would have been less original.[28]

The 1878 Baedeker guide to Paris granted Leonardo a paragraph but Raphael almost a page. It called the *Mona Lisa* 'the most celebrated work of Leonardo in the Louvre'. Though 'unfinished' (as in Vasari's view) and 'darkened', 'the face still delights us with the wonderful charm of its smile'.[29]

Pater, indifferent to guidebooks, took his cue not only from the French writers but also from Swinburne, whose essay on images of women in Michelangelo ('Notes on Designs of the Old Masters at Florence'), published in the *Fortnighly Review* on 1 July 1868, he had studied very closely.[30] Swinburne showed Pater how one could comment on a work of art. It was not necessary to spend time describing details or explaining techniques. One did not need to attain Gautier's expertise – a demanding task for Pater, who had written no art criticism before. All that was needed was to convey one's impressions, make allusions, hazard audacious generalisations and, above all, package it in beautiful prose. Pater admitted that there was plenty of useful work scholars could do, 'but a lover of strange souls may still analyse for himself the impression made on him by those works'.[31] Swinburne provided an obvious model to follow.

Swinburne's own reaction to Pater was generous. As he wrote to Dante Gabriel Rossetti: 'I liked Pater's article on Leonardo very much. I confess I did fancy there was a little spice of my style as you say, but much good stuff of his own, and much of interest.'[32]

Swinburne was not only the crucial link between the French and the British; he would also influence Gabriele D'Annunzio, the leading admirer of the *Mona Lisa* in Italy (see pages 163–6). Swinburne's admiration for Gautier was considerable. He dedicated several of his poems to him – all included in the commemorative volume *Le Tombeau de Théophile Gautier* (1873). Swinburne, who liked morbid themes, was also a great admirer of the Marquis de Sade and of Baudelaire, both then barely known in Britain.[33] Respectable Britain reacted on cue:

> All that is worst in Mr. Swinburne belongs to Baudelaire … the offensive choice of subject, the obtrusion of unnatural passion, the blasphemy, the wretched animalism … that any sane man, least of all an English poet, should think this dunghill worthy of importation![34]

Thus fulminated the writer and essayist Robert W. Buchanan, now totally forgotten except for such attacks on major poets. Swinburne, who loved sexual degradation and self-flagellation (a practice picked up at Eton, not in Paris), was fascinated by strong and powerful women: 'One of the great charms of birching lies in the sentiment that the flogee is the powerless victim of the furious rage of a beautiful woman.'[35] Unsurprisingly, he was completely besotted with the cult of the *femme fatale*. He wrote numerous poems on the usual array of women of lust and perverse licentiousness, from Cleopatra ('The queen whose face was worth the world to kiss', in 'Laus Veneris') to 'the mystic and sombre Dolores', whom he calls 'Our Lady of Pain' – a provocatively blasphemous inversion of the Virgin Mary – whose sins are 'seventy times seven' (in 'Dolores', dedicated to Baudelaire):

> O lips full of lust and laughter,
>
> Ah, feed me and fill me with pleasure,
> Ere pain come in turn

The list of (un)suitable women also included the Roman Empress Faustine (in 'Dedication'), Astarte, the Phoenician goddess of love (also in 'Dolores'), and Lucrezia Borgia, Swinburne's favourite *femme fatale* and the dedicatee of 'A Ballad of Life'. To these we could add the no fewer than twenty-two Queens of Pleasure in 'The Masque of Queen Bersabe'.[36] In 'The Triumph of Time' he invoked the Mother of the Sea, 'fed with the lives of men … cruel of heart … thou art older than earth', in a way reminiscent of Pater's later 'she is older than the rocks among which she sits'. Last but not least there is what Swinburne called his 'sunflower poem', 'The Complaint of Monna Lisa'.[37]

Pater's purple prose annoyed some of his contemporaries, who regarded him as a grandiloquent amateur. Margaret Oliphant thought it a mixture of sense and nonsense, and added the cutting remark, 'a failed Ruskin'.[38] George Eliot concurred.[39] W.J. Courthope dismissed Pater's essay: 'The picture is made the thesis which serves to display the writer's extensive reading and the finery of his style.'[40] And an anonymous American reviewer wrote that what Pater attributed to Leonardo reflected essentially his own emotional responses to *La Gioconda*.[41]

All this may have been true, but the critics were routed, and Pater's prose lived on. Style – and timing – was what mattered. Pater's words and ideas about the painting became popular precisely because they were a reflection of his impassioned reaction expressed in an enthralling style. 'There is only one man in this century who can write prose,' said Oscar Wilde, adding, half in jest, that he never travelled without Pater's *Renaissance*.[42] The *Mona Lisa* had not yet become canonised as the most famous picture in the world, but Pater propelled it decisively in that direction. He made the painting known to readers who had never seen it. What's more, he made them want to see it.

The translation into French of Pater's essay (in the *Mercure de France* of September 1894) ensured a wider diffusion throughout the Continent, where French was still the *lingua franca* of intellectuals. However, even from an art-historical point of view, Pater's contribution had merits that were recognised later by specialists. Marcel Brion, in 1952, wrote that Pater had grasped that Leonardo had tried to portray the eternal feminine – as if that had not been common currency in France for some time previously.[43] C. Puelli's 'Leonardo e il volto della Gioconda' (1959) is, substantially, a Paterian analysis spiced up with a little Freud.[44] Kenneth Clark, in his 1961 introduction to *The Renaissance*, wrote that 'even today we cannot improve on Walter Pater's characterisation of Leonardo da Vinci.'[45] He was still of the same opinion in 1973, though by then a little put off by Pater's rhetoric.[46] Richard Carpenter announced that 'her mute wisdom, which is at once love and knowing, seems both aged and ancient'. She could be a 'mistress or a mother . . . Yet she is also a witch and thus casts a spell which carries within its strangeness something predatory and deadly' – all in 1963.[47] Webster Smith, as recently as 1985, noted that Pater had been the first to call attention to the affinity of the sitter with the landscape behind her.[48] And in 1992 Giancarlo Maiorino praised Pater's commentary for finding in Mona Lisa 'ten thousand experiences', adding that 'her smile will always mean too much for anybody trying to steal any one of its meanings.'[49]

Pater's influence and his purple prose continue, over a hundred years later, to find their way into 'arty' publications:

> We look into eyes that are deep chasms of life. We sense the excitement of da Vinci, the scientist, discovering a truth. We feel the breath of life running through his *Mona Lisa* . . . we see the full majesty, power and beauty of his ideal woman. Through the eyes of da Vinci, the scientist, we know *Woman*.[50]

But the greatest plaudits for Pater occurred at the turn of the twentieth century. G.K. Chesterton, the well-known creator of Father Brown, in his far less entertaining *The Victorian Age in Literature* (1913) regarded Pater as a prose stylist as fine as Ruskin, an aesthete who wanted to be both a Christian and a pagan and who had almost succeeded:

> Certainly, the almost successful summit of all this attempt is Pater's superb passage on the Monna Lisa; in which he seeks to make her at once a mystery of good and a mystery of evil. The philosophy is false; even evidently false, for it bears no fruit to-day. There never was a woman, not Eve herself in the instant of temptation, who could smile the same smile as the

mother of Helen and the mother of Mary. But it is the high-water mark of that vast attempt at an impartiality reached through art . . . [51]

Oscar Wilde, in 'The Critic as Artist', a fictional conversation first published in the *Nineteenth Century* in 1890, grasped the creative role of a talented critic armed with a 'mighty and majestic prose':

> Who . . . cares whether Mr. Pater has put into the portrait of Monna Lisa something that Lionardo [sic] never dreamed of? The painter may have been merely the slave of an archaic smile, as some have fancied, but whenever I pass into the cool galleries of the Palace of the Louvre, and stand before that strange figure 'set in its marble chair in that cirque of fantastic rocks, as in some faint light under sea,' I murmur to myself, 'She is older than the rocks among which she sits . . .' And I say to my friend, 'The presence that thus so strangely rose beside the waters is expressive of what in the ways of a thousand years man had come to desire . . .;' and he answers me 'Hers is the head upon which all the ends of the world are come, and the eyelids are a little weary . . .'[52]

Wilde realised full well that Leonardo had never tried to put into the portrait 'the animalism of Greece, the lust of Rome', etc., but for that very reason, 'the criticism which I have quoted,' he added, 'is criticism of the highest kind. It treats the work of art simply as the starting-point for a new creation.'[53]

A scene similar to that evoked by Wilde found its way into Somerset Maugham's 1939 novel *Christmas Holiday*. Leslie and Venetia Mason visit the Louvre with their children. He is a wealthy art connoisseur, she the daughter of a professional painter. They stop by the *Mona Lisa*: '"Words fail me to express what that picture always makes me feel," she said, with a sigh.' Her husband entreats her:

'Can you remember that bit of Pater's, Venetia? He hit the nail on the head and no mistake.' Mrs. Mason, a faint, enigmatic smile on her lips, in a low but thrilling voice repeated the celebrated lines that two generations ago wrought such havoc on the aesthetic young ... They listened to her in awed silence. She broke off, and in her natural voice said brightly: 'Now let's go and look at the Raphael.'[54]

In 1915, in his autobiographical novel *On Human Bondage*, Maugham had used a tone a shade more respectful, but only just. In a Paris restaurant, a discussion is raging. British art students disparage Raphael, worship the Impressionists. One declares: 'Whenever I open a paper and see Death of a Great Victorian, I thank Heaven there's one more of them gone. Their only talent was longevity.' They decide to burn, metaphorically, forty Great Victorians, including Carlyle, Ruskin, Tennyson, Dickens and many others. At last comes Walter Pater. '"Not Walter Pater," murmured Philip. Lawson stared at him for a moment with his green eyes and then nodded. "You're quite right, Walter Pater is the only justification for *Mona Lisa*."'[55]

Later, Philip is taken to see the *Mona Lisa*:

He looked at it with a slight feeling of disappointment, but he had read till he knew by heart the jewelled words with which Walter Pater has added beauty to the most famous picture in the world; and these now he repeated to Miss Price. 'That's all literature,' she said, a little contemptuously. 'You must get away from that.'[56]

Other literary references were less directly allusive. Pater's Mona Lisa merges with other fictional *femme fatales* and seeps into the collective unconscious of literary elites. The substitutability of the Mona Lisa for any typical dangerous female (Helen of Troy, Cleopatra, Salomé, Lucrezia Borgia, etc.) confirms that she had been received into this magic circle. All of these women, however, had acquired their 'qualifications' in pre-existing myths, legend or history – all except Mona Lisa. There was not the remotest historical substance for her transformation into a dangerous woman. None of the conceivable historical identities of the sitter (Lisa Gherardini, Isabella Gualanda, Isabella d'Este, etc.) had been a renowned seductress. The painting itself contains not the slightest indication that it is the representation of a lustful woman or an enchantress. The identification of Mona Lisa with the disquieting women of the past is a totally arbitrary and utterly modern construction.

At a certain stage in this process of artistic definition it becomes difficult, almost impossible, to change the meaning attributed to and thence acquired by a painting. The world is stuck with the identification of the *Mona Lisa* with a mysterious woman. Novelists, under constant pressure to distinguish themselves from their rivals, cannot simply repeat established clichés as if they had discovered them. Gautier and Pater had not used a cliché, they had invented it. All that was left to others was either to ignore the *Gioconda*'s smile or to use it for what it had become, a cultural reference point, recognisable by their potential readers though perhaps still unknown to a wider public.

By the end of the nineteenth century the smile of the *Mona Lisa* had become part of the numerous cultural references which were present in literary texts and which have, as one of their functions, that of creating a feeling of fellowship between writers and readers. It is as if the writer is telling the reader: 'I know you know what I am alluding to because I write for clever and knowing people; people like you, people like us.' Yet, the more a reference is repeated, the greater force it acquires – until eventually it becomes a true cliché and begins to be disparaged or parodied by intellectuals. Until then it is part of the selected and elegant language of a relatively narrow circle. Almost certainly the schoolboy Marcel Proust was conscious of this when he referred in 1898 to the 'beautiful' letters written by his friend Lucien Daudet as having the 'mysterious smile of an epistolary Vinci'.[57]

In the decades following the publication of Pater's essay, interpretations of the mysterious Mona Lisa multiplied. In 1909 they even became themselves an object of study, when Salomon Reinach assembled in a somewhat ironical essay what had been said about the *Mona Lisa* by 'intelligent people', all 'amateurs of the sous-entendus and quintessence'.[58]

Pater's or Gautier's influence cannot be readily determined. Oscar Wilde, for instance, had learned to love the Renaissance while sitting at Pater's feet at Oxford. He later disparaged him, and when Pater died, commented, 'Was he ever alive?' Yet, in prison, Wilde asked for Pater's posthumous and unfinished *Gaston de Latour*.[59] Wilde was also a great admirer of Gautier, and was enthralled by *Mademoiselle de Maupin*, 'the golden book of spirit and sense, that holy writ of beauty', he wrote in 1885.[60] Wilde belonged to a group of young aesthetes who idolised French writers such as Balzac, Flaubert, Gautier and Baudelaire and belittled the established British ones – including George Eliot, Charlotte Brontë, Dickens and Thackeray. He deeply admired Swinburne, however – at least until he turned into a Tory patriot.

Wilde's poem 'The New Helen' (1881) is indebted to Swinburne, but the Aphrodite it describes has something of Pater about her: she has 'mocking eyes', 'sea-washed lips' and lies in a stream 'deep brooding on thine ancient memory'.[61] In 1874, shortly after the publication of Pater's essay, Wilde began to write a long poem, 'The Sphinx', which he completed only twenty years later. Was it inspired by Swinburne's 'Dolores', by Baudelaire, or by Pater's *Mona Lisa*? Or just by a vague decadent sensuality pervading all the writers Wilde esteemed. The Sphinx of his poem is the symbol of ageless profligacy. The poem abounds with veiled allusions to Pater's *Mona Lisa*. Its opening lines are:

> In a dim corner of my room for longer than my
>   fancy thinks
> A beautiful and silent Sphinx has watched me
>   through the shifting gloom.

She is unquestionably 'older than the rocks':

> Inviolate and immobile she does not rise she does
>   not stir
> For silver moons are naught to her and naught to
>   her the suns that reel.

Pater's 'what in the ways of a thousand years men had come to desire' became, in Wilde's poem, 'A thousand weary centuries are thine'. The rhythmic, almost biblical, Paterian use of 'and', as in '*And* learned the secrets of the grave; *and* has been a diver in the deep seas, *and* keeps their fallen day about her', is reproduced by Wilde over twenty times: '*and* you have talked with . . . *And* you have looked on . . . *And* did you watch . . . *And* drink . . .'. The theme of the wanton and passionate dominatrix pervades Wilde's poem: 'Who were your lovers? who were they who wrestled for you in the dust?' – as does the Sphinx's smile: 'How subtle-secret is your smile! Did you love none then?' She accepts the sexual advances of the god Ammon, yet retains her sexual supremacy: 'And with your curved archaic smile you watched his passion come and go.' 'Archaic' is how Wilde had described the smile of the *Mona Lisa* in his 'The Critic as Artist', quoted above.[62] The Sphinx of the poem encompasses the Mona Lisa and all the threatening females which haunt men's lives, hence the warning:

> . . . Get hence! I weary of your sullen ways,
> I weary of your steadfast gaze, your somnolent
>   magnificence.
>
> Your eyes are like fantastic moons that shiver in
>   some stagnant lake,
> Your tongue is like a scarlet snake that dances to
>   fantastic tunes . . . [63]

Wilde, however, was already moving towards sending up a metaphor that was coming dangerously close to becoming trite. In his poem 'Humanitad' (1881), he writes of 'Mona Lisa smiling through her hair', a gentle reference unencumbered by the usual imagery of Medusas, Sphinxes and *tutti quanti*.[64]

The image was ready for parody. In Wilde's 1887 short story 'The Sphinx Without a Secret' the narrator meets in Paris an old acquaintance, Gerald Murchison, looking distraught. Murchison explains: he was in love with a mysterious woman now dead. He shows a photograph. The narrator continues, Pater-like:

> I examined it carefully ... Its beauty was a beauty moulded of many mysteries ... – and the faint smile that just played across the lips was far too subtle to be really sweet.
> – Well, he cried impatiently, what do you say?
> – She is the Gioconda in sables, I answered.

Murchinson continues his story. He had decided to marry the woman, but one day, by chance, he happened to observe her as she surreptitiously entered a dingy house in a shabby street. Later that evening, when confronted by him, she claimed she had spent the day at home. Feeling deceived, he left in anger, and refused to see her again. After her death from an illness, Murchison returned to the strange house, only to be told that his beloved had rented the room herself and that all she ever did there was to sit quietly and read books. He is still mystified. It is for the narrator (Wilde) to explain:

> 'My dear Gerald, Lady Alroy was simply a woman with a mania for mystery. She took these rooms for the pleasure of going there with her veil down, and imagining she was a heroine. She had a passion for secrecy, but she herself was merely a Sphinx without a secret.'

The trend, once set, seemed unstoppable. Ronald Firbank, in many ways a minor version of Wilde, and like him an *habitué* of the Café Royal, a dandy, an aesthete, a homosexual, an admirer

of Gautier, introducing – in his 1905 *A Study in Temperament* –
a painting, could not resist describing it as a Pateresque madonna
in whose 'wearied eyelids' are gathered 'the sins and sorrows of
the whole world'.[66]

It had taken some effort to transform Mona Lisa into a dangerous woman. In the late 1830s, before Gautier et al. had set to
work, she was desired by her few admirers with naïve, almost
teenage passion, as in Charles Coran's 'Le Portrait de la Joconde'
(late 1830s), which concludes:

> *Combien d'amants allaient courtiser sa Joconde?*
> *J'eu mon heure; un matin tout me favorisa;*
> *j'était prés d'elle au Louvre; à mes côtés personne;*
> *Je brave la consigne. – O Léonard, pardonne*
> *Un baiser sur la main de ta Monna Lisa!*

> How many lovers wooed his [Leonardo's] *Gioconda*?
> I had my turn; one morning, luck was on my side;
> I was near her, in the Louvre; no one near me;
> I broke the rules – forgive me, Leonardo
> – and kissed your Mona Lisa's hand.[67]

Lisa's fame continued to be literary, for literature was still
the fastest way of communicating the importance of a painting.
Literary references to the *Mona Lisa*, its mystery and its smile
suggest a self-reinforcing mechanism: writers, when using a
famous painting in a story, choose one that is well-known. This
adds to the notoriety of the painting and makes it more likely to
be selected by another writer.

Take, for instance, Henry James's 1873 short story 'The Sweet-
heart of Mr Briseux'. The female narrator visits the Louvre and,
inevitably, stands 'before the inscrutable Joconde, a picture dis-
agreeable to most women'. Her companion, an inept painter,
announces that he will copy it, aware though he is of the difficulty.
The woman has a better suggestion: paint my portrait, she says,
I shall be just as difficult. In so doing she is playing at being the
awkward woman, troublesome and mocking, a 'real' Mona Lisa.

The painter tries, fails and gives up. Another painter, poor but more talented, comes along and offers to finish the portrait. He succeeds and gains great fame. As a result the young woman never sees him again, but she consoles herself: she has acquired some kind of immortality . . . just like Lisa Gherardini.[68] The idea that a woman could gain immortality by being portrayed by a great artist makes another appearance in James's 'The Madonna of the Future' (also 1873). Discussing an American painter, once promising, but who never sold a picture, a character recalls, 'The women were all dying to sit to him for their portraits and be made immortal, like Leonardo's Joconde. We decided that his manner was a good deal like Leonardo's – mysterious, inscrutable, and fascinating.'[69]

James returned to this theme again in 'Confidence' (1880), where a painter, Bernard Longueville, sketches a young woman, Angela, sitting on a terrace with a strange background in the distance. The sitter 'seemed to desire to present herself as a beautiful tormentress'. Later she is described as sitting 'with her hands crossed in her lap, and on her lips a kind but inscrutable smile'.[70]

These were youthful works, but the *Mona Lisa* idea and even her pose continued to fascinate Henry James in his later fiction. This is how Madame de Vionnet, the embodiment of enchanting Europe, is introduced in *The Ambassadors* (1903): 'She was seated, near the fire, on a small stuffed and fringed chair . . . and she leaned back in it with her hands clasped in her lap and no movement, in all her person, but the fine prompt of her deep young face.' Later the American protagonist, Lewis Lambert Strether, who hails from Woollett, Massachusetts, notices: 'Her head, extremely fair and exquisitely festal, was like a happy fancy, a notion of the antique, of an old precious medal, some silver coin of the Renaissance . . . he could have compared her to a goddess still partly engaged in a morning cloud, or to a sea-nymph waist-high in the summer surge.' And later still, 'the way her slightly thicker veil was drawn . . . the composed gravity of her dress ... the quiet note, as she sat, of her folded, grey-gloved hands'. 'It was,' to Strether's mind, 'as if she sat on her own ground ... while all the vastness and mystery of the domain stretched off behind'.[71]

A further reference to a widely diffused image can be found in James Joyce's *Portrait of the Artist as a Young Man* (1916), where the author's *alter ego*, the young Stephen Dedalus, troubled by sexual thoughts, imagines he is contemplating a young woman:

> She seemed like one whom magic had changed into the likeness of a strange and beautiful seabird ... Her bosom was a bird's soft and slight, slight and soft as the breast of some darkplumaged dove ... She was alone and still, gazing out to sea; and when she felt his presence and the worship of his eyes her eyes turned to him in quiet sufferance of his gaze, without shame or wantonness. Long, long she suffered his gaze and then quietly withdrew her eyes from his.

The effect on Stephen is immediate:

> Heavenly God! cried Stephen's soul, in an outburst of profane joy ... Her image had passed into his soul for ever and no word had broken the holy silence of his ecstasy. Her eyes had called him and his soul had leaped to the call. A wild angel had appeared to him, the angel of mortal youth and beauty ...[72]

Ten years later Stephen, still obsessed by sex, remembers the young woman and the street song, a villanelle, he had composed for her:

> Conscious of his desire, she was waking from odorous sleep, the temptress of his villanelle. Her eyes, dark and with a look of languor, were opening to his eyes. Her nakedness ... enfolded him like water with a liquid life: and like a cloud of vapour or like waters circumfluent in

space the liquid letters of speech, symbols of the element of mystery, flowed forth over his brain . . .

> and the words of the song came back to him:
> And still you hold our longing gaze
> With languorous look and lavish limb!
> Are you not weary of ardent ways?
> Tell no more of enchanted days.[73]

Is this an allusion to Pater's *Mona Lisa*, to 'the presence that rose thus so strangely beside the waters', to the temptress who elicits 'strange thoughts and fantastic reveries and exquisite passions'? And the line from the song, 'Are you not weary of ardent ways?' – is it inspired by Wilde's 'I weary of your sullen ways' (in 'The Sphinx'), or by Swinburne's poems and ballads? It is hard to distinguish between the coincidental convergence of male fantasies and the existence of a common literary language, between an unconscious inspiration and a deliberate one. Stephen's schooldays may be behind him, but – as Hugh Kenner noted – his prose still 'courts Newman and Pater'.[74] And Joyce had conjured up the *Mona Lisa* for the reader by inserting, some ten pages before the song, a reference to it: Stephen, in the middle of a discussion on art, exclaims, 'Is a chair finely made tragic or comic? Is the portrait of Mona Lisa good if I desire to see it?'[75]

In an earlier essay on the poet James Clarence Mangan, Joyce overtly mimicked Pater's prose when discussing the role of imaginative beauty in poetry:

> A scenery and a world have grown up about her face, as they will about any face which the eyes have regarded with love. Vittoria Colonna and Laura and Beatrice – even she upon whose face many lives have cast that shadowy delicacy, as of one who broods upon distant terrors and riotous dreams, and that strange stillness before which love is silent, Mona Lisa . . . [76]

Eventually the literary world emancipated itself from Paterian prose (as Stephen Dedalus would do in *Ulysses*) and from the identification of the *Mona Lisa* with the *femme fatale*. Mona Lisa had entered the collective unconscious. A new chapter was about to open. The portrait was about to be discovered by popular culture, an event that would mark its history in the twentieth century. The reaction of the intellectual classes to their loss of control over the image of the painting was to transform it into kitsch, or into a game of internal references whose decoding would always remain ambiguous.

There is some innocence in nineteenth-century literary celebrations of the *Mona Lisa*: intellectuals acclaimed the painting, unaware that it would soon be appropriated by popular culture. It is difficult to imagine a late-twentieth-century avant-garde poet announcing, without a hint of irony, that his ideals of beauty were the Venus de Milo or the *Mona Lisa*, when these are constantly besieged by droves of tourists on package tours. Yet these were precisely Mallarmé's avowed preferences in 1867: 'they seem to be and *are* the two great sparkles of Beauty on this earth', he wrote, adding the usual comments on mysterious smiles.[77]

Similarly, in 1900 Marcel Proust compared the smile 'so particular' of the golden Virgin of Amiens (the *Vierge Dorée* – the statue on the southern portal of the cathedral) to that of 'her sister' the *Joconde*. In his bedroom, he wrote in the *Mercure de France*, he kept a photograph of each. That of the *Joconde* had only the beauty of a masterpiece, while that of the Golden Virgin had taken the melancholy of a memory.[78]

By the turn of the century the terrain opened up by Gautier had been well ploughed. The *Gioconda*'s smile had become an attribute to be pinned on any female combining dangerous charm and deviousness. Giulia Belcredi, a character in Élémir Bourges's best-selling novel *Le Crépuscule des dieux* (1884), is an Italian soprano who hides her perfidious nature and her thirst for power and riches behind the charm of her smiles. Bourges describes her as possessing a 'masculine spirit', like some famous sixteenth-century Italian enchantress, 'a woman made to live in those bloody times, to dominate some Italian court, to engage in wars, politics, intrigues, poisons, and poems and to be painted by a Leonardo'.[79]

In Jean Lorrain's novel *Trés russe* (1886) – dedicated to Bourges – the *femme fatale* Madame Livitinof is not from Italy but from Russia, the land of 'snow . . . furs and swans'.[80] In her past 'there is a little of everything: mud, gold and blood'.[81] She explains to Mauriat, the man whose crazy passion she has done everything to inflame, that she spurns his advances 'Because chastity is the extreme desire.' In pronouncing these words 'a wicked smile, the disquieting smile of the *Gioconda*, simultaneously painful and cruel, separated her thin lips'. She adds, 'To be always desired is never to grow old.'[82]

At times the references to *Mona Lisa*, and especially to Pater's Mona, verge on the parodic. In E.M. Forster's *A Room with a View* (1907), Lucy Honeychurch's supercilious fiancé Cecil notices that the trip to Tuscany has 'worked some marvel' in Lucy. She now accepts him, though he can't understand why. She has turned mysterious. It is almost as if she has been imbued by the *chiaroscuro*:

> It gave her light, and . . . it gave her shadow . . . Soon he detected in her a wonderful reticence. She was like a woman of Leonardo da Vinci's, whom we love not so much for herself as for the things she will not tell us . . . She reminded him of a Leonardo more than ever; her sunburnt features were shadowed by fantastic rocks; at his words she had turned and stood between him and the light with immeasurable plains behind her.[83]

The metaphor (dangerous woman = Mona Lisa) was rapidly turning into a cliché, yet writers held on to it. Some attempts were made to recast the *Gioconda* in a less threatening light – a sort of *embourgeoisement* of the *Mona Lisa*. In 1908 the critic René Bonnamen started off with a plausible position: the painting in the Louvre is not a portrait but an invented image.[84] Leonardo, he claimed, had begun a real portrait, a naked *Gioconda* such as the one at the Hermitage, a coarse and rather insolent courtesan who offers her naked bust to all 'with enthusiastic ardent lust'. Then Leonardo resolved to rescue this wanton woman. Everything was recast. The eyes, the eyelids and the mouth no longer proclaimed an erotic urge. The smile became sweet and familial. A veil was drawn to protect her from profane gaze. Clothes covered 'the small breasts, the soft arms'. The result was the *Mona Lisa* we all know and love. Leonardo performed this purifying rite because, continued Bonnamen, he understood the role a woman should have in a man's life: to reassure him that he is loved.[85] This – apparently – had been 'proved' by modern philosophy and science, and Leonardo was a modern man and a scientist. That is why we feel at home with him. Of course, hard intellectual work can lead to melancholia. Fortunately, we – men of culture – can lift our eyes and take comfort by contemplating our beloved companion, sitting by our side. Naturally – I am still paraphrasing Bonnamen's views – she is not able to comprehend the importance of our 'virile labours' or of our intelligence, which alone enables humankind to lord it over all things and all matter. The role of the beloved companion is to safeguard humankind by procreating and raising the new generation. In other words, Mona Lisa, far from being the Romantics' seductress, turns out to be an exemplary mother and a devoted spouse – probably what Lisa Gherardini was in real life. Her smile, maintains Bonnamen, far from being sarcastic, is light-hearted. It is the smile of a woman who lovingly teases her man for innocuous faults she finds amusing.[86]

As was to be expected, Bonnamen's efforts were in vain. Threatening women are so much more interesting than tranquil housewives. Some women also accepted the convention. Madame Perdrield-Vaissière, in a poem of 1902 dedicated to the playwright

Edouard Schuré, starts off with an intimation of equality: 'We are alone, the two of us, Joconde,' before succumbing to 'Beautiful and mysterious image, you attract me,/smile, Joconde! In your gaze, I have found again/all that is secret, all that is the infinite, all that is life!'[87]

Clearly, once an image has been successfully established, it is difficult to displace or alter it, particularly when the constant expansion of mass culture guarantees that what has become a stale cliché for some is a stunning novelty to others.

Mona Lisa had some time to go before becoming truly global. In Italy, for instance, even at the end of the nineteenth century she had not yet become a proper *femme fatale*. There, the name '*La Gioconda*', which translates as 'the happy one', could be used without any reference to the *Mona Lisa*, as was the case, for instance, in Almicare Ponchielli's famous 1883 opera of that name, on a text by Arrigo Boito. This tells the dramatic story of a female ballad singer of pure and noble spirit who is in love – unrequitedly – with a gentleman. The opera contains not the slightest Leonardian hint.

In Gustavo Strafforello's *Il primo amore di Leonardo da Vinci* (1871), one of the rare popular novels fictionalising the life of Leonardo, the painter is made to fall in love with Angela, the daughter of Verrocchio, his teacher, and not with Lisa.[88] But even in France the term '*Joconde*' did not automatically bring the portrait to mind. For instance, Mathilde Alanic's *La Romance de la Joconde* (1908), imbued with Catholic morality, takes its title from an aria.[89] Maurice Montégut's *Les Chevauchées de la Joconde* (The Rides of the Joconde, 1901) was prefaced by a disclaimer: the book was about neither 'the Mona Lisa Vinci immortalised; nor the divine Ariosto's joyful hero'.[90]

Twenty years later it is unlikely that Montégut would have resisted the temptation to turn his Joconde into a Mona Lisa. His is the mildly erotic story of a beautiful courtesan who gives herself to others because 'it would be a sin to keep for oneself treasures that could enchant a crowd'.[91] Her generosity extends even to the infirm, the poor and the old. An elderly vagabond receives the gift with gratitude: 'Be blessed for ever . . . I part with a light heart, a soul in bloom . . . now I can die: I have known Beauty.'[92]

Until Gabriele D'Annunzio (1863–1938) 're-imported' her, Leonardo's *Mona Lisa* had been almost ignored in Italy. *The Last Supper* was regarded as the greater work. As Sandra Migliore demonstrated in her excellent survey in 1994, Italians, except for the D'Annunziani, were immune to the European attempt to see the *femme fatale* in Mona Lisa. They sought to demystify their *Gioconda* as just a Florentine gentlewoman painted wonderfully well by a great painter.[93] At the end of the nineteenth century the most popular interpretation of Leonardo in Italy was neither Gautier's nor Pater's but a positivist reading that emphasised Leonardo the scientist and the philosopher. Later, there was even a somewhat nationalist reaction against the idea of Leonardo as a universal genius. In 1919, during the commemorations of the four hundredth anniversary of the death of the painter, the historian Francesco Orestano declared Leonardo to be typically Italian, neither 'narrowly empiricist' like the English, nor 'abstractly rationalist' like the French, nor 'furiously transcendental' like the German.[94]

D'Annunzio's position was different. The usual suspects – Gautier, Swinburne, the French and English Decadent writers, the pre-Raphaelites – fascinated him.[95] Regarded in his day as the leading Italian poet, especially by himself, D'Annunzio was essentially an imitator and an importer.[96] His Renaissance was derived from Ruskin and Pater, both far more congenial to him than the stodgy produce of the Italian academy. His themes were borrowed from Baudelaire, Swinburne and Gautier: androgyny, sadomasochism, decay, lust, blood, the Orient, antiquity, etc. His philosophy was part Nietzsche, part Oscar Wilde. Yet the form of his poetry, with its uncommon effervescence, its baroque opulence of words, its extraordinary musicality, its astonishing command of the language, is utterly original. Until D'Annunzio, the

Italian study of Leonardo consisted either in scholarly and erudite tomes dealing mainly with his scientific feats or potted biographies and essays culled from foreign texts. D'Annunzio's Leonardo was, unmistakably, the exciting Leonardo of mysterious smiles and threatening Medusas.

Like his French and English paragons, D'Annunzio was prodigal with his references to the works of the great Italian painters of the Renaissance. His poem 'Al poeta Andrea Sperelli' (his *alter ego*), from 1889, has as its main theme Leonardo's 'Ambiguous Being', a woman whose gaze causes indefinable anxiety, whose lips restlessly smile. Beyond her visage rises 'a resplendent irrigated land under a sweet sky'. She addresses the young poet, who is, of course, lovesick and suffering: 'In vain, in vain, young man, you try to unravel me. My great secret is not for mortals.' And she ends with: 'Oh you who suffer, your suffering is harrowing; but you will never know why I smile' – '*ma non saprai giammai perché sorrido*'.[97] It may not have been self-evident that D'Annunzio was talking about Mona Lisa – indeed, the She-Being declares, 'I am the Sphinx and the Chimera.' However, such was the interconnection between all these fantasies that when the *Mona Lisa* was stolen from the Louvre on 21 August 1911, D'Annunzio promptly abbreviated the poem, adding 'La Gioconda' to the title. He then published it on 25 August in *Il Giornale d'Italia*, claiming that he had written it on the very day the painting was stolen, as if he had had a kind of strange premonition (hoping no one would remember that it had been published in 1889).[98]

D'Annunzio could just as well have used his 1890 poem 'Gorgon', about his encounter with an aristocratic lady on whose mouth

> appeared the smile, so radiant and so cruel, the Divine Leonardo represented on his canvases. That smile contrasted melancholically with the sweetness of her elongated eyes; it gave a superhuman charm to the beauty of female heads the great Vinci loved.

(*Ne la bocca era il sorriso*
fulgidissimo e crudele
che il divino Leonardo
perseguì ne le sue tele.
Quel sorriso tristamente
combattea con la dolcezza
de' lunghi occhi e dava un fascino
sovrumano a la bellezza
de le teste feminili
che il gran Vinci amava.)

This patrician lady is sitting – where else? – on a loggia. Attracted by the presence of the poet, she turns and looks directly at him. Inevitably, she smiles. He falls in love, she smiles again and departs. And he is left desperate: '*o signora, voi, voi sola;/voi che tanto avrei amata!*' 'Oh lady, you, only you, you whom I would have loved so much!'[99]

D'Annunzio liked using Leonardesque references. In 1895 he published a novel called *La Vergine delle rocce* ('The Virgin of the Rocks'), and in 1899 a tragedy in five acts called *La Gioconda*. The hero of the latter is Lucio Settàla, a sculptor who, torn between his duty to his wife Silvia, and his mistress and model Gioconda, decides that his art (and hence the model) must come first. The wife, dutiful as ever, sacrifices herself – or rather her hands, burnt in the act – to rescue her husband's work. In spite of the title and the use of a model called Gioconda, the theme is not Leonardian but the classic dilemma between artistic vocation and marital duty, with the former winning effortlessly. There was an autobiographical – and self-serving – element in the play, for it had been conceived as a vehicle for D'Annunzio's mistress, the great *diva* Eleonora Duse, who had recently displaced his wife. The play was a flop.[100]

D'Annunzio's work and his references to the *Mona Lisa* were part of the more general reception of the theme of the *femme fatale* in Italian popular culture. The terrain had been prepared not by the intelligentsia but rather by the spread of popular novels with dark and threatening heroines. D'Annunzio himself became really obsessed with the *Mona Lisa* only after it had been stolen and thus become more widely known. He pinned to the wall of his study in his eccentric home by Lake Garda some of Leonardo's aphorisms, and placed an engraving of the *Mona Lisa* in the boudoir of his mistress Luisa Baccara.

Around the end of the nineteenth century, in European culture, the Mona Lisa's smile had become the central feature of the painting, an almost automatic starting-point for all those who thought about the portrait of Lisa Gherardini – as is still the case today. The 'mysterious smile', at least among the cultural elites on both sides of the Atlantic, was well-established. It was still unknown, however, to the majority of the Western middle classes. In 1900 Baedeker told tourists that 'the most celebrated of the treasures of the Louvre' was the Venus de Milo. The *Mona Lisa*, however, was 'the most celebrated female portrait in the world, the sphinx-like smile of which has exercised the wits of generations of poets and artists and still fascinates in spite of the darkened condition of the canvas'.[101]

Some, of course, had begun to debunk all this. In his essay on Leonardo, 'Introduction à la méthode de Léonard de Vinci', written around 1894 for the *Nouvelle revue*, Paul Valéry wrote, 'The "smile of the Joconde" thinks about nothing . . . it is Leonardo who thinks for me.'[102] In 1891 the French novelist and politician Maurice Barrès wrote that Leonardo's smiling women 'smile at the trouble we take to find out what attracts their attention'.[103] To no avail: references to the smile among refined connoisseurs of the arts multiplied – and not just in Europe. In 1884 Ernest Fenollosa, the Boston-based scholar of Japanese art, travelling with Kakuso Okakura, the celebrated author of *The Book of Tea*, uncovered an eighth-century gilded statue of Kannon, the Buddhist deity of mercy, in the temple of Horyuji near Nara, in Japan. His reaction was to write that the lips of the androgynous statue formed a smile 'not unlike that of Da Vinci's Mona Lisa'.[104] Fenollosa was committed to the view, then still controversial, that

Japanese art was as valuable as that of the West. It therefore mattered to him to link an unidentifiable Japanese sculptor to Leonardo, connecting East and West and eight centuries of artistic development.

The *Mona Lisa* gained wider popularity with the publication of Dmitri Merezhkovsky's *The Resurrection of the Gods* (1900). This was a fictionalised biography of Leonardo, with a plot and dialogue, marketed as a novel. The Russian author used all the available sources and then filled in the gaps with his imagination. Leonardo, a father figure to his assistants, is the celebrated scientist, the creator of *The Last Supper*, a curious mind who cannot finish anything. As hardly anything was known about Mona Lisa, the chapter that dealt with the painting of the portrait was either made up from scratch or followed in the footsteps of the nineteenth-century writers previously mentioned. Thus Mona Lisa's husband is described as more interested in a new breed of Sicilian cows than in her charms.[105] She pines for a past admirer who died on the battlefield, and turns down all other suitors. She is now obviously in love with Leonardo; so much so that *she begins to look like him*, and, obviously, so does the portrait he is painting. Thus the androgyny theme, somewhat dormant in Gautier, now comes to the fore. It would become a strong motif in the twentieth century.[106] Mona Lisa, Leonardo realises, possesses a special type of intelligence: feminine intelligence, a kind of 'prophetic wisdom'.[107] Leonardo proclaims his love in the only way he can: by painting her portrait and producing an immortal masterpiece.

Merezhkovsky's special contribution was to have articulated the crucial element of the nineteenth-century view of the painting: it was no longer 'simply' the product of the mind of Leonardo, but a joint venture. The model is elevated, so that the created becomes equal to the creator. Lisa is no longer regarded as passively and patiently allowing the male gaze to reproduce her living features on a flat wooden surface. Leonardo's ambiguous sexuality, like Lisa's, facilitates this fantasy. As in all such stories, the woman dies young, before the irreparable outrage of time can change her appearance. In Merezhkovsky's story Lisa dies in Lagonegro, near Potenza in southern Italy, in 1506, at the age of twenty-seven while accompanying her insensitive husband on a business trip. Such is the power of the media, as we would now say, that reality adapts itself to it. On 28 August 1991 the leading southern Italian daily, the *Gazzetta del Mezzogiorno*, retold the story of Merezhkovsky's 'discovery'. The good citizens of Lagonegro, delighted with such unexpected glory, decided to exploit it to the full.[108] The town became a tourist centre marketing *Mona Lisa* souvenirs, and is now brimming with *Mona Lisa* plates, postcards and a Monna Lisa wine. Tourists, on their way to somewhere else, stop for another encounter with 'history'.

Merezhkovsky's successful book inspired Francesco Cazzamini Mussi and Marino Moretti to write a four-act drama in verse, *Leonardo da Vinci*, in 1909.[109] It had also influenced Edouard Schuré's important play *Léonard de Vinci* (1905), in which Leonardo's modernity is directly attributed to his encounter with Lisa Gherardini.[110]

The play opens in Leonardo's laboratory in Milan. Leonardo is a driven and busy man who has no time for women and does not notice that, around him, the place is teeming with jealousies and intrigues.[111] Deeply implicated in these is Lodovico's young mistress Lucrezia Crivelli (whose portrait by Leonardo, *La Belle Ferronnière*, is in the Louvre). She finds consolation in the friendship of a young Florentine lady, Monna Lisa, who has an air of mystery about her. Lucrezia implores her: 'Your past, your present, your future, everything is a mystery to me.'[112] Lisa explains that she was forced to marry Il Giocondo, but was disgusted by him the first night she spent with him. 'I wanted to kill myself,' she says.[113] She ran away, and in this new world she had found the man to whom she should give herself and who would be her master. 'Who is he?' asks Lucrezia. She replies: 'It is the greatest of men.' 'Is it Leonardo?' asks Lucrezia.[114] Lisa replies:

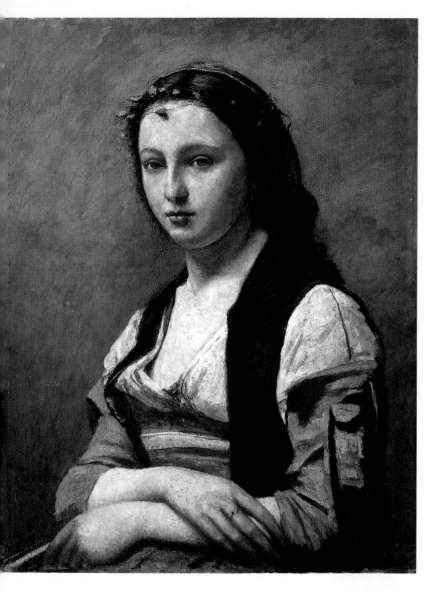

15. *La Femme à la perle* by Camille Corot (1869, Louvre). Corot painted this portrait of
Berthe Goldschmidt in the now traditional 'Gioconda' pose as a tribute to Leonardo.
The painting was acquired by the Louvre in 1912 while the real *Mona Lisa*, stolen in
1911, was still missing.

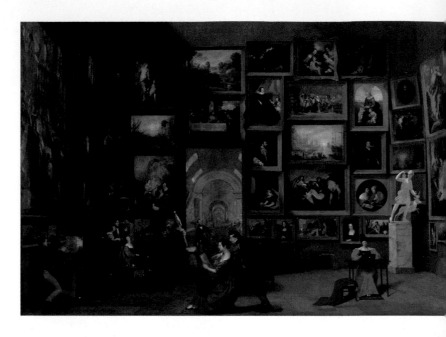

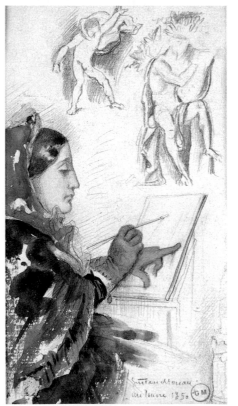

16. *The Gallery of the Louvre* by Samuel F.B. Morse (1833, Musée americain, Giverny). Morse, better known as the inventor of the eponymous code, depicted paintings in the Salon Carré of the Louvre for fellow Americans unable to see the originals. He included all his favourites: Poussin, Titian, Van Dyck, Rubens, Rembrandt, Guido Reni, Murillo, as well as the *Mona Lisa*.

17. *Lady Copyist at the Louvre* by Gustave Moreau (1850, Musée Gustave Moreau, Paris). In the nineteenth century, most of the copyists were women. Copying artworks was deemed ideally suited to them, and morally preferable to drama or music. In fact the museum was, and still is, a fertile place for pick-ups. The novelist Champfleury (1821-89) provided useful tips: spot an enticing female copyist, settle down to paint next to her, chat her up near closing time so that the conversation can continue outside the museum.

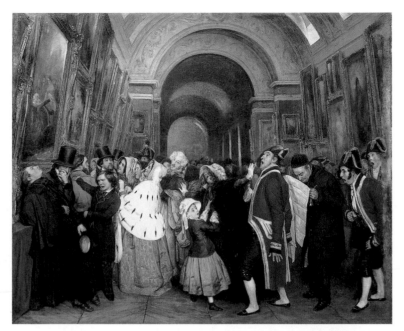

18. *Quatre Heures au Salon* by François Biard (*c.*1847, Louvre). A guard announces that the annual Salon in the Grande Galerie of the Louvre is about to close. The Parisian *nouvelle bourgeoisie*, curious to see for themselves what the aristocracy had deemed of great value, would take their children to visit the Louvre after a stroll in the gardens of the Tuileries.

19. *The Salon Carré and the Grande Galerie of the Louvre* by John Scarlett Davis (1831, British Embassy, Paris). Many representations of the masterpieces of the Louvre did not include the *Mona Lisa*, not then regarded as a particularly interesting painting.

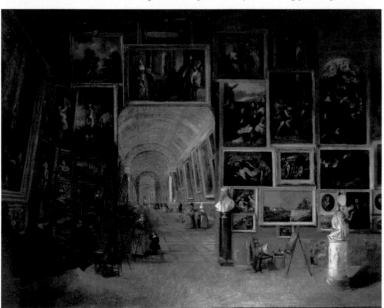

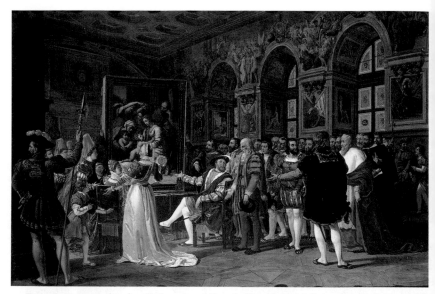

22. *François I recevant dans la salle des suisses à Fontainebleau la grande Sainte Famille de Raphael* by Charles Lemonnier (1814, Musée des Beaux-Arts, Rouen). The king is shown surrounded by his entire court, including famous painters and writers, admiring the masterpiece he has just acquired. He appears to invite Leonardo – on the right – to share in the general admiration, but the old man seems unenthusiastic and a little envious.

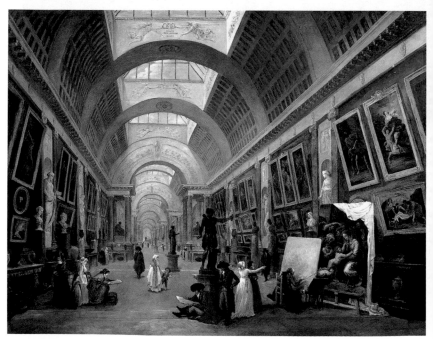

23. *Project for the new Grande Galerie* by Hubert Robert (1796, Louvre). Robert, the Louvre's Chief Curator of Pictures, produced a vast canvas in which he imagined how the Grande Galerie would look once it had become a vibrant museum. In the forefront, in pride of place, Raphael's *Holy Family* is devoutly copied by various artists. Nearby are paintings by Guido Reni and Titian. Of Leonardo and the *Mona Lisa* there is no trace.

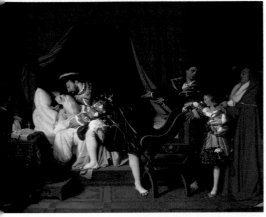

24. *The Death of Leonardo in the Arms of King François I* by Jean-Auguste Dominique Ingres (1818, Musée du Petit Palais, Paris). This is the best-known of the many death scenes of Leonardo. Death scenes were a popular genre, amounting to pictorial biographies. The artist would fill the picture with the images and works of those who had been important in the life of the central character. As in modern biographical films, they blended history and fiction to produce a more exciting narrative.

25. RIGHT *Raphael Being Introduced to Leonardo,* engraving by Paul-Prosper Allais, after a painting by Aimée Pagès (1845, Bibliothèque nationale de France). This is the first known picture representing Leonardo painting the *Mona Lisa*. Only the engraving by Allais now survives.

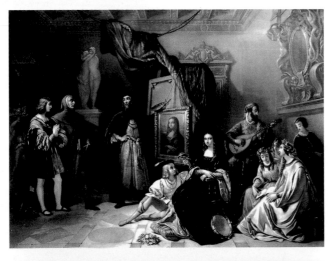

26. BELOW *Leonardo che ritrae la Gioconda* by Cesare Maccari (1863, Istituto per le Belle Arti, Siena). By the 1860s the *Mona Lisa* was at the centre of a literary cult. Maccari chose this theme for a competition of the Siena Institute of Fine Arts. He won, and the Institute kept the painting. As Maccari was a protégé of the director it is possible that he was informed that such a theme would have a good chance of winning.

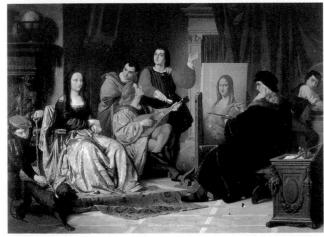

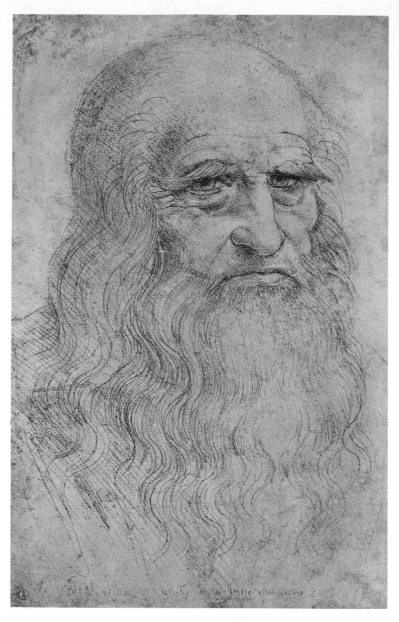

27. *Self-portrait* (?), Leonardo (1512-13?, Biblioteca Reale, Turin). This highly stylised portrait of a wise old man is the best-known representation of Leonardo, but the evidence that it is a self-portrait is very thin. Here Leonardo looks like Moses or God the Father, with long white hair and beard, strong and manly, the quintessence of the sage. By the end of the nineteenth century this had become the archetypal image of Leonardo.

'When I first cast my eyes on one of his paintings I knew he was my Master. His gaze encountered mine and he became the king of my heart, the sole Lord of my life.' Lucrezia is alarmed: 'You poor wretch, his gaze is of steel and his heart of ice.' 'How do you know?' asks Lisa. 'Vesuvius, always smouldering, is a poor volcano. But snow-covered Mount Etna inwardly foams with the fire of the world.' 'Don't you know that Leonardo has never loved a woman, that he will never be in love?' says Lucrezia.

However, when Schuré's Leonardo finally contemplates Mona Lisa for the first time he says:

> In this one visage I find the Medusa and the Madonna. In this sad smile, I find the profound science of Good and Evil. What does this gaze want when it probes into my heart with the rays of infinite tenderness and the cruel dart of doubt? Oh secret of the soul, Oh sphinx of nature, I thought I could quell you with my potions and my metal grips. You mock me in the enigma of these eyes. You smile in the corners of this sinuous mouth.[115]

Now madly in love with Mona Lisa, Leonardo starts to paint her portrait. 'It will be our child,' he tells her. She replies, 'Yes, but a strange child who mocks his parents, an immortal child deriding his ephemeral parents.'[116] Lisa dares Leonardo to elope with her. As he wrestles with this temptation, envoys from the Florentine Republic arrive, demanding that he should return immediately to show his experiments with human flight before the Grand Council. Science beckons: 'My wings call me, Lisa. Don't try to cut them off.' They part. Desperate, Lisa asks Sidonia, who dabbles in alchemy, to help her die with a potion. Sidonia suggests poisoning her husband instead. Lisa agrees, but at the last minute she drinks the potion herself. As she dies she says, prophetically:

> Leonardo, our eternal nuptials are about to commence.
> I am becoming the Immortal One, the ever-present

Spouse, the Lady of Victory . . . A dying swan will bring
you with his last song our first kiss . . . your Gioconda's
smile.[117]

In the final scene Milan has fallen to the French. Outside
Leonardo's home a mob has gathered, believing him to be a
sorcerer. Leonardo thinks Lisa has run away with another man,
but Sidonia tells him the truth: she died in love with him. As the
mob destroys Leonardo's works, he opens a letter Lisa had given
him with the request that it should be read only after her death.
He reads:

> O great Leonardo!
> The supreme truth is beyond your science
> I have found the divine secret in my suffering;
> No one can enter, alone, the paradise of his dreams.
> Save a heart, if you can, and you shall be saved!
> Love, not science, is the key to truth and happiness.

Disconsolately, Leonardo looks at the finished portrait of Mona
Lisa, then turns to his friends: 'This woman . . . now dead.' But
suddenly a magic sun fills the room with light. 'She is reborn,'
they exclaim. The play ends here, engulfing the positivist dream of
the supremacy of science, another telltale sign that the nineteenth
century was over.

Merezhkovsky's book influenced one of the great theorists of
the twentieth century: Sigmund Freud declared it to be among
his favourite books. And Mona Lisa was not going to miss out on
psychoanalysis. Freud's celebrated treatment of Leonardo (1910)
concentrated not on the Gioconda but on St Anne, the mother
of Mary, represented with her daughter on her lap and the child
Jesus playing with a lamb. Freud linked this to a dream Leonardo
had in which a bird of prey, a *nibbio* (kite in English), had put
its tail in his mouth when he was a baby. Unfortunately, the
German version Freud used translated '*nibbio*' as '*Geier*', the German word for vulture, instead of '*Hüngeier*' or '*Milan*' (kite).
This led Freud to develop a series of associations based on the

image of the vulture in Egyptian mythology. The Egyptians worshipped a Mother Goddess, Mut, represented by a vulture. Freud thought he could detect in the pleats of St Anne's clothes the representation of a vulture. The tail of the bird was, or so Freud thought, a representation of the phallus of the mother that the child supposes she possesses.[118] Leonardo was illegitimate and grew up with his mother, hence his mother-fixation and his presumed homosexuality.

Freud then moves on to the 'strangely beautiful face of the Florentine Mona Lisa . . . This smile has called for an interpretation, and it has met with many of the most varied kinds, none of which has been satisfactory.'[119] He takes it as an 'indisputable fact' that the smile 'exercised no less powerful a fascination on the artist than on all who have looked at it for the last four hundred years'.[120] Freud's 'solution' is that the smile awoke in Leonardo something that had lain dormant in his mind: the smile of his mother. Stimulated by this smile, he reproduced it on St Anne, the mother of Mary.[121] This would, of course, confirm the now commonly held view that men seek in the women they love the mother they have lost to their father.

Many critics of Freud's foray into psycho-history concentrated on the mistaken translation which led to the mother–vulture construct. Freud himself became aware of his gaffe in 1923, but refused to modify the essay, though he often revised other, more significant works.[122] The main weakness of his analysis, however, was due to his rudimentary understanding of Renaissance history, as Meyer Schapiro, the most important of these critics, has shown.[123] What matters here, however, is the fact that Freud accepted the entire nineteenth-century construct of the *Mona Lisa*, quoting directly and uncritically texts by Angelo Conti, a follower of D'Annunzio and Ruskin, Pater and others. In other words, he built his analysis on the foundation of the nineteenth-century literary myth of the *femme fatale*.[124] Freud also provided novel interpretative possibilities, and some of his insights found their way into Kenneth Clark's biography of Leonardo. By insisting on the child narcissistically finding himself in the mother, he contributed to various attempts to see in the *Mona Lisa* a self-portrait; by looking for clues about the artist in the painting, he set the scene for a new direction in art-historical studies.[125]

Leonardo, of course, was a suitable subject for analysis. This famous universal genius, who was also illegitimate, raised by a lone parent and possibly homosexual, must have had problems. Perhaps he was also a sadist (constructed instruments of death, did not like children, drew grotesque caricatures . . .), he was certainly a vegetarian (to over-compensate for his repressed sadism . . .), and was unable to complete anything (what else but a death wish . . .). Quite clearly a complex personality, waiting to be unravelled.[126]

The *Mona Lisa* had something to smile about. She (or it) was about to enter the twentieth century armed with formidable credentials and a diverse array of supporters and admirers. In 1800 the painting was known only by a tiny group of connoisseurs, none of whom was prepared to declare it the best painting in the whole world. A hundred years later it had been dissected, examined, discussed by and made the object of the fantasies of the literary and artistic intelligentsia of the nineteenth century. It transpired that almost anything could be read into the features of the unknown woman. In the age of democracy, this anonymity – neither a Venus nor a queen nor a Virgin Mary – turned out to be a positive advantage. Helped, unquestionably, by the enormous development of technology, it was well poised to exploit and be exploited by the new global means of mass communication. Press and advertising, tourism and popular novels, songs and television would carry her far beyond the bounds of any hitherto conceivable artistic renown.

CHAPTER SEVEN

Mona Kidnapped

Notoriety, fame, celebrity may require individual ability, some competence, even cunning. Being a genius is help- ful, though not essential. What is fundamental is to be seen, noticed, discussed and to be the centre of attention, of debate, of controversies, of mysteries. The cardinal principle is to use and exploit all available communication systems.

By the beginning of the twentieth century, the *Mona Lisa* – a passive object, as one should periodically remind oneself – had achieved considerable fame. It would have been included in any list of the world's best-known paintings. In the course of the subsequent decades it outdistanced its rivals and became a global icon. In 1900, however, there was still some way to go. Though it had been widely copied, engraved, used in fiction, lionised as the quintessential Woman, and its creator revered as the Universal Man, it was still known only by a relatively narrow elite.

Nineteenth-century culture had been dominated by intellec- tuals who developed many of the basic themes of later popular mass culture: crime and horror stories, science fiction, popular music, the serialised saga, the popular press, variety shows. Real expansion, however, required both technological advances and changed social conditions. In the 1850s books were still relatively expensive. The mass press was in its infancy. Photography had just appeared. Literacy was far from universal and educa- tion still limited. The world of high culture still jealously shielded its secrets from the uneducated hordes. Museums erected intimidating barriers which made many visitors conscious of being outsiders.[1]

By the end of the century this narrow bourgeois world was breaking down. And not by revolution, as the Marxists believed it would, but by the combination of a relentless struggle for social progress and the development of capitalism. Commodities that had been the prerogatives of the bourgeoisie became available to a wider world. This process, which became truly global only towards the end of the twentieth century, was then under way only in parts of the United States and the most advanced countries of Europe: Britain, Germany and – last but not least – France, home of the first great department stores.

The world of culture was at the centre of this transformation. Books we still read today became bestsellers. Dickens's *Pickwick Papers* (which first appeared in serial form in 1836–37) sold, in book form alone, some 800,000 copies in its first forty years.[2] Zola's gloomy description of working-class degeneration, *l'Assommoir*, sold 145,000 copies between 1877 and 1902. The *Tour de la France par deux enfants* by G. Bruno (pseudonym of Madame Fouillée) – no longer read now, but for years used in all French schools – sold eight million copies in the same period.[3]

A formidable new power arose, the popular press. In 1870, in Paris alone, thirty-seven dailies sold a total of one million copies a day, the largest four accounting for 600,000 sales.[4] Ten years later, two million copies were being sold each day, with the *Petit Journal* selling half a million.[5] New printing techniques and better means of distribution played their part. Between 1870 and 1914 the French railway network trebled while the price of a daily paper, in real terms, was halved. In the same period, male illiteracy in France dropped from 20 per cent to 4 per cent. By 1914 the four largest dailies (the *Petit Journal*, the *Petit Parisien*, the *Matin* and the *Journal*) sold 4.5 million copies every day – cornering three-quarters of the market.[6] In Britain, Alfred Harmsworth's *Daily Mail* sold nearly a million copies a day by 1900.[7]

As early as 1895 the illustrated supplements of the *Petit Journal* and the *Petit Parisien* sold a million copies each.[8] In 1910 an illustrated daily, the *Excelsior*, began to appear in Paris. In Britain the *Illustrated London News*, founded in 1842, the first newspaper to depend for its appeal almost entirely on its illustrations, delighted respectable middle-class families.[9] The more popular *Titbits* sold some 600,000 copies per issue by the end of the century. In 1873 the Italian publisher Treves brought out the *Illustrazione Italiana*. By 1900 the Sunday illustrated *Domenica del Corriere* (owned by the powerful *Corriere della Sera* group) was well established. In Germany *Gartenlaube*, founded by Ernst Keil in 1853, had a circulation of 100,000 by 1860, and almost 400,000 by 1880.[10] In the USA the number of magazines leapt from seven hundred to more than three thousand between 1865 and 1885.[11] What appealed to these publications' new readership were human interest stories, the feats of adventurers and explorers, events surrounding royalty and celebrities, wars – especially colonial wars – and crime. How could the *Mona Lisa* penetrate this new world? How could it become known to those millions who were not aware of her mysterious smile, and who had barely heard of the Renaissance, or even of Leonardo? Some illustrated magazines published pictures of the occasional work of art, including the *Mona Lisa* – for instance *l'Illustration* on 26 April 1911 – but a photograph of such an unprepossessing woman, on its own, not linked to an event, was unlikely to strike the popular imagination.

What was required was a startling and newsworthy incident. Early in the morning of 21 August 1911, Vincenzo Peruggia, a thirty-year-old Italian painter-decorator who had been working at the Louvre, provided the painting with a unique opportunity. It was a Monday – the weekly closing day.[12] Peruggia removed the *Mona Lisa* from the sixteenth-century Italian frame donated in 1909 by the Comtesse de Béarn, wrapped it up under his coat and took it away.[13]

There had been premonitory signs. In August 1905 the French Ministry of Foreign Affairs told its embassy in Austria-Hungary to investigate a letter received from Vienna, signed by one Albert Ranieijko, containing threats against the *Mona Lisa*. The embassy found nothing to cause concern.[14] On 24 July 1910 the satirical *Le Cri de Paris* claimed that the painting was a copy, and the original had been stolen. It was a joke. Around the same time a journalist had tested the Louvre's security by spending the night in a sarcophagus. Earlier, a small but heavy statuette of the Egyptian divinity Isis had been stolen.

The Louvre – in a state of shock – remained closed for a week. The government sacked the Director of the Musées Nationaux, Théophile Homolle (on holiday at the time of the theft), along with the head guard, and disciplined the security guards.[15] An administrator with a security and police background replaced the unfortunate Homolle, a noted scholar.

These steps, of course, did not stop the outcry. The press would not let go of such a good story. In Italy there was massive coverage – after all, claimed patriots, it's our painting. The front page of the *Domenica del Corriere* of 3–10 September 1911 had a drawing, full spread, of two thieves removing the picture above the caption '*Come sia stato possibile l'impossibile*' – 'How the impossible has been possible'.

The *Petit Parisien* – now claiming to be the largest-circulation daily in the world with 1.4 million copies sold – came out with a banner headline, '*La Joconde a disparu du Musée du Louvre*', over a large picture of the stolen painting (23 August). Below the headline was the caustic comment '. . . *il nous reste le cadre*' ('. . . we still have the frame'). The article – with various features on the second page – made it clear that it was a tragic loss: 'The absolute truth is that there never was a more perfect picture.' The *Mona Lisa* was part of the national heritage: 'This *Joconde* was really ours. Will we ever see her smile again?' It was stressed that this was no 'ordinary' Renaissance masterpiece but the unusual portrait of a mysterious woman, painted by a genius and deploying a strange smile. It was not just a theft. It was abduction, almost a rape.

The papers dealt with the story according to the unwritten rules of traditional journalistic and popular narratives: they mourned the loss and hyped the painting (one cannot grieve for trivial damages). Then they speculated: was the mysterious thief a possessive art-lover, a deluded fanatic in love with Mona Lisa? Was he a reclusive eccentric millionaire?[16] It was also necessary to blame someone: who else but the Louvre and its poor security – at the time the museum had fewer than 150 guards. The poet Guillaume Apollinaire joined in with the final insult: 'The Louvre is less secure than a Spanish museum.'[17]

This line of narrative kept papers like the *Petit Parisien* going for nearly three weeks, with the *Joconde* reproduced almost daily on the front page. The story fascinated all social classes, now subjected to an accelerated course in Renaissance art. The *Petit Parisien* explained who Leonardo was, how the painting had been acquired by France, that the model was a Lisa Gherardini (doubts had not yet been expressed), that it was painted around 1501–03, and so on. All the well-known anecdotes by Vasari, including that of Lisa being entertained with songs and music while Leonardo painted her, were recycled. The *Petit Parisien* mentioned the enigmatic smile in virtually every issue. Gautier's fantasies were finally reaching millions. Indeed, on Monday, 28 August the *Petit Parisien* paraphrased – on the front page – Gautier's words of 1867, 'She makes you feel like a schoolboy before a duchess.' It also made up a few myths, for example alleging that the celebrated Romantic poet and playwright Alfred de Musset had once been allowed to realise his dream and spend the night, alone, with the *Mona Lisa*.[18]

The weekly *l'Illustration* of 26 August came out with a full-spread picture of the *Mona Lisa*; Leonardo had been in love with her, it claimed.[19] But the front page was entirely taken up with a photograph of the Minister for War, M. Adolphe Messimy (who was not smiling). A week later *l'Illustration* published the picture of the empty space on the Louvre wall and reassured its readers: 'For some months we have been working towards providing you with a colour reproduction of the Joconde. In two weeks' time it will be available to our readers.'[20] On 23 September the promise was fulfilled. Unfortunately I cannot report on the quality of the reproduction because it had been stolen from the copy of the newspaper which I consulted at the Bibliothèque Nationale; a helpful librarian's note explains that this new rapine was discovered on 15 December 1961.

When the Louvre finally reopened, a week after the theft, on 30 August, Parisians displayed a sense of personal grief, as if a well-loved celebrity had died. In larger numbers than ever before they went to the museum to contemplate the empty space and inspect the hooks that had held the *Joconde*.[21] Outside, peddlers, smiling unenigmatically, were doing a roaring trade selling postcards and reproductions of the *Mona Lisa*. Later that week a ceremony – almost a wake – was held at Leonardo's last home, at Clos Lucé in Amboise.[22] On 18 September the *Petit Parisien* published a front-page picture of the Louvre's most recent acquisitions, Jack and Milord, two fierce-looking guard dogs.

Connected stories kept the reporters going for a while; it was discovered that the well-known poet Apollinaire had tried to return through a newspaper two Phoenician statuettes stolen from the Louvre in May 1911.[23] Could he have stolen the *Mona Lisa* too? It later turned out that the thief of the statuettes had been a friend of his. He had done it as a dare and had left them with Apollinaire. The poet, though disapproving and angry, had kept them. When the *Mona Lisa* was stolen he panicked, and considered throwing the statuettes in the Seine; then, advised by Picasso, he decided to return them. The police arrested him, kept him in custody for a few days, then released him. On his way to a celebration party he called in at the *Paris-Journal* to hand in an article entitled 'My Life in Prison'.[24]

Eventually, the *Joconde* faded from the news. The story

was getting cold, and another had materialised: the assass-
ination on 14 September of the Russian Prime Minister Piotr
Stolypin.

The theft had, indeed, been a good story, but it did not have
the same impact everywhere. In England it was not regarded as
a major cultural loss. The *Athenaeum* – a review grandly subtitled
'a Journal of English and Foreign Literature, Science, the Fine
Arts, Music and the Drama' – dealt with the theft in twelve lines
(26 August 1911), but dedicated fifteen to the revised attribution
of Holbein's Dresden Madonna. The *Illustrated London News* of
2 September had on its front page a drawing of a ship at sea
threatened by a tidal wave – not the reporting of an actual disaster,
but the launch of a special series on shipwrecks. Mona Lisa was
relegated to page ten, though with a full-spread black-and-white
picture. A lengthy caption announced: 'As hard to sell as the
Towers of Nôtre-Dame: the lost Leonardo.' Note: 'the lost Leonardo', not 'the lost *Mona Lisa*'. The painter was better known
than the picture. As the caption explained:

> its disappearance caused far greater sensation than did
> that of Gainsborough's 'Duchess of Devonshire' years
> ago; a fact not to be wondered at, for it is one of the
> most famous, if not *the* most famous, of paintings in
> the world.

The *Illustrated London News* was not inward-looking. It
devoted ample space to foreign news. At the time of the theft it
had features on and pictures of the new Portuguese president, a
new Italian admiral, the new Canadian prime minister, fighting
in Turkey and the Italian invasion of Tripoli. Its main constraint
was the range of pictorial material available. No picture, no story.
Once it had reproduced the *Mona Lisa*, there was not much else
to do. There was a small news item in the issue of 4 November,
and on 9 December it printed a double-spread colour picture of
Mona Lisa's face (no background) – like a *Playboy* centrefold –

describing the smile as 'enigmatic'. The magazine explained that though it had published a picture immediately after the theft, it was confident that many readers might want to keep a colour version.

In France, popular culture exploited the theft to the full. The Louvre's security was regularly lampooned in songs, postcards, cabarets and variety shows. At the Olympia, the most popular theatre in Paris, the comic duo Rip and Bousquet entertained the crowds with a satirical act: a Louvre guard is dusting a priceless statue. He lets it fall, breaking it. Unfazed, he simply dusts it away while clumsily dropping more statues and pictures. Friends and casual acquaintances drop in to 'borrow' items to decorate their homes. Tourists are asked: 'How about a Murillo, or would you prefer a Rembrandt, or a Raphael?'[25]

A locksmith in the rue Ménilmontant placed in his shop window a cartoon of the *Mona Lisa*, eyes rolling, head shaking and secured by a large padlock. A few verses were added: '*Elle avait un p'tit cadenas,/mais le Louvre n'en avait pas*' (She had a small padlock, but the Louvre didn't have it).[26]

Satirical postcards appeared almost immediately. One showed a thief running away with the painting while a guard sleeps. Another depicted the *Mona Lisa* smiling broadly with the caption: 'Now happy to be on the loose – after four centuries.' Another, printed in Milan, showed Mona Lisa running away, cocking her nose.[27]

Less than two weeks after the theft a short humorous film about the theft was projected on the gigantic screen of the Omnia Pathé. Among the spectators on 10 September were Franz Kafka and Max Brod, who the previous day had also visited the bare wall at the Louvre. *Nick Winter et le vol de la Joconde* lasted only five minutes. Kafka was amused, and so was Brod, who gave us this account:

> The action takes place in the Louvre. Everything is imitated wonderfully well, the paintings the sculptures

and, in the middle, the three hooks that held the *Mona Lisa*. They call a funny detective; a shoe button leads him onto a false trail; disguised as a shoeshine boy he forces passers-by to have their shoes cleaned; Croumolle is arrested [Croumolle is, of course, Homolle, the Museum Director]; the button belonged to him. Then, the climax: while everyone is running around, the thief returns, the Joconde under his arm, puts it back, and removes a Velázquez. No one notices. Then the Joconde is found with a message: 'Sorry, it's my poor eyesight. I wanted the picture next to it.'[28]

Cabaret songs satirising the event, often using new lyrics to old tunes, became almost instantly available. The *Petit Parisien* reported three being sold on the streets within days of the theft. Most were light-hearted and irreverent, with no sense that a terrible fate had befallen France's artistic heritage. The *Mona Lisa* was usually described as a fun-loving girl, a little bored in the stuffy Louvre. In one song she is found in a low dive. She explains – in strict Parisian argot:

> *Mon poteau*
> *Embrasse-moi, j'suis pas bégueule.*
> *J'm'ennuyais beaucoup dans ce palais.*
> *Un soir que le gardien criait*
> *'On ferm'! . . .' j'ai répondu: 'ta gueule! . . .'*
> *Et j'suis carapatée tout' seule.*

(Roughly: 'Hi mate, give us a kiss, I ain't squeamish. I was very bored in that palace. One evening, when the guard shouted "closing time", I said "up yours" and made myself scarce.')[29]

Another song, 'L'as-tu vue? la Joconde!!', after mocking, as usual, the security ('It couldn't be stolen, we guard her all the time, except on Mondays'), wondered whether this '*suave Joconde au sourire angélique et moqueur*' was not simply fed up with the visitors. It ended: 'Soon they'll nick the Venus de

Milo.' The smile also made an appearance in 'La Joconde en balade', published with a photo taken from the *Petit Parisien*, while a poster advertising a cabaret in 1913 had the caption, 'I smiled at the Louvre. Now I am merry at the Moulin de la Chanson.'[30]

A year later the magazine *Comoedia illustré*, a fortnightly dedicated to the theatre, published photographs of the twelve leading stars of the Paris stage, including Caroline Otéro and Mistinguett. Each had a full-page spread, wearing Mona Lisa clothes and smiling under the banner headline: '*Les sourires qui nous restent*' ('the smiles still with us').[31]

Thus the popular press, songs and postcards all contributed to the diffusion of the features of the *Mona Lisa*, and to the idea that the portrait's key attribute was a famous smile. It was the start of an unstoppable and self-reinforcing trend which has lasted to this day.

Not all reactions to the theft were humorous. In the Third Republic no scandal, however minor, could avoid becoming politicised, and the opposition was quick to exploit the government's discomfiture. On 23 August the ultra-nationalist and anti-Semitic *Action française* directed its initial wrath at the Louvre's director, Homolle, a supporter of Dreyfus (and by implication a Jew-lover) and his deputy Benedite, 'a Jew, quite by chance'.[32] The following day, the headline demanding the resignation of Homolle was more brutal: 'a director of the Jewified organisation of national museums'.[33] A day later, Leon Daudet, the editor, in a leading article entitled 'Le Louvre enjuivé' ('the Jewified Louvre'), raged that the entire art world was in hock to the Jews. On the fourth day *Action française* was still at it. Its art critic, the respected Louis Dimier, claimed that the lax security was a result of the democratic values of the Third Republic, of which he strongly disapproved. What do you expect if you open the doors of the Louvre to all and sundry? What do you expect if you allow the Louvre to be run by the Jews, like the rest of the country?

The Republic of the Jews has transformed the museum into a bazaar. Homolle, who has been sacked, was in their pockets. This regime is the cause of the loss of the Joconde, gloriously acquired by our kings, and part of our national heritage since François I.[34]

The rest of the artistic world reacted in a more temperate way. Some used art: George-Daniel de Monfreid painted a portrait of Anna Filiabelli in the now classic three-quarter position – but facing to the right – and called it *Souvenir de la Joconde* (1913, now at the Musée du Petit-Palais). The art review the *Grande Revue* wondered how the *Mona Lisa* compared to paintings by other Old Masters, Titian, Rembrandt and Velázquez. How great was the loss? Over two issues it published the replies of France's best-known painters.[35] Some adopted a suitably grieving approach. 'It was like losing a dear friend,' said several. Jacques-Emile Blanche remarked that, though it was not one of his favourites, he felt 'humiliated and diminished not to have any longer among us such a masterpiece'. Charles Léandre called it 'the most impressive portrait of all time'. Many others called it a 'masterpiece', including Félix Edouard Vallotton (who had used the pose in his own work). Georges Rochegrosse thought it a 'sacrilege' even to ask the question. Some resorted to the usual clichés: 'It represented Eternal Womanhood, the most perfect union of science and sentiments' (Pascal Dagnan-Bouveret). René Poxet declared 'the loss of the mysterious smile which allures us and seduces us' to be a catastrophe. 'A national calamity, nay, a universal one,' added Diogène Maillart. Jacques Drésa sent a prayer: 'Oh! May she return to us, our Joconde, fountain of hope, of strength, of life. May she be returned even if it costs us a king's ransom!'

But others – while not denying it had been a serious loss – were less perturbed. Georges d'Espagnat thought it was lucky that the thief had not taken the paintings hanging on either side (a Tintoretto and a Giorgione): 'Those are real paintings.' Another preferred Rembrandt's *Bathsheba* and Leonardo's *St Anne with Virgin and Child* (Georges Rouault's favourite). Maurice Chabas thought the *Mona Lisa* could not compete with works by Titian and Velázquez. Kees Van Dongen (whose *La Parisienne de Montmartre* (1903), now at the Musée Malraux, has some *Gioconda* qualities about it) adopted a frivolous tone: 'It is a pretty good picture with some exceptional qualities, but everything, eventually, comes to an end so why miss her? In any case she has no eyebrows and a funny smile. She must have had nasty teeth to smile so tightly.' Othon Friesz took the matter more seriously:

> Poussin or Lorrain are much better, the *Mona Lisa* is ... technically fine, but cold ... Once shorn of the useless literature which surrounds it, it will stay in our memory only because teachers and parents have spoken highly of Leonardo when we were children ... its mournful smile fails to attract me ... not as good as Watteau, Velázquez or Rembrandt.

For Auguste Gorguet it was not even as good as Frans Hals. Francis Jourdain, who preferred Rembrandt's *Bathsheba*, Vermeer's *Lacemaker* and Ingres's *Madame Rivière*, criticised the religious adoration of crowds, who only venerate dead artists, and predicted that when Auguste Renoir's *Portrait de Madame Charpentier* (not enigmatic, he said, but deeply moving) was hanged where the *Joconde* had been, the public would drool over a masterpiece that now left them cold. Georges Delaw hoped that the entire contents of the Louvre and all other museums would be stolen. And, last but not least, Lucien Lévy-Dhurmer claimed Mona Lisa was better off now because she was no longer subjected to the stares of the ignorant and the narrow-minded.

In all, some fifty painters had replied. Thirty thought the loss had been a catastrophe. The others did not rate the *Mona Lisa* among the best paintings in the Louvre. Many of those polled were modernists eager to demonstrate their non-conformist views and manifest their disdain of received 'bourgeois' opinion sanctioned by the Academy. As the *Mona Lisa* was beginning to reach a wide public, the world of culture was distancing itself.

The months passed by. It was assumed that the painting would never be recovered. In 1913 it was no longer listed in the Louvre catalogue. Raphael's *Baldissare Castiglione* – the portrait of a middle-aged man in the *Mona Lisa* pose – took the place of the *Joconde*. Official *Mona Lisa* postcards were still being sold, but with a sad new caption: 'Stolen on 22 August 1911'. In March 1912 the Louvre acquired the best-known modern homage to the *Mona Lisa* – Camille Corot's *La Femme à la perle*. It may have been some kind of consolation.

Comments on the *Mona Lisa* began to sound like obituaries. In this genre, the friends and admirers of the dear departed make claims that would previously have appeared excessive. Devotees such as the writer and Leonardo-idolater Joséphin Péladan lamented the disappearance of what he called 'The Painting', 'as the Bible is The Book'. 'In a thousand years,' he wrote, 'people will ask of the year 1911: "what did you do with the Joconde?"'[36] But men are fickle, and Péladan himself proposed as a worthy successor to the *Mona Lisa* Leonardo's *St John*, a 'brother lost in the space of the Grande Galerie, ignored by the crowds'.[37] It was now, he said, 'the most beautiful painting in the world'.

Meanwhile the priceless painting had been kept in a box under the stove in Peruggia's lodgings. In 1912 he had gone – without the *Mona Lisa* – to London to see the famous art dealer Joseph Duveen, who thought he was a hoaxer and sent him away.

By the end of 1913 the story had been forgotten by most of the public, particularly outside France. No one impersonated Mona Lisa at a major charity ball held at the Albert Hall in London on 3 December, though guests were supposed to dress after world-famous paintings. On 29 November the *Illustrated London News*, in its massive coverage of the event, previewed, over two pages, fifteen society ladies, dutifully dressed up.[38] There was a Filippo Lippi Angel Gabriel, a Fra Angelico angel,

Vermeer's *Lady with Pearl Necklace*. Other favourites were women by Millais, Velázquez, Guido Reni, Rembrandt, Rubens, Reynolds and Van Dyke. The *Illustrated London News* dealt again with the event in its next two issues (6 and 13 December), adding various Chinese and Greek impersonations and a stunning Flora from Botticelli's *Spring*. Mona Lisa, so easy to impersonate, was absent. There were no ladies sufficiently prescient to be photographed wearing a veil, a simple Renaissance dress, and smiling enigmatically.

The recovery of the painting followed a script which few journalists or novelists could have improved upon. On 29 November 1913 Alfredo Geri, an antique dealer in Florence, received a letter signed 'Leonardo'. Its author claimed to want to 'return' the painting to Italy in exchange for 500,000 lire to cover 'expenses'. 'Leonardo' hinted at a patriotic motivation, the desire to return an Italian treasure stolen by foreigners.[39] Encouraged by the Director of Fine Arts, Corrado Ricci, and by the Curator of the Uffizi, Giovanni Poggi, Geri replied that he wanted to see the painting. 'Leonardo', i.e. Vincenzo Peruggia, complied, and left Paris by train with the *Mona Lisa* in a box. He arrived in Florence on 12 December, and checked in at the modest Albergo Tripoli-Italia. Geri and Poggi examined the back of the painting, and found the correct Louvre inventory number. They convinced Peruggia to allow them to take it to the Uffizi to be examined further. There was a small delay when the hotel receptionist stopped them – he thought they were removing one of the hotel's pictures. The 'artwork' of the Albergo Tripoli-Italia was evidently better protected than that of the Louvre. At the Uffizi, a photograph of the original to hand, Geri and Poggi examined the *craquelures* – the numerous cracks in the paint, estimated to number some 500,000 on the *Mona Lisa*, which provide the 'fingerprint' of old paintings. Satisfied they had the real thing, they convinced Peruggia to return to the hotel and wait for his reward, then called the police.

The enormous press coverage that ensued reminded everyone

of the stories and anecdotes they had read in 1911 but had since forgotten. At first, some expressed doubts that the Italian authorities would return the painting to France. There had been a wave of nationalism following the conquest of Libya, the most recent addition to Italy's new empire. Gabriele D'Annunzio, probably upset not to have had the idea of stealing the picture himself, praised Peruggia in *Il Marzocco* of 21 December 1913. Peruggia was now in prison, the poet wrote,

> far for ever from his *Gioconda*. He who dreamed of honour and gratitude; he, the avenger of Napoleonic thefts. He who kept Leonardo's *Gioconda* in Paris for two years, deceiving the French police, and then took her across the border back to Florence. Do you understand? Back to Florence where she was born, near the Palazzo Vecchio, by the sounds of the bells of Giotto's campanile, able to see the cypresses of San Miniato . . . Only a poet, a great poet, could dream such a dream.[40]

The Italian government did not heed these calls and quickly reached an amicable understanding with the French, who agreed to let the *Mona Lisa* be exhibited in Florence, Rome and Milan before its return to Paris.

Just as the theft had made the Parisians aware of possessing such a masterpiece, the recovery made the Italians proud of 'their' *Mona Lisa*. Huge crowds gathered at the Uffizi to see the famous painting, some with tears in their eyes.[41] There were plenty of photo-opportunities for the press. The *Illustrated London News* of 20 December produced several pages of photographs and included a special supplement with a double-page spread. In the following issue the entire front page showed the *Mona Lisa* at the Uffizi guarded by policemen while experts examined it. Unwilling to let go of the story, the issue of 3 January 1914 had another full-page picture of the painting – the third in a row. In addition, on the facing page it published photographs showing the identical position of the now-famous *craquelures*. There were no doubts. It was the genuine article.

Mona Lisa stayed in Florence until 19 December 1913. The following day – under armed guard – she travelled to Rome to be officially handed back to the French authorities. The commentary appended to the photo reportage by the Rome correspondent of *l'Illustration* captured the mood. She (it is always 'she', *elle*, never 'it') left Florence, travelling like a queen in a purpose-built padded box with a guard of honour. At each stop special agents in civilian clothes surrounded the train. In Rome she was welcomed at the station by functionaries who took her to the Ministry of Education. Then the king, Victor Emanuel III, and a long line of deputies, senators and civil servants visited her. At a private ceremony the Italian Foreign Minister handed her back to the French Ambassador. The Director of the Louvre was present to check the authenticity of the painting, the famous *craquelures*. Speeches were made about the friendship between the two countries (though they were in rival power blocs competing for European supremacy). She was then taken to the French Embassy in the Piazza Farnese. *L'Illustration* rejoiced: 'At last she is French again.'[42] At the embassy it was the turn of the Queen, the entire diplomatic corps and various personalities to pay their respects. Finally she was taken (23–27 December) to the Villa Borghese to be seen by crowds of happy Romans.

On her way back to France the *Mona Lisa* was exhibited in Milan (29 December) to the delight of crowds estimated at 60,000, before arriving, finally, in Paris on 31 December.[43] At the Gare de Lyon, crowds gathered hoping to catch a glimpse.[44] Further ceremonies took place, each providing more photo-opportunities. At the École des Beaux-Arts, after further checks, the painting was the object of a special three-day exhibition before being returned to the Salon Carré at 10 a.m. on 4 January 1914. That Sunday long lines of Parisians filed to catch a glimpse of *their* painting. The celebrated novelist Colette, invited to the private showing at the Beaux-Arts, described the scene in her column in

Le Matin. To see her, Colette wrote, had not been easy. Most of her fellow guests were 'armed to the teeth' with photographic equipment. The visit proceeded between flashes of magnesium and frivolous comments: '"Did you know she had such a plump lower lip?" "Yes, but look: her right hand is less well executed than her left!" They discover her. They invent her ... They would like to love her for more than for her looks and attribute to her – who lacks for nothing except eyebrows – imaginary failings.'[45]

Lucie Mazauric, the art expert who during the Second World War would look after the *Mona Lisa* and other Louvre pictures evacuated from Paris, recalled her visit to the Louvre in 1914. She was then a '*petite provinciale*', accompanied by her parents, eager to see the newly found *Mona Lisa*: 'I could not see much because of huge crowds. But I remember a smell. It was like being in a perfumery shop. All the elegant ladies of Paris had gathered to visit the Joconde.'[46]

The *Mona Lisa*'s new renown rubbed off on the supporting cast. Vincenzo Peruggia obtained his fifteen minutes of fame. The illustrated daily *Excelsior* of 14 December 1913 placed his picture at the centre of a *récit-photo*, or photographic story. Like a comic-strip, a sequence of photographs (using actors) illustrated the succession of events from the removal of the painting from the Salon Carré to its exit from the museum's Porte Visconti.

For the press, it must be said, Peruggia was something of a disappointment.[47] Instead of the sophisticated international art thief celebrated in popular novels he was, quite clearly, a classic loser. Even his criminal record was trivial. Once he had tried to rob a prostitute. Incompetent to the last, he failed miserably. She resisted (he was only five feet three inches tall), and he was arrested and jailed for a week.

At his trial in Italy Peruggia tried to play up the patriotic element, claiming that he had been upset to see so much Italian art in foreign hands and complaining of the racism of the French, who called him '*macaroni*'. At first he had intended to steal

Mantegna's *Mars and Venus (Mount Parnassus)*, because he had
heard some visitors enthusing about it at the Louvre. Then, hearing others favouring the *Mona Lisa*, he decided to take it because it
was much smaller and could be hidden under his coat.[48] Gautier,
Michelet, Pater and co. would have approved, but Mantegna may
have missed a golden opportunity, and only because his painting
was ten times bigger than the *Mona Lisa*.

Peruggia's defence lawyer quite shrewdly explained that, in the
end, no one had lost anything. The newspapers and postcard
peddlers had boosted their sales. The Louvre had acquired even
more renown. The return of the picture had improved the
hitherto tense diplomatic situation between France and Italy.
Alfredo Geri, the antique dealer who had been instrumental in
returning the *Mona Lisa*, got the 25,000 francs promised by the
Friends of the Louvre, whose membership, meanwhile, had vastly
increased. (Geri objected to the 'paltry' sum – he had hoped for
a percentage of the value of the painting!)

Peruggia was treated leniently. The prosecutor had asked for
a sentence of three years; he got twelve and a half months. His
death, in September 1947, was widely reported as that of 'the man
who stole the *Mona Lisa*'.

Giovanni Poggi, the Uffizi Director, died in 1961, aged eighty-
two. During the Second World War he had worked indefatigably
to save Italian artworks from the Nazis. A scholar of some importance, he had edited for years the *Rivista dell'arte*, but the many
obituaries he received – including one in *The Times* – gave far
more space to his 'recovery' of the *Mona Lisa* (in which he played
a limited role).[49] The Albergo Tripoli-Italia shortly afterwards
changed its name to the Hôtel La Gioconda. It is still in business,
still in via Panzani.

The delay between the theft and the recovery ensured that the
Mona Lisa received massive coverage both when it was stolen
and when it was found. The recovery provided the story with a
happy ending. A painting had been turned, anthropomorphically,
into a person, a celebrity. The fantasies of previous generations

of intellectuals and writers had been projected onto a wider public. The press had transformed the *Mona Lisa* from a passive object into a real being, endowed with emotions and feelings. Thus the illustrated theatre magazine *Comoedia Illustré* put on its cover a colour picture of the painting with a commentary that used the language of the stage: 'After an exciting Italian tour, *la Joconde* makes a brilliant comeback at the National Theatre of the Louvre.'[50]

The French street-song industry returned to the *Mona Lisa* with customary speed. Within days of the recovery Gaston Bergeret had put new words to the famous tune of 'Sous les ponts de Paris' and called it 'La Joconde est r'venue' ('The *Joconde*, she's come back'). The cover of the song sheet had a large picture of Mona Lisa – a face now increasingly recognisable. The same tune was also used for Francis Izenic's 'Enfin!! Ca y est!! Elle est retrouvée la Joconde'. The tone remained light-hearted and mocking.[51]

A new series of funny postcards appeared: Mona Lisa arriving at the station in Paris and demanding to be taken to the Louvre; Mona Lisa leaving Milan (an Italian card advertising the Gond-rand removal firm); Mona Lisa beaming, holding a baby, a handsome Italian in the background (the mystery explained); Mona smiling broadly and visibly pregnant with the caption '*La giocondissima*'. Some professional painters tried to take the matter seriously: in 1914 William Nicholson painted *The Return of Mona Lisa*, showing the crowds gathering in the Louvre to witness the re-hanging of the painting. The theme helped it to sell for £150,000 at Agnew's in 1990.

With its irreverent treatment of an art masterpiece, popular culture, in 1913 as in 1911, spawned a new industry: the systematic ridiculing of High Art through postcards. Today, it is almost impossible to find a shop selling art postcards without a stock of *Mona Lisa* send-ups.[52]

While popular culture was having fun, there was a backlash from the intellectual elites against the increased popularity and renown of the *Mona Lisa*. Hitherto it had been 'their' discovery. Now, even the readers of the *Petit Parisien*, the devotees of cabarets and people who had never been to a picture gallery knew all there was to know about the enigmatic Mona Lisa. The aesthete's position had been illustrated by Joris-Karl Huysmans in his influential 1884 novel *À Rebours*. The neurotic protagonist, des Esseintes, disgusted with his Rembrandts because they are becoming so annoyingly popular, exclaims: 'The best tune in the world becomes vulgar and unbearable as soon as the public sings it . . . the work of art that provokes wide enthusiasm becomes . . . for the initiated, polluted, banal, even repellent.'[53] For some it had become necessary to distance themselves from the unseemly razzmatazz which now surrounded the *Mona Lisa*. The masterpiece they had loved was rapidly becoming kitsch. The distinctive prerogative of critics – setting trends and deciding what is fashionable – was being eroded. Originality, after all, is of some importance to the profession. Outside France there were supercilious comments. In England, within days of the recovery, the upmarket *Saturday Review of Politics, Literature, Science and Art*, which had made no comment about the theft, devoted a perceptive, though damning, editorial to the *Mona Lisa* myth:

> . . . without the legend of the wicked smile, the fate of Leonardo's masterpiece would hardly have thrilled the average intelligent citizen of these islands. The public must have a story to relish its old masters. Either they must recall a naughty reputation . . . or they must be connected with a crime, like Gainsborough's Duchess; or they must cost a dreadful amount of money, like the National Gallery Raphael . . . La Gioconda lacked a story until the formula of the smile was invented . . .
>
> An evil day . . . in one tremendous passage of denunciation Pater tore her character to shreds. He saw in the smile . . . something demoniac and sinister . . . the legend grew until every American and English visitor to the Louvre made a point of staring for ten

minutes on the half-ruined picture, in the hope of reading new depravity into the smile.[54]

Roberto Longhi, only twenty-three at the time, but on his way
to becoming the most influential Italian art historian and critic
of the twentieth century, launched an attack on the *Mona Lisa*
and Leonardo in the periodical *La Voce*. The article, called 'Le
due Lise' – dedicated to politicians, princes, professors and 'all
those who do not think with their heads' – declared Leonardo
to be grossly overrated. The *Mona Lisa* was an 'admixture of
different styles'. Her puffiness suggested an inner emptiness. The
pose was dreadful. Who is this wretched woman who, squeezed
between a balcony wall and a chair, vainly attempts to strike an
elegant posture by setting her arm parallel to the viewers while
letting her hand hang down? The silly veil made everything look
flat, including the greenish landscape, which was little more than
an 'Antarctic fantasy'.

There was, however, 'another Lisa', Longhi went on, warming
to the theme. 'For this second Lisa, should she ever be stolen and
then found, you won't find ten people troubling themselves. Yet,
of the two, she alone is Art. She is by Renoir [see plate 33].'[55]

The masses – along with Walter Pater – were also put in their
place by Bernard Berenson. Unlike Longhi he was already famous,
celebrated as the greatest art connoisseur of his time. Writing in
1916, he recollected the time when, as a young man, he had tried
to like the *Mona Lisa*,

> Leonardo's 'supreme creation', as I was taught to regard
> it . . . I would spend the hours of long summer days
> trying to match what I was really seeing and feeling
> with the famous passage of Walter Pater, that, like so
> many of my contemporaries, I had learned by heart.

When finally he 'dared come into conflict with the powers of
a shaman so potent . . . as Walter Pater', all he really saw in the
Mona Lisa was

The estranging image of a woman beyond the reach of
my sympathies . . . disdainfully unlike the women I had
hitherto known or dreamt of, a foreigner with a look
I could not fathom, watchful, sly, secure, with a smile
of anticipated satisfaction and a pervading air of hostile
superiority . . . I argued with myself many scores of
times that the landscape was mysterious and fascinating
. . . And besides, were not four centuries unanimous in
repeating that *Mona Lisa* was one of the very greatest,
if not absolutely the greatest achievement of artistic
genius?

Thinking his views would change, he too joined 'the secular
chorus of praise'. When he heard the painting had been stolen
he found himself

saying softly 'If only it were true!' And when the news
was confirmed, I heaved a sigh of relief. I could not
help it. The disappearance of such a masterpiece gave
me no feelings of regret, but on the contrary a sense
of long-desired emancipation . . . She had simply
become an incubus, and I was glad to be rid of her.
But I did not dare even then. Who was I to lift up
my feeble voice against the organ resonances of the
centuries?[56]

Berenson eventually emancipated himself from those resonances. Yet, I wonder. His Mona Lisa has a 'sly' look, her smile a
'pervading air of hostile superiority'. Is there not still a little
shade of Gautier and co. here? Nevertheless, Berenson could now
declare, with evident satisfaction, that he was among those 'few
. . . who have autonomous artistic selves; for art, being for most
people the eminent domain of "prestige values", is the chosen
paradise of humbug'.[57]

Heavyweight literary giants joined in to express their disdain
for the popular icon. T.S. Eliot, in a few pages, managed to
castigate Goethe, Coleridge, Shakespeare, Pater and Leonardo. In

'Hamlet and his Problems', an essay published in 1920, he drubbed Goethe and Coleridge as critics who 'substitute their own Hamlet for Shakespeare's'. He was 'thankful that Walter Pater did not fix his attention on this play' which, far from being Shakespeare's masterpiece, is 'most certainly an artistic failure'. He concluded with what he felt had to be the final put-down. *Hamlet* was 'the *Mona Lisa* of literature'.[58]

This attitude was making its way even into middlebrow fiction. In Somerset Maugham's *Christmas Holiday*, Leslie and Venetia Mason (whom we encountered in the previous chapter) visit the Louvre with their children and make straight for the *Mona Lisa*. Maugham comments disdainfully: 'The four of them stood in front of the picture and with reverence gazed at the insipid smile of that prim and sex-starved young woman.'[59]

The theft added considerably to the baggage of anecdotes concerning the *Mona Lisa*. Decades later, any new comment or information on the picture sent the journalists scurrying to their clippings. In addition to the usual Vasari stories and the quotes from Gautier, Pater and co. they found the exciting story of the theft, by then all but forgotten. They realised, once again, that the lady in question was not just a pretty picture. She had an interesting past. The clipping files multiplied, ensuring that each anecdote would be faithfully reproduced at each subsequent development in the history of the painting.

The growing popularity of the *Mona Lisa*, however, did not rely on a single event.[60] So far, the theft had been mainly a French story. Mona Lisa had not yet gone global.

Thus the 1914 Baedeker guide to Paris called it 'the best known female portrait in the world' – as it had in 1911 – and added only that since its recovery it had become even better known.[61] The 1924 edition dropped the reference to the theft and reprinted, without changes, its 1911 comment.[62] The 1922 *Larousse universel*, in its entry for the *Joconde*, mentions the mysterious and disturbing smile but not the theft.[63]

Being stolen may be a good marketing ploy, but it does not

always work. Paintings are still stolen from the Louvre, but how many remember that on 3 May 1998 it was the turn of Corot's *Chemin de Sèvres*? In 1977 some nine thousand paintings were stolen in France alone; most, of course, were neither famous nor valuable.[64] The *Guardian* of 8 January 2000 reported an impressive list of stolen masterpieces, including Picasso's *Head of a Woman (Dora Maar)* – vaguely reminiscent of the *Mona Lisa* – and major works by Rembrandt and Vermeer from the Isabella Steward Gardner Museum in Boston in 1990, a Turner stolen in 1994, a Titian in 1995, and a Cézanne taken from Oxford's Ashmolean Museum on the first day of the millennium.

Important events intervene to interrupt the continuity of memories. Months after the *Mona Lisa* was recovered, the Great War engulfed Europe. It was followed by an influenza epidemic that resulted in more deaths than the war itself. Seen in its proper historical context, it is unlikely that the fate of even a major painting could have remained for long in the public mind. As all advertisers and politicians know, the key to lasting fame and popularity is not a single fifteen-minute episode, but constant repetition.

In the 1920s, however, the *Mona Lisa* was remembered not only by those who had known her all along, and those who are always 'in the know', but also by a new generation of popular writers. They prudently realised that, if mentioning the painting, it was useful to jog their readers' memory. Emmanuel Bourcier's *Comment j'ai retrouvé la Joconde*, ('How I Found the *Joconde*') is a highly fictionalised account of the theft, almost a novel. The author, approached by someone claiming to have the real *Joconde*, says that he 'vaguely remembered the business about the theft'.[65] L. Roger-Milès, in a footnote to his *Léonard de Vinci et les Jocondes* (1923), wrote that the theft, which had caused so much commotion at the time, was now, twelve years and a long war later, little more than a *fait-divers*: 'we can barely remember the name of the thief.'[66]

The theft had been a major building-block in the construction of the *Mona Lisa*. Other people, as we shall see, joined the enterprise. Some consciously, others not, but none able to foresee the long-term consequences of their actions – as is always the case with history.

CHAPTER EIGHT

Exploiting the Theft

Intellectuals were getting a little bored with Mona Lisa. The fickle public had almost forgotten her. Yet the notoriety acquired by its theft might have sufficed to preserve the picture in the pantheon of works familiar to the general public. Eventually, tourism, advertising and television would have further entrenched the *Mona Lisa* and other 'favourites' in the canon of Great Works, particularly as the twentieth century did not recruit many new painters to the narrow circle of revered Old Masters. The nineteenth century was less conservative: it rediscovered Vermeer, Piero della Francesca, Botticelli, El Greco and others.

Of course, the *Mona Lisa* might have been subjected to the vicissitudes of fashion – the fat years of celebrity being followed by lean years of benign neglect. This may happen in the future. In art, as in most things, it is difficult to stay at the top all the time, though it is easier to stay there than to make it to the top in the first place. The history of artistic taste is not only the history of the rehabilitation of faded and forgotten glories, once great but now despised. It is also the history of downward slides into oblivion.

It is reasonable to assume that, after its recovery, the popularity of the *Mona Lisa* would have settled at a 'normal' level. It might have been 'downgraded' (I use the word with some hesitation) to the level of Leonardo's *Lady with an Ermine* or *St Anne with Virgin and Child*. These are hardly minor works: art critics and historians regard them as masterpieces, and they are much admired by visitors. Both Cecilia Gallerani and St Anne are prettier than Mona Lisa, but neither picture is even remotely in her league. And unlike them, the *Mona Lisa* continued to thrive on the oxygen of publicity.

Between the wars the flame of Mona Lisa's celebrity was kept alive by both the avant-garde and popular fiction. The first affected to deride it. The second used it as a hook on which to hang stories. Both exploited it to attract attention and sell their own artistic wares.

Of those who quickly realised that the theft provided an opportunity for self-advertisement, D'Annunzio – who never let a bandwagon pass by without jumping on it – must rank as the most eccentric and the least successful. By 1920 he was dangerously close to being yesterday's man in literature, out of touch with both high modernism (Joyce, Eliot and Proust) and the irreverent avant-garde, while disdaining the new successful middle- and lowbrow writers who were increasingly crowding the market. We have seen (page 164) how D'Annunzio had changed the title and the date of an old poem to suggest that it had been written on the day the *Mona Lisa* was stolen. This great prima donna could not bear to be left out, and even attempted to implicate himself in the theft. During his armed expedition to recover for Italy the disputed port of Fiume from Yugoslavia (1920), an event that gave him the national and international fame he craved so ardently, he wrote a short essay, 'Portrait de Loÿse Baccaris' (Luisa Baccara was his mistress). This slight work was published in France in 1925 in a limited edition. D'Annunzio's translator and devotee André Doderet wrote in the introduction of their meeting at Fiume. With the international crisis at its height, D'Annunzio assured the credulous Doderet that Peruggia had brought him the stolen *Mona Lisa* when he was living in France before the war.[1] The claim was repeated in the essay, where D'Annunzio wrote that the 'sublime thief' had shown him the painting 'wrapped in a blanket like those used in stables'. He continued: 'I began to hate Mona Lisa's spongy hands: I had them under my eyes for days on end, forced to hold metaphysical discussions with the thief.'[2] The idea of Vincenzo Peruggia discussing metaphysics with anyone is somewhat absurd.

D'Annunzio had assembled a large collection of clippings from French and Italian magazines and newspapers regarding the theft, a sign of his obsession.[3] This took an artistic form: perhaps, he thought, a film could be made of it. Until the war he had shown no interest at all in the cinema – an inferior art, he believed, if it was an art at all[4] (later he mellowed and allowed his plays to be turned into successful films). In 1920 he prepared a film treatment of some twenty pages, with a good title: 'L'uomo che rubò la Gioconda' ('The Man who Stole the *Gioconda*') – a fictionalised development of his essay.[5]

The complex plot, set in 1911, involves a painter, Peter van Blömen, who dabbles in metaphysics and alchemy. He invents a devilish magic substance made with human organs, and plans to use it to bring to life the fantasies emanating from the *Gioconda*: 'a work of art, almost magic, that has captured the imagination of poets for centuries. Generations of dreamers and thinkers have created around it an atmosphere of incalculable intensity.' In Paris he entices a young Tuscan, Lunelli, to help him steal the *Mona Lisa*. Lunelli had been working in the Louvre, preparing casts of artworks to be sent to the 'famous poet' Gabriele D'Annunzio (who thus hoped to star in the film), one of 'the most perceptive admirers of the *Gioconda*', then in self-imposed exile in France. The picture stolen, van Blömen and Lunelli take it to D'Annunzio, leaving (so envisages the script) a 'long-haired romantic' young police investigator weeping disconsolately before the void left by the missing painting.

As D'Annunzio contemplates the stolen *Mona Lisa*, his mistress, the beautiful Sonia, becomes jealous at once – such is the power of feminine intuition. For the experiment to succeed, van Blömen privately explains to D'Annunzio, a human heart is required. That is what the unsuspecting Lunelli is there for. They'll have to catch him, though, because he has disappeared into the woods, seduced by Sonia, who wants to get her own back on D'Annunzio. The couple are found in a passionate embrace. Enraged, D'Annunzio kills Lunelli while Sonia runs into a forest fire and is incinerated. The still-throbbing and warm heart of the young Italian enables the *Gioconda* to acquire human form. The 'Maestro' (i.e. D'Annunzio), having lost Sonia, can at last possess Mona Lisa, his life's passion, whose smile had always intrigued him. Had he not written a poem with the line 'You will never know why I smile' (see page 164)? Lisa, who has meanwhile stopped smiling, has to listen to D'Annunzio explaining how he had tried to find her in numerous women, searching for her smile on all the lips he kissed: 'Let me possess you! I have nothing left.' This amazing seduction technique fails miserably. As the poet tries to touch her, Lisa smiles and disappears. Her image also dissolves from the painting, leaving only the landscape. The devilish van Blömen takes the panel away, confident that she will return. D'Annunzio is left disconsolate. He has lost, in one night, both Sonia and Lisa.

The story ends with Mona Lisa back in the Louvre, surrounded by happy crowds. In the midst of the rejoicing, D'Annunzio turns up carrying Sonia's ashes, which he throws at the mysterious smile, screaming, 'For you I deserted her.' They take him away, while the crowds gather again around the 'perpetual charm'.

D'Annunzio's film, of course, was never made, and his attention-seeking claims about having seen the stolen *Mona Lisa* never taken seriously. He had understood, however, the new possibilities offered by the theft. Fiction does not have to accept the ending provided by real life. Events such as the assassinations of John F. Kennedy and Martin Luther King, or the death of a royal princess, have produced interesting theories – all more exciting than the likely truth. Accounts of plots and conspiracies sell far better than those of boring routine crimes. Master criminals are far more alluring than the second-rate losers who are usually involved in real-life murders and robberies. Vincenzo Peruggia had let the press down by being so uninteresting. Apparently he had not been charmed by the mysterious smile. He may never even have heard of it, or have realised he could not pass for a Romantic poet or Decadent aesthete.

But if the thief was not interesting, the theft was. Perhaps a gang of real international art thieves had simply used Peruggia. Perhaps the *Mona Lisa* that had been recovered was not the real one. Perhaps the painting in the Louvre had been a copy all along, or a fake. Stories about fakes are fascinating. Forgers are endearing creatures – as long as we have not bought their works – because they fool the experts. The history of art is replete with fakers, but usually they concentrate their efforts on really prolific painters, such as Camille Corot, whose estimated three thousand works are dwarfed by the estimated eight thousand paintings in the United States alone.[6] This only made stories about real and false *Mona Lisa*s all the more alluring.

The theft provided excellent opportunities for cranks and fantasists. Once it was realised that the history of the picture was full of gaps, many rushed to fill them in, find secrets and solve mysteries. Of course, many Renaissance works have an uncertain history, but by now the *Mona Lisa* was special. Besides, it is not very difficult to come up with an alternative history if the available facts are few and far between. Historians do this all the time.

Experts were certain that the painting recovered in Florence was the one that had been stolen: the evidence (particularly the *craquelures*) was overwhelming. Facts, however, are seldom a defence against wishful thinking. And the occasional discomfiture of experts is always greeted with delight. After the theft, copies of the *Mona Lisa* hitherto regarded as mere replicas turned up, with their supporters claiming that they were the real *Mona Lisa*. In 1915 a John R. Eyre eagerly embraced the highly tentative hypothesis that Leonardo had painted two *Mona Lisa*s.[7] The one he kept ended up in the Louvre; the other he handed over to Francesco il Giocondo. This second – and better – *Mona Lisa* was now in Isleworth, just west of London, the proud property of one Hugh Blaker (Mr Eyre's stepson).[8] Years later, the Isle-

worth *Mona Lisa* turned up in the collection of a Henry F. Pulitzer, who published, at his own expense, a booklet entitled *Where
is the Mona Lisa?* (c.1967).[9] This was the story of 'a great love
which had not changed ... since I first met the lady ... I have
courted this lady for twenty-six years before I could call her my
own and bring her to my home.'[10] He had purchased the 'real'
Mona Lisa in 1962 by selling his house with all its contents,
including much of his collection of paintings. As he candidly
admits, John Eyre had convinced him. Pulitzer died in 1979 –
unable to prove he had the real *Mona Lisa*.

The Pulitzer *Mona Lisa* even ended up in a *roman noir*, the
French equivalent of the hard-boiled genre. In Georges Pierquin's
Du Mouron pour la Joconde (1985), Marilyn, a member of a team
pursuing a gang of forgers, evidently knows a thing or two about
Renaissance art. She remarks that in a reproduction of the *Mona
Lisa* (her favourite painting) in an art book, the side columns
are quite visible, unlike the one in the Louvre. She notices this
because she always looks at the picture as a whole, and not,
like others, only at the famous smile. It turns out that the
picture in the book is the second *Mona Lisa* Leonardo painted.
A footnote in the novel explains that this is fact, not fiction, and
that another *Mona Lisa* belonged to the British art dealer Henry
Pulitzer.[11]

The hunt for the 'real' *Mona Lisa* had begun, and others joined
the fray. In 1954 Raymond Hekking, an antique dealer from Grasse
in southern France, used the D'Annunzio story to cast doubt on
the authenticity of the Louvre *Mona Lisa*. He claimed to own the
real painting, and found his own 'art expert' to back his claim.
This *Joconde de Nice* received wide coverage and was still being
reported in newspapers ten years later, by which time it had been
displaced by fresher claimants.[12]

In October 1972, Lord Brownlow announced that the real *Mona
Lisa* had been in his family's possession for two centuries, and
was now in his country home in Grantham, Lincolnshire (birthplace of another famous lady). Claims on behalf on the Brownlow

Mona Lisa had been made as early as 1933, but not prior to the theft.

Some museums tried to upgrade their copies. In 1961 Professor Matvey A. Gukovsky of the University of Leningrad cautiously claimed that the *Colombina*, a *Mona Lisa* copy attributed to Melzi, at the Hermitage, had been painted 'mainly' by Leonardo and only completed later by Melzi.[13]

The USA too had its 'real' portrait: the Vernon *Mona Lisa*. The evidence was that in 1797 William Henry Vernon, an American friend of Benjamin Franklin, had bought in Paris a sixteenth-century copy of the painting, or maybe (even better) had received it from Queen Marie-Antoinette before her execution in 1793.[14] The Vernon *Mona Lisa* had always been regarded as a copy, but so strong was the wish that it should be genuine that when it was exhibited at the Otis Institute in Los Angeles in July–August 1964, an 'attributed to Leonardo' note was appended to it. On 12 January 1995 it was sold at Sotheby's New York for $552,500. More recent copies regularly turn up at auctions, but seldom fetch more than a few thousand dollars. It was estimated that between £4,000 and £6,000 would be required to secure a seventeenth-century copy at Christie's on 20 February 1986, the same for another copy at Phillips' two years later. In July 1994 the 'Houston' *Mona Lisa* was offered for sale at Christie's with an estimate of only £1,200–1,800.

The media eagerly and widely reports all odd claims. To justify such coverage the claim must appear to be taken seriously. A certified Salvatore Rosa found in the attic would not generate a fraction of the coverage of a doubtful *Mona Lisa*. The Pulitzer claim, enhanced by a lavish press party at Claridge's, made the front page of both the *Daily Express* and *Paris-Jour* (10 January 1967) and was reported by most of the world press. There is a set pattern to these stories. Initially, the crank is never a crank, but an 'art dealer' or a 'serious collector', usually 'respected'. Experts, previously cautious ('Well, it *could* be a Leonardo, but on the other hand . . .'), become, for a while, 'world' experts, their prudent 'on the other hand' thrown to the wind. When the hype is at its height, the papers prepare their readers for the inevitable backlash ('"Claim bogus", say experts'). This generates a second round of articles, written with particular zest by the papers that had missed out on the original story. The 'real' *Mona Lisa*, it now turns out, was a fake. 'Most' experts now think that it was painted with the wrong paint, on the wrong surface, in the wrong way, in the wrong century, and, above all, not by Leonardo or even by a distant relative of his. The story is filed away. The file gets bigger still, waiting, like some insatiable beast, for the next episode.

The Louvre has tried, not always successfully, to quell these eternal rumours. In 1928 it subjected the *Mona Lisa* to further tests, all of which confirmed that the picture returned was the one stolen. But the temptation is irresistible. When a newspaper decides to publish an article on fakes, the picture editor, with uncanny originality, illustrates it with a photograph of the *Mona Lisa* and a caption like 'Is it a fake?'[15]

The public is eager for such stories. Some try to participate in the game. They write to the Louvre with their own theories about the 'real' *Mona Lisa*, or 'the second *Mona Lisa*', or the identity of the sitter. With characteristic French courtesy the curators unfailingly reply, profusely thanking their correspondent for the precious information, which will 'enrich our considerable documentation'. The letters are dutifully filed away to await the supercilious comments of future historians – such as this one.

It is in fiction and the more speculative non-fiction (novels that dare not speak their name) that the theft has been used with particular vigour. An otherwise routine detective story about an art theft becomes a little more marketable if the stolen painting is the world-famous *Mona Lisa*. Some of these stories are very slight, such as Pierre Fontaine's 'Le Dernier amoureux de la Joconde' (in *l'Européen*, 29 May 1936), where Sir Mac Call, a highly stereotyped Scottish laird, falls in love with Mona Lisa and convinces an art thief to steal the painting.

A more interesting slant that provoked a whole stream of stories was provided by an interview in the *Saturday Evening Post* of 25 June 1932. A so-called 'Marquis of Valfiero' told the journalist Karl Decker that it was he who had stolen the *Mona Lisa*, in order to be able to convince some rich (but presumably not very clever) collectors that the copy they were being offered was the real thing. Then Valfiero, through his accomplice Vincenzo Peruggia, returned the authentic *Mona Lisa* to the Louvre, while telling each deluded millionaire that the picture the museum had was a fake, but that the Louvre was pretending, for political reasons, that it was genuine. The story was fairly unlikely, but this did not stop the *Sunday Express* from coming up with a similar one a year later (6 August 1933), with a Jack Dean 'confessing' to the theft rather than Valfiero.[16]

This angle was too good to be forgotten. Seymour V. Reit's *The Day they Stole the Mona Lisa* (1981) could be described as imaginative non-fiction. The foreword is fairly typical: 'The narrative may read like detective fiction, but it decidedly isn't. Everything described in these pages happened: the people are real people; so, too, are the names, places, times and events.'[17] Eduardo Valfiero is a shadowy, impeccably dressed Argentinean who, with the help of a talented forger, produces Murillos at the drop of a hat. Valfiero's original plan is to return the *Mona Lisa* once he has sold various copies as the genuine article, but Peruggia, his accomplice, decides to take it back. The 'evidence', typically, consists merely in establishing that a particular sequence of events *could* have occurred.

Eduardo Valfiero also turns up as the charming international con-artist hero of Robert Noah's novel *The Man who Stole the Mona Lisa* (1998). The theft of the picture is to be the crowning feat of his career. Valfiero wants to ensure that after his death his young wife Rosa Maria will have enough money to live on in the style she deserves. Stealing the *Mona Lisa* becomes a sort of life insurance.[18]

Martin Page's 1984 novel, also called *The Man who Stole the*

Mona Lisa, had a different angle, blending, as the publisher's blurb put it, 'history and fiction into an ingenious thriller'.[19] Here the American millionaire on whose behalf the painting is stolen is none other than the financier and art collector John Pierpont Morgan. Morgan tells the famous art thief Adam Worth (notorious for having stolen Gainsborough's *Duchess of Devonshire*) that what fascinates him about the *Mona Lisa* is not the smile but the eyes: 'You can walk back and forth in front of her countless times, and those approving, loving eyes follow you at every moment.'[20] (It is commonly believed that this is one of the *Mona Lisa*'s remarkable attributes, but in reality the effect can be obtained from any portrait.) Worth, a master impersonator, joins the decorators at the Louvre, pretending to be Vincenzo Peruggia (who has been drugged), and steals the painting. The plot grows in complexity, involving a restorer's replica of the *Mona Lisa* and Morgan blackmailing the French government into starting the First World War.

Wolf Mankowitz's witty 1987 *Gioconda* is of a different order. The tongue-in-cheek narrative has no pretence of historical accuracy, but the author, a well-known art critic, multiplies cultural references to amuse the *cognoscenti*. There is, of course, the traditional gentleman-thief, Daniel Lavine; a London art-dealer; a Texan art collector and many others. The tone is set in the opening paragraphs, where an American tourist, 'her head heaving like a tortoise', reads, 'in a low dull voice', the famous Pater passage from her guidebook. Upon reaching the lines 'her eyelids are a little weary', she says, 'My eyelids are a little weary too. Let's go get some coffee. This place is really hard on the feet.'[21] There is the Paris chief of police who goes to consult Freud in Vienna about the personality of the thief: '"Do you think it possible, Herr Professor, that the culprit could be a Jewish intellectual?" "I doubt it," Freud snapped, biting his cigar. "The *Mona Lisa* is essentially a Christian mother. Jewish mothers are distinctly different." '[22] The thief takes the *Mona Lisa* to a master-forger who is known as 'the last of the Pre-Raphaelites'. He is a very angry man: 'To be totally out of fashion and short of funds due to the chicanery of dealers promoting insane daubs to the cretinous public . . . does not improve a disposition always inclined to the choleric.'[23]

The story of the theft has also been used for language teaching. *Marcel and the Mona Lisa* (1991), by Stephen Rabley, was devised for students in their first year of learning English.[24] Marcel is a (French) mouse, and a detective. He jumps into the bag in which the thief has concealed the *Mona Lisa* (who, obviously, smiles at him) and ends up in Venice, where the picture is handed over to Signor Spandini. Marcel manages to get hold of the rolled-up *Mona Lisa* (for the purposes of this story, Leonardo used a canvas) and delivers it to the police.

Chris Greenhalgh's *Stealing the Mona Lisa* (1994) is a collection of poems, none on the *Mona Lisa*, let alone the theft. There is, however, one about making love to Marilyn Monroe ('The Night I Met Marilyn') which contains the lines: 'and what happened later that evening/I have never related./It would have been like stealing the *Mona Lisa*.' The poem ends, sarcastically, with the unreliable narrator announcing that he will reveal all in his forthcoming book.[25] Jasper Johns's *Racing Thoughts* (which has a *Mona Lisa* in the left-hand side) is used as the cover illustration.

Ramsey Montgomery's *The Mona Lisa is Missing!* (1988) is one of those children's books (reading age: ten and up) where the reader, about to visit Paris, seeing the *Mona Lisa* being 'the high point of the trip', can choose between different plot sequences and twenty-two different endings ('If you choose to follow the van turn to page 61').[26]

Boris Bergman's *Un Tatami pour Mona Lisa* (1999) is a Jewish crime story set in New York. The investigator, Ramon Berkovitch, is following the trail of Noburo, a Japanese tycoon who has stolen the *Mona Lisa*. But what the thief has taken is a fake because the book believes, as many do, that the Louvre keeps the real painting hidden: 'You don't seriously think that they would exhibit it like this. With all these clumsy tourists . . .'[27]

Laurent Charnin's *La Joconde assassinée*, published in 1991 but set in 2000, has as its hero and heroine François La Fourme, a 'rather enigmatic journalist', and Sister Claire, the somewhat unconventional Mother Superior of the Congregation of the Daughters of Chastity. Sister Claire looks like Mona Lisa, and has the same 'restrained and enigmatic smile'.[28] In the novel the *Joconde* is abducted by Muslim fundamentalists, who threaten to destroy it unless the French government hands over a blasphemous writer. With their demands they enclose a picture of the *Mona Lisa* with a *chador* on her head and a mosque in the background.[29] Michel Noir's *l'Otage* ('The Hostage', 1998) has a similar theme: terrorists have already destroyed the Winged Victory and the Venus de Milo. They now threaten to blow up the *Joconde*. Will they succeed?[30]

In a 1979 French comic strip an attempt is made to steal the *Mona Lisa* when it is supposed to be lent to the British Museum.[31] It had been stolen earlier by a gang in the American *Li'l Abner* strip.[32] The 1965 Franco–Italian film *On a volé la Joconde*, directed by Michel Deville, has George Chakiris as the gentleman thief who plans to steal the painting. The object of his lust is Marina Vlady, who keeps a bordello where all the girls are dressed as Mona Lisa.

Children get less exciting, if more informative, accounts. Designed for the seven-to-eleven age-group, Cyriel Verleyen's *The Theft of the Mona Lisa* (1976) tells the story of how Leonardo painted the portrait, embedding in young minds a number of doubtful, if familiar, notions: from Leonardo dying in the arms of François I to the idea of the enigmatic smile – 'For three hundred years people looked at the smile on the face of the *Mona Lisa* and puzzled over the reason for it' – before getting to the story of the theft, which it assumes was caused by Peruggia's patriotism.[33]

By far the most ingenious plot involving multiple *Mona Lisa*s is Bob Shaw's 'The Gioconda Caper' (1988), a short story in the hard-boiled style of Hammett and Chandler, with a little post-modern irony.[34] The hero is Phil Dexter, a 'private psi' (a detective who uses psychic powers). The amazingly beautiful Carole Colvin – a 'tall creamy blonde' – turns up seeking his help. She has found a *Mona Lisa* among her father's old things. It is strikingly similar to the original in the Louvre – Dexter gets genuine Leonardo psychic vibrations – save for a tiny detail: her hands are apart, not cradled together. Eventually the couple find, in a cave near Milan, a large heap of *Mona Lisa*s, each in a slightly different pose. Near them is a strange circular machine resembling a large wheel, lying on its side. The *Mona Lisa*s are attached to the wheel, facing its centre, where a sentry-box with two small holes at eye level completes the structure. They realise that Leonardo, the amazing universal genius, had invented the cinema, but had to rely on the technology available in the Renaissance: oil paint and wooden panels. The *Mona Lisa* hanging in the Louvre is only the first frame of the world's first movie. The machine is still working. The film starts with Lisa revealing one breast and making it perform, in the words of the hero, 'one of the classiest circular swings I had seen since . . . I witnessed Fabulous Fifi Lafleur windmilling her tassels'. This trick accomplished, Lisa returns to her classic *contrapposto* position, one hand upon the other, and resumes, of course, her smile. The mystery haunting generations of writers is thus resolved: Lisa was performing a Renaissance striptease.[35]

As we saw in the previous chapter, such irreverence towards an icon of high culture started much earlier, in the streets and cabarets of Paris when songs and stage acts sent up the whole mystique that had enveloped Leonardo and his great work.

The so-called avant-garde took the same direction, more or less unconsciously. While cartoonists had no pretensions to be 'real' artists – they made fun of high culture for the sake of it, with no intention of destroying it – the avant-garde (Dadaists, Futurists and Surrealists) had greater ambitions. They pretended to make fun of high culture, but were in reality deadly serious. Their number one enemy was the revered culture of the past.

Marinetti's *The Futurist Manifesto* (February 1909) declared that a car could be far more beautiful than the Winged Victory of Samothrace: 'Why should we look over our shoulders if we want to break down the mysterious doors of the Impossible? . . . We want to glorify war – sole hygiene of the world – and militarism, patriotism, and the contempt for women.' Article Ten of the Manifesto announced: 'We want to destroy museums, libraries, all kinds of academies and fight against moralism, feminism . . .'[36] Museums were particularly singled out for derision: they were nothing but graveyards, and should be visited only once a year: 'Once a year we could bring flowers to the Gioconda, I will grant you that . . .'

Marinetti's aim was to challenge bourgeois conventions – what the French call '*épater les bourgeois*', which roughly translates as 'leaving the bourgeoisie flabbergasted'. The ploy worked, and Futurism became an 'overnight success and an international scandal'.[37] Some established critics, realising that outrage was expected of them, refused to play the game. André Marty, reviewing Marinetti's play *Le Roi Bombance* when it opened in Paris in 1909, wrote: 'One can feel a powerless desire to shock [*épater*]; one could almost say that to protest would be to give it too much credence.'[38] The play, which used as characters the digestive organs of the human body, was a complete flop. Nevertheless, Marinetti ended his days as a member of Italy's Royal Academy – appointed by Mussolini.

The Futurists, as well as the Dadaists and the Surrealists, were unwittingly developing a form of irreverence towards high culture that would be widely used by advertisers. In 1915 Marinetti's friend and fellow leading Futurist Ardengo Soffici described in his diary his reaction to a poster advertising a new laxative potion called 'Gioconda' (see plate 46): 'I saw on a wall written in large white letters on a blue background: Gioconda: Acqua Purgativa Italiana. Below, the dull face of Monna Lisa. Finally! Here [i.e. in Italy] too we are beginning to produce some good art criticism.'[39]

The artistic avant-garde recruited from both ends of the

political spectrum. Marinetti became an early supporter of Fascism; others became Communists or anarchists. All used parody and the appropriation of clichés as a 'rhetorical strategy . . . to undermine the belief in the permanence of social values'.[40] The Dadaists took established icons, '. . . the *Mona Lisa*, a Rembrandt painting, the Venus de Milo . . . cannibalising, disfiguring or defacing them, in order to defy dominant aesthetic and social codes, such as the untouchability of the work of art, the originality of the artist'.[41] It was a kind of creative iconoclasm that may have met a popular need to demystify high art, a habit so ingrained that it is rare not to overhear irreverent remarks about famous paintings when one is visiting an exhibition or a museum.

Iconoclastic behaviour requires, by definition, that the icon to be destroyed is widely revered and known. The earliest known example of such jocular use of the *Mona Lisa* to undermine artistic excellence occurred well before the inter-war avant-garde set to work. In 1887 the illustrator Sapeck (Eugène Bataille) produced for Coquelin Cadet's book *Le Rire* a Mona Lisa with a clay pipe in her mouth, surrounded by wreaths of smoke – a joke aimed at the so-called *fumistes* (literally 'smokists', bullshitters) by one of their leading lights (see plate 35). The *fumiste* was a kind of bohemian prankster who 'internalises Universal Stupidity by postulating the illusory nature of values and of the Beautiful, hence his denial of the established order and of official hierarchies'.[42]

The *Mona Lisa* was being transformed into a metaphor for High Art. Only thus could it become a major target for profanation. One such act occurred in 1914 at an exhibition in Brussels, then one of the centres of Europe's avant-garde. One painter, B.B. Col, now quite forgotten, represented Mona Lisa with a cigarette hanging from her lips, her arms full of fruit and vegetables. The punning title, *Jo féconde*, compounded the mockery.[43] Others joined the fray. In 1915 Jean Metzinger produced a pastiche of the *Mona Lisa* called *Contrasts*. In 1913 the French *Almanach Vermot* showed a cubist *Mona Lisa*. Of greater import was Kasimir Malevich's *Composition with Mona Lisa* (1914, see plate 37). The feeling that prevails in this collage is disapproval rather than scorn. The cult surrounding the recovered *Mona Lisa* was for Malevich an example of false artistic consciousness. The *Mona Lisa* is situated deep inside the collage, with two red crosses, one on the face, the other on the cleavage, as marks of rejection.[44] A few years later, Malevich painted the picture that should have ended all pictures – but didn't – a white square on a white ground (Museum of Modern Art, New York).

Five years later, in 1919, Duchamp took a postcard of the *Mona Lisa* and drew on her face a moustache and a goatee beard (see plate 36). He had been developing the idea that as art could only be defined by its context, it could be made out of anything at all, including what he called a 'ready-made', such as a urinal (*The Fountain*, Arturo Schwartz Collection, Milan). Context was like the miracle of transubstantiation: it could transform anything. If a vulgar wafer can become the Body of Christ, a urinal can become a work of art, provided it is so regarded by an artist and positioned in an art gallery.[45]

In adding a beard and a moustache to the *Mona Lisa*, Duchamp was 'making free with a work of art whose popular fame had reached mythic proportions [. It] was bound to appear provocative.'[46] Though Duchamp's act now appears, at best, mildly amusing, at the time it caused consternation, particularly because Duchamp compounded the sacrilege by calling the result *L.H.O.O.Q.*, letters which, if spelt out in French, make *elle a chaud au cul* ('she is hot in the arse'). If read out in English, without aspirating the H, it makes the sound 'look'.

Nowadays even rotting animals in formaldehyde do not shock many people; those who are shocked provide artists and gallery owners with gratifying publicity. But in Duchamp's day assaults on convention provoked more dismay. Thirty years later *L.H.O.O.Q.* was still causing anxiety, at least in some quarters. T.H. Robsjohn-Gibbins's *Mona Lisa's Mustache*, a rambling book published in 1948, argued that the Surrealists 'proposed to destroy utterly the entire universe erected by western logic, by inducing the superstition that reality was not reality as it was conceived by Western logic and the normal mind'. By depicting the Mona Lisa *'with a mustache'* (the author's emphasis) the Surrealists hoped that the 'bourgeoisie would begin to teeter between what was real and what was hallucination'.[47]

We now know that the bourgeoisie was made of sterner stuff. Surrealism, as Luis Buñuel wrote in his memoirs, was always far less subversive than it imagined; it was 'the bourgeoisie revolting against the bourgeoisie'.

To superimpose a moustache on a face is a typical schoolboy prank indicating mockery. When Gautier said that, before the *Mona Lisa*, 'we feel timid, like schoolboys in the presence of a duchess', he was building up an icon. When Duchamp chose to behave like a schoolboy, he was questioning its value. His friend the artist Francis Picabia wanted to publish *L.H.O.O.Q.* in the March 1920 issue of his Dadaist magazine *391*. As Duchamp had taken his postcard to New York, Picabia got hold of another *Mona Lisa* postcard, added the moustache, and published it with the caption 'Dada Painting by Marcel Duchamp . . .', forgetting the beard. Duchamp's card had temporarily become as 'unique' as Leonardo's *Mona Lisa*. Later he explained that he intended *L.H.O.O.Q.* to be an aggressive response to the curiosity he had aroused among the members of Picabia's circle, deliberately using 'the symbol of everything that was sacred in museum art'. He also followed Freud in raising the issue of Leonardo's homosexuality by 'masculinising' the *Mona Lisa*.[48] There are numerous interpretations of *L.H.O.O.Q.*, mostly from a Freudian perspective: the facial hair stresses the androgyny of the painting, the male side of the *Mona Lisa* (androgyny is a major theme of Duchamp). Perhaps the beard is a transfer of Lisa's pubic hair to her face. Perhaps Duchamp wanted to remind us that, in some way, Mona *is* Leonardo.[49]

Duchamp's idea was simple and effective. *L.H.O.O.Q.* is still the best-known send-up of the *Mona Lisa*. It may not be Duchamp's most important or significant work, but it made him universally popular. In the early 1920s his fame in New York was unmatched by that of any other living artist. He had become the man who put the moustache on the *Mona Lisa*. Paradoxically, this was, of course, a direct tribute to the renown of the *Joconde*. As Kenneth Clark said, 'Nobody feels compelled to paint a moustache on the upper lip of Hélène Fourment.'[50] Through Duchamp, the avant-garde had symbolically acknowledged that Leonardo's revolutionary portrait had become a synecdoche – a metaphor where a part of the whole stands for the whole. As the expression 'the Crown' stands for the whole institution of the monarchy, so the *Mona Lisa* had progressed from being the expression of enigmatic femininity to representing the entire tradition of Western art, indeed of culture in general. Thus in 1985 Jean Glavany, President Mitterrand's adviser on sport, called his book advocating the union of cultural and physical excellence *La Joconde et Platini*. Michel Platini, the great French footballer, stood for *corpus sanum*, a sound body; Mona Lisa for *mens sana*, the sound mind.[51]

The *Mona Lisa* had become a painting even ignorant people had heard of. Did Leonardo, up in the heavens, in the Old Masters' quarters, smile with satisfaction, exclaiming, 'Michelangelo, Raffaello, Tiziano, eat your heart out'?

In 1930 Duchamp bought another postcard and replicated his stunt. He gave it to the Surrealist poet Louis Aragon, later a Communist. In the 1970s, Aragon in turn donated it to Georges Marchais, the Secretary-General of the French Communist Party – an organisation whose appreciation of avant-garde art has been somewhat limited. Perhaps this was Aragon's last Surrealist gesture.

In 1941 Duchamp – unable to let the *Mona Lisa* go – reproduced separately just the moustache and beard of *L.H.O.O.Q.* In 1944 he went to a New York notary and had his *L.H.O.O.Q.* authenticated. Now it was truly unique. Leonardo had never signed his *Mona Lisa* or taken it with him to a lawyer, Renaissance Florence lacking such bourgeois conventions.

In 1965, probably prompted by the great success of the recent exhibition of the *Mona Lisa* in the United States (see pages 244–5), Duchamp produced a new version of *L.H.O.O.Q.* The invitations for his own American retrospective exhibition consisted of playing cards with the effigy of the *Mona Lisa*, unmodified but for the inscription '*LHOOQ rasée*' (shaved). Leonardo's *Mona Lisa* had now become that of Duchamp, without the moustaches. One such card is now at the New York Museum of Modern Art; another was offered for sale at Christie's in May 1996 with an estimate of $10–12,000.

Duchamp had set a trend. Other renowned icons of high culture, notably the Venus de Milo, would receive similar treatment from Dali, Man Ray, Magritte and others. Hundred of (less original) artists followed in Duchamp's footsteps. There were, inevitably, homages to the 'homage' Duchamp had paid to Leonardo. As he had used Leonardo, others used him – such as Lucio Del Pezzo with his 1962 tempera *Omaggio a Duchamp*: a *Mona Lisa* superimposed on a larger *L.H.O.O.Q.* In 1965 Jean-Jacques Lebel produced a *Portrait de Monna Lisa et de sa doublure Rrose Selavy* ('Rrose Selavy', a pun on 'Eros, that's life', was Duchamp's feminine *alter ego*). Lebel painted just a Groucho Marx moustache on a white circle with, at the top, a reclining naked woman. Most of these remakes were forgotten – in this business it pays to be in on the act early – but they further consolidated the supremacy of the *Mona Lisa*.

In 1963 Salvador Dali objected to Duchamp's 'ultra-intellectual aggression' in giving the *Mona Lisa* facial hair. It was, he wrote, an act of rebellion against a feminine image, masculinising it by defacing it.[52] Dali had presumably forgotten that in 1953 he had told the photographer Philippe Halsman that he had always wanted to look like Mona Lisa. Halsman suggested a photomontage: a Mona Lisa with Dali's moustache. At first, Dali demurred: Duchamp had been there before. Halsman insisted: 'It will be *your* moustaches, *your* eyes and *your* big hands counting money.' Dali accepted, and his dream was realised (see plate 42).

Duchamp also provided André Gide with an idea for his characterisation of the cultural anarchist Armand in his 1925 novel

Les Faux-Monnayeurs ('The Counterfeiters'). Armand, preparing the first issue of the avant-garde review *Le Fer à repasser*, declares: 'There are loads of works that we admire on trust because everyone admires them and because no one has said, or has dared say, that they are stupid. For instance, on the cover of the issue, we will have a reproduction of the *Joconde* with a pair of moustaches. You'll see, pal, it will be terrific.' 'Does that mean,' asks his friend, 'that you think the *Joconde* stupid?' 'Not at all, my dear (though I don't find it all that amazing). You don't understand. What is stupid is the admiration it receives. *Le Fer à repasser* will have the duty to ridicule this worship.'[53]

Museums had become the main target of the avant-garde just as they were becoming open to a wider public. Duchamp, shortly before his death in 1968, said: 'When I go to a museum I am never amazed or astonished or curious in front of a painting . . . I hardly ever go to museums. I have not been to the Louvre in twenty years. It does not interest me. I would take issue with those who have decided that some pictures should be in the Louvre and others should not.'[54]

Duchamp soon became genuinely bored and embarrassed by the hype surrounding modern art. Coherent to the last, he gave it up and spent the remaining forty years of his life in what he thought was a more absorbing occupation: playing chess. He became acclaimed as a genius, as the man who had changed art in the twentieth century, and his work was exhibited in the museums he despised. People contemplated his urinal with awe. Far from demolishing Leonardo, Duchamp had become almost like him.

Gide's *Les Faux-Monnayeurs* had captured well the elitist attitude manifest in the Dadaist movement and its follow-ups. The avant-garde artist, like the artists of the past, was still a superior spirit endowed with special gifts, able to distinguish between what is and what is not art while the despised masses follow, like sheep, the lead of the establishment. When they sent up the *Mona Lisa*, it was art; when caricaturists and cabaret singers did it, they were just caricaturists and cabaret singers.

Be that as it may, even the culturally deprived were now becoming accustomed to the *Mona Lisa*. Fernand Léger illustrated such familiarity in his *La Joconde aux clefs* (1930, see plate 38). He recognised that the *Mona Lisa* was no longer only an icon of high culture but also a household name, an object as familiar as a bunch of keys. His avowed intention was to paint alongside the keys (his own) something that would be 'its absolute opposite':

> I go out and what do I see in a shop window? A postcard of the *Joconde*! I understood at once. This is what I needed. What could be of greater contrast to the keys ... The *Joconde*, for me, is an object like any other.[55]

Léger believed that by reducing the *Mona Lisa* to an object (or, in his terms, *elevating* it to that rank) he was helping to liberate the 'popular masses, giving them the possibility of thinking, seeing, educating themselves, enabling them to enjoy the ... novelties of modern art'.[56]

Léger, who joined the French Communist Party in 1945, after years as a sympathiser, became increasingly aware that he had over-romanticised the notion of 'the people'. In 1950 he complained that museums closed too early: 'Late closing days were introduced. The workers turned up. But they all lined up for the one painting they wanted to see: the *Joconde*; she was the "star", like at the movies. Result: null and void.'[57]

Léger had started his artistic life despising the Renaissance. Its dogmatic commitment towards reproducing reality had, he felt, done untold harm to art, and it had destroyed the great art of the Middle Ages.[58] In 1952 – three years before his death – he must have given up the fight. He agreed to paint the scenery and design the costumes for a ballet to be performed at Amboise to celebrate the five hundredth anniversary of the birth of Leonardo da Vinci.

The contribution of the artistic avant-garde to the global marketing of the *Mona Lisa* was considerable. Of course, the real mass audience materialised only when these techniques were adopted by the advertising industry. But in the USA the appreciation of modern art was rapidly expanding. Duchamp in particular had acquired great fame, as had the *Mona Lisa*, the painting taken to represent the whole of the Italian Renaissance and, indeed, the whole of traditional art. Lisa had now acquired a secure foothold in the USA. Globalisation was just around the corner.

In 1928 the young Communist poet Nazim Hikmet left Moscow to return clandestinely to Turkey, but was caught and detained at Hopa, by the Black Sea. In prison he wrote a long poem, 'Jokond ile Si-Ya-Ou' ('The *Gioconda* and Si-Ya-Ou'). The poem – a mixture of lyricism and irreverence, magic realism before its time – tells the story of Si-Ya-Ou, a young Chinese who falls in love with Mona Lisa. It opens with a familiar theme. Mona is bored at the Louvre: 'to visit a museum is fine,/to be an object in a museum is dire'. Then she notices Si-Ya-Ou's frequent visits. She hears him ask:

> Those who crush our rice paddies under the tracks
>   of their tanks,
> Those who stroll in our cities like emperors from
>   hell,
> Do they belong to the species that has also created
>   you?

Suddenly, Si-Ya-Ou stops coming. Mona Lisa realises the French have deported him. Feeling sad, she curses Leonardo for inflicting upon her a permanent smile: 'May Leonardo's bones be used as brushes by a cubist painter.' Driven by love, she escapes from the Louvre and reaches China, where she witnesses the massacre of the Communists by the troops of the Kuomintan and the death of her Si-Ya-Ou.

> And so it was that in Shanghai, on this day of death
> The Florentine Gioconda lost
> A smile more famous than Florence.

Mona Lisa takes up the struggle against imperialism as an audacious guerrilla fighter. She is arrested and tried by a French military court. An art expert pleads on her behalf: 'This is the famous Mona Lisa. The great Leonardo painted her . . . think of the Renaissance . . .' But the military court does not care about art, and orders that Mona Lisa be shot at dawn. Rather than let her suffer such a fate, her comrades set her on fire. Enveloped in the red glow of the flames, the Gioconda dies, her heart smiling, her face laughing.[59] Hikmet, a member of the guard of honour at Lenin's funeral in 1924, and one of the great voices of Turkish poetry, remained in prison for twenty-two years, not being released until 1950. He did not see the *Mona Lisa* until 1958, during his first trip to Paris. He died in Moscow in 1963.

A patriotic Mona Lisa can also be found in the short story 'Mona Lisa', written in September 1937 by Ba Jin, a prominent Chinese writer. A French woman takes her meals with her young son in a Shanghai restaurant. She has the 'look of Leonardo's Mona Lisa . . . There was a smile on her face, with yet a hint of loneliness to it.' The Japanese have recently shot down her husband, a daring air pilot. Now 'Mona Lisa' feels strongly: 'I would want my husband to give his life for the happiness of his fellow-countrymen, when all China is in uproar with anger and the time has come to repay blood debts in blood.'[60]

In some instances the twentieth-century exploitation of Mona Lisa was merely a development of nineteenth-century themes, enhanced by the notoriety the theft had brought about. For example, in 1914 Max von Schillings composed the opera *Mona Lisa*, to a libretto by Beatrice Dovsky (first performed in Berlin in 1915). Lisa Gherardini – a classic *femme fatale* – has a lover called Giovanni. When her husband unexpectedly returns, Giovanni hides. The increasingly convoluted plot ends tragically, with the unintended death of Giovanni and with Lisa murdering her husband.[61]

Often the name 'Mona Lisa' functions as a lure to attract an audience. Raymond Souplex's trivial *Autour de la Joconde*, a one-act play first performed in Paris on 5 October 1933, is about a bourgeois couple having an argument. The audience is invited to laugh at the expense of the wife, who thinks that Rembrandt painted the *Mona Lisa* and Milo sculpted the Venus.[62]

In Aldous Huxley's story 'The Gioconda Smile' (in his 1920 collection *Mortal Coils*; later versions use *The Gioconda Smile* as the overall title), the 'Gioconda' is Miss Janet Spence, a 'virgin of thirty-six' who fancies the lazy Henry Hutton. It is Henry, 'in a moment of half-ironical flattery', who once referred to her 'Gioconda smile'. Janet took the compliment seriously, and 'always tried to live up to the Leonardo standard'. This is enough to provide the story with its catchy title. Janet is poisoning Henry's ailing wife with arsenic, convinced that, once widowed, Henry will marry her. When the wife dies, Janet's hopes are dashed. Henry had been having a secret affair with a younger and prettier woman all along, and he now marries her. Janet had not even crossed his mind. Having discovered how insensitive men can be, the revengeful Janet accuses Henry of his wife's murder. An inquest is held, and traces of arsenic are found in the body. Henry, who had a motive, is arrested, tried and executed. Now Janet can smile again – Gioconda-like. This was hardly Huxley's best work, but it was adapted for the stage (performed for the first time in New York in 1950),[63] and in 1966 it was turned into a film in Germany.

Schillings's opera and Huxley's short story addressed themselves to a relatively up-market audience. This was not the case with Georges Spitzmuller, author of a string of popular novels. His *Les Amours de François I et de la Joconde* was published in 1920 by the Paris-based Fayard, in their famous series *Le Livre populaire*. At sixty-five centimes per volume, the printers, who were earning 3.45 francs an hour, could easily afford it themselves.[64]

Spitzmuller tells the imaginative story of the sex life of King François I and Mona Lisa. She turns up only two-thirds of the way through the book, after François has already fallen in love with another woman, a blonde of 'almost superhuman' beauty who, unfortunately, is abducted and severely wounded by an arrow. As she dies in the arms of the king, she flashes a final 'angelic and divine smile'.[65] François is sad, but not too depressed: in Italy he had met the pope, who had shown him the portrait of an enigmatic woman. It was, the pope had said helpfully, the portrait of the famous Gioconda (misspelled throughout the book as 'Giochonda') painted by Leonardo. François is attracted by it. As the plot thickens, Mona Lisa, who is also Leonardo's mistress, joins the king in France, with her husband in hot pursuit. François is eager to meet 'this adorable creature with her exciting eyes and her lascivious smile'.[66] Lisa is easily seduced by the handsome king, whose love for all things Italian is legendary. Meanwhile the husband, realising that all those who have looked at the portrait of his wife have fallen in love with her, attempts unsuccessfully to destroy it.

In the middle of the nineteenth century Jules Michelet had written, 'This portrait attracts me, revolts me.'[67] The sentiment had now become common. It could be assimilated into a work of popular literature without being relinquished by the more traditional intelligentsia. Ortega y Gasset, whose elitism harked back to pre-mass society, repeated in the 1930s what had already been said some eighty years earlier: the smile repels and attracts; the *Joconde* is the symbol of extreme femininity, she is mother, daughter, wife, sister. She is the counterpart of Don Juan, and so on. A few weeks after the theft he had called the portrait the representation of Nuestra Señora del Descontento (Our Lady of Discontent). It depicted, he wrote, 'temptation itself', for Mona Lisa showed those who looked at her something desirable that was other than themselves, making them long for an ideal.[68]

It was now generally accepted that the *Mona Lisa* was not an ordinary masterpiece. Its status was enhanced in multifarious ways, sometimes imperceptibly, as if some invisible marketing agency had been charged with the long-term historical task of promoting the painting. Its predominance was increasingly taken for granted. It represented all the great masterpieces of Western art. The press coverage compounded this. Thus when, during the Second World War, the *Mona Lisa*, along with all the other important Louvre paintings, was provided with central heating in the manor houses to which it had been evacuated, the headline was: '*On installe le chauffage central pour la Joconde*' ('Central heating installed for the *Mona Lisa*').[69]

Yet, for Mona Lisa, the best (or the worst) was yet to come. In the second half of the twentieth century, the mass society that had taken its first steps at the end of the nineteenth came into its own. People became wealthier and better educated, better informed and better travelled. When Walter Pater wrote that the *Mona Lisa* was the 'symbol of the modern idea', he could not have imagined that every advance of modern society – mass travel, advertising, popular culture – would contribute to make his 'lady of the rocks' far more famous than any other lady in the world.

CHAPTER NINE

Lisa Goes Pop

Iconoclastic attacks on the *Mona Lisa* have been 'one of the surest (if most perverse) tributes that other artists have paid the painting'.[1] The same can be said of less metaphorical forms of iconoclasm, such as vandalism.

On 30 December 1956 Hugo Unzaga Villegas, a forty-two-year-old Bolivian, threw a stone at the *Mona Lisa*, slightly damaging its elbow. The following day, the story was covered by almost every newspaper in the world, from the *East Anglian Daily Times* to the *Royal Gazette* of Bermuda and the Polish *Zycie Warszawy*. The newspaper cuttings fill three large boxes carefully preserved in the Louvre documentation centre.[2] A psychiatric report on Villegas by Dr Gouriou (14 January 1957) found that the man was insane, heard strange voices, and had intended to murder the Argentinean dictator Juan Perón, but went instead for the less well protected *Mona Lisa*. Though the event was certainly newsworthy, it could not produce on its own more than one or two paragraphs of copy, at least on the first day. But newspapers fill the available space with relevant items from their file of clippings and with quotes obtained from accessible and serviceable experts.

Anyone could come up with a view of the attack, even years later. In 1963 Salvador Dali provided his own 'Freudian' interpretation: imagine, he wrote, a naive Bolivian visiting the Louvre. He perceives the museum as a whorehouse full of naked, shameless statues – these Rubenses, this naked flesh. He notices, hanging on a wall, the portrait of his own mother. What is she doing in a place like this? She too must be a whore. What's more, she is smiling ambiguously at him. He has two options: the first is to run away with the portrait and hide it, piously, where it cannot be found; the second is to assault it.[3] Dali has a point. It is difficult to imagine an attack on Raphael's *Baldissare Castiglione* (though he could look like someone's father). Usually, men who attack pictures attack those representing women

Unzaga Villegas's stone ensured that selected aspects of the *Mona Lisa* story would be told all over again; in particular, the story of the theft, along with a couple of lines from some well-known cultural sources – usually Freud, since by the 1950s Gautier and Pater were no longer household names. Then one could dwell on any of the three canonical mysteries: Why is the smile enigmatic? Who was the model? Is the Louvre *Mona Lisa* authentic?

Nothing could be simpler than to get a few experts to come up with apparently controversial comments on any of the above. *Mona Lisa* stories are among the easiest for the press to cover. Name recognition is very high among readers. The few who had not heard of it could be authoritatively informed that it was the best-known picture in the world, painted by a universal genius. The controversies surrounding it were of importance only to specialists, yet were of interest even to those who, quite rightly, did not really care who was the model. Stories about the *Mona Lisa* could be classed as 'cultural' while being of interest to both ends of the market.[4]

As a marketing instrument working on behalf of the *Mona Lisa*, Hugo Unzaga Villegas's blow had an effect comparable to Marcel Duchamp's moustaches, and produced even greater coverage. Besides, Lisa's 'high culture' association with Leonardo continued to bear fruit. Throughout the twentieth century the reputation of Leonardo had grown exponentially – largely because of its scientific connection. He was the kind of scientist everyone felt familiar with, even without knowing what it was he had discovered or invented. The four hundredth anniversary of his death (1919) had been a relatively muted affair, but the five hundredth anniversary of his birth (1952) was widely celebrated. By then Leonardo had 'won' the popularity contest against his traditional rivals Raphael and Michelangelo. The evidence is all around us, in the imperceptible but systematic, and often unwitting, promotion of Leonardo's image. Neither Raphael nor Michelangelo, for instance, benefits from a pre-installed screensaver on Microsoft Windows 98 software. 'Leonardo', 'Raphael' and 'Michaelangelo' (sic) as well as 'Donatello' were the names given in 1984 by Kevin Eastman and Peter Lairdin (both had studied art history at university) to their enormously successful Teenage Mutant Ninja Turtles, a comic-book strip which led to toys, games and a television animation series. The leader of the Turtles was, of course, Leonardo.[5]

Raphael in particular has suffered from his failure to produce a strikingly popular piece of work such as Michelangelo's *David*. Raphael's life has never been turned into a best-selling book, as Michelangelo's was in Irving Stone's *The Agony and the Ecstasy* (1961), later adapted into a successful film starring Charlton Heston (1963).

In the nineteenth century Lisa travelled on the back of the better-known Leonardo, but in the twentieth she became bigger than her creator, particularly in the mass market, where, as all advertisers know, the real money is made. In 1934 Cole Porter wrote the song 'You're the Top' for his famous show *Anything Goes*, in which the Mona Lisa smile was – inevitably – included in the list of items that are 'the top':

> ... You're the Nile;
> You're the Tower of Pisa;
> You're the smile
> on the *Mona Lisa* ...

Ella Fitzgerald has sung it (beautifully), and so have Fats Waller, Dionne Warwick, Barbra Streisand and many others. The idea that *Mona Lisa* was 'the top' became a matter of course, even in chess: the grand master Eduard Gufeld called his greatest triumph his 'Gioconda game'.[6]

An even greater hit than 'You're the Top' (in which Lisa shared the honours with other 'tops') was the song 'Mona Lisa', by Jay Livingston and Ray Evans. Nat 'King' Cole made it famous, singing it in the film *Captain Carey USA* (1950), for which it gained the Academy Award for best song. Cole's wife Maria had objected to his recording the song, feeling than an 'offbeat thing about an old painting wouldn't go'.[7] Nat insisted, and was proved right: 'Mona Lisa' resolved, at a stroke, his financial problems. It hit the number one spot on the US charts in July 1950, and became the biggest-selling record of the year. Five other singers, less well-known than Cole, also made it into 1950's top three hundred by singing 'Mona Lisa': Don Cherry (No. 53), Charlies Spivak (198), Harry James (192), Ralph Flanagan (243) and Dennis Day (249).[8] The song has since been recorded by Pat Boone, Bing Crosby, Marlene Dietrich, Elvis Presley, Paul Anka, Conway Twitty, Donny Osmond, Tom Jones, Julio Iglesias, Englebert Humperdinck and many others. Jazz versions have included those by Sonny Rollins and, in Japan, Masabumi Kibuchi. It has been included in a French compilation of songs about women called '*de l'éternel féminin*', sung by Tino Rossi, whose distinctive rolling 'r', Mediterranean intonation and Italianate tenor voice were still fashionable in France in the 1950s.[9] But Nat King Cole's remained the classic version. Almost forty years after his untimely death in 1965, anyone tuning to an 'easy listening' radio station is still highly likely to hear it.

> Mona Lisa, Mona Lisa, men have named you.
> You're so like the lady with the mystic smile.
> Is it only 'cause you're lonely they have blamed you?
> For that Mona Lisa strangeness in your smile?
> Do you smile to tempt a lover, Mona Lisa?
> Or is this your way to hide a broken heart?
> Many dreams have been brought to your doorstep

They just lie there and they die there.
Are you warm, are you real, Mona Lisa?
Or just a cold and lonely, lovely work of art?

Nearly a hundred years had gone by since Théophile Gautier had created 'his' *Mona Lisa*. The image had now travelled across the oceans, and turned into the lyrics of a song. Well over a million people bought it in 1950 alone. Tens of million listened to it. A great black American singer, backed by a powerful cultural industry, had made the Florentine lady more famous than ever. Would Gautier, if he could witness the event, smile in his turn, surprised at the distance travelled by that 'strangeness in your smile' from the relatively enclosed art world of mid-nineteenth century Paris? Yet perhaps, seen from a wider perspective, Gautier's and Nat King Cole's worlds were not so far apart: both were selling dreams, both partaking of the modern imagination and of its overwhelming urge to be fascinated by romantic love, by its fantasies, its mysteries, its strangeness and its familiarity.

In 1986 the song made an appearance in Neil Jordan's film *Mona Lisa*. This harsh, gritty film has nothing to do with Leonardo's picture, even indirectly. It starred Bob Hoskins as George, a kind-hearted ex-con who becomes the bodyguard and driver of Simone (Cathy Tyson), a high-class prostitute with whom he becomes infatuated in spite of her initial contempt for him, and for herself ('Having me is nothing, George – any prick can have me'). George, struggling against his subordinate status, insists on listening to a song on his car's tapedeck. It's Nat King Cole's 'Mona Lisa'. Eventually Simone forces him to switch it off. She does not wish to be reminded that, like the Mona Lisa of the song, she is all alone.[10]

Livingston and Evans's has remained the most famous of the songs using a Mona Lisa theme. If you phone the Hotel Monna Lisa in Florence and are put on hold, what you hear is Nat King Cole's voice singing 'Mona Lisa, Mona Lisa, men have named you . . .' Of course, Mona Lisa has more than one song. In Germany Willy Forst sang 'Warum lachelst du, Mona Lisa?' ('Why do you smile, Mona Lisa?'), appropriately used in the film *Der raub der Mona Lisa* ('The Abduction of *Mona Lisa*'). In 1975 it was the turn of the Alexandria-born Greek singer Demis Roussos with 'Schön wie Mona Lisa (Wenn ich ein Maler wär)', that is, 'Beautiful as Mona Lisa (When I was a Painter)'. In Italy, Umberto Tozzi sang 'Il mistero di Lisa' (1977):

> *In un vuota sala del Louvre*
> *siamo soli io e te.*
> *l'allarme suona, portami via,*
> *Lisa è la mia follia.*
> *Lisa Lisa . . .*

> (In an empty room at the Louvre
> we are alone, you and I.
> The alarm sounds. Take me away!
> Lisa is my madness.)

In French cabarets the intellectual *chanteuse* Barbara sang an ironic 'La Joconde', originally composed for a 1957 French television documentary by Henri Gruel and Jean Suyeux:

> *C'est moi que je suis la Joconde.*
> *Mon sourire vient d'outre-tombe.*
> *Attendez que le vernis tombe.*
> *Attendez la fin du monde*
> *Et je sourirai sous les bombes.*

> (It is I who am the *Joconde*.
> My smile, it comes from the after-life.
> Wait until the varnish crumbles.
> Wait until the end of the world.
> And I shall smile underneath the bombs.)

Nor did Mona Lisa escape the attention of Bob Dylan (1966):

Inside the museums, Infinity goes up on trial
Voices echo, this is what salvation must be like after
  a while
But Mona Lisa musta had the highway blues
You can tell by the way she smiles.[11]

Nor could we forget Elton John's 'Mona Lisa and Mad Hatters' (1972):

While Mona Lisas and Mad Hatters,
Sons of bankers, sons of lawyers,
Turn around and say good morning to the night,
For unless they see the sky,
But they can't, and that is why
They know not if it's dark outside or light.

Or his 1985 'Wrap her Up' (from the album *Ice on Fire*):

There are ladies, illegal X's
Mona Lisas, well connected
They may be shady, English roses
Blue blooded, turned-up noses.

By 1988, in 'Mona Lisa and Mad Hatters Part 2', Elton John sings that while 'Spanish Harlem still sounds good to me ... Yeah, Mona Lisa's getting older'.

Robert Charles Voice went for a (very) slightly more intellectual approach: his '3D Mona Liza' throws in a cultural reference to Frans Hals's *The Laughing Cavalier*:

Your canvas is getting faded,
your eyes have lost the shine.
Your frame is housing woodworm,
Though your smile still freezes time.
See, the doors are closing,
the clock is striking nine.
Climb out of your picture frame
And climb on in mine.

Oh, Madame, I like your brushwork,
It's a pleasure to be near.
Will you accept the compliment
From a laughing cavalier?

Increasingly the name is used without any other references to the painting, except, at most, a veiled reference to the smile. We have moved a long way from Lisa Gherardini and Leonardo's picture. The name has become detached from its origin and takes on a life of its own.

In 1988 Slick Rick (Rick Walters) chanted, with rap-like aplomb:

It was one of those days, not much to do,
I was in downtown, with my old school crew.
I went into a store to buy a slice of pizza,
and bumped into a girl whose name was Mona Lizza.

In the *Cut Killer* remix compilation (Sony) these lyrics are countered with the 1960s hit 'Walk on by'. Less original was Shawn Colvin's 1997 British pop 'You and the *Mona Lisa*': 'I love you the most. There is sweet mystery. There is nothing in between you and Mona Lisa.' More successful was the Swedish singer Carola, who included in her song 'Främling' ('Stranger'), runner-up in the 1983 Eurovision Song Contest, the words 'Mona Lisa has her smile and you too hide a secret'.

In 1993 *Leonardo the Musical: A Portrait of Love* opened in London. In 2000 another musical, *Da Vinci*, written, composed and directed by Christian Schittenhelm, opened in Paris. The advertising poster reproduced just the hands of the *Mona Lisa*, by then so well known as not to warrant further explanation. It announced Marco Valeriani in the role of Leonardo and Léa La Liberté as Mona Lisa, and claimed to have the support of the Louvre, keen to 'bring to life the paintings'. Partner in the enterprise was the City of Paris, which, according to the brochure, 'spontaneously encouraged the initiative from the very beginning of it's [sic] conception'. The sponsors were the Japanese firm

ARITA Porcelain, which contributed to the event 'by bringing to it it's [sic] refined Japanese creativity and it's [sic] cultural history which dates back to 1616'. The lighting 'associates Leonardo's sanguine technique with paintings and drawing of the Japanese painter, Yoshinobu Toïdé'.

By the 1990s 'Mona Lisa' had just become someone's name. Thus in 1992 Jacques Higelin, a midly *engagé* French rock singer, famous in the francophone world but less so elsewhere, sang 'Mona Lisa Klaxon': 'I know only one girl called Mona Lisa Klaxon. She lives in an island surrounded by crocodiles and ghosts, she is black like ebony and plays the trombone.' Similarly, in Carlos Santana's chart-topping 'Smooth' (2000) there is no longer any connection with the Louvre *Mona Lisa*: 'But you stay so cool/My Muñequita, my Spanish Harlem/Mona Lisa/You're my reason for reason.'

However, the smile had not disappeared from pop music. On the album *Bang Bang Boom* (2000) by Moffatts, the average age of whom is sixteen, the second song starts, 'Early morning, I've got Mona Lisa by my side, what's the story behind that devious smile?', while in the video 'Tulsa, Tokyo and the Middle of Nowhere' (1998) the seventeen-year-old lead singer of Hanson is seen by the entrance to the Louvre shouting 'Mona Lisaaaa.'

In literature, the Mona Lisa smile had become an almost idiomatic expression indicating a range of possible enigmatic behaviour. Thus in D.H. Lawrence's short story 'The Lovely Lady' (1932), the 'wonderfully preserved' Pauline Attenborough (she is seventy-two) has 'a gay look like a Leonardo woman who could laugh outright'. That is her outward persona, to be deployed with those she liked. With them 'she was her lovely and changeless self, that age could not wither, nor custom stale: so bright and kindly and yet subtly mocking, like Mona Lisa who knew a thing or two'.[12]

In Stella Gibbons's Second World War novel *Westwood* (1946), the canonic status of the *Mona Lisa* is questioned. The heroine, Margaret, a schoolteacher with cultural pretensions, shows her friend Hilda her bedroom. Hilda expresses powerful dislike of a reproduction of the *Mona Lisa*: '. . . honestly, I don't know how you can bear to have that fat pan looking at you when you wake up in the morning. It would brown me off for the day.' Such is the power of this criticism that Margaret can defend herself only weakly: '"It's beautiful," said Margaret, but even as she spoke a faint doubt assailed her. Was it?'[13]

That the smile could mean different things to different people is made clear by Lawrence Durrell in *Justine* (1957). The narrator tells of old Scobie, who has, hanging next to the crucifix on the wall behind his bed, a small print of the *Mona Lisa*, 'whose enigmatic smile has always reminded Scobie of his mother'. But the narrator has another view: 'For my part the famous smile has always seemed to me to be the smile of a woman who has just dined off her husband.'[14]

The smile could become an inward one, as when one smiles to oneself, in secret. Lakey, one of eight young Vassar women, all members of 'The Group' in Mary McCarthy's famous novel of 1963, is an enigmatic lesbian with a 'faint smile in the depth of her green eyes', who 'never enlarged on a suggestion, and for this had been named the Mona Lisa of the Smoking Room'.[15]

Even Jean Paul Sartre used the smile to describe his grand-mother's absorption in the pleasures of reading:

> She would settle herself by the window, in her winged armchair, put on her spectacles, sigh with pleasure and weariness, and lower her eyelids with a delicately vol-uptuous smile which I have since discovered on the lips on the *Mona Lisa*.[16]

Until recently, traditional popular fiction tended to use *Mona Lisa* themes fairly closely related to the painting's historical con-text (the Renaissance) or to well-trodden images such as the mystery of the smile. Mona Lisa was used to make an ordinary love plot more interesting in Serge Raffalovich and H.M. Mons's 1935 *La Joconde: Le Roman d'amour de Léonard de Vinci et de*

Mona Lisa. In this romantic story Mona Lisa has become, after her marriage to Francesco il Giocondo, one of the most desirable women in Florence, enjoying, without ever succumbing to, temptation. Her husband is, of course, a bore.[17] (The disparagement of Giocondo, incidentally, is a staple element in all accounts of the Mona Lisa story throughout the nineteenth and twentieth centuries. In reality we know virtually nothing about his private life – for all we know he might have been incredibly handsome, witty and a formidable lover.) Having seen Leonardo at a public meeting, Lisa convinces her husband to commission the portrait so that she can see Leonardo regularly. He loves her too, but they never sleep together. The novel's authors, aware that by then Lisa's features were well known, accept that she was not a classic beauty. They note her 'puffy' cheeks, her 'too broad' forehead and her 'wrinkled' eyes, but add that, nonetheless, she possessed charm and a strange seductiveness.

We have seen how a similar theme has been used previously, for instance in Schuré's 1905 drama *Léonard de Vinci* (see pages 168–70). One of the effects of such narratives, as well as of much of the Romantic commentary of the nineteenth century, recycled in the twentieth, has been to give Mona Lisa an increasingly leading role in the story of the painting. We have thus witnessed the transformation of an inert object into a protagonist. Mona Lisa's passivity had taken two forms. In the first place we are dealing with an object, the product of the labour of a individual, Leonardo. In the second we are dealing with the role of the sitter, who by definition co-operates, if at all, in a totally subordinate role to the creation of the work. Her function is to acquire the characteristics of an object, almost pretending to be one, renouncing her individual will and consenting to take the shape (the position) indicated by the painter. This is a clearly 'gendered' position. The (usually) male painter is the true creator, who demands of the (usually female) sitter that she become an object. As the painting has become a story, and an ever-developing one at that, a reversal of positions has occurred. Lisa becomes increas-

ingly active. Leonardo moves (relatively speaking) into the background. This is more evident in popular fiction, such as the
Raffalovich and Mons novel, because the genre dictates that it
should be the woman who imparts the knowledge of the importance of romantic love (and the suffering it can bring) to the
man. This convention starts with the biblical story of Adam and
Eve. It is Eve who is the motor force. It is she, and not Adam,
who changes position. From being a mere rib of Adam's she
turns into the primeval cause of their expulsion from a changeless
world. It is Eve, not Adam, the woman, not the man, who kick-
starts humanity into history.

Leonardo, though constantly lionised for centuries, is only an
inventor and creator of *things*, objects without souls. He is someone who takes a living person and transforms her into an object.
He is an imitator of nature, a maker of surrogates. Lisa (the
imagined Lisa, of course) does the opposite. Leonardo wants to
turn her into an object; she turns him into a human being. This
can only be made to happen by using narrative forms, whether
fictional (including songs), or semi-fictional versions of art criticism, such as those of Gautier and Pater. All of these, leaving aside
subjective aesthetic considerations, have a fundamental point in
common: they create a woman with human attributes.

In the second half of the twentieth century we witnessed a
kind of backlash. Mona Lisa became an object once again, as her
features were used and distorted by an endless succession of
painters, advertisers and caricaturists. It is the revenge of the
artist. Leonardo's *Mona Lisa* (the painted object, not the imagined
woman) is again a model, passively allowing itself to be whatever
others want it to be.

Increasingly, fictional stories, particularly after the Second
World War, when the name was well established, simply inserted
the magic words 'Mona Lisa' or 'Gioconda' into the title, adding
some perfunctory references to smiles or enigmatic behaviour to
the text. For instance, Guy Fau's *Le Sourire de la Joconde* (1961)
is a mystery story involving double identities, the hunt for Jewish

gold hidden from the Nazis and the Marseilles underworld. The title was justified by the author providing the female protagonist with a 'beauty immortalised by the Italian painters of the Renaissance', a 'disturbing smile, a smile of an angel or a demon', and, finally, a lover who tells her she has the smile of the *Mona Lisa*, adding, for the cultural improvement of the reader: 'I wonder about the hidden meaning of the famous smile. Some critics are not even sure of the real identity of the sitter.'[18]

One of the most successful of the hard-boiled crime novels published by the *Fleuve Noir* imprint was San-Antonio's *Passez-moi la Joconde* (1954), which had sold some 550,000 copies by 1988. The only mention of the *Joconde* occurs at the end of the novel when San-Antonio (the author is also the hero) discovers that the head of a criminal gang is a beautiful woman. When she is discovered she poisons herself with a potion hidden inside her ring, like a Renaissance heroine. San-Antonio exclaims: '*Elle a trop lu de romans policiers, la Joconde!*' ('She read too many crime stories, the Joconde!').[19]

In Daniel Odier's *Gioconda* (1984) the eponymous heroine is a young American searching for her roots and soul in a voyage of discovery in Mexico. Her 'only treasure' is a newspaper clipping of the *Mona Lisa*, given to her by her dying grandmother.[20] Otherwise she just sleeps around and has her portrait painted by an artist and lover whose name, distressingly, is Ken.

Between the wars too, however, the name was used as a marketing ploy. Thus in Albert Boissière's *La Joconde aux enchères* (1929), Roland, to resolve the financial predicament of his aristocratic family, must marry a rich English heiress whose name is Nelly and who, of course, looks like a horse (this is a standard Continental stereotype). The novel's title is justified by having a psychic black jazz musician telling a cabaret audience that someone is thinking of stealing the *Mona Lisa*. This, however, turns out to be Grazia, a capricious young Italian woman, and a 'living enigma' even to her parents. Her nickname is, of course, 'Joconde'.[21]

Children's books featuring the *Mona Lisa* are a special case.

They began to appear in some numbers only when the popularity of the painting had become overwhelming. The *Mona Lisa* may have limited appeal for children, but their parents, who are the buyers, may be attracted by the illusion of educational side-effects for their offspring. Thus these books stick closely to some of the established themes. For instance, Jocelyne Zacharezuk's *l'Escapade de Mona Lisa* (1994) is the story of the magic disappearance of Mona Lisa from the actual painting. She leaves behind the land-scape, the rocks etc., and returns to Florence. Two teenagers, Frédéric and Marie-Ange, find her there, among the tourists, and they become friends. This gives Lisa the opportunity to impart a few art-historical anecdotes, such as that she was entertained while posing. Eventually she is re-integrated into the Louvre pic-ture. There are some in-jokes for the benefit of better-informed parents: the Louvre guard is called Duchamp, and the book ends with Frédéric saying to Marie-Ange: 'This woman loves being an enigma.'[22]

Catherine Ternaux's *Le Secret de la Joconde* (1997) is for nine-year-olds and above and has a nine-year-old heroine, Amandine Toupet, who loves drawing and painting. One night Amandine goes to the Louvre to discover the real secret of the *Mona Lisa*. She finds Lisa with her eyes closed, mouth open and snoring. She wakes up, and they start chatting. The main plot of the story concerns the attempted theft of the painting, and its rescue by Amandine. During the course of the action Mona Lisa tells Aman-dine that Leonardo had invented a magic powder which, if mixed with paint, has the power to bring a painting to life; that she did not like the landscape behind her; that Leonardo had found her quite exigent and jealous of other women. Leonardo had realised an artist's life could be quite a bother, and never painted again.[23]

The Mona Lisa Mystery (1981) by Pat Hutchins involves Hamp-stead Primary School's Class 3, on a bus trip to Paris the main purpose of which is to see the Eiffel Tower and the *Mona Lisa*. The children witness the theft of the painting, and investigate. Eventually it is recovered, hidden in the bandages of the allegedly bad leg of a woman impersonating one of the teachers (for the purpose of this book and its readers, the *Mona Lisa* is, once more, on canvas).[24]

Along the same lines but for younger children, and with a manifestly pedagogical aim, is James Mayhew's *Katie and the Mona Lisa* (1998). Katie is taken to the Louvre by her grandma. She is invited by Mona Lisa (bored with smiling all the time, and grateful for the visit) to join her inside the painting, and from there onto a little escapade inside various famous Renaissance paintings, with Mona Lisa calling the little girl '*bambina*' and exclaiming '*Mamma mia!*' At the end of the story, grandma, who had dozed off, asks Katie what she would like for supper: '"Pasta and ice-cream," said Katie . . . And she smiled a secret smile, just like Mona Lisa.'[25]

In Jamila Gavin's short story 'Mona' (2001), a Mars Bar-eating pet Vietnamese pot-bellied pig is called Mona after 'a painting of a beautiful woman with a mysterious smile', as her owner's mother explains. A thief steals the family car, but is scared out of his wits when he sees the piglet on the back seat with its 'black face, with great big floppy ears, a nose more like a snout and two beady eyes which gleaned like a demon. It smiled – a mysterious smile.'[26]

Historical novels are never out of fashion. Among the more recent in a long stream to refer to the *Mona Lisa* is E.L. Konigsburg's *The Second Mrs Gioconda* (1975). Here the leading role is taken by Salai, Leonardo's assistant. There is dialogue with lines such as 'Hey, Leonardo.' Much of the action takes place at the court of Lodovico il Moro, with Leonardo painting the portraits of the duke's mistresses. In the last pages the action shifts to Florence. A timid and uncouth merchant turns up at Leonardo's home and asks Salai whether he thinks Leonardo will deign to paint the portrait of his second wife. Salai is about to turn him down, then he looks at Lisa, and realises 'there was something haunting about this lady's look, something that only Leonardo could capture in paint'.[27] The rest, as they say, is history.

The Private Life of Mona Lisa (1976) is by Pierre La Mure, an author who compares himself to Tolstoy. The plot, however, is quite unoriginal. Civil strife in Renaissance Florence provides some of the background. Lisa had been in love with Giuliano de Medici, but marries the older Francesco il Giocondo. Giuliano ask Leonardo to find Mona Lisa and paint her portrait, but dies before it is finished. This is why Leonardo takes the portrait with him to France. Thus a number of art-historical mysteries are resolved at a stroke.[28]

Mona Lisa could hardly have been ignored by the comic strip – its appearance in *Li'l Abner* has been noted, and it has also been used in *Mandrake the Magician*. The genre is particularly popular in France, where in 1969 the BD (*bande-dessinée*, the French term for comic strip) *Time is Money*, by Alexis and Fred, told the story of a mad scientist, Stanislas, who has invented a time machine. His idea is to travel back to the Renaissance and convince Leonardo to sell him the *Mona Lisa*. The sad truth he discovers is that – contrary to received wisdom – Leonardo is a ne'er-do-well who has never thought about taking up painting, and Mona Lisa is a rather bovine and heavy-set woman who never smiles. When Leonardo is convinced to draw her the results are disastrous: he just can't draw.[29]

Mona Lisa could not possibly miss out on one of the most successful literary genres, romantic fiction. The market leaders in this field are Harlequin Books, part of a Canadian conglomerate that also controls the British publishers Mills & Boon. By 1998 they were selling 160 million books a year, in twenty-four languages.[30] Some of the larger French publishing houses followed suit with romantic series of their own, such as Presse de la Cité with their *Collection Turquoise*. The French ownership makes very little difference to the strict adherence to a set formula: the heroine is a nice young woman who is genteel but not rich, and probably a virgin. She is invariably blonde. Her mother is always dead, but there is a father she loves dearly. The man she fancies is always dark, has a prestigious job or a title, and is sexually experienced. However, he has some character defects, possibly because he is temporarily infatuated with the heroine's rival, who is a brunette and no longer a virgin. The story consists in establishing how the nice blonde will rescue her man from the clutches of the brunette and give him the chance to improve himself. As these novels, rather prudently, never go into post-marital life, we never get to find out whether or not she succeeds. Georgina Hardy's *Aimez-vous la Joconde?* (1981) adheres religiously to the formula. The blonde heroine is called Monna Lisa because her father (a widower who runs a bookshop) had a passion for the famous portrait. She works at the Louvre, and pays a visit to the *Mona Lisa* every day. This is where she meets Lucas Cramer (possibly the author's little joke, a reference to Leonardo's great contemporary Lucas Cranach), a handsome and wealthy architect who teaches at MIT. He approaches her with '*Aimez-vous la Joconde?*' She knows at once that this is Mr Right: he has dark hair, tanned skin and white teeth. Unfortunately he also has a relationship with a sexy and beautiful South American woman, the dark-haired Dolorès. By the time Cramer gets round to ditching Dolorès and finding true love with Monna, the readers have been given some basic information on the Louvre, Leonardo and the famous portrait.[31]

From romantic fiction we move to post-modern cyberpunk sci-fi and William Gibson's cult 'sprawl novel' *Mona Lisa Over-drive* (1988).[32] A Cleveland prostitute, Mona Lisa, is rebuilt thanks to biotechnology to look like the international pop star Angela Mitchell, whose brain has been implanted with biochip devices. Angela is described as 'the most famous face in the world', and after her surgery Mona Lisa 'looked at the face in the mirror and tried on that famous smile'.[33]

Georgina Hardy's *Aimez-vous la Joconde?* and Gibson's *Mona Lisa Overdrive* share a Mona Lisa theme, but little else. Though their different audiences are equally aware of who and what the Mona Lisa is, *Aimez-vous la Joconde?* takes the popularity of the painting as a fact of life not to be questioned. Its attitude is self-comfortingly elitist: noble spirits endowed with a special sensitivity, such as the heroine and the hero – and by implication the readers – can understand the *Mona Lisa* better (its mysterious charm, etc.) than the uncomprehending hordes of tourists. Ideologically, we are still in the nineteenth century. It is all a matter of knowing what to say. This is a novel that appeals to the uncomplicated in us, to our desire to be told a straightforward story with a recognisable backdrop. Gibson's novel, by contrast, has an intricate plot, difficult or impossible to follow (I found it impossible). Nevertheless it has the merit of conjuring up disturbing images. Its relationship to the *Mona Lisa* (save for the title) may appear to be minimal, but it raises directly the question of what it is that constitutes celebrity and fame. The prostitute Mona Lisa has her face reshaped so that she will look like a celebrity, even though she is dimly aware that this may cost her her life: a powerful organisation wants Angie Mitchell dead. To be a celebrity can be dangerous. One is not in control of the consequences of one's appearance, even when technology offers one the possibility of being somebody or something else. *Mona Lisa Overdrive* thus speaks directly to the issue of Leonardo's *Mona Lisa*, for neither the creator nor, of course, the sitter, has willed the consequences of his or her enterprise. The *Mona Lisa* we see in the Louvre is no longer Leonardo's, and has never been Lisa Gherardini's.

CHAPTER TEN

Lisa Goes Global

W hen François I invited Leonardo to come to France in 1516, he was reinforcing a link between art and politics that had ample and consolidated precedents. Over the following centuries artists gained considerable independence, but the state never relinquished all control. Through censorship it regulated what could and should be produced. Through public money and patronage it encouraged some artists at the expense of others. The market, however, became increasingly important, as did the views and opinions of the cultural establishment. The state, particularly the democratic state, had to take account of both.

The French state, of course, had always given special emphasis to culture as a political instrument. For much of the twentieth century however, France, as a republic, lacked charismatic figures able to play, even remotely, a role resembling that of the monarchs and personalities of the past. There had been no François I, Louis XIV, or Napoleon. Then came Charles de Gaulle, the wartime hero elected President in 1958.

In the USA, though politics had long been personalised, there had been relatively little presidential use of art and artists. Few were inclined or able to play the Renaissance President. Then came John F. Kennedy (elected in 1960). He surrounded himself with enough intellectuals to grace his 'court' with the name of 'Camelot'. Most of this was just the hype of a sycophantic press, but in the modern age, that can matter more than reality.

By the early 1960s France, under de Gaulle, appeared to have acquired a new sense of direction. The Algerian war had ended. A peace treaty with Germany was signed, and France became the centre of an increasingly integrated Europe. The French atom bomb provided a symbolic fig-leaf for an independent foreign policy. But the appearance of grandeur disguised the reality of cultural decline.

Kennedy, like de Gaulle, called for a new course in international affairs; but there was considerable friction between the two countries. For America to lead the free world, it needed compliant partners. France demurred. Its relationship with the United States followed a complex path, alternating disagreements on matters of substance (NATO, nuclear policy, *détente*, Cuba) with symbolic gestures of good will. The visit of the *Mona Lisa* to Washington in 1963 was one of these. From a wider historical perspective it did not do much for US–French relations, but it did a lot of good to the renown of the *Mona Lisa*, now way ahead of any potential rival as the most famous work of art in the world.

The architect of this initiative was André Malraux, de Gaulle's Minister of Culture – *maître-penseur* for some, mountebank on the make for others.[1] De Gaulle had massive support among the French electorate at large, but not among the intelligentsia. The creation of a Ministry of Culture under Malraux was a deliberate attempt to woo the intellectuals. Malraux was 'one of them': a prize-winning novelist, an art critic and a former Resistance fighter. As an administrator he was a nullity; as a showman he was without peer.

John and Jacqueline Kennedy visited Paris in 1961. They charmed de Gaulle, a difficult man with deeply-rooted prejudices against *les anglo-saxons*. Jackie Kennedy was fascinated by Malraux. She had read his books with admiration, and now this larger-than-life character was showing her around the Louvre. No boring minister he, but a true intellectual with a view on everything, especially the arts.

In 1962 Malraux repaid the visit. At a press conference a

journalist asked if there was any chance of the *Mona Lisa* being exhibited in the United States. Malraux's reply was encouraging. Usually in such matters, nothing is left to chance. The question is planted in advance, the reply studied in all its implications. This time, however, it seems the idea caught Malraux's fancy at once. He would become the man who brought the *Mona Lisa* to America.[2]

The Louvre, of course, protested. The risks were too great. The five-hundred-year-old piece of wood might crack at the slightest change in temperature. Most experts agreed. The American painter Georgia O'Keeffe, though recognising that the trip would do much for the arts in the USA, was among them.[3]

But politics, as usual, came first. The preparations for the *Mona Lisa*'s visit took several months, giving the press many opportunities to dwell on the elaborate precautions being taken. All the familiar *Mona Lisa* stories were also resurrected: the theft, the attack with a stone, Vasari, Freud, Duchamp, the copies, the replicas, the claims and counterclaims.[4] There was no question of sending the *Mona Lisa* by plane, not in 1963. 'She' had to travel by ship, like a queen. She was taken to Le Havre, escorted by a motorcade, and 'welcomed' by the captain of the liner *S.S. France* – the shipping company immediately used the event for an advertising campaign. She was then installed in a specially arranged first-class compartment, in a purpose-built waterproof box that would float if the ship sank.[5] In other words, she was safer than the passengers and the crew – after all, the world is full of sailors, but there is only one *Mona Lisa*. The press, especially the illustrated press, lovingly related such details. Not since the theft had the portrait figured so prominently across the world.

On 14 December 1962 Mona Lisa embarked for her first extra-European trip. On arriving in New York she was reverently placed in an ambulance fitted with special springs and escorted by armed secret service agents, and went through the Lincoln and Baltimore Harbor tunnels, cleared of all traffic, before arriving at the National Gallery in Washington.[6]

On 8 January 1963 a glittering welcoming party was held at the gallery in the presence of *le tout Washington*. Photographers, of course, juxtaposed the radiant smile of Mrs Kennedy with the 'enigmatic' one of Mona Lisa. De Gaulle stayed in France – there was room for only one star. There was also a special dinner at the French embassy, attended by President Kennedy. This was a further symbolic gesture of good will: it is not customary for the American President to attend parties at foreign embassies. On the menu was *Poires Mona Lisa*, a dessert specially created for the occasion. In 1919 Marcel Duchamp had added moustaches to Mona Lisa. By 1963, no one thought it odd to name a dish of poached pears swaddled in hot chocolate sauce and bundled into pastry after a Renaissance masterpiece.

The painting remained on public view at the National Gallery from 10 January until 3 February. It was then shown at the New York Metropolitan Museum, where it remained until 4 March. *Paris-Match* (19 January 1963) wrote that 11,250 people a day had viewed the painting, giving each one an average of twelve seconds in which 'to see the smile'. The press piled on the figures: on 17 February the *Observer* in London declared that Mona Lisa had been seen by 250,000 people in the previous week (thus more than trebling the *Paris-Match* figures), at the rate of thirty seconds per person. The *New Yorker* countered with the calculation that visitors took an average of four seconds each to contemplate Mona Lisa – Leonardo's careful *sfumato* had taken four years.[7] Events of this kind engender their own stories. A particularly maudlin one attracted Malraux's attention: a young man, stopped for trying to smuggle his dog into the exhibition, explained tearfully, 'I wanted Foxy to be the only dog in the world to have seen the *Mona Lisa*.'[8] Thirty-six art lovers from North Carolina chartered a plane with a *Mona Lisa* effigy on the fuselage and flew to Washington DC to see the portrait.[9]

By the end of its American stay the *Mona Lisa* had been seen by over 1.6 million people. Hundreds of thousands had waited in the cold and the rain to catch a glimpse of it. The modern craving for authenticity is such that when, just over a year later, in July–August 1964, a faithful sixteenth-century copy of the portrait (the Vernon *Mona Lisa* – see page 204) was exhibited at the Otis Institute in Los Angeles, only a few hundred people turned out, though the weather was pleasantly Californian.[10] Authenticity, the key concept of tourism, means that one only waits for hours in order to 'experience' the *real* thing.[11] As Mary McCarthy wrote in 1974: 'Today, originals are demanded. Every town, every college must have originals for its museum. The old plaster casts ... that stocked the provincial museums of my childhood have vanished without a trace.'[12] This disparagement of copies is modern, but not recent: Charles Blanc, Director of the École des Beaux-Arts from 1870 to 1873, created a Museum of Copies to provide a comprehensive history of art, but it remained open only a few months, and was closed by his successor.

In some circumstances, however, to the culturally deprived (or the culturally mature) a copy may be sufficient. In November 1979 the French sent a sixteenth-century replica of the *Mona Lisa* to Bulgaria on the occasion of a Leonardo da Vinci exhibition celebrating 'the harmonious development of the human personality'. Exhibited separately to make room for the large number of people who wanted to see it, it was even attacked by a vandal.[13]

The trip to the United States was the final component in the 'nationalisation' of the *Mona Lisa*. Few thought it odd that France should send as a representative of its artistic patrimony and heritage an Italian portrait of an Italian lady. Besides, no single exemplar of French art – short of dismantling the Eiffel Tower and shipping it across the Atlantic – would have had the same effect. France, of course, simply assumed that she was fulfilling her destiny as the universal bearer of universal values. Americans understood the concept, and accepted it readily. Like the French, they had the legitimate presumption that their revolution spoke to the whole world.

The exhibition had obvious political and cultural aims, but it also contributed to the further metamorphosis of the portrait into the People's *Mona Lisa*. To like it or appreciate it or have a view about it, it was no longer necessary to be an art connoisseur or an intellectual, or to have any qualification. Though neither grand nor impressive, it had become like Niagara Falls, the Eiffel Tower, the Grand Canyon, the Great Wall of China or the Pyramids: a great wonder one just *had* to see.

Sending art abroad would soon become commonplace. In 1964 Malraux would send another part of 'French' heritage, the Venus de Milo, a Greek goddess by an unknown Greek sculptor, to Japan (it returned slightly chipped).

A decade later, in 1974, de Gaulle's successor Georges Pompidou agreed to send the *Mona Lisa* to Japan, and it was exhibited at the Tokyo National Museum from 17 April to 11 June. On the way back it stopped in Moscow for a further exhibition. There were protests at the political use of the *Mona Lisa*.[14] Only two years before, Michel Debré, the Gaullist Minister of Defence (and Mayor of Amboise) had declared his opposition to sending the *Mona Lisa* to London to celebrate British entry into the European Economic Community, declaring, rather oddly, 'One does not send an Italian masterpiece to represent France abroad.'[15]

The main effect of the debate was to keep Mona Lisa in the news until her Tokyo exhibition. This time she went by plane. The French reporting of the Japanese trip reflected the same barely concealed supercilious attitude that had been exhibited towards the Americans. The latter, as everyone knew, were the masters of the universe, able to walk on the moon or blast the planet to smithereens; but the poor wretches, though keen to learn, had no culture. As for the Japanese, few could deny that they were heirs to an ancient and refined civilisation, but little was known of it in the West save for swords, samurais and raw fish. Nevertheless, it was conceded that they had 'caught up with the West' – i.e. had become rich, and were good at making cars and tiny radios. What is more, they were paying for the *Mona Lisa* trip. In addition, perhaps, they might buy Concorde.

The presence of Japanese tourists in Europe was even then

regarded as massive, a common misconception, lasting to this day. In the prejudiced minds of Europeans, the Japanese had exchanged position with the Americans as unthinking international mass-travellers. This perception of Japanese preponderance was due to their greater visibility: in reality, even in 1999 they accounted for only 5 per cent of visitors to the Louvre, the same as the total for Canada and Australia, whose combined population is just over a third that of Japan. The Americans constitute the largest foreign contingent, with 20 per cent, followed by Italians, British and Germans (each with roughly 6 per cent).[16]

The Americans had been the first to make jokes about themselves: a famous cartoon in the *New Yorker* showed a middle-aged American couple rushing into the Louvre and asking the guard, 'Which way to the *Mona Lisa*? We're double-parked!'[17] The humorist Art Buchwald recounted how he bettered a twenty-year-old record by visiting the Louvre – i.e. the Venus, the Winged Victory and the *Mona Lisa* ('Everyone knows the rest is junk') – in five minutes nineteen seconds, under 'perfect tourist conditions'.[18]

The Japanese, like the Europeans and the Americans before them, were enthusiastic about the *Mona Lisa*. The press, as usual, tried to overwhelm its readers with statistics, in particular, once again, the number of seconds available for each visitor to view the picture. The *Japan Times* of 28 April 1974 put the average daily turnout for the first week at 18,881. The authorities – it was claimed – had allowed ten seconds per person.[19] If the Tokyo Museum remained open for ten hours per day, and the turnout for the first week was the norm, each visitor passing by the painting would have had 1.9 seconds. This may seem a little rushed, but was perhaps sufficient to enable everyone to feel sanctified by the experience, just like medieval pilgrims who, after waiting for hours, were allowed to approach the sacred crypt and behold the holy relics.[20]

To speed things up the Japanese museum authorities banned

the physically handicapped: wheelchairs, crutches, walking sticks and Zimmer frames would only slow the procession of worshippers. There were protests. A woman sprayed paint on the protective glass. The authorities relented and set aside one day for the disabled. On another occasion eight activists of the Japanese women's liberation movement denounced the Japanese Ministry of Culture for 'alienating the masses from the *Mona Lisa*'.[21]

There was massive merchandising of the picture in Japan. In 1963 this trade had still been in its infancy, and the trip to the United States had generated only an ephemeral fad for a Mona Lisa look, with the French actress Michèle Mercier posing as Lisa to advertise Paris hairdresser Désfossé's new cut.[22] US hairdresser Michel Kazan used actress Susan Strasberg to launch his own version, though both suffered from heavy competition from new and old *femmes fatales* – Jackie Kennedy and Cleopatra (in the Elizabeth Taylor film version). There were also reports of a mild scramble in the fashion, jewellery and cosmetic trades to cash in on the *Mona Lisa*.

By the time of the Tokyo trip, merchandising had blossomed. The industry had become aware of the rich potential of the ancient business of selling souvenirs to pilgrims and visitors. The previous year the Chinese had sent two pandas to a zoo in Japan, and fortunes were made selling stuffed soft toys. From a business perspective, there are no differences between pandas and Monas. Consequently *Mona Lisa* dolls, posters and cards were sold in large quantities, and the enigmatic smile was seen everywhere.[23]

Mona Lisa's visit to Japan coincided with some of the first uses of computer gadgetry: the Japanese claimed to have established what she might have sounded like. At the push of a button, a computerised Lisa Gherardini would say, in Japanese uncontaminated by the slightest trace of Florentine intonation: 'Hi, my name is Lisa and I am known as the Gioconda.'

In his formal speech to open the exhibition in Tokyo, the French Minister of Culture Alain Peyrefitte said that it was the best painting from the best museum in the world. (One does not become Culture Minister in order to be modest about one's country.) The *Mona Lisa*, he added, represented the two great traditions of Western culture. The first was the classical aesthetic tradition of formal beauty (i.e. Greece). Mona Lisa was a beautiful woman, the pose was beautiful, and the landscape was beautiful too. She also represented, he continued, the Christian tradition, that of spiritual beauty. Her smile was serene, almost saintly.[24] Thus there was something in the painting for everyone. At a stroke, Gautier's mocking woman, Pater's pagan goddess and Michelet's secular icon were disposed of in favour of the Universal Mona Lisa.

The Louvre curators, who had again opposed the trip, had insisted that the painting be encased in a special box while it was being transported, and behind protective glass while it was being exhibited. When it returned to Paris, they could hardly deny it the same treatment at home. It was repositioned in the Louvre in a bulletproof box, the only artwork to be so protected. Its main rivals, the Venus de Milo and the Winged Victory, were left at the mercy of psychopaths and vandals, like everything else. Lisa remained alone in her fortress. Soon the Louvre guards demanded signposts directing visitors to the *Mona Lisa*, the Venus and the Winged Victory. They did not want to spend their entire working lives showing tourists the way to the *Joconde*.

The era of mass exhibitions began at about the same time as the *Mona Lisa*'s first trip. It was becoming clear that the growth in education, travel and economic prosperity would be beneficial to museums and exhibitions. Contrary to widespread fears, television, the cinema and the ease of art reproduction had not killed museums. Indeed, seeing images of foreign countries and their artistic heritage made people want to go and see for themselves.

Mass tourism is a recent phenomenon. In the late 1940s, only 3.1 million British workers had two weeks' holiday a year. Ten years later the figure was over twelve million. In 1971, only a third of British adults had ever been abroad; ten years later only a third had not been.[25] In the 1960s, international travel was still expensive, and the amount of foreign currency one could take abroad was often restricted: most European countries did not abolish exchange controls until the 1990s. Only after 1970 were there wide-bodied jets able to carry over four hundred passengers.[26] By the 1990s, travel and tourism had become one of the most important industries in the world. It accounted for at least 6 per cent of the world's GDP, employing at least 127 million people around the globe. This was the result of an astonishing growth: in 1950, twenty-five million international trips were taken; by 1996 this had increased to 592 million.[27]

Most of this took place within the developed world. The USA, the greatest exporter of tourists, was also the leading earner, receiving in 1995 $61 billion from foreign visitors. France and Italy did very well too: each gained $27 billion, making them, in terms of *per capita* earnings, the top tourist countries in the world, followed by Spain and the United Kingdom. In 1999, over sixty million tourists visited France.[28] In the future the numbers will grow even further: political and economic changes have brought new arrivals from Russia, Eastern Europe, China, Korea and Latin America.

So-called cultural tourism expanded to the benefit of the great art-rich capitals of Europe: Rome, London, Venice, Florence and, of course, Paris. Most tourists seldom spend more than a few intense and exhausting days in a city, and follow the suggestions of guidebooks, guides and friends. In Paris it would be unusual for a first-timer not to go to the Eiffel Tower and visit the Louvre – which before the creation of the Pompidou Centre and the Musée d'Orsay was the only Parisian museum of international popular fame. Even now it is, by far, the French museum with the highest proportion of foreign tourists. In the 1960s the Louvre had one million visitors a year, increasing to nearly three million in the 1980s.[29] By 1998, the number had grown to six million – the same as Washington's National Gallery, and more than the British Museum, neither of which, unlike the Louvre, charges its visitors a penny for entry.

Who are these visitors? They are predominantly young: 63 per cent are under thirty-five, 40 per cent under twenty-five. They are also predominantly female: 58 per cent. Fewer than half have been to the Louvre before. In 1998, 39 per cent of the adult French population and 71 per cent of the inhabitants of greater Paris had been to the Louvre. Some of them, eventually, skip the obligatory visit to the *Mona Lisa* and discover for themselves the museum's other splendours. But imagine the benighted tourist experiencing Paris for the first time. So much to do, and so little time: the Eiffel Tower, the cafés, the restaurants, the Seine, the shows, the shopping, and all that culture – and the Louvre is such an enormous museum, especially after its expansion in 1993. On average, foreign tourists spend just over three hours in the Louvre – at least, that is what they claim in surveys. In these circumstances, a dash to the *Mona Lisa* is almost unavoidable before taking in the Venus, the Winged Victory and the Egyptian antiquities. After this the Louvre is 'done', and there is still some time in which to contemplate the 'junk', as Art Buchwald facetiously put it – Rubens and Rembrandt, Vermeer and Veronese, Caravaggio and Cranach.

For some, the *Mona Lisa* is a disappointment: so small, so many people around it. For others it is an unforgettable experience, as it was for Mary, a sixteen-year-old girl from Swinton, near Rotherham in Yorkshire, who visited the Louvre in 1978 and wrote to the curator:

> I saw in this portrait women of all ages, girls playing with their dolls, dressing up, the love of women for their man, their children, home art, their own skills, simple things which give enjoyment to a woman, cooking, sewing, knitting, crochet and lace work. There was no vice or corruption . . . It was such a beautiful revelation that I thought that I had worked so long to see the picture, that my imagination had played tricks with me . . . [30]

Twenty years later, in October 1999, another young woman, Gina Shaw from Washington DC, wrote, this time to a website (www.epinions.com):

> I arrived at the Musée du Louvre prepared to be under-
> whelmed . . . Call me easily manipulated, but I couldn't
> tear my eyes away . . . I understood, at last, why this
> painting was legendary, eternal. I felt that I had connec-
> ted with the work, the artist and the subject in a way
> I couldn't have done had I been focused on my photos
> or video.

A Latin American poet, Rosario Castellanos, captured her own experience in her 'Looking at the *Mona Lisa*' (1970s):

> But I'm only one of those dumb little tourist ladies,
> One of those who gets a travel agency
> To invent a 'package tour' for her.
> And a monolingual to boot!
> Who's come to contemplate you
> And you smile, mysteriously
> As is your obligation. But I can read you.
> That smile is mockery. It mocks me and every
> One of us who believe that we believe that
> Culture is a liquid one imbibes at the source,
> A special symptom one contracts
> In certain contagious places, something
> One acquires by osmosis.[31]

Thanks to mass production of copies and the vast numbers of postcards available (and bought and sent thanks to the increase in travel and tourism), everyone, not just the likes of Marcel Proust, can have Mona Lisa in the bedroom. Those who want 'proper' copies in oil on canvas keep professional copyists busy. One claims to have painted the *Mona Lisa* 255 times.[32]

What did artists make of this? In the early 1960s Andy Warhol had already started his visual commentary on mass production and celebrities: his Marilyn Monroe (*Twenty-five Colored*

Marilyns, 1962), his Elvis Presley (1964), his Campbell's soup tins (1961–62). The American visit of the *Mona Lisa* led him to produce what would remain until the 1980s his only multiple use of a painting: *Thirty are Better than One* (see plate 44).[33]

It is tempting to see Duchamp's influence in Warhol and in the many other paintings that use or misuse the *Mona Lisa*. This should be resisted. While Duchamp's *L.H.O.O.Q.* could be regarded – in 1919 – as an attempt to subvert high culture, by the 1960s the *Mona Lisa* was no longer high culture, but a popular cultural icon. It was no longer just another precious object, enclosed in the aloofness of a solemn museum, away from the untutored masses. Debunking it was no longer an option. Warhol was percipient: Lisa had become like Elvis and Marilyn, a media projection. The hundreds of painters who used it as a theme were not subverting anything. They were using the *Mona Lisa* to advertise themselves and their works – while, of course, further consolidating its position as the best-known painting in the world.

Some had started relatively early. In 1948 Jean Dubuffet painted *La Joconde* (now at the Galerie Daniel Varenne in Geneva). The Colombian Fernando Botero painted *Mona Lisa Age Twelve* in 1959, and returned to the theme with his 1978 *Mona Lisa* (see plate 43).

The *Mona Lisa* was adopted by all the pioneers of Pop Art: Robert Rauschenberg's *Untitled* (*Mona Lisa*, c.1952, Collection Ethel Redner Scull, New York) was so successful as to spur him to produce a large number of *Mona Lisa*s, among them a series of ceramics in Japan which included *Pneumonia Lisa*. In 1960 it was Magritte's turn. His *La Joconde* (see plate 45), characteristically, does not represent the *Joconde* – that would have been unnecessary, for we all know how it looks. The foregrounded central motif is a typical Magritte sky of clouds enclosed in a shape. Two pleated curtains (another recurrent theme) flank it; at the side, near the bottom, is a ball with a horizontal slit – a mouth? A smile? A vagina? Or something even more enigmatic? The Hungarian Sándor Bortnyk had a rather striking *Mona*

Lisa (*Mona Lisa in the Twentieth Century*, 1953) with bouffant, shoulder-length hair, long black gloves and bare shoulders, drinking an espresso with skyscrapers in the background – part of a set of four, including a *Mona Lisa* after Cézanne and one after Van Gogh. In 1964 the Romanian Daniel Spoerri produced an artwork consisting of an ironing board resting on a chair with an iron on top. The object to be ironed was the *Mona Lisa*. The ironing board was, presumably, a Rembrandt, as the entire construct was labelled *Using a Rembrandt as an Ironing Board*.[34] Here 'Rembrandt' stands for any museum masterpiece, and hence for the *Mona Lisa* as well – a target and a point already identified by the Futurists and the Dadaists some fifty years previously. Pop artist Jasper Johns also had a go. In 1968 he produced the lithograph *Color Numeral No. 7*, which contains an image of the *Mona Lisa*, and in 1984 *Racing Thoughts*, where the *Mona Lisa* is placed alongside other images culled from the life of the artist and the influences on his art. Johns continued for years to use the *Mona Lisa* as a source of inspiration for his comments on the history of painting. Tom Wesselman, in his Great American Nudes series of 1962, also placed the *Mona Lisa* alongside other common objects – as Léger had done thirty years before. In 1964 the British Pop artist Peter Blake made a silk-screen collage of the *Mona Lisa* surrounded by pictures clipped at random from newspapers.

In 1965 there was a real avalanche of *Mona Lisa* derivations, including Erico Baj's *The Revenge of Mona Lisa* (with the face of Duchamp), Mark Brusse's *Le Jeu de la Joconde*, Lourdes Castro's *Le Contour de la Joconde*, and works by Gudmundur Erro, Robert Filliou, Jean Jacques Lebel, Peter Klasen, Milva Maglione, Jacques Monory and many others.[35]

In September 1974 London's Nicholas Treadwell Gallery held an exhibition of recent works inspired by *Mona Lisa*. Some thirty artists took part in 'The Mona Lisa Show'.[36] The real pioneers, though not all the artists may have been aware of it, were neither Duchamp nor Warhol, but the designers of the funny postcards which had appeared during the saga of the theft. Indeed, many of the works at the Treadwell Gallery were not so different from postcards sending up Mona Lisa. She was shown in a sheepskin coat, woollen headscarf and sunglasses, with a camera hanging around her neck; viewed from behind, in stockings; and as a young 'punk' version of herself (bleached blonde, bare-breasted and sporting a pair of black boots). She was depicted in a see-through blouse astride a motorbike; with a giant apple hiding most of her face (*Magritta Lisa*); masturbating (*Kiss me Lisa*); petting on the back seat of a car seen in the rear-view mirror; as a little girl showing her knickers (*Mona Lolita*); as a label on a bottle next to a reclining sunbather (*Just Another Product*); enjoying cunnilingus (*Well, What do you Think she had to Smile About?*); in bed with Leonardo (*Leo and Mona*). Such an exhibition, far from exhausting the trend, was just a symptom of an unstoppable industry that is twice derivative: it builds on Duchamp's 'homage' to Leonardo as well as on the *Mona Lisa* itself.

Much of this work falls into overlapping categories: the send-up *à la* Duchamp, with Mona Lisa skiing, cross-eyed, playing tennis, etc.; her sexualisation by undressing her or placing her in various erotic positions; and, finally, her technologisation by using electronic equipment (photocopying computers, printers, etc.).

Some of these works, of course, are rather ingenious. George Castaldo added curlers in the 'Misguided Masterpieces' postcard series (1994), while Rick Meyerowitz turned her into a gorilla (*Mona Gorilla*, 1971). Jacques Poirier's *Dos de La Joconde* (1991, see plate 51) shows the back of the wood panel of the *Mona Lisa*, on which the unseen and imagined restorer has left his unfinished working-man's lunch: baguette, camembert, a bottle of wine. In the irreverent creation of the comic-strip designer Georges Pichard, Lisa has a ring in her nose, a torn dress, her breast defiantly exposed, a joint between her lips. In 1990 the Egyptian artist Arys Archimbaud drew a stylised Mona Lisa vaguely resembling the extra-terrestrial hero of Steven Spielberg's film *ET*. She was called, appropriately, *Mona Futura*, and sported a large dangling Egyptian earring. She had been preceded by the Tunisian artist Alyssa,

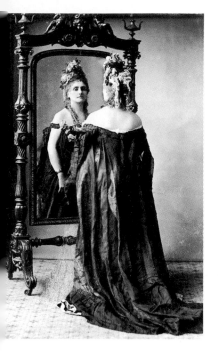

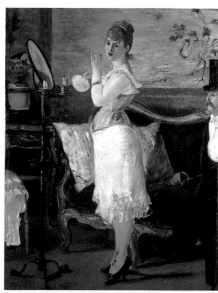

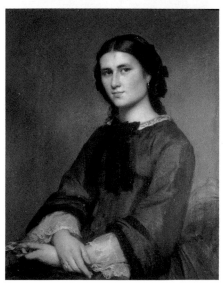

ABOVE The Countess of Castiglione (Musée Unterlinden, Colmar). The Countess, wishing to personate the new *femme fatale*, had hundreds [of] photographs taken of herself in 1856-65 in a [va]riety of extravagant clothes: a deliberate presen[tat]ion of her own person as a highly desirable [sex]ual object.

ABOVE RIGHT *Nana* by Edouard Manet (1877, [Ku]nsthalle, Hamburg). As the uses of the *femme [fat]ale* image expanded, the range of variations [be]came wider and were used by writers, painters [an]d, in the twentieth century, film-makers. Manet [pa]inted the Nana of Zola's *l'Assomoir*, who later [be]came the heroine of the eponymous sequel. [Na]na, though neither enigmatic nor mysterious, [in]flamed men's passion and caused their undoing.

RIGHT *La Jeune fille à l'oeillet* by Hippolyte-[Jea]n Flandrin (1858). Théophile Gautier, always on [th]e lookout for *femmes fatales*, found in this [att]ractive woman 'something strange, mysterious, [an]d disturbing, the eyes have a sphinx-like malice, [he]r severe mouth betrays an imperceptible smile [...] In front of this figure as with certain of [Le]onardo da Vinci's canvases, you feel a little ill at [ea]se; she seems to belong in another sphere.'

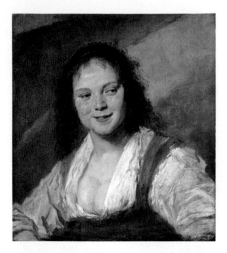

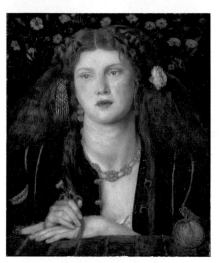

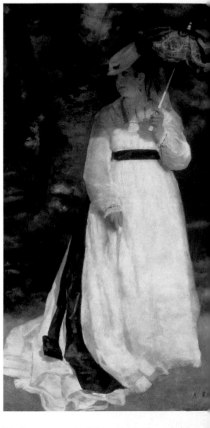

31. TOP Franz Hals, *La Bohémienne* (*c*.1630, Louvre). The Louvre acquired this painting in 1869. By then the Parisian men of letters had selected the *Mona Lisa* as their ideal *femme fatale*. In any case this gypsy girl's smile is too inviting and unambiguous.

32. ABOVE *Bocca Baciata* ('The Kissed Mouth') by Dante Gabriel Rossetti (1859, Museum of Fine Arts, Boston). The pre-Raphaelite followed the fashion for enigmatic and moody females. The title originates in a sonnet by Boccaccio: 'Bocca baciata non perde ventura' ('The mouth that has been kissed stays lucky'). Swinburne thought the painting 'more stunning than can be decently expressed'. It was commissioned by Rossetti's friend George Price Boyce who had become obsessed by the model, Fanny Cornforth.

33. ABOVE RIGHT *Lise with a Parasol* by Auguste Renoir (1867, Folkwang Museum, Essen). After its theft in 1911, the *Mona Lisa* had become too well-known for sophisticated young art critics, such as Roberto Longhi. He contrasted *Mona Lisa* unfavourably to Renoir's *Lise*: 'For this second Lisa, should she ever be stolen and then found, you won't find ten people troubling themselves. Yet, of the two, she alone is Art.'

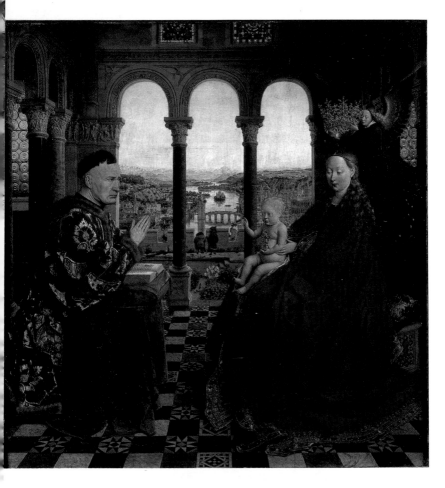

34. *La Vierge du Chancelier Rolin* by Jan Van Eyck (*c.*1436, Louvre). In the nineteenth century, this Flemish masterpiece hung next to the *Mona Lisa*. With its Virgin sitting down, in three-quarter view and with a complex landscape in the background, it belongs to a tradition that influenced Leonardo's famous portrait.

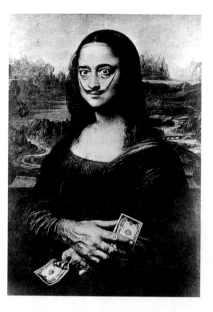

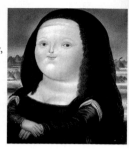

42. LEFT *Mona Lisa with Dali's Moustaches*, photomontage by Philippe Halsman (1953). When Dali told the photographer Philippe Halsman that he had always wanted to look like Mona Lisa, Halsman suggested a photomontage: a *Mona Lisa* with Dali's moustaches. At first, Dali demurred: Duchamp had been there before. Halsman insisted: 'It will be your moustaches, your eyes and your big hands counting the money.' Dali accepted, and his dream was realised.

43. In the Colombian Fernando Botero's *Mona Lisa* (1978), a South American view, complete with smoking volcano, has replaced the original landscape, and Mona Lisa has acquired the caricatural and grotesque aspect of Botero's painting of the female figure. 'In art,' he wrote, 'as long as you have ideas and think, you are bound to deform nature. Art is deformation.'

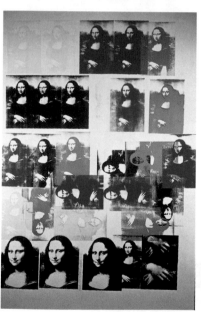

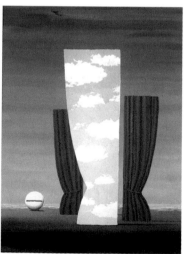

44. *Thirty are Better than One* by Andy Warhol. In 1963 Warhol had already started his visual commentary on mass production and celebrities: Marilyn Monroe, Elvis Presley, and Campbell's soup. The American visit of the *Mona Lisa* led him to produce his first serialisation of a painting.

45. *La Joconde* by René Magritte (1960, private collection, Paris). Magritte's *Mona Lisa*, characteristically, does not represent the *Joconde* – by then everyone knew how it looks. The central motif is a typical Magritte sky of clouds enclosed into a shape. Two pleated curtains flank it. Near the bottom, another recurrent Magritte motif, a ball with a horizontal slit. Is it a mouth? A smile? A vagina? Or something even more enigmatic?

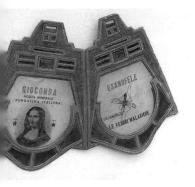

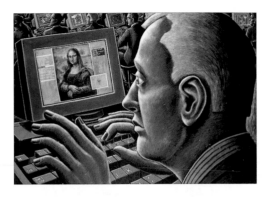

46. LEFT One of the first commercial uses of the *Mona Lisa* (1915): the label for Gioconda Acqua Purgativa Italiana, a laxative water which was also a protection against malaria. 'Finally! Here [in Italy] too we are beginning to produce some good art criticism,' sarcastically wrote the Futurist Ardengo Soffici.

47. RIGHT *Leonardo*, by P.J. Crook. Computer and electronics firms have relied heavily on the ubiquitous effigy in their advertising. Almost any article explaining how computers can modify or manipulate pictures will use the *Mona Lisa* as an example.

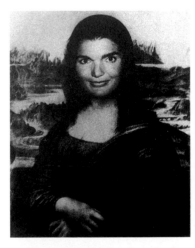

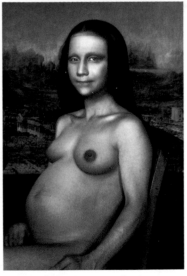

48. Almost every celebrity of note has been 'monalised'. This is Jacqueline Kennedy, who played host to the *Mona Lisa* during its visit to Washington D.C. in 1963. The press did not fail to draw parallels between the modern beauty of Jackie Kennedy (and her smile) and that of Mona Lisa.

49. *Mona Lisa in Pregnancy* by Yasumasa Morimura (1998). In April-May 1999 the White Cube Gallery in London presented three new works by the Japanese artist Yasumasa Morimura, boasting that they would 'radically metamorphise Leonardo's *Mona Lisa*'. By then there had been well over three hundred uses of the *Mona Lisa* by painters, and many more by advertisers. *Mona Lisa in Pregnancy* has the original hairstyle and landscape, but has the artist's face for Lisa's and the body of a naked pregnant woman.

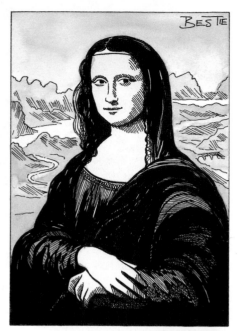

BESTIE

MONA WAS TRYING NOT TO SMILE AS
SHE WAITED FOR HER SILENT FART
TO REACH LEONARDO.

50. LEFT Since the 1980s Jocondologues have collected thousands of postcards inspired by the *Mona Lisa*. Many are, of course, humorous. In 1992 the British cartoonist Steve Best came up with his own impressive solution to the century-old enigma of the mysterious smile.

51. BELOW *Dos de la Joconde* by Jacques Poirier (1991, Galerie Alain Daune, Paris). Poirier shows an accurate reconstruction of the back of the wood panel of the *Mona Lisa*, where an imagined restorer has left his unfinished working-man's lunch: a typically French baguette, camembert, and bottle of wine.

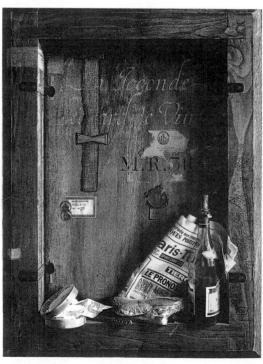

whose Mona Lisa appears in full Tunisian dress with even more massive earrings (c.1967). The French painter Jean Ache has rendered the portrait in the style of various artists including Gauguin, Picasso, Modigliani and Léger. In 1985 Greg Constantine, in his cartoon series *Leonardo Visits Los Angeles*, had 'Leo and Lisa on Valium Driving their Volvo on the Ventura'.[37] In London, in April 2000, the Saatchi exhibition 'Ant Noises', an anagram homage to its controversial predecessor 'Sensation', included an elephant-dung-encrusted African Mona Lisa by Turner Prize-winner Chris Ofili.[38]

In an apparent attempt to set a record, the self-styled French electronic painter Artus Pixel has announced his intention to produce, by 2003, 1001 versions of the *Mona Lisa* for a 'Viva Mona Lisa!' exhibition. Readers can check his progress on www.arkonet.fr/vivamonalisa/. Pixel had already printed a number of cards of his own creation, with Mona Lisa as Mickey Mouse, Napoleon, Captain Lisa, *Macdona Lisa* (with hamburgers), *Marchéluna Mona* (as a moon rocket), Tintin (*Tintina Lisa*), Marianne (*Républica Lisa*), with the European flag (*Europa Lisa*), as Batman (*Batmona Lisa*), *Money Lisa* (surrounded by banknotes), *Mona Frenchette* (baguette, beret, Eiffel Tower in background), *Punketta Lisa* (as punk), as Elvis (*Rocka Lisa*). In 1977 Jean-Pierre Yvaral, another electronic painter (and the son of the Hungarian-born French painter Vasarely), began using a computer to synthesise the *Mona Lisa* in electronic pixels (based on the intensity of colours). In 1985 he presented nineteen such *Mona Lisa*s at the Forum des Halles in Paris. He had chosen it, he says, because 'It was one of the two or three best-known paintings in the world.'[39]

One would think that the deformation of revered masterpieces could no longer shock anyone, but there are exceptions. In 1996 a museum specialising in billboards, the Conservatoire Régional de l'Affiche, near Locronan (Brittany), used, to advertise its collection, a 'derivation' of *Mona Lisa* called *La Joconde dans tous ses états* ('The *Mona Lisa* in a Terrible State', 1994), which represented her smoking a joint. This threw the regional president into a terrible state too. Afraid that Mona Lisa would incite the young to smoke cannabis, he forced the museum to withdraw the poster. Naturally the museum and the poster thereby obtained more publicity than they could ever have hoped for.[40]

In April–May 1999 the White Cube Gallery in London presented three new works by the Japanese artist Yasumasa Morimura that 'will radically metamorphise Leonardo da Vinci's *Mona Lisa*' – according to its handout. One of them, *Mona Lisa in Pregnancy* (1998, see plate 49), has the original hairstyle and landscape but substitutes the artist's face for Lisa's and the body of a naked pregnant woman.

In the visual arts, as in all cultural fields, it is not unusual for artists to be inspired by other artists. Repetition works. Modern art has become increasingly self-referential: Manet used Giorgione for his *Le Déjeuner sur l'herbe* (1861), Francis Bacon used Velázquez's *Pope Innocent III* for his famous triptych, Ingres's *Odalisque* has been widely used. Picasso, regarded as the greatest painter of the twentieth century, never ceased using material handed down from his predecessors from antiquity to modern times. Hence his systematic revisitations of famous paintings such as *Les Femmes d'Alger* (1954–55), Velázquez's *Las Meninas* (1957) and his own version of Manet's *Le Déjeuner sur l'herbe* (1960–61). But he never tried the *Mona Lisa*.

Those who did are a large contingent: nearly three hundred since 1960, according to the findings patiently collected by the indefatigable Jean Margat, the world's leading *jocondologue* – and even that figure is almost certainly only the tip of an iceberg.[41] Of these, nearly a hundred have been produced in the 1990s, excluding mass production *à la* Artus Pixel, Yvaral and others. It is much easier to copy than to create. Citation has become an art form, and the Louvre is a massive databank of templates. Museums, said the critic Bernard Ceysson, are like stud farms, providing masterpieces whose function is to generate derivations.[42] As Thierry de Duve put it, discussing Duchamp, 'The

Louvre is the *Mona Lisa* Bank. All artists, even, or especially, the *enfant terrible* of the avant-garde, draws cheques on tradition.'[43] It is almost as if, unable to match the achievements of the Old Masters, all that is left for those who come later is to pay them a backhanded form of respect and homage.

The art establishment has responded to the multiplication of *Mona Lisa*s with a mixture of silence and anxiety. Lorne Campbell's *Renaissance Portraits: European Portrait-Painting in the Fourteenth, Fifteenth and Sixteenth Centuries* (1990) has no *Mona Lisa* among its 267 illustrations. A reviewer in the *Burlington Magazine* wrote: 'It must be the first book on Renaissance painting that does not even illustrate the lady.'[44] Art magazines such as *Museum News* have been urged to refuse to carry advertisements which feature works of art.[45] One of these showed Mona Lisa wearing white suntan ointment on her nose to illustrate the perils of ultraviolet radiation.[46]

At times the absence of a brand name is the only way of distinguishing the derivations constituting 'art' (a problematic term at the best of times) from those which constitute advertising. Pop artists like Rauschenberg have claimed that 'Times Square is America's greatest work of art,'[47] and mass consumption has reached the stage where ordinary people buy products for their image rather than for their function – as the aristocracy used to do. Advertising strategists, explained Fredric Jameson in 2000, are true 'Freudo-Marxists'.[48] They desperately try to link eroticism to what they sell: not only clothes and cosmetics, but also cars, computers, even lawnmowers. Items are libidinised when put on sale: 'It is not jeans you buy, but the sculpted buttocks which model them in the advertisements.'[49] Advertisers need to use instantly recognisable symbols, the more universal the better. As production becomes global and local tastes and identities become subsumed in a wider culture, the advertising industry follows, searching constantly for universal symbols. The notion that art has a universal value may well be one of those nineteenth-century ideas whose time has come. We may not have an agreed definition of art, but there are universally recognisable images of what is art, and the *Mona Lisa* is one of them. In 1991 the anthropologist Signe Howell reported that during her fieldwork in the mountains of Nepal she found a large reproduction of the *Mona Lisa* hung on a wall in a lodge. She dismissed claims that great art transcends cultural boundaries by pointing out that the adjacent pictures portrayed the Swedish pop group Abba, Michael Jackson and the King of Nepal.[50] It is likely, though, that the *Mona Lisa* will outlive them all. Such universalist qualities made it almost inevitable that the *Mona Lisa* would become the advertisers' dream painting.

The modern advertising industry had modest origins. Until the end of the nineteenth century, the image of advertising was even shabbier than it is now, still being associated with misleading and fraudulent claims for products such as patent medicines. This somewhat parasitic enterprise depended for its expansion on the large-scale production of homogeneous branded goods. The problem was to establish distinctions between similar competing products. The use of art in advertising was a way of linking a unique, high-quality object to the less than unique commodity being promoted. Though a greater market share was the object of the exercise, some advertisers had additional, nobler, motives. For instance the great American advertiser Ernest Elmo Calkins said in the 1920s that advertising provided an 'opportunity to expose millions of people to fine works of art', and that 'advertising art, reaching millions of people, was in effect the poor man's picture gallery'.[51]

One of the earliest uses of art in advertising depended on personal taste and preference. Thomas J. Barratt, son-in-law of Francis Pears, the manufacturer of soap and beauty products in Victorian Britain, and an art lover, devised a range of publicity schemes to beat the competition. He convinced Lillie Langtry, the most popular actress of the London stage (and, as was well known, the mistress of the heir to the throne), to endorse Pears' soap. But his greatest achievement was to use John Everett Millais's *Bubbles* as an advertisement (1886). This painting shows a nauseatingly pretty curly-headed child looking at the soap bubbles he has just blown. Millais, though the most successful painter in Britain, could not resist the lure of a wider dissemination of his work. The art world reacted with predictable hostility, and even three years after Millais's death in 1896 the matter was still the subject of debate in *The Times*.[52] But Pears' soap made *Bubbles* famous to this day, and the picture was turned into postcards and jigsaw puzzles.[53]

Barratt had been a pioneer. Even in the United States, advertising would give greater emphasis to the written word than to the visual aspect until at least the 1930s. The realisation that images could say several things at the same time dawned only gradually.[54] Advertisers, like politicians, often have a contradictory message to convey: the product is new, modern, and hence better than anything else; the product is of high quality, hence somewhat connected to tradition, to the good old days, before commodities became standardised and when craft production prevailed.

Advertisers found modern art particularly appropriate to this difficult juggling act. Some of it appeared to be amusing and ironic, thus contributing to the entertainment value without which advertising is a substantially dull affair, which most people would avoid. Besides, much modern art has no obvious meaning, and can be used in any way one wants.

Since the 1960s, when advertising started its massive global expansion, the advertisers' favourite painters have also been the best-known: Magritte, Picasso and Dali. Magritte's work, at least after the 1930s, escapes clearly defined interpretations. It is a mix of ironic clichés and familiar things in unusual setting.[55] But Old Masters too were used: Vermeer's maid pouring milk found herself advertising Chambourcy yoghurt; Michelangelo's *David* was seen wearing Levi's jeans. The hand of Michelangelo's God creating Adam can be used by anyone by simply inserting the object to be advertised at the end of His finger.

The *Mona Lisa* fitted many of the parameters set by advertisers. Although it was not new, it certainly represented high quality, because it was after all high culture. Once Duchamp and others had distorted it in various amusing ways, advertisers could follow, adding a touch of modernity. It was also extremely well known, and had 'open text' qualities.

There are very few recorded examples of advertisements using the *Mona Lisa* before the theft in 1911, although one such appeared in 1910, for leather straps made by the Milan-based firm Massoni & Moroni.[56] It is safe to assume that no improper use of the product was suggested.

After the theft the *Mona Lisa* was used to advertise a clothing store in Tours (in 1911) and the digestive qualities of the Italian Gioconda bottled water (1915). Later the Mona Lisa corset appeared in the USA – '100% nylon horsehair' – as advertised in *Charm and Mademoiselle*. Italy came up with Gioconda hand cream. The painting was also used to sell the aperitif Select, '*l'aperitivo degli intenditori*' ('the aperitif of the connoisseur'). Fascist pride can be detected in the Italian textile company Snia Viscosa's advertisement of 15 December 1938: a drawing of the *Mona Lisa* with, in the background, the firm's factories and the caption 'the everlasting vitality of our race finds strength in the glories of our past and our contemporary achievements'.

In the 1950s one could find British-made condoms sold in Spain (Gioconda Liquid Latex – 'guaranteed for five years'), Spanish and Italian oranges (a Spanish Mona Lisa mandarin was bought in London as recently as 1999), the Italian-made cheese Robiolina Gioconda, boiled sweets, chocolate, cigars (Holland), stockings (USA), hairpins (France), gramophone styluses (Germany), soap (Romania) and matches (Argentina). In most instances the product's association with the painting amounted to little more than it being named 'Mona Lisa' or 'Gioconda'. This was only the early phase of a massive expansion.

The advertising industry, contrary to the image it likes to project, is not particularly innovative. Its main achievement has been to raise the cost of entry into a particular market. However, its more successful practitioners are skilled at identifying, early on, what is likely to turn into a trend or a fashion. Acumen and luck, more than creativity, are what is required. And everyone gets a second chance – contrary, again, to the insiders' view of the trade. When a fashion or an idea looks like being productive, the entire industry joins in, and when it does so it reinforces the general trend. Advertising is a world where it is believed that if everyone does the same thing, then everyone can win, while seeming to be always alert to original ideas. It is the sweet revenge of the conformist. This self-validating success is evident in the case of the *Mona Lisa*. Its uses in advertising before its rise to global fame were, as we have seen, minimal. Its trips to Washington and Tokyo had confirmed its position as the world's best-known picture. The fundamental reason it has remained at the top ever since is that it has been promoted by the advertising industry.

Since the 1960s Mona Lisa has advertised Air India flights to Paris (1962), chocolate, champagne, Pitterson rum from Martinique (1986), the Spanish orange drink Naranjada Casera (1990), Mona Lisa Wigs (USA, 1966), a blood-testing kit for Hepatitis B (France), the French ground coffee Grand Expresso Italien (a double case of frenchification), the delicious Egyptian sweet halawa, Doncella cigars (1977), a dental prosthesis, Italian air-conditioning equipment (illustrated with Mona Lisa wearing a woollen scarf and ear-muffs), pitted Californian black olives, the 1989 Taipei Trade Show, the gay store 'Don't Panic' in London's Soho, Renault's Twingo car, Rembrandt toothpaste (with Mona Lisa proud of her shiny teeth, and the caption 'she has discovered Rembrandt', thus mentioning two Old Masters for the price of one), and DiaMed, a medical device for analysing blood and urine samples. In 1991 a rather plump Mona Lisa was advertising Ajinomoto's Pal Sweet Diet drink, while an Oriental-looking one was seen drinking Café de Colombia alongside a bemused museum guard. She made the front cover of the Italian magazine *Motociclismo* (May 1996), sitting astride the new Aprilia motorbike, model Leonardo 125, bare legs well in evidence. In June 1997 the French women's magazine *Quo: Les Clés de la vie quotidienne*

used a naked model with Mona Lisa's face superimposed to advertise a feature on how to seduce men. Mudd, the UK's biggest-
selling cosmetic face-mask, represented Mona Lisa with a mud
mask and the caption 'No wonder she's smiling. She knows the
secret to perfect skin.' Marriott's Renaissance hotels used her
with the slogan 'A Renaissance Person wants a hotel staff who's
mastered the art of making guests smile.' Her image has appeared
on the Swiss chocolate Zoom.[57] She has been depicted holding
an intra-uterine device with the caption: 'Before insertion of the
Mona Lisa-CU375 the enclosed instructions should be followed
carefully.'[58]

Computers and electronics firms have a strong penchant for
the *Mona Lisa*. Epsom, Honeywell and Compaq have all used the
ubiquitous effigy. It has been seen on the front cover of *Computer*,
the cultural electronic supplement of the Roman daily *La Repub-
blica* (20 November 1997); the Argentinean magazine *Noticias*
(1997); *Micro* (1998); *Dream* (1998); and the catalogue of a salon
for computer-assisted manufacturing (1994, Paris). Metatools, a
software firm in Carpinteria, California, demonstrated the flexi-
bility of its products by showing twelve distortions of the *Mona
Lisa*. Almost any article explaining how to use computers to
modify or use pictures will probably use the *Mona Lisa* as an
example.

It is difficult to quantify the advertising uses of the *Mona
Lisa* accurately. A rough count, based on Jean Margat's findings,
suggests that the average for the 1970s was twenty-three a year.
This more than doubled in the 1980s and 1990s (to fifty-four).
In other words, since 1980 there has been a new utilisation of
Leonardo's portrait of Lisa Gherardini every week. These figures,
like everything that concerns the *Mona Lisa*, are bound to be an
underestimate, for they reflect only the documentation actually
sent to or collected by the Louvre.

Since the time of the theft various objects connected with the
Mona Lisa have been offered for sale, beginning with a *Mona
Lisa* doll (price 1.75 francs) which was included in the list of 'toys

of the year' advertised in *l'Illustration* of 22 December 1911. When the painting was recovered a Mona Lisa cake-tin made its appearance; on the cover the Mona Lisa is holding two babies, suckling one of them, with the caption 'the return of the *Joconde* after an absence of nine months'.[59]

In France alone some twenty-five Mona Lisa hotels, cafés, pizzerias and restaurants have been traced – including the bar of the Hôtel Louvre in Paris. Others have been seen in Belgium, Tunis (a pastry shop), Boston, California, Brazil, Morocco and Winnipeg. Mustang in Nepal has a Hotel Mona Lisa. In rue St. Martin in Paris there is a bookshop called Mona Lisait. In New York's Greenwich Village there is a fine pizzeria called Mona Lisa. On Wilshire Boulevard in Los Angeles there is a Mona Lisa lingerie shop. At Legoland in Windsor (England) there was, in 1998, a large *Mona Lisa* reproduction made out of Lego bricks. There is a *Mona Lisa* fridge magnet, an inflatable *Mona Lisa*, a *Mona Lisa* mousepad, a *Mona Lisa* clock (Japan, 1977) and a hashish tin with Mona Lisa smoking a joint on the lid. The *Mona Lisa* decorates the Old Masters Deodorant Block Holder.[60]

The Galerie Perrine Masselin, a Paris shop specialising in '*art ludique*' (amusing art), offered for sale a *Mona Lisa* necklace of stupendously ludicrous taste, presumably destined to be a present for someone who collects kitsch – the designer is Liliane Müller. In the USA, for $14 you could buy a 'Mona-Dada-Lisa' mug with Duchamp's moustaches and goatee – as you fill it with hot beverage Duchamp's sacrilegious additions disappear, Leonardo's masterpiece is restored and you can drink with artistic integrity. $26 will obtain the Giggling Mona Lisa Pillow: 'Squeeze this beautiful pillow and Mona lets loose a peal of laughter. Machine washable.'

The *Mona Lisa* has also offered an easy option for cartoonists trying to represent celebrities as mysterious, enigmatic and seductive. The renown of the painting ensures that the simple substitution of the features of any celebrity for those of Lisa

Gherardini will amuse almost all the readers. The Amis de Mona Lisa, an international association of self-styled Jocondomaniacs based in France – their motto: *Jocondophiles du monde, unissez-vous* – has attempted to list the *Mona Lisa* cartoons.[61] But a definitive inventory could not possibly be reached without a massive investigation throughout the world and a vast research budget (and surely the money could be better spent in other ways . . .). However, the data at our disposal confirms the relatively recent origins of the craze. Only fifteen to twenty caricatures and drawings were produced before the Second World War, a few more in the period 1945–65, and then there was a massive explosion in the last thirty to forty years.[62]

Almost anyone who is anyone has been 'monalised': from Jackie Onassis to Stalin to Tony Blair (sporting an enormous smile, by cartoonist Steve Bell in the *Guardian*, 14 August 1998). A *Mona Lisa* John Major was seen during the 1997 election holding a piece of paper representing the Maastricht Treaty and a Union Jack. All the American presidents since Kennedy have been done, as have Hillary Clinton, the Mexican President Carlos Salinas (1995), most of the numerous Italian prime ministers including Bettino Craxi and Silvio Berlusconi,[63] most British prime ministers – including, of course, Mrs Thatcher – the German chancellors Helmut Kohl, Helmut Schmidt and Willy Brandt, Lech Walesa (as Monalidarność in 1990), and most of the women of the British royal family: the Queen; Princess Anne; Diana, Princess of Wales; and also the Prince of Wales. And, of course, film stars and celebrities from Brigitte Bardot to John Lennon and Woody Allen.

Mao Tse-tung, whose image at one moment in history was as ubiquitous as that of Lisa, has been monalised in various ways, notably by Marcel Laverdet, with *La Joconde rouge* in 1979.

The *New Yorker* gave Monica Lewinsky the *Mona Lisa* treatment (Mona = Monica, *and* the same initials) in its issue of 8 February 1999. The accompanying article comments: 'In Monica we have taken to seeing anything or anyone we care to; the innocent brought low, the sexual independent, the retrograde temptress.'

Many French politicians have had the same honour, starting with former Prime Minister Edouard Herriot in 1938 on the cover of *Le Rire*, by the caricaturist J. Sennep. Almost all the others, however, have been 'monalised' since the 1960s. There has been Malraux, of course, de Gaulle (regularly, notably one of the general as a concierge in Mona Lisa guise barring the British from the Hôtel Europe),[64] Georges Pompidou (as *Monna Elysa* in *Le Canard enchaîné* of 3 October 1973), Valéry Giscard d'Estaing, François Mitterrand, Jacques Chirac, most prime ministers and, indeed, any politician adopting an ambiguous position (an almost unavoidable necessity) – including Michel Rocard, Edith Cresson, Raymond Barre and Edouard Balladur.[65]

It is possible for non-celebrities to see what they would look like as Mona Lisa by using a traditional fairground technique: the insertion of their head in a hole carved in a wooden panel reproducing the painting. This writer saw a version of this contraption in July 2000 opposite the entrance to the Musée d'Orsay in Paris. Of course, in the age of digital cameras and electronic scanners one can obtain better results at home. We can look forward to a world where every human being will be able to monalise him or herself.

Philately took a keen interest in the *Mona Lisa* after its visit to Washington, though the West Germans were the first, with a *Mona Lisa* stamp back in distant 1952. Others followed later, including Aden in 1967, Albania in 1969, Butan in 1972, Bulgaria in 1980, Hungary in 1974, Jordan in 1974, North Korea in 1981, Mali in 1969, Paraguay in 1971, Qatar in 1967, Ras El Khaima (a Gulf state) in 1968, Togo in 1972 and the Yemen Arab Republic in 1969.[66] Neither religion nor culture nor politics unites this group of countries in any way – further evidence of the universal status gained by the *Mona Lisa*. France joined them only on 26 March 1999, when it produced three 'art' stamps: Delacroix's *Liberté guidant le peuple* (10 francs) and – equitably at 5 francs each – the Venus de Milo and the *Mona Lisa*.

Postcards have followed the same pattern as advertising, artistic derivation and stamps. After a flurry of cards at the time of the theft, the incidence returned to 'normal' until 1970. In the 1990s, the collector Robert Crespin produced a list of 983 postcards, overwhelmingly French. Almost all are post-1980. Another French collector, Gérard Neudin, the owner of a formidable collection of 100,000 postcards, says there are a few *thousand* inspired by *Mona Lisa*. Many are, of course, humorous. In 1992 the British cartoonist Steve Best came up with his own solution to the century-old enigma with a cartoon bearing the caption: 'Mona was trying not to smile as she waited for her silent fart to reach Leonardo'.

Mona Lisa has also been prominently displayed as a cover girl on many magazines. The satirical *l'Assiette au beurre* can claim to have been the first, in April 1902. Since 1980 she has appeared on the Italian *Epoca*, *Radiocorriere*, *Panorama* and *Espresso*; the German *Der Spiegel*; the French *l'Express*, *Paris-Match*, *Pariscope*, *Le Figaro* magazine, *Le Nouvel observateur*; the British *Sunday Times* supplement, *Sunday Telegraph*, *Radio Times*, *Punch*; the American *Ms*, the *New Yorker* and many more. It has been used on record sleeves, including *Gould Plays Bach* (1983) and the Beatles' *Sergeant Pepper's Lonely Hearts Club Band* (1967, artwork by Peter Blake). It was regularly used as a cartoon in the celebrated British television comedy series *Monty Python's Flying Circus*.

Two *Mona Lisa* games have been traced to 1912, and there have been over fifty since the 1950s. Some are ordinary board games, others pseudo-psychological tests (choose a hat for Mona Lisa and find out about your sexuality) and educational games – including a teach-yourself-English game consisting of identifying parts of the human body using the *Mona Lisa*.

A *Mona Lisa* bead-curtain was seen in Saigon in 1995; in 1976 she was painted on an American barn by a professional barn-painter,[67] and on the dialling disc of a Kuwaiti telephone (1983). A photograph of the *Mona Lisa* hangs in a humble church in Armenia – possibly believed to be a madonna.[68]

In September 1997 a *Mona Lisa* postcard was inserted amidst the floral tributes left by members of the public for Diana, Princess of Wales.[69]

In 1983 Tadahiko Ogawa, a Japanese artist from Kyoto, made a copy of the *Mona Lisa* completely out of toast, *Mona in Toast*.[70] The Munich-based artist Christina David will paint *Mona Lisa* miniatures on your fingernails for £35.[71] In 1989 Will Ashford, a 'Land Artist', produced a gigantic image of the *Mona Lisa* (61 metres × 43 metres) with manure-controlled grass, in California – where else?[72]

Mona Lisa has attracted her share of eccentrics. In 1981 the press took a keen interest in the career of a Léon Mekusa, an entrepreneur who, having fallen in love with the painting, sold his firm and took a job as a Louvre guard. He explained that he regarded being able to greet the *Mona Lisa* before anyone else in the morning as such a privilege that he had asked not to be paid. Every evening he talked about his love for the *Mona Lisa* to his wife, Angela. It happened that Angela was an amateur painter, and to humour her husband, or because the insanity is infectious, she painted over forty *Mona Lisa* derivations, including one with her Léon in the full uniform of a Louvre guard. An exhibition of her works which opened on 7 November 1997 was called 'Mon mari, la Joconde et moi'.[73]

More disturbing has been the experimentation of the French 'performance artist' Orlan, who underwent plastic surgery in 1990 in order to look like the Mona Lisa. The video-recorded operation constituted her artwork. Originally she had planned to have it broadcast live, with worldwide satellite connections, but the organisers of the contemporary arts festival in Paris at which the event was to take place vetoed the project.[74] If *Newsweek* of 6 January 1975 is to be believed, a Japanese woman, Reiko Ishii, had surgery to become a Mona Lisa lookalike before Orlan, and an undated Associated Press report tells the story of another Japanese woman, twenty-one-year-old Yukie Tamura, who appeared on television after such an operation 'wearing a medieval dress'.

Then there are the poems and love letters, often addressed simply to 'Mona Lisa, Louvre, Paris'. One was sent in 1994 from Her Majesty's Prison in Exeter, England, to 'Mona Lisa, Epsom, Surrey'. It was redirected, 'Not known at this address, try the Louvre Paris France'. It starts, 'Dear Mona, This is your Dad . . .'[75] Some send her postcards with news of themselves, as if she were an old friend.

Numerous correspondents claim to have discovered the solution to her identity, or secret codes hidden in the painting. There is an irrepressible desire to solve mysteries. The world, as we know, is full of them – some real, many invented, and to be a problem-solver has always been gratifying. It can lead to fame and renown. Detectives are among the greatest modern fictional heroes. Well before them, fairy tales and mythological stories celebrated and honoured those who resolved riddles. The *Mona Lisa*, as we have seen, has presented quite a few mysteries. Anyone who solves, or claims to have solved, one of them is guaranteed instant, if ephemeral, fame. The headline 'Mystery of the Smile Explained' appears with great regularity, if not monotony, in the international press. Very few people genuinely care deeply about the matter (and who can blame those who do not?), but almost everyone has some curiosity about the *Mona Lisa*, because of its fame. This makes the story ideal: it is completely inoffensive, is of general interest, and will be almost immediately forgotten, thus ensuring its regular recycling.

Some of the *Mona Lisa* mysteries are connected with the identity of the sitter (see Chapter 1). My conclusion is that the evidence is too scanty for us to arrive at any firm identification. We shall never know – not that this will stop people from trying. And there is always the remote possibility that some new evidence will be unearthed.

One of the most popular theories is that the *Mona Lisa* is in fact Leonardo's self-portrait. Such claims were made at the beginning of the twentieth century, and have remained current. For instance, in 1913 the painter Maurice Vieuille claimed that while the lower half of the face is that of a woman, the upper half is that of a man. And not just any man: 'That gaze, it is Vinci's.'[76] However, it is only since the 1952 X-ray examination carried out by Madame Magdalene Hours, the director of the Louvre laboratory, that the androgyny theme, first ventilated in the nineteenth century, has really blossomed.[77]

In that year, on the five hundredth anniversary of the birth of Leonardo, the art critic Georges Isarlo claimed that Mona Lisa was a transvestite. He had come to this conclusion after watching a college play in which a male actor was dressed as a woman,[78] and expanded on his theory in a widely reported book in 1956.[79] On the basis of Isarlo's claims, in June 1953 the New York journal *Sexology* published a picture of Mona Lisa with cropped hair, looking like an effeminate young man – as many young men with longish hair would in female dress – with a veil. In 1986 Lillian Schwarz, a computer-art scientist working at Bell Laboratories in New Jersey, 'conclusively' proved that the *Mona Lisa* was a self-portrait of the young Leonardo.[80] This prompted the London *Daily Telegraph* to report the news with the headline 'Mona Lisa "was Leonardo in drag"' (19 December 1986). The reaction of Mr Freeberg, a curator at the National Gallery in Washington DC, was optimistic: 'The *Mona Lisa* will survive this crap.'[81]

The *Mona Lisa* became a toy with which one could play. In 1993 a French-Canadian artist, Suzanne Giroux, vastly enlarged the smile, shifted it vertically and pointed out that this made the face look strikingly like the curvaceous back of an adolescent male – another 'sign' of Leonardo's homosexuality. Her work was exhibited at the Fair of International Contemporary Art at the Grand Palais in Paris.[82] This was taken seriously – perhaps it was meant to be – by the Italian magazine *Il Bel Paese* (March 1996), which tried to discredit it by showing that surprising results can be obtained by magnifying details of any painting: by changing the axis of the magnified elbow of the child Jesus in Raphael's *La Belle jardinière* (also at the Louvre), for example, it could appear as an anus or a vagina.

In the 1970s photocopying machines were used to create – in a largely pre-computer age – what the French call *électrographie*, and the rest of the world 'Copy Art'. This consists of deforming pictures by moving them or changing the intensity of the light during photocopying, or by manipulating the machine. Needless to say, most of the examples used to advertise this technique, which did not survive the advent of desktop computers, were scowling Mona Lisas.

Thanks to computers and a technique called 'image morphing', it is now possible to distort pictures and photographs so they can be viewed from a different perspective. A profile can thus be made to 'turn around' and face the viewer directly. Workers in this field have demonstrated their achievements by eliminating Leonardo's *contrapposto* and making Lisa sit up straight.[83]

John Asmus, of the University of California at San Diego, using computer enhancement techniques, claimed that Mona Lisa originally wore a necklace (which I failed to spot in the pictures accompanying the 1986 article).[84] In 1992 a French art student used a computer to 'remove' Mona Lisa from her own portrait, thus transforming Leonardo into a landscape painter. He won a prize.[85] That, however, had already been done in 1965, without computers, by the Italian artist Guido Biasi in his ironically titled *Mona Lisa Without Landscape* – in fact a landscape without Lisa.

The *Mona Lisa* craze was spotted, years before advertisers set to work on it, by observant minds. In 1959 the self-styled 'Jocondologue' Jean Margat produced a *Treatise of Jocondology*, the first phase of a systematic collection of assorted monalisiana.[86] A little earlier, in 1957, Henri Gruel and Jean Suyeux made an iconoclastic French television documentary making fun of the *Mona Lisa* obsession: it was broadcast only after being reduced to fourteen minutes by the censors. At that time it was still considered disrespectful to make fun of a masterpiece in the mass media:[87] angry tourists nearly lynched the film crew when they were spotted filming three gigantic deformed portraits of the *Mona Lisa* in the courtyard of the Louvre.[88] However, the documentary won a prize at the Cannes Film Festival.

In 1990 the organisers of the football World Cup, held in Italy, used Mona Lisa as the tournament's symbol, placing a ball in her hands. British television's Channel Five used the *Mona Lisa* to promote the programme *The Female Orgasm* – occupying an entire page of the *Guardian* of 9 September 1999.

Mona Lisa played a part in the Second World War when her smile was used as a coded message to the French Resistance by the BBC World Service: '*La Joconde garde son sourire*' ('The *Joconde* keeps her smile'). Later she also took part, so to speak, in the 'class struggle': on 12 February 1992 freelance French 'cultural' workers (musicians, actors, etc.) demonstrating for the right to be treated, for social security purposes, like salaried employees, staged a sit-in in the Louvre by the *Mona Lisa*. Some chained themselves by its side.[89] In 1995, employees of the French Ministry of Culture used her effigy (with raised fist) in a demonstration against the government's austerity plan.[90]

Inevitably, the sex industry has not left the *Mona Lisa* alone. In 1957 the Paris nightclub La Fontaine de Quatre Saisons put on a show called *Jocond' Folie* in which dancers dressed as Mona Lisa performed a striptease.[91] The *International Herald Tribune* (12 May 1974) reported another Parisian strip show called 'The Coquettish Smile of Mona Lisa'. There is a website advertising the services of one Mona Lisa, born in 1970 and raised in Tacoma, Washington: 'There is no mystery about the smile on this lascivious lady – she's most likely thinking about sex . . . an incendiary sexual performer who has never met a man that she couldn't wrap around her little finger.'[92]

The so-called 'mystery' of the smile – as we have seen, largely a nineteenth-century invention – became in the twentieth century the preoccupation of men of science rather than art historians and critics. The trend seems to have started in 1955, when a Genoa daily reported that a local dentist had attributed Mona Lisa's expression to a toothache. In the same year a 'London critic' announced that she was deaf, and that her enigmatic expression was due to the effort of trying to hear what Leonardo was telling her.[93]

More substantial, and better reported, because it had the imprimatur of an influential medical journal, was the 1959 claim of Dr Kenneth D. Keele, a respected Leonardian, that Mona Lisa was pregnant, and that anyone who has observed a pregnant woman sit down and turn to one side would realise it.[94] An enlargement of the thyroid gland had caused the 'almost puffy' neck. Far from being mocking or enigmatic, the smile signalled the placid satisfaction of pregnancy.[95] His conclusion was that 'Leonardo created his ideal picture of motherhood.'[96]

Dr Étienne Maigret, writing in 1962, was more harsh: though Mona Lisa was 'a woman of normal anatomic proportions', she was clearly crossed-eyed, hence her strange expression.[97] According to Dr F. Becker-Christensen, a Danish specialist in congenital facial paresis, the wry smile was caused by an asymmetrical hypofunction of the facial muscles.[98] A copy of his article was sent to the Louvre in 1975 by another Danish doctor, Johan Schioldann Nielsen of the Department of Psychiatry at Odense University Hospital, who also supplied an article, 'The Enigmatic Smile of Mona Lisa', which he had published in the same journal.[99] Dr Nielsen claimed that Leonardo was a neurotic who had found his mother's smile in Mona Lisa's enigmatic look – exactly what Freud had written some sixty-five years previously.

As medical interest expanded, Mona Lisa's health deteriorated. In 1989 Dr Kedal Adour, a Californian specialist, diagnosed a facial paralysis known as Bell's Palsy. His view was that Leonardo never finished the portrait 'because of the ever-changing relation between the eye blink (and its associated motion, upward twitch of the upper lip) and a deepening of the nasolabial fold when the forehead moves upward'.[100]

Things could only get worse. In 1991 the press drew attention to the findings of Professor Jean-Jacques Comtet of Lyon: Mona Lisa was hemiplegic (spastic); bits of her brain had gone. With her right arm and shoulder paralysed she could not sit in any other way.[101] Now we know why Leonardo was obliged to use the *contrapposto* position. Dr Comtet was described by the *Daily Mail* of 27 April 1991 as a 'world-renowned expert on hands'. The headline was ' "Tragic secret" behind that Mona Lisa smile'. Lisa's problems were not over. Later in 1991 Professor Harno Nakamura, a Japanese scientist, established that a slight excrescence or nodule on the corner of her left eye was due to excess cholesterol.

Not to be outdone, the dentists returned to the fray. In 1992 Joseph E. Borkowski, a professor of operative dentistry, stated that the expression of Mona Lisa is common to people who have lost their front teeth, and that a close examination of the lip area shows a scar not unlike that left by a blow from a blunt object.[102] We are thus left with new mysteries: did Leonardo knock Lisa about because she refused to sit still? Was she a battered wife? Further research is required, and no doubt more findings will be forthcoming. One can only marvel, however, at the advances in medical science. If we believe all these reports, it should be quite unnecessary to submit oneself to medical visits, dental X-rays or even pregnancy tests. All that is required is to send one's photograph to all and sundry, then wait confidently for an expert diagnosis.

Perhaps the smile was just due to the boredom of sitting for long hours (or years). In September 1999 it was widely reported that Filippo Surano, an Italian doctor, had discovered, once more, the secret of the enigmatic smile: it was due to a compulsive gnashing of the teeth. According to Dr Surano Mona Lisa suffered from bruxism, an unconscious habit of grinding the teeth during sleep or periods of mental stress. This would probably lead to mouth and kidney infections and nephritis, causing her hands and face to swell.[103] Had she seen the front cover of the *Journal of the Indiana Dental Association* (Fall 1994), on which she is shown beaming with a full smile, she might have been interested in the feature inside on implant dentistry.

There may well be something in all of this. Dentistry was not well developed in the sixteenth century, and few people had gleaming white teeth – one of the many reasons teeth are hardly ever shown in portraits. At least Lisa was spared the further deterioration which occurred in dental health in later centuries, after the advent of cheap sugar and the increasing consumption of chocolate in Europe.[104]

The growth of the Internet, by democratising communication, will no doubt accelerate the multiplication of ingenious hypotheses and the growth of the *Mona Lisa* industry. Websites such as the appropriately named www.monalisamania.com ask web surfers to 'Enter your Mona Lisa Theory below. When your [sic] finished please click *Submit*.' And the theories come, thick and thin, to this and other *Mona Lisa* websites. Here is a startling one sent in 1999:

> One evening I was admiring my new Mona Lisa desktop background and it occurred to me with a shock that she bears a terrifying resemblance to [the Hollywood actor] Michael Douglas. This is in fact because Michael Douglas is a distant descendant of the woman whom Leonardo Da Vinci painted, and knowing this he had plastic surgery to make himself look more like her in the hope that it would further his career.[105]

In October 2000 there were 93,800 web pages on 'Mona Lisa' and another 2,110 on 'Joconde'. Readers will forgive this writer for having looked at only a tiny fraction of them, but there is such a thing as *Mona Lisa* fatigue. Further evidence is unnecessary. The fame of the painting bearing the Louvre inventory number 779 has surpassed all imaginable boundaries. And the time has come to draw some conclusions.

I have tried to map out the complex origins and development of this global craze. The assumption underlying this study is that though aesthetic considerations have a place in the story, it is not a large one. People have not decided, independently of their social and cultural context, that Leonardo's *Mona Lisa* is the most beautiful painting in the world, nor did they decide for themselves that the smile it portrays has particular qualities. Its renown and meanings have been the product of a long history of political and geographical accident, fantasies conjured up, connections made, images manufactured, and luck – 'little cell by cell', as Pater put it.

Like many others I often wondered, 'Why her?' This, I felt, was the one 'mystery' really worth solving. It was not a metaphysical problem. It did not require special insights into the Meaning of Art or the Soul of Man. It was a historical problem, to be solved by using the ordinary methods of historians: accumulating evidence, sifting facts and making connections. It does not require a particular artistic sensibility, or 'scientific' knowledge, let alone medical expertise. All that is necessary is to take nothing for granted.

One of the duties of the historian – or so I feel – is to examine the origins of our own opinions and preferences. Why do we like what we like? Why do we want what we want? Why have certain images from the past survived? There is an element of chance and individual choice involved in this, but much of what we believe is due to the tyrannical weight of the past. Questioning it is part of the modern condition.

Questioning why the *Mona Lisa* has become so famous begins with the assumption that the reasons for its fame were external to it. No single cause or explanation gives us an adequate answer. The fact that it ended up in Paris was decisive, but many other paintings ended up in Paris. Being painted by Leonardo mattered a great deal, but Lucrezia Crivelli, Ginevra de' Benci and Cecilia Gallerani – all prettier than Lisa Gherardini (at least by conventional standards) – were also painted by Leonardo. The famous smile, now almost universally regarded as the *Mona Lisa*'s most distinctive feature, is in reality barely perceptible, and is not unusual. The theft in 1911 gave the *Mona Lisa* considerable renown, but many other paintings have been stolen and gained only ephemeral fame. The crucial factor in transforming the *Mona*

Lisa into a global icon has been its deployment in advertising, merchandising and by later artists. But advertisers and artists would not have used it had it not already been regarded as the most famous painting in the world. We must not forget that the *Mona Lisa* was regarded as a masterpiece by many of Leonardo's own contemporaries, including Raphael, and by Vasari (although he never actually saw it). Few paintings were as widely copied in the sixteenth and seventeenth centuries. Artists knew it was a special portrait long before modern intellectuals engaged with it.

Nothing has a single cause. The present status of the *Mona Lisa* is the result of a complex historical process in which many people had a role to play: Leonardo, who painted it; Francesco il Giocondo, who commissioned it; François I, who brought Leonardo to France. Then there were those who transformed the Louvre from a royal palace into a public museum; the intellectuals who wrote enticing things about the *Mona Lisa* and propagated the idea of her mysterious powers and smile. Then there was Vincenzo Peruggia, who stole it; Malraux and de Gaulle, who used it to represent French culture; the press that never grew tired of writing about it; all those who sang about her, drew her, distorted her and made fun of her; all the 'solvers' of enigmas; all those who visited her and told their friends that her eyes follow you everywhere; and all those who exploited her fame, not realising or caring that in so doing they were adding to it.

The cultural establishment – like all elites – has always been ambivalent about any product of high culture that acquires mass fame. It is as if one of the defining features of high culture is that it should be beyond the masses. Close to this position, but pretending to be on the other side, are the populists, who say (while disbelieving it) that everything is as good as everything else: a Tintin comic-strip is as good as a Botticelli, Hollywood films as good as Shakespeare. The masses are patted on the back and patronisingly told: 'Your stuff is fine, it's just as good as ours, really.' The big divide is thus reinforced and everyone kept in their traditional place. The story of the *Mona Lisa* confounds all of these positions: it demonstrates that something can be both a classic of Western art and pop, hip and cool.

Besides, nothing is static. What we read, what we see, what we experience, changes our perceptions. When I started this work, I did not find the *Mona Lisa* a particularly beautiful painting. Now I do. I think I know why she is famous. I still do not know why she smiles. But neither does anyone else.

NOTES

CHAPTER ONE

1 Ginger Danto, 'Taking Mona Lisa's Temperature', in *ARTnews*, September 1991, pp.99–101.
2 Kenneth Clark, 'Mona Lisa', in *Burlington Magazine*, March 1973, p.150.
3 Paul Barolsky, '*Mona Lisa* Explained', in *Sources: Notes in the History of Art*, Vol.13, No.2, 1994, pp.15–16.
4 Ibid., p.15.
5 Giorgio Vasari, *Le Vite de' più eccellenti pittori, scultori e architetti*, Newton, Rome, 1991, p.564.
6 Ernst Gombrich, *The Story of Art*, Phaidon, London, 1989, pp.227–8.
7 Nielsen–CRA survey directed by Renato Mannheimer, Istituto per gli Studi sulla Pubblica Opinione, Milan, 11–13 February 2000.
8 Report in *Connaissance des arts*, June 1974.
9 *Paris-Match*, 13 July 1984.
10 See *Hamburger Abendblatt*, 26 October 1989.
11 Federico Zeri, *Derrière l'image*, Rivages, Paris, 1988, p.153.
12 See an account of the debate in *Nuances*, No.18, October 1998.
13 Vasari, op. cit., p.564.
14 Meyer Schapiro, 'Leonardo and Freud: An Art-Historical Study', in *Journal of the History of Ideas*, Vol.17, No.2, April 1956, p.165.
15 Umberto Eco, *Opera aperta: Forma e indeterminazione nelle poetiche contemporanee*, Bompiani, Milan, 1995, pp.35–6. The first version of this essay was originally conceived in 1958.
16 Leonardo da Vinci, *Leonardo on Painting*, ed. Martin Kemp, Yale University Press, New Haven and London, 1989 (henceforth cited as *Leonardo on Painting*), p.149.
17 Baldassare Castiglione, *Il cortegiano*, Mondadori, Milan, 1991, p.47; English translation, here slightly modified, *The Book of the Courtier*, Penguin, Harmondsworth, 1967, p.67, where 'sprezzatura' is translated as 'nonchalance'.
18 Jacob Burckhardt, *The Civilization of the Renaissance in Italy*, Phaidon Press, London, 1960, pp.219–21.
19 Ibid., p.210.
20 Daniel Arasse, *Leonardo da Vinci: The Rhythm of the World*, English trans., Konecky and Konecky, New York, 1997, p.408.
21 E.H. Gombrich, 'Portrait of the Artist as a Paradox', in *New York Review of Books*, 20 January 2000, p.8.
22 Raymon Bayer, *Léonard de Vinci: La Grâce*, Félix Alcan, Paris, 1933, p.200.
23 Ibid., pp.215–16.
24 This was Eugène Müntz's view;

see his *Léonard de Vinci: l'Artiste, le penseur, le savant*, Hachette, Paris, 1899, pp.417–19.

25 Baedeker, *Paris et ses environs*, Leipzig and Paris, 1914, p.119.

26 André-Charles Coppier, 'La "Joconde" est-elle le portrait de "Mona Lisa"?', in *Les Arts*, No.145, January 1914.

27 Vasari, op. cit., p.555.

28 Frank Zöllner, 'Leonardo's Portrait of Mona Lisa del Giocondo', in *Gazette des beaux-arts*, March 1993, p.132.

29 Ibid., p.118.

30 Vasari, op. cit., p.564.

31 Zöllner, op. cit., pp.115–38.

32 Ibid., p.120.

33 Kenneth Clark, *Leonardo da Vinci*, Penguin, Harmondsworth, 1989, p.172. See also Clark, 'Mona Lisa', in *Burlington Magazine*, op. cit., pp.144–50.

34 Martin Kemp, *Leonardo da Vinci: The Marvellous Works of Nature and Man*, Dent, London, 1981, pp.268–70.

35 For a recent example of the two-Lisas theory see Jérôme de Bassano, 'Le Mythe de la Joconde', in *Bulletin de l'Association Léonard de Vinci*, No.16, March 1978 pp.21–3.

36 Zöllner, op. cit., p.122.

37 On this important drawing see Françoise Viatte, *Léonard de Vinci: Isabelle d'Este*, Éditions de la RMN, Paris, 1999.

38 Müntz, op. cit., p.371.

39 Viatte, op. cit., p.23.

40 See Raymond Stites, 'Monna Lisa Monna Bella', in *Parnassus*, January 1946, pp.7, 10, 22–3; Hidemichi Tanaka, 'Leonardo's Isabella d'Este: A New Analysis of the Monna Lisa in the

Louvre', in *Annali dell'Istituto Giapponese di Cultura in Roma*, No.13, 1976–77.

41 Adolfo Venturi, 'La pittura del cinquecento', in *Storia dell'arte italiana*, Vol.IX, Hoepli, Milan, 1925; and *Enciclopedia Italiana*, Treccani, Rome, 1933.

42 Carlo Vecce, *Leonardo*, Salerno editrice, Rome, 1998, p.257.

43 Ibid., pp.324–36.

44 Vasari, op. cit., p.565.

45 Carlo Vecce, 'La Gualanda', in *Achademia Leonardi Vinci*, Vol.3, 1990, p.64.

46 Ibid., pp.335–6.

47 Carlo Pedretti, *Leonardo: A Study in Chronology and Style*, Thames and Hudson, London, 1973, pp.135–7.

48 Carlo Pedretti, 'Storia della Gioconda di Leonardo da Vinci con nuove congetture sulla persona ritratta', in *Bibliothèque d'humanisme et Renaissance*, Vol.18, 1956, pp.171–82.

49 See *Il Giornale dell'Emilia*, 1 November 1953.

50 See www.italica.rai.

51 Stendhal, *Histoire de la peinture en Italie*, Gallimard Folio, Paris, 1996, p.207.

52 See André Chastel, *Un cardinale del Rinascimento in viaggio per l'Europa*, Laterza, Bari-Rome, 1995 (originally *Le cardinal Louis d'Aragon: Un voyageur princier de la Renaissance*, Fayard, Paris, 1986). There is an English version of de Beatis's diary: *The Travel Journal of Antonio de Beatis: Germany, Switzerland, the Low Countries, France and Italy, 1517–1518*, introduction by John R. Hale, The Hakluyt Society, London, 1979.

53 Chastel, op. cit., pp.75, 85.

54 The Italian text used here is in the *Catalogue raisonné des oeuvres de Léonard de Vinci au Musée du Louvre et dans les collections françaises*, in *Homage à Léonard de Vinci*, Musée du Louvre édition MN, Paris, 1952, p.xxi.

55 Janice Shell and Grazioso Sironi, 'Salaì and Leonardo's Legacy', in *Burlington Magazine*, February 1991, pp.98–100.

56 Cassiano's description is cited at length in Janet Cox-Rearick, *Chefs-d'oeuvre de la Renaissance: La Collection de François Ier*, Albin Michel, Paris, 1995, p.153. Cassiano's diaries were republished in Paris in 1885 in the original Italian with the title *Le Château de Fontainebleau en 1625 d'aprés le commandeur Cassiano del Pozzo*.

57 Cox-Rearick, op. cit., p.123.

58 Kemp, op. cit., plate 71, p.264.

59 Shell and Sironi, op. cit., pp.95–108; this was republished with minor changes as 'The Gioconda in Milan', in *I leonardeschi a Milano: Fortuna e collezionimo*, Atti del convegno internazionale Milano, 25–26 September 1990, Milan, 1991.

60 Alessandro Vezzosi, *Leonardo da Vinci: Arte e scienza dell'universo*, Electa/Gallimard, Trieste, 1996, p.167.

61 Shell and Sironi, op. cit., p.102.

62 We owe this information to Father Pierre Dan, author of *Le Trésor des merveilles de la maison royale de Fontainebleau*, 1642.

63 Sylvie Béguin, 'La Joconde et le démon', in *Connaissance des arts*, 1991, pp.62–9.

64 Gabriel Séailles, *Léonard de Vinci: L'artiste et le savant: Essai de biographie psychologique*, Perrin et cie, Paris, 1892, p.473.

65 Janice Shell, *Léonard de Vinci*, Réunion des musées nationaux, Paris, 1993, p.32.

CHAPTER TWO

1 Daniel Arasse, *Le Détail: Pour une histoire rapprochée de la peinture*, Champs-Flammarion, Paris, 1996, pp.68–72.

2 *Journal des arts*, 28 August 1998.

3 These tests were carried out by Magdeleine Hours. They are available in Louvre Folder Inv 779. See also her published report, 'Radiographie des tableaux de Léonard de Vinci', in *Revue des arts*, No.4, 1952, pp.227–35.

4 Stendhal, op. cit., p.207.

5 Jean-Pierre Cuzin, reported in 'Quand Monna Lisa fait sa toilette', in *Paris-Match*, 3 June 1997.

6 Kemp, op. cit., p.266. The diptych in question is the double-panelled portrait of Federigo da Montefeltro and Battista Sforza, c.1472.

7 *Leonardo on Painting*, p.147.

8 Paolo Bernini, 'Women under the Gaze: a Renaissance Genealogy', in *Art History*, Vol.21, No.4, December 1998, p.581.

9 Kemp, op. cit., p.265.

10 Carlo Starnazzi 'Leonardo in terra di Arezzo', in *Studi per l'ecologia del Quarternario*, No.17, 1995, pp.7, 24.

11 Kemp, op. cit., p.266.

12 David Alan Brown, 'Leonardo and the Idealized Portrait in Milan', in *Arte Lombarda*, no.67, 1983–84; also Arasse, *Leonardo da Vinci*, op. cit., p.394.

13 Vasari, op. cit., p.81.

14 Charles Hope, 'A Wind from the West', in *New York Review of Books*, 2 December 1999, pp.11–13.

15 John Pope-Hennessy, 'The Portrait in the Renaissance', The A.W. Mellon Lectures in the Fine Arts, 1963, National Gallery of Art, Washington DC, Bollinger Series XXXV, 12, Pantheon Books, New York, 1966, p.60.

16 Zaremba Filipczak, 'New Light on Mona Lisa: Leonardo's Optical Knowledge and his Choice of Lighting', in *Art Bulletin*, Vol.59, No.4, December 1977, p.519.

17 Vincent Pomarède, *La Joconde*, Prat/Europa, Paris, 1988, p.58.

18 Lisa Jardine, *Worldly Goods: A New History of the Renaissance*, Macmillan, London and Basingstoke, 1997, pp.10–11.

19 *Le Monde*, 29 June 1991.

20 Pomarède, op. cit., pp.39, 63.

21 *Leonardo on Painting*, p.88.

22 Karl Jaspers, *Leonardo, Descartes, Max Weber: Three Essays*, Routledge and Kegan Paul, London, 1965, p.9.

23 *Leonardo on Painting*, p.87.

24 Ernst Gombrich, *The Story of Art*, Phaidon, Oxford, 1989, p.228.

25 Barolsky, op. cit., p.14.

26 Luba Freedman, 'Raphael's Perception of the *Mona Lisa*', in *Gazette des beaux-arts*, November 1989, p.171.

27 Schneider and Flam, op. cit., p.16.

28 Pope-Hennessy, 'The Portrait in the Renaissance', op. cit., p.112.

29 I have relied here on what is by far the most convincing analysis of Raphael's debt to Leonardo, namely Luba Freedman, 'Raphael's Perception of the *Mona Lisa*', op. cit., pp.169–82.

30 Ibid., p.172.

31 Cox-Rearick, op. cit., pp.124–6.

32 Marie-Antoinette Fleury, *Documents du Minutier Central concernant les peintres les sculpteurs et les graveurs au XVIIe siècle (1600–1650)*, Vol.1, Paris, 1969.

33 NAAF 1892, p.198, No.47, in Louvre folder Inv 779.

34 Mireille Rambaud, *Documents du Minutier central concernant l'Histoire de l'art (1700–1750)*, Vol.2, Paris, 1971, p.781.

35 See E. Dacier, *Catalogue de la vente Gaignat (1769)*, Paris, 1921.

36 Philip Fehl, 'In Praise of Imitation: Leonardo and his Followers', in *Gazette des beaux-arts*, July–August 1995, p.1.

37 David Alan Brown, *The Young Correggio and his Leonardesque Sources*, Garland, New York, 1981.

38 Fehl, op. cit., p.8.

39 On de Bagarris see Cox-Rearick, op. cit., pp.100–1.

40 Müntz, op. cit., p.421; also A. Brejon de Lavergnée, *l'Inventaire de Le Brun de 1683: La Collection des tableaux de Louis XIV*, Éditions de la Réunion des musées nationaux, Paris, 1987, p.44 (the original document is in the Biblioteca Barberini, Rome LX, No.64, fol.192, V 194 V).

41 F.-A. Gruyer, *Voyage autour du salon carré au musée du Louvre*, Paris, 1891, p.34; and Charles Clément, *Michel-Ange, Léonard de Vinci, Raphael*, Michel Lévy Frères, Paris, 1861, p.222.

42 Roger de Piles, *Abrégé de la vie des peintres avec des réflexions sur leurs ouvrages*, 1691, cited by Jean Suyeux, 'Le Testament de Léonard', in *Le Gnomon: Revue*

Notes

internationale d'histoire du
notariat, No.88, June–July 1993,
p.6. This carefully researched
paper provides the most detailed
factual information on the
vicissitudes of the *Mona Lisa* in
the sixteenth to eighteenth
centuries.

43 Lépicié, *Catalogue des tableaux
du Roy*, Tome 1, Paris, 1752.

44 See *Musée du Louvre: Janvier
1797–June 1797: Procés du Conseil
d'administration du Musée
Central des Arts*, in Yveline
Cantarel-Besson, *Notes et
documents No.2*, RMN, Paris,
1992.

CHAPTER THREE

1 See the entry for the Louvre in
Diderot and D'Alembert,
Enclycopédie, Cramer, Geneva,
1772, Vol.9, pp.706–7, where it
is suggested that the king's
pictures should be moved to the
Louvre.

2 Andrew McClelland, 'The
Musée du Louvre as a
Revolutionary Metaphor During
the Terror', in *Art Bulletin*,
Vol.70, No.2, June 1988,
pp.300 3.

3 Text of document in Geneviève
Bresc, *Mémoires du Louvre*,
Gallimard and RMN, Paris,
1989, pp.170–1.

4 Germain Bazin, *Trésors de la
peinture au Louvre*, Éditions
Somogy, Paris, 1962, p.78.

5 *Notices des principaux tableaux
recueillis dans la Lombardie par les
commissaires du gouvernment
francais*, Decembre 1797;
information in Foureolle, *Livres
Rares*, Paris, 1998 where this
catalogue was advertised for sale.

6 Germain Bazin, *The Museum
Age*, Desoeer, Brussels, 1967,
pp.186–7.

7 Originally published by Baxter,
Oxford, 1816, it has been
reprinted in photo-facsimile by
Garland Publishers, New York,
1978, in their 'Significant Minor
Poetry' series.

8 John C. Eustace, *Classical Tour
Through Italy*, Vol.2, Hawman,
London, 1813, p.60.

9 Bazin, *The Museum Age*, op. cit.,
p.177.

10 Ibid., p.171.

11 Jean-Pierre Cusin, 'Au Louvre,
d'aprés les maîtres', in *Copier
Créer: De Turner à Picasso: 300
oeuvres inspirées par les maîtres
du Louvre* (exhibition
catalogue), Réunion des Musées
Nationaux, Paris, 1993, pp.31–4;
henceforth cited as *Copier Créer*.

12 Eugène Delacroix, *Journal
1822–1863*, Plon, Paris, 1980,
p.737, entry for 9 March 1859.

13 Cusin, 'Delacroix copié', in
Copier Créer, pp.250–5.

14 Cusin, 'd'Aprés les Florentins',
in ibid., pp.274–5.

15 Delacroix, op. cit., pp.384, 603.

16 Jean-Pierre Cuzin, 'Autour de la
Joconde', in *Copier Créer*,
pp.412–15; see also pp.416–20.

17 Cusin, 'd'Aprés les Florentins',
in *Copier Créer*, pp.275ff.

18 Dupuy, op. cit., pp.44–5.

19 Léon Lagrange, 'Du Rang des
femmes dans les arts', in *Gazette
des beaux-arts*, October 1860,
pp.40–3.

20 See Champfleury, *l'Artiste*, 1844,
pp.210, 212, cited by Marie-Anne
Dupuy, 'Les Copistes à l'oeuvre',
in *Copier Créer*, p.49.

21 Dominique Poulot, 'La Visite au
musée: Un loisir édifiant au

XIXe siècle', in *Gazette des beaux-arts*, May–June 1983, p.189.

22 Gérard Monnier, *l'Art et ses institutions en France: De la Révolution à nos jours*, Folio-Gallimard, Paris, 1995, p.133.

23 Bresc, op. cit., p.122.

24 Émile Zola, 'Édouard Manet' (1867), in *Oeuvres Complètes*, Vol.12 (*Oeuvres critiques* 3), ed. Henri Mitterrand, Cercle du livre précieux, Paris, 1969, p.842.

25 Émile Zola, *l'Assommoir*, Livre de Poche, Paris, 1979, pp.88–90.

26 Poulot, op. cit., p.189.

27 Marie-Anne Dupuy 'Les Copistes à l'oeuvre', in *Copier Créer*, pp.44–7.

28 Pierre Angrand, 'L'État mécène: Période autoritaire du Second Empire (1851–1860)', in *Gazette des beaux-arts*, May–June 1968, pp.304–6.

29 Russell M. Jones, 'American Painters in Paris: The Rate of Exchange 1825–48', in *Apollo*, February 1992, p.73.

30 Clément de Ris, 'Musée du Louvre', in *l'Artiste*, 15 January 1849.

31 See the report in the art review *Le Cabinet de l'amateur II*, 1843, pp.551–2.

32 Ministère de l'intérieur, *Notice des tableaux exposés dans les galeries du Musée Nationale du Louvre*, ed. Frédéric Villot, 1ère partie, Écoles d'Italie, Musées nationaux, Paris, 1849, p.108.

33 Germain Bazin, *La Peinture au Louvre*, Éditions Somogy, Paris, 1966, p.61.

34 Villot, op. cit., p.104.

35 Kenneth Clark, *Another Part of the Wood*, Hodder and Stoughton, London, 1976, p.47.

36 Charles Clément, *Michel-Ange, Léonard de Vinci, Raphael*, op. cit., pp.220–2.

37 Valeria Ramaciotti Donato, 'I decadenti e la Gioconda: ambiguità e polivalenza di un simbolo', in *Studi francesi*, Vol.21, No.61–2, January–August 1977, pp.70–98; see p.74.

CHAPTER FOUR

1 See Martin Kemp, 'Clark's Leonardo', introduction to Kenneth Clark, *Leonardo da Vinci*, op. cit., p.7.

2 See Shearer West (ed.), *Italian Culture in Northern Europe in the Eighteenth Century*, Cambridge University Press, 1998.

3 Charles Clément, *Michel-Ange, Léonard de Vinci, Raphael*, op. cit., pp.47–8.

4 Arnold Hauser, *The Social History of Art: Vol.2, Renaissance, Mannerism, Baroque*, Routledge, London, 1999, p.60.

5 Charles Hope, 'In Lorenzo's Garden', in *New York Review of Books*, 24 June 1999, p.65.

6 Raymond Lebègue, 'Les Artistes italiens de la Renaissance et les écrivains français du temps', in *l'Art et la pensée de Léonard de Vinci*, Communications du Congrés International du Val de Loire (7–12 July 1952), Etudes d'Art Nos.8,9,10, Paris–Alger 1953–54, pp.213–21.

7 E.H. Gombrich, *New Light on Old Masters: Studies in the Art of the Renaissance*, University of Chicago Press, 1986, p.125.

Notes

8 Barrie Bullen, 'Walter Pater's "Renaissance" and Leonardo da Vinci's Reputation in the Nineteenth Century', in *Modern Language Review*, Vol.74, 1979, pp.268–80.

9 These figures are crude indicators: a book entitled *From Duccio to Picasso* would add to Picasso's (and Duccio's) total but not to Michelangelo's or Leonardo's.

10 These were the so-called 'Milan manuscripts'. Leonardo's student and heir Francesco Melzi dispersed the collection of Leonardo's writing. It took centuries to piece it together again.

11 J.B. Bullen, *The Myth of the Renaissance in Nineteenth-Century Writing*, Clarendon Press, Oxford, 1994, p.173. Venturi's lecture was published in French as *Essai sur les ouvrages physico-mathématiques de Léonard de Vinci*.

12 See Bertrand Gille, *Les Ingénieurs de la Renaissance*, Seuil Points, Paris, 1978, pp.83–127, for the contributions of Taccola and Francesco di Giorgio; pp.129–75 for a thorough reconsideration of Leonardo amounting to a debunking of nineteenth-century claims of exceptional originality; on the superiority of Leonardo's method of reasoning see p.193.

13 Richard Schofield, 'Leonardo's Milanese Architecture: Career, Sources and Graphic Techniques', *in Achademia Leonardi Vinci*, Vol.4, 1991, pp.111–57; the citation is on p.120.

14 Gille, op. cit., p.141.

15 Clark, *Leonardo Da Vinci*, op. cit., pp.140

16 Maria Vittoria Brunoli, 'The Sculptor', in Anna Maria Brizio, Maria Vittoria Brugnoli and André Chastel, *Leonardo the Artist*, Hutchinson, London, 1981, p.102.

17 Gombrich, op. cit., p.43.

18 Vasari, op. cit., p.565.

19 Ibid., p.559.

20 This point is made by Leonid M. Batkin, *Leonardo da Vinci*, trans. from the Russian by Gabriele Mazzitelli, Laterza, Bari–Rome, 1988, p.193.

21 Ivor B. Hart, *The World of Leonardo da Vinci, Man of Science, Engineer and Dreamer of Flight*, Viking Press, New York, 1961.

22 Some have tried to explain it away by claiming that it was badly copied by Salai from a Leonardo original; see Augusto Marinoni, 'La Bicyclette', in Ladislao Reti (ed.), *Léonard de Vinci: l'Humaniste, l'artiste, l'inventeur*, Laffont, Paris, 1974, pp.288–9.

23 Charles H. Gibbs-Smith, *Aviation: An Historical Survey from its Origins to the End of World War II*, HMSO, London, 1985, pp.8, 21; see also his amply illustrated *The Inventions of Leonardo da Vinci*, Phaidon, Oxford, 1978, pp.13–14.

24 Leonardo da Vinci, *L'uomo e la natura*, introduction by Mario De Micheli, Feltrinelli, Milan, 1991, p.5.

25 See introduction in Brizio et al., op. cit., pp.14–15.

26 Serge Bramly, *Léonard de Vinci*, Lattès, Paris, 1988, p.33.

27 Clément, op. cit., p.174.

28 Batkin, op. cit., p.210n.
29 Stendhal, op. cit., pp.220–1; the claim about Bacon was taken from the Venturi lecture mentioned above. The Leonardo–Bacon parallel became increasingly frequent later in the century; see for instance Hippolyte Taine, *Voyage en Italie*, Édition complexe, Brussels, 1990, p.216, and Théophile Gautier, *Les Dieux et les demi-dieux de la peinture*, Morizot, Paris, 1864, p.5.
30 Stendhal, op. cit., p.181.
31 Batkin, op. cit., p.28.
32 Anna Maria Brizio, 'The Painter', in Brizio et al., op. cit., p.35.
33 *Leonardo on Painting*, pp.52–68.
34 Ibid., pp.13–15.
35 Jardine, *Worldly Goods*, op. cit., p.242.
36 One of Michelangelo's descendants, Michelangelo il Giovane, published an anthology in 1623, heavily edited and in many instances completed by himself; see the editorial note in Michelangelo, *Rime*, Mondadori, Milan, 1998, p.xlvi.
37 Vasari, op. cit., p.563; see also Batkin, op. cit., p.35.
38 Vasari underlined this quality of Leonardo's in ibid., pp.558, 561.
39 Burckhardt, op. cit., p.81.
40 Ibid., p.84.
41 Edgar Quinet, *Les Révolutions d'Italie*, in his *Oeuvres complètes*, Vol.2, Hachette, Paris, 1904, pp.132–3.
42 Jules Michelet, *Oeuvres complètes: Vol.7, Histoire de la France au seizième siècle: Renaissance et réforme*, ed. Paul Viallaneix, Flammarion, Paris, 1976, p.83.
43 Ibid., p.52; when younger he had been enthusiastic about the Middle Ages.
44 Ibid., p.54.
45 George Eliot, 'Brothers in Opinion: Edgar Quinet and Jules Michelet', in *Coventry Herald and Observer*, 30 October 1846, reprinted in *Selected Essays, Poems and Other Writings*, Penguin, Harmondsworth, 1990, p.261–2.
46 Arsène Houssaye, *Histoire de Léonard de Vinci*, Didier et cie, Paris, 1869, p.8.
47 F.-A. Gruyer, *Voyage autour du salon carré au musée du Louvre*, op. cit., p.15.
48 Baedeker, *Paris and its Environs*, Leipzig, 1900, p.111.
49 Houssaye described this saga in op. cit., p.293–320, see also the account in Müntz, op. cit., p.485.
50 Clément, op. cit., p.238.
51 Séailles, op. cit., p.169.
52 Stendhal, op. cit., p.224.
53 Alfred Dumesnil, *l'Art italien*, Giraud, Paris, 1854, pp.134, 143.
54 René Bonnamen, *La Question de la Joconde: Problème Vinciens*, Imprimerie Legendre, Lyon 1908, pp.24–6; this pamphlet was originally published as an article in the influential *Grande revue*, 25 September 1908; for Michelet see op. cit., p.259.
55 De Micheli, op. cit., p.24.
56 B. Couret, 'Il y a 500 ans naissait l'ouvrier de l'intelligence Léonard de Vinci', in *Avant-garde*, 14 May 1952.
57 Raymond Williams, *Culture and Society*, The Hogarth Press, London, 1987, p.84.

Notes

58 See Peter Gay, *The Naked Heart*, Vol.4 of *The Bourgeois Experience: Victoria to Freud*, HarperCollins, London, 1996, pp.102–12.

59 Ibid., pp.153–4.

60 *Leonardo on Painting*, pp.38–9.

61 Ernst Kris and Otto Kurz, *Legend, Myth, and Magic in the Image of the Artist*, Yale University Press, New Haven and London, 1979, esp. Introduction.

62 Raymonde Moulin, 'La Genèse de la rareté artistique', in *Ethnologie française*, Vol. 8, No.2–3, 1978, p.241.

63 Bruno S. Frey and Werner W. Pommerechne, *Muses and Markets: Explorations in the Economics of the Arts*, Blackwell, Oxford, 1989, p.103.

64 John Russell Taylor and Brian Brook, *The Art Dealers*, Hodder and Stoughton, London, 1969, p.137.

65 André Malraux in *Les Voix du silence*, La Galerie de la Pléiade, Paris, 1951, p.370.

66 Yves Renouard, 'Léonard de Vinci et la France', in *Bulletin de l'Association Léonard de Vinci*, No.17, April 1979, p.25.

67 Michelet, op. cit., p.435.

68 See De Micheli, op. cit.

69 Roberto Paolo Ciardi, 'Leonardo Illustrato: genio e morigeratezza', in *L'immagine di Leonardo: Testimonianze figurative dal XVI al XIX secolo*, ed. Roberto Paolo Ciardi and Carlo Sisi, Giunti, Florence, 1997, p.29. This is the catalogue of an exhibition held in June–September 1997 in Vinci. Stendhal reports the anecdote of Charles V but, interestingly, does not accept Vasari's account of Leonardo's death; see his *Histoire de la Peinture en Italie*, op. cit., pp.59, 225.

70 Stendhal, op. cit., p.191.

71 J.W. Goethe, *Italian Journey*, trans. W.H. Auden and Elizabeth Mayer, Penguin, Harmondsworth, 1970, pp.375–6.

72 Ciardi, op. cit., p.30.

73 The catalogue of the exhibition *L'immagine di Leonardo*, op. cit., provides many similar examples.

74 Ciardi, op. cit., pp.33–4, and Giovanna Damiani, 'La biografia illustrata', in ibid., p.112.

75 Federico Tognoli, 'Leonardo: maschera e volto', in *L'immagine di Leonardo*, p.64.

76 At the Museum in Vinci there are engravings of the 'self-portrait' by G.D. Campiglia (1754), Carlo Lasinio (c.1789) and Zocchi (c.1766).

77 Cited in De Micheli, op. cit., p.18.

78 Richard Turner, *Inventing Leonardo: The Anatomy of a Legend*, Macmillan, Basingstoke and London, 1995, pp.90–1.

79 Lord Terlinden, 'Léonard de Vinci dans la gravure flamande', in *l'Art et la pensée de Léonard de Vinci*, op. cit., pp.364–8.

80 Charles Dickens, *Pictures from Italy*, Penguin, Harmondsworth, 1998, p.95.

81 Letter to Alice Swinburne, 31 December 1863, in Swinburne, *Letters*, ed. Cecil Y. Lang, Yale University Press, New Haven, 1959–60, Vol.1, p.91.

82 Cited in Nicholas Boyle, *Goethe: The Poet and the Age: Vol.I, The Poetry of Desire*, Oxford University Press, 1991, p.512.

83 Goethe, *Italian Journey*, op. cit., p.166.

84 Turner, op. cit., p.95.

85 Marcel Proust, 'Aprés la guerre', in *Essais et articles*, Gallimard, Paris, 1971, p.275.

86 Clark, *Leonardo da Vinci*, op. cit., pp.144, 149.

87 Batkin, op. cit., p.147.

88 Text translated and published in *Achademia Leonardi Vinci*, Vol.10, 1997, pp.141–5; see p.144.

89 Stendhal, op. cit., p.181; see also his *Journal*, entry of 6 November 1811, in *Oeuvres intimes*, Gallimard Pléiade, Paris, 1955, p.1179, where he praises Morghen's engraving.

90 See letter in *Oeuvres intimes*, 25 October 1811.

91 Stendhal, op. cit.; the section on Leonardo is on pp.171–225, the sub-sections on *The Last Supper* on pp.181–201.

92 Ibid., pp.175, 206–7.

93 Ibid., p.209.

94 This review and those that follow are reprinted in the French edition of Stendhal, op. cit., that I am using; see pp.512–14.

95 Ibid., pp.515–20.

96 Ibid., p.517.

97 Ibid., pp.523–4.

98 Ibid., pp.524–7.

99 Ibid., pp.527–47. The original piece appeared in Vol.32, No.64, October 1819.

100 Ibid., p.547.

101 Ibid., p.549.

102 C.W. Thomson, 'Note sur la diffusion de l'Histoire de la peinture en Italie jusqu'en 1833', in *Stendhal Club*, No.15, 15 April 1971.

103 Christina Toren, 'Leonardo's *Last Supper* in Fiji', in Susan Hiller (ed.), *The Myth of Primitivism: Perspectives on Art*, Routledge, London, 1991, p.261.

104 Charles Lamb, 'Lines on the celebrated picture by Leonardo da Vinci, called the Virgin of the Rocks', in *The Poetical Works*, Moxon, London, 1836.

105 Felicia Dorothea Browne Hemans, *The Works of Mrs. Hemans*, seven volumes, Blackwood, Edinburgh and Cadwell, London, 1839.

106 See Théophile Gautier, *Voyage en Italie*, Charpentier, Paris, 1875, p.58, originally in *La Presse*, 2 October 1850.

CHAPTER FIVE

1 Charles Blanc, 'La Joconde de Léonard de Vinci gravée par Calamatta', in *Gazette des beaux-arts*, February 1859, p.164.

2 André Chastel, 'Un Tableau difficile', in *Vraiment faux*, Fondation Cartier pour l'art contemporain, Jouy-en-Josas, 1988, p.91.

3 See Henri Focillon, 'Les Graveurs de la Joconde', in *Revue de l'art ancient et moderne*, Vol.30, 1911, pp.365–78. Focillon, writing in the 1930s, maintains that there were no engravings of the *Mona Lisa* before the nineteenth century; see 'La Joconde et ses interpretes', in his *Technique et sentiment: Études sur l'art moderne*, Henri Laurens, Paris, 1931, p.83.

4 Blanc, op. cit., p.165.

5 See Mario Praz's pioneering essay (1930) in *La carne, la morte e il diavolo nella letteratura romantica*, Sansoni, Florence, 1966; and George Boas, 'The *Mona Lisa* in the

Notes

History of Taste', in *Journal of the History of Ideas*, Vol.1, No.2, April 1940, pp.207–24.

6 Sara F. Matthews Grieco, 'The Body, Appearance, and Sexuality', in Natalie Zemon Davis and Arlette Farge (eds), *A History of Women: Renaissance and Enlightenment Paradoxes*, The Belknap Press of Harvard University Press, Cambridge, Massachussetts, 1993, p.65.

7 Françoise Borin, 'Judging by Images', in ibid, pp.193–4.

8 Alcuin Blamires (ed.), *Woman Defamed and Woman Defended: An Anthology of Medieval Texts*, Clarendon Press, Oxford, 1992, pp.100–2.

9 Carolyne Larrington, *Women and Writing in Medieval Europe*, Routledge, London, 1995, p.227.

10 For a wider treatment see Olwen Hufton, *The Prospect Before Her: A History of Women in Western Europe: Vol.1, 1500–1800*, HarperCollins, London, 1995, Chapter 8, 'Kept Mistresses and Common Strumpets', esp. pp.308–9.

11 Praz, op. cit., p.173.

12 Edmond et Jules de Goncourt, *Journal: 1851–1863*, Vol.1, Fasquelle et Flammarion, Paris, 1956, p.719.

13 The case is made by Marcel Sauvage in *Jules et Edmond de Goncourt: Précurseurs*, Mercure de France, Paris, 1970, pp.133–50.

14 Sainte-Beuve, *Volupté*, 1834, quoted in Praz, op. cit., pp.209–10.

15 Cited in Bram Dijkstra, *Idols of Perversity: Fantasies of Feminine Evil in Fin-de-siècle Culture*, Oxford University Press, 1986, p.13.

16 Charles Baudelaire, *Fusées: Mon coeur mis à nu: La Belgique déshabillée*, Gallimard, Paris, 1986, p.73.

17 In Théophile Gautier, *Emaux et camées*, Gallimard, Paris, 1981, p.55; originally published in *Revue de Paris*, 1 January 1852.

18 Gustave Flaubert, *Mémoires d'un fou: Novembre et autres textes de jeunesse*, Flammarion, Paris, 1991, pp.422, 407–8. In a letter to Louise Colet (28 October 1853) Flaubert wrote: 'How right I was not to publish it.'

19 Praz, op. cit., p.229.

20 Jules Renard, *Journal: 1887–1910*, Gallimard–Pléiade, Paris, 1965, p.510, entry for 17 November 1898.

21 Cited in Praz, op. cit., p.229.

22 Anne Higonnet, 'Immagini di donne', in Geneviève Fraisse and Michelle Perrot (eds), *Storia delle donne: L'Ottocento*, Laterza, Roma–Bari, 1998, p.293.

23 Jules Barbey d'Aurevilly, *Les Diaboliques*, Gallimard, Paris, 1973, p.25.

24 J.-K. Huysmans, *À Rebours*, GF-Flammarion, Paris, 1978, p.106.

25 Heard and reported by the Louvre curator Sylvie Béguin, 'Un illustre sourire', in *Vraiment faux*, op. cit., p.86; but see also 'La Joconde: Ombres et lumières', in *Journal des chefs-d'oeuvre de l'art*, No.3, 1963, where the same claim is made.

26 Gustave Planche, 'Étude sur l'art et la poésie en Italie: Léonard de Vinci', in *Revue des deux mondes*, Vol.20, September 1850, pp.854–79.

27 Maxime Du Camp, *Théophile Gautier*, Hachette, Paris, 1890, p.80.

28 See Baudelaire's article on Gautier in *l'Artiste*, 13 March 1859, collected in *l'Art romantique*, GF–Flammarion, Paris, 1968, p.238.

29 Michael Clifford Spencer, *The Art Criticism of Théophile Gautier*, Librairie Droz, Geneva, 1969, pp.1–3.

30 Théophile Gautier, *Salon de 1847*, Hetzel, Paris, 1847, p.153.

31 Robert Snell, *Théophile Gautier: A Romantic Critic of the Visual Arts*, Clarendon Press, Oxford, 1982, p.127.

32 *Leonardo on Painting*, p.144.

33 Anita Brookner, *The Genius of the Future: Essays in French Art Criticism*, Cornell University Press, Ithaca, New York, 1971, p.1.

34 For a treatment of Gautier on women see Natalie David-Weill, *Rêve de pierre: La Quête de la femme chez Théophile Gautier*, Librairie Droz, Geneva, 1989.

35 It is included in the collection *Emaux et camées*, op. cit.

36 Théophile Gautier, *Le Roman de la momie*, Livre de Poche, Paris, 1997; see pp.68 and 250 for the idea of 'retrospective desire'.

37 Théophile Gautier, *Récits fantastique*, GF-Flammarion, Paris, 1981, p.238.

38 Ibid., p.124.

39 Théophile Gautier, *Mademoiselle de Maupin*, GF-Flammarion, Paris, 1966, pp.228–9.

40 *Leonardo on Painting*, pp.26–7.

41 See Vernon Lee, *Supernatural Tales*, Peter Owen, London, 1987; the citation is on p.108. See also Christa Zorn, 'Aesthetic Intertextuality as Cultural Critique: Vernon Lee Rewrites History through Walter Pater's La "Gioconda" ', in *Victorian Newsletter*, No.91, Spring 1997, pp.4–10.

42 Gautier, *Récits fantastique*, op. cit., pp.61–2.

43 Théophile Gautier, *Spirite*, Nizet, Paris, 1970, p.84.

44 Gautier, *Voyage en Italie*, op. cit., p.69.

45 See Théophile Gautier, *Exposition de 1859*, ed. Wolfgang Drost and Ulrike Henninges, Carl Winter Universitätsverlag, Heidelberg, 1992, p.129 (originally in *Le Moniteur universel*, 13 July 1859).

46 Maurice Aubert, *Souvenirs du salon de 1859*, Tardieu, Paris, 1859, p.219.

47 Théophile Gautier, *Les Beaux arts en Europe*, Vol.1, Michel Lévy, Paris, 1855, p.165. Ingres's painting is now at the Musèe Condé, Chantilly.

48 See Gautier's article in *La Presse*, 28 August 1850. The painting, known as *Lady in Ermine*, was painted by El Greco in c.1577–78. It is now at Pollock House in Glasgow.

49 See his contributions to *Le Moniteur universel*, 7 May and 25 June 1859, now in Gautier, *Exposition de 1859*, op. cit.

50 Gautier, *Les Dieux et les demi-dieux de la peinture*, op. cit., p.14.

51 Gautier, *Voyage en Italie*, op. cit., p.344.

52 Joanna Richardson, *Théophile Gautier: His Life and Times*, Max Reinhardt, London, 1958, p.49.

53 Théophile Gautier, *Correspondance générale, Vol.X: 1868–1869*, ed. Claudine Lacoste-Veysseyre, Librairie

Notes

Droz, Geneva–Paris, 1996,
pp.20–1.

54 See *Le Moniteur universel*, 26
November 1855.

55 Théophile Gautier, 'Les
caricatures de Léonard de
Vinci', in *l'Artiste*, 12 April 1857,
p.21.

56 Théophile Gautier, *Guide de
l'amateur au musée du Louvre*,
Charpentier, Paris, 1882, p.26.

57 Ibid., p.27.

58 Gautier, *Les Dieux et les demi-
dieux de la peinture*, op. cit.

59 Ibid., pp.24–5.

60 Gautier, *Mademoiselle de
Maupin*, op. cit., p.83.

61 Edgar Quinet, *Les Révolutions
d'Italie*, in his *Oeuvres complètes*,
Vol.2, Hachette, Paris, 1904,
p.133.

62 Praz, op. cit., pp.189–90.

63 Anne Higonnet, 'Le donne e le
immagini, apparenza,
divertimento e sopravvivenza',
in Fraisse and Perrot, op. cit.,
p.282.

64 Joseph Lavallée, *Catalogue de la
Galerie du Musée Napoléon*,
Vol.11, ed. Filhol, 1828, in
Louvre folder Inv 779.

65 Jules Verne, *Monna Lisa*,
l'Herne, Paris, 1995.

66 H. Taine, *Nouveaux essuix de
critique et d'histoire*, Hachette,
Paris, 1901, p.352.

67 Clément, op. cit., p.220.

68 Gruyer, op. cit., pp.42–6.

69 Dmitri Merezhkovsky's novel
The Resurrection of the Gods was
published in Russian in 1900.

70 Houssaye, *Histoire de Léonard de
Vinci*, op. cit., p.127.

71 Séailles, op. cit., p.142.

72 Carlo Predetti has attempted,
bravely but unconvincingly, to
dispute these views in his

'Quella puttana di Leonardo', in
Achademia Leonardi Vinci, No.9,
1996, pp.121–39.

73 Clark, 'Mona Lisa', in *Burlington
Magazine*, op. cit., p.149.

74 Stéphane Michaud, 'Idolatrie
rappresentazioni artistiche e
letterarie', in Fraisse and Perrot,
op. cit., pp.130–54.

75 Gautier, *Guide de l'amateur au
musée du Louvre*, op. cit.,
pp.28–9.

76 Ibid., p.28.

77 Jean-Jacques Rousseau,
Confessions, trans. J.M. Cohen,
Penguin, Harmondsworth, 1960,
p.28.

78 Cited in Ramacciotti Donato,
op. cit., p.72; originally in O.
Redon, *A Soi-même: Journal
1867–1915*, Floury, Paris, 1922.

79 Séailles, op. cit., p.471.

80 André Malraux, *Le Miroir des
limbes*, in *Oeuvres complètes*,
Vol.3, Gallimard Pléiade, Paris,
1996, p.621.

81 Séailles, op. cit., p.141.

82 Baedeker, *Paris and its Environs:
Handbook for Travellers*,
London, 1878, p.103.

83 Ibid., p.96.

84 Baedeker, *Paris et ses environs*,
Leipzig, 1911, p.100.

85 Jeanne de Flandreysy, *Femmes et
déesses*, Société d'éditions
littéraires et artistiques, Paris,
1903.

86 Théophile Gautier, *Tableaux de
siège, Paris 1870–1871*,
Charpentier, Paris, 1871, p.348.
The passage was also cited in
Baedeker, *Paris et ses environs*,
1911, p.100.

87 See entry for 'Leonardo' in
Vol.XX of *Enciclopedia italiana*,
op. cit., p.875.

88 On this portrait see M.

Rzepinska, 'The "Lady with the Ermine" Revisited', in *Achademia Leonardi Vinci*, Vol.6, 1993, pp.191–9.

89 Walter Pater, *The Renaissance*, Oxford University Press, 1998, p.71.

90 Müntz, op. cit., pp.196–8.

91 See Osvald Sirén, *Leonardo da Vinci*, Stockholm, 1911 (English trans.: *Leonardo da Vinci: The Artist and the Man*, Yale University Press, New Haven, 1916); and Francesco Malaguzzi-Valeri, *La Corte di Lodovico il Moro*, Vol.3, Hoepli, Milan, 1917.

92 Dumesnil, *l'Art italien*, op. cit., pp.123ff.

93 Clément, op. cit., p.221.

94 Michelet, op. cit., p.83.

95 Ibid., p.84.

96 Hayden White, *Metahistory: The Historical Imagination in Nineteenth-Century Europe*, Johns Hopkins University Press, Baltimore, 1975, p.140.

97 Jules Michelet, *Journal, Vol.3: 1861–67*, ed. Claude Digeon, Gallimard, Paris, 1976, entry for 26 August 1861.

98 See review reprinted as an appendix to Michelet, op. cit., pp.645–7.

99 Taine, *Voyage en Italie*, op. cit.; see Vol.1, pp.216–18 and Vol.2, p.226.

100 Taine, *Nouveaux essaix de critique et d'histoire*, op. cit., p.351.

101 Houssaye, *Histoire de Léonard de Vinci*, op. cit., p.332.

102 Ibid., p.334.

103 Cited in Pierre Marcy, *Guide populaire dans les musées du Louvre*, Librairie du Petit Journal, Paris, 1867, pp.26–7.

104 George Sand, 'La Joconde de Léonard de Vinci gravée par Louis Calamatta', in *La Presse*, 8 December 1858. She says her aim was to help Calamatta; see letter to Émile Aucante of 3 December 1858 (in George Sand, *Correspondance, Vol.15*, ed. George Lubin, Garnier, Paris, 1981, pp.194–6).

105 Last but not least in *Paris-Match*, 3 June 1997: 'Quand Monna Lisa fait sa toilette'.

106 de Flandreysy, op. cit., p.27.

107 Séailles, op. cit., pp.472–4.

108 Ibid., pp.471–2.

109 Ibid., p.472.

110 Jaspers, *Leonardo, Descartes, Max Weber*, op. cit., p.11.

CHAPTER SIX

1 *The Oxford Book of Modern Verse 1892–1935*, ed. W.B Yeats, Clarendon Press, Oxford, 1936, p.viii.

2 Mark Jeffreys, 'The Mona Lisa and the Symbol of Ideas: Pater's Leda as Mother to Yeats's Helen', in *Colby Quarterly*, Vol.29, No.1, 1993, pp.20–32; see esp. pp.26–7. On Pater's influence on Yeats see Edward Engelberg, *The Vast Design: Patterns in W.B. Yeats's Aesthetic*, Catholic University of America Press, Washington DC, 1988.

3 Clark, 'Mona Lisa', in *Burlington Magazine*, op. cit., p.148.

4 Praz, op. cit., p.227.

5 Walter Pater, *The Renaissance*, Oxford University Press 1998, pp.79–80; the 'ends of the world are come' is a biblical reference (*Corinthians I*, 10:11).

6 Rita Severi, 'The Myth of

Leonardo in English Decadent Writers', in *Achademia Leonardi Vinci*, Vol.5, 1992, p.100.

7   Gustave Flaubert, *La Tentation de saint Antoine*, Flammarion, Paris, 1967, p.132.

8   Andrew Wilton, 'Symbolism in Britain', in *The Age of Rossetti, Burne-Jones and Watts: Symbolism in Britain* (exhibition catalogue), ed. Andrew Wilton and Robert Upstone, Tate Gallery Publishing, London, 1997, p.18.

9   All these paintings are listed in *The Age of Rossetti, Burne-Jones and Watts*, op. cit.

10 See Ramacciotti Donato, op. cit., pp.71–2.

11 Germain d'Hangest, *Walter Pater: l'Homme et l'oeuvre*, Didier, Paris, 1961, Vol.1, pp.192–5. This massive *doctorat d'état*, some eight hundred pages long, accepts the influence of Gautier on Pater; see Vol.1, pp.357–8.

12 Billie Andrew Inman, *Walter Pater's Reading: A Bibliography of his Library Borrowings and Literary References, 1858–1873*, Garland Publishing, New York and London, 1981, p.335.

13 Ibid., pp.xi–xii, 78, 189, 195.

14 Barrie Bullen, op. cit., p.279.

15 See Pater's hint in *Renaissance*, op. cit., p.76.

16 Clément, op. cit., p.221.

17 Pater, op. cit. p.68.

18 Percy Bysshe Shelley, *Complete Poetical Works*, Oxford University Press, 1970, p.583.

19 George Sand, 'La Joconde de Léonard de Vinci gravée par Calamatta', op. cit.

20 Umberto Eco, *Il pendolo di Foucault*, Bompiani, Milan, 1988, p.17.

21 This is included in the collection *Sonnets of the Wingless Hours*.

22 E. Cobham Brewer, *The Dictionary of Phrase and Fable*, new and enlarged edn, Cassell and Co., London, 1894.

23 J.B. Bullen, op. cit., p.173.

24 Bayle St. John, *The Louvre, or Biography of a Museum*, Chapman and Hall, London, 1850, pp.328, 353.

25 See Baedeker, *Paris and its Environs*, London, 1878, pp.116ff.

26 Cited by J.B. Bullen, op. cit., p.174.

27 John Ruskin, in *The Cestus of Aglaia* (1865), in *The Complete Works of John Ruskin*, George Allen, London, 1905, Vol.19, p.129.

28 Tim Hilton, *John Ruskin: The Later Years*, Yale University Press, New Haven and London, 2000, pp.41, 201ff, 236, 293.

29 Baedeker, *Paris and its Environs*, London, 1878, p.112.

30 Inman, op. cit., p.169.

31 Pater, op. cit., p.64.

32 To Dante Gabriel Rossetti, 28 November 1869; in Swinburne, *Letters*, Vol.2, op. cit., p.58.

33 See Swinburne, 'Charles Baudelaire', in *Spectator*, 6 September 1862, and his poem 'Ave Atque Vale', dedicated to Baudelaire.

34 Cited in Introduction to *Baudelaire in English*, ed. Carol Clark and Robert Sykes, Penguin, Harmondsworth, 1997, p.xxx.

35 Cited in Praz, op. cit., p.202.

36 For more details see David G. Riede, *Swinburne: A Study of Romantic Mythmaking*, University Press of Virginia,

Charlottesville, 1978, pp.52ff.
37 A. Swinburne, *Collected Poetical Works*, Vol.1, Heinemann, London, 1935, pp.338–43, originally in the *Fortnightly Review*, February 1870, Vol.7, pp.176–80, and hence one year after Pater. He refers to it as his 'sunflower poem' in a letter to Edmund Gosse of 6 April 1877, in *The Letters of Algernon Charles Swinburne*, ed. Edmund Gosse and Thomas James Wose, Heinemann, London, 1918, Vol.2.

38 Margaret Oliphant, 'Pater's History of the Renaissance', in *Blackwood's Edinburgh Magazine*, November 1873, pp.604–9.

39 See her letter of 5 November 1873 to John Blackwood in *The George Eliot Letters*, Vol.5, ed. Gordon S. Haight, Yale University Press, New Haven, 1954–55.

40 W.J. Courthope, 'Modern Culture', in *Quarterly Review*, No.137, October 1874, p.411.,

41 See 'Recent Literature', in *Atlantic Monthly*, Vol.32, October 1873, pp.496–8.

42 Richard Ellmann, *Oscar Wilde*, Hamish Hamilton, London, 1987, pp.80, 284.

43 Marcel Brion, *Léonard de Vinci*, Albin Michel, Paris, 1952, p.465.

44 C. Puelli, 'Leonardo e il volto della Gioconda', in *Revue des études italiennes*, No.1, January–March 1959, pp.47–53, where, unfortunately, Pater is referred to as 'Peter'.

45 Kenneth Clark, 'Introduction' to Walter Pater's *The Renaissance*, Collins, London, 1961, pp.11–26.

46 Clark, 'Mona Lisa', in *Burlington Magazine*, op. cit., p.148.

47 Richard B. Carpenter, 'The Mythical Nature of Leonardo Da Vinci's "Mona Lisa" ', in *Sewanee Review*, Vol.71, No.3, July–September 1963, pp.502–4.

48 Webster Smith, 'Observations on the *Mona Lisa* Landscape', in *The Art Bulletin*, Vol.67, No.2, June 1985, p.184.

49 Giancarlo Maiorino, *Leonardo da Vinci: The Daedalian Mythmaker*, Penn State Press, State College Pennsylvania, 1992, p.271.

50 Florence Purvis, 'La Femme universelle', in *Impresario: Magazine of the Arts*, July–August 1966, pp.31, 35.

51 G.K. Chesterton, *The Victorian Age in Literature*, Thornton Butterworth, London, 1938, p.71.

52 *The Works of Oscar Wilde*, Collins, London and Glasgow, 1948, pp.967–8. Wilde cites the famous passage at greater length.

53 Ibid., p.968.

54 W. Somerset Maugham, *Christmas Holiday*, Heinemann, London, 1939, p.213.

55 W. Somerset Maugham, *Of Human Bondage*, Heinemann, London, 1961, pp.280–1.

56 Ibid., p.301.

57 Marcel Proust, letter of 23 March 1898 to Madame Daudet in *Correspondance*, Vol.2, ed. Philip Kolb, Plon, Paris, 1976, p.229.

58 Salomon Reinach, 'La Tristesse de Mona Lisa', in *Bulletin des musées de France*, Vol.2, 1909, pp.17–22.

59 Ellman, op. cit., pp.49, 469.

60 Ibid., p.252.

61 *The Works of Oscar Wilde*, op. cit., p.717.

62 Ibid., p.967.

63 'The Sphinx', in ibid., pp.812–21.

64 'Humanitad', in ibid., p.788 (line 358).

65 'The Sphinx Without a Secret', in ibid., pp.215–18.

66 See Severi, op. cit., p.102.

67 In *Les Poésies de Charles Coran*, Vol.1, Le Puy, 1895, pp.8–9; also cited by Sandra Migliore, *Tra Hermes e Prometeo: Il mito di Leonardo nel decadentismo Europeo*, Leo S. Olschki, Florence, 1994, p.28. Coran was then just over twenty.

68 I was made aware of this and the story which follows by reading Adeline Tintner's 'Henry James's Mona Lisa', in *Essays in Literature*, Vol.8, No.1, 1981, pp.105–8.

69 Henry James, *The Madonna of the Future and Other Tales*, Macmillan, London, 1880, p.23.

70 Ibid., p.107.

71 Henry James, *The Ambassadors*, Penguin, Harmondsworth, 1994, pp.157, 173, 189.

72 James Joyce, *A Portrait of the Artist as a Young Man*, Viking, New York, 1969, pp.171–2.

73 Ibid., p.223.

74 Hugh Kenner, 'O, an Impossible Person', in Mary T. Reynolds, *James Joyce: A Collection of Critical Essays*, Prentice Hall, Englewood Cliffs, New Jersey, 1993, pp.100–1.

75 Ibid., p.214.

76 *The Critical Writings of James Joyce*, ed. Ellsworth Mason and Richard Ellmann, Faber and Faber, London, 1959, p.79. The essay was published in May 1902 in *St. Stephen's*, the unofficial magazine of University College, Dublin.

77 Stéphane Mallarmé, letter of 17 May 1867, in *Correspondance Vol.1: 1862–1871*, Gallimard, Paris, 1959, p.246; also cited in Ramacciotti Donato, op. cit., p.80.

78 Marcel Proust, 'Ruskin a Notre-Dame d'Amiens', in *Mercure de France*, Vol.34, April–June 1900, p.65; reprinted in the collection *Pastiches et mélanges*, published in 1919. I was made aware of this by reading Cynthia J. Gamble, 'A l'ombre de la vierge dorée de la cathédrale d'Amiens: Ruskin et l'imaginaire proustien', in *Gazette des beaux-arts*, May–June 1995.

79 Élémir Bourges, *Le Crépuscule des Dieux*, Christian Pirot, Saint-Cyr-sur-Loire, 1987, pp.68–9. Inspired by Wagner's opera, the novel tells the story of a noble family undermined by lust and folly; it was filmed by Luchino Visconti in 1969 as *The Damned*.

80 Jean Lorrain, *Trés Russe*, Hubert Julia, Rouen, 1986, p.76. Bourges and Lorrain are both cited in Praz, op. cit., pp.311, 321.

81 Lorrain, op. cit., p.29.

82 Ibid., p.59.

83 E.M. Forster, *A Room with a View*, Penguin, Harmondsworth, 1979, pp.107–8.

84 René Bonnamen, *La Question de la Joconde: Problème Vinciens*, Imprimerie Legendre, Lyon, 1908, pp.12–13; also published as an article in the *Grande revue*, 25 September 1908.

85 Ibid., pp.23–4.

86 Ibid., pp.29–33.

87 J. Perdrield-Vaissière, *Le Sourire de la Joconde*, Librairie de la Plume, Paris, 1902.

88 Gustavo Strafforello, *Il primo*

amore di Leonardo da Vinci,
Lampugnani, Milan, 1871; cited
in Migliore, op. cit., p.45.

89 Mathilde Alanic, *La Romance de
la Joconde,* Plon, Paris, 1908.

90 'Ni de Mona Lisa qu'éternisa
Vinci/Ni du joyeux héros du
divin Arioste', in Prologue to
Maurice Montégut, *Les
Chevauchées de la Joconde,*
Olendorff, Paris, 1901.

91 Ibid., p.6.

92 Ibid., p.245.

93 Migliore, op. cit., pp.141–9.

94 See his *Per il IV centenario della
morte di LdV 11.5.1919,* cited in
ibid., pp.150–1.

95 For a deeper analysis see
Migliore, op. cit., pp.155–93.

96 For D'Annunzio's well-
documented plagiarisms see
Praz, op. cit., pp.233ff.

97 This poem was later published
in the collection *La Chimera;* see
Gabriele D'Annunzio, *L'Isottèo:
La Chimera,* Mondadori, Milan,
1996, pp.196–9.

98 Pier Marco De Santi cites this
second version, clearly unaware
of the antecedents, in 'La
Gioconda rubata "Tu non saprai
giammai perché sorrido" ', in
Achademia Leonardi Vinci,
No.111, 1990, p.77.

99 'Gorgon', in D'Annunzio,
op. cit., pp.75–9.

100 Laura Granatella, ' "La
Gioconda" dannunziana:
creazione fatale', in *Otto/
Novecento,* Vol.12, Nos.3–4, 1988,
pp.129–39.

101 Baedeker, *Paris and its Environs,*
op. cit., p.96 for the Venus, and
p.112 for the *Mona Lisa.*

102 Paul Valéry, *Cahiers,* Vol.II,
Gallimard–Pléiade, Paris, 1974,
p.929.

103 See 'Trois stations de
psychotérapie', in *l'Oeuvre de
Maurice Barrès,* Vol.2, Plon,
Paris, 1965, p.345.

104 Cited by Christopher Benfey in
'Tea with Okakura', *New York
Review of Books,* 25 May 2000,
p.43.

105 I have used a recent Italian
edition of this book, the only
one currently in print: Dimitri
Mereskovskij, *Leonardo da Vinci:
La vita del più grande genio di
tutti I tempi,* Giunti, Florence,
1998, p.235.

106 Ibid., pp.237–9.

107 Ibid., p.252.

108 In the Louvre folder (Inv 779)
there is an undated letter from
the public library of Lagonegro
saying that they had read
Merezhkovsky's book and
wished to develop a local
awareness of Lisa's sad end in
the town.

109 See Migliore, op. cit., p.56.

110 Édouard Schuré, *Léonard de
Vinci,* in *Le Théâtre de l'âme,*
Perrin, Paris, 1905. Schuré was
influenced by his Italian
mistress Margherita Albana-
Mighety.

111 Ibid., p.35.

112 Ibid., Act 2, Scene 2.

113 Ibid., p.89.

114 Ibid., pp.89–94.

115 Ibid., p.105.

116 Ibid, p.167.

117 Ibid., p.212.

118 Sigmund Freud, 'Leonardo da
Vinci', in *Art and Literature,*
Vol.14 of the Pelican Freud
Library, Penguin,
Harmondsworth, 1990, pp.185–7.

119 Ibid., p.200.

120 Ibid., p.202.

121 Ibid., p.204.

Notes

122 See Peter Gay, *Freud: A Life for our Time*, Macmillan, London, 1989, pp.273–4.

123 Meyer Schapiro, 'Leonardo and Freud: An Art-Historical Study', in *Journal of the History of Ideas*, Vol.17, No.2, April 1956, pp.147–78.

124 See Leonardo Ceppa, 'Freud e il sorriso della Gioconda', in *Belfagor*, Vol.44, No.5, 1989, pp.590–1.

125 Of course, if one really wants, one can find almost anything in the details of paintings; see Arasse, *Le Détail*, op. cit., pp.394–6.

126 See, for instance, the essay by the Argentinean psychoanalyst Giovanni Dalma, 'Tendenze tanatiche in Leonardo: Saggio su di un aspetto della sua personalità', in *Nevrasse*, Vol.50.

CHAPTER SEVEN

1 See Zola's perceptive description of the visit of Gervaise's wedding guests to the Louvre in *l'Assommoir*, op. cit., pp.88–90.

2 Richard D. Altick, *The English Common Reader*, University of Chicago Press, 1957, p.383. All book and press statistics are unreliable – these figures and those that follow are purely indicative.

3 Bruno Lasselle, *Le Triomphe de l'édition: Histoire du livre*, Vol.1, Gallimard, Paris, 1998, p.58.

4 Pierre Albert, 'La Presse française de 1871 à 1940', in Claude Bellanger et al., *Histoire générale de la presse française*, Vol.3, PUF, Paris, 1972, p.137.

5 Ibid., p.234.

6 Ibid., p.297.

7 Raymond Williams, *The Long Revolution*, Harper and Row, New York, 1966, p.203.

8 Albert, op. cit., p.303.

9 Celina Fox, 'The Development of Social Reportage in English Periodical Illustration During the 1840s and Early 1850s', in *Past and Present*, No.74, February 1977, p.91.

10 David Blackbourn, *The Fontana History of Germany 1780–1918: The Long Nineteenth Century*, Fontana Press, London, 1997, p.277.

11 Anthony Davis, *Magazine Journalism Today*, Heinemann, London, 1988, pp.7–8.

12 The correct spelling was almost certainly 'Perugia', like the city in Umbria.

13 For an account of the theft see Jérôme Coignard, 'On a volé la Joconde', Adam Biro, Paris, 1990.

14 Ministère des affaires étrangères, 'Affaires diverses: Menaces contre la Joconde', Autriche Hongrie/Série D, Carton 16, Dossier 3 – all in Louvre folder Inv 779.

15 'Le Vol de "la Joconde" ', in *Le Bulletin de l'art ancient et moderne*, No.514, 2 September 1911, p.227.

16 Josephin Péladan, 'La Joconde et le saint Jean', in *La Revue hebdomadaire*, No.36, 9 September 1911, p.247.

17 See his article in *l'Intransigeant*, 24 August 1911, reprinted in Guillaume Apollinaire, *Chroniques d'art 1902–1918*, Gallimard, Paris, 1993, pp.248–9.

18 *Le Petit Parisien*, 27 August 1911.

19 *l'Illustration*, 26 August 1911, pp.150–1.

20 *l'Illustration*, 2 September 1911.

21 See picture in *Le Petit Parisien*, 30 August 1911.

22 See Paul Ginisty's leader column, *Le Petit Parisien*, 4 September 1911; also Gustave Babin, 'Le Pelerinage à Amboise', in *l'Illustration*, 23 September 1911.

23 *Le Petit Parisien*, 30 August 1911.

24 Cecily Mackworth, *Guillaume Apollinaire and the Cubist Life*, John Murray, London, 1961, pp.133–5.

25 The *Excelsior*, 7 October 1911, has a transcript of the show with illustrations on pp.3–4.

26 Reported in *Le Cri de Paris*, 23 January 1912.

27 See Louvre folder Inv 779, Margat collection; collection of the Museo Virtuale Leonardo da Vinci, Vinci; and Enrico Sturani, 'Le Gioconde: Ritratti infedeli', essay in appendix to Marcello Vannucci, *Il furto della Gioconda: Vincenzo Peruggia e la sua storia*, Novecento, Palermo, 1993.

28 Cited in Hanns Zischler, *Kafka va au cinéma*, trans. from German by Olivier Mannoni, Cahiers du cinéma, Paris, 1996, pp.73–6. The book also contains four stills from the film.

29 'Le Vol de la Joconde', words by F. Bossuyt, music by D. Berniaux, word sheet published by Berniaux in 1911.

30 Louvre folder Inv 779, 'Le Vol'.

31 File in Louvre folder Inv 779.

32 'La Joconde volée', in *Action française*, 23 August 1911.

33 'Un Directeur des Musée Nationaux enjuivé', in *Action française*, 24 August 1911.

34 Louis Dimier, 'La "Joconde" volée', in *Action française*, 26 August 1911. An anonymous and irritated handwritten note attached to the clipping in the Louvre archives says that Dimier was obviously secretly delighted by this 'malheur républicain', this republican reverse. Of Dimier's standing as an art historian there is little doubt: see Jacques Foucart, 'Louis Dimier et la pratique de l'histoire de l'art, d'aprés sa chronique de l'Action française (1910–1913)', in *Gazette des beaux-arts*, March 1999, pp.145–72; the author describes Dimier as eccentric and flamboyant, but does not mention his anti-Semitism.

35 See *Grande revue*, Vol.15, No.17, 10 September 1911, esp. pp.121–6, and No.18, 25 September 1911, esp. pp.351–68. The results were widely reported.

36 Joséphin Péladan, 'La Joconde: Histoire d'un tableau', in *Les Arts*, No.121, January 1912, pp.2–7, with a large picture of the *Mona Lisa*; see also his 'La Joconde et le saint Jean', cited above.

37 The painter Maurice Vieuille also nominated the *St John* as the best replacement for the *Mona Lisa*; see his lecture 'Léonard et la Joconde', in Saint-Helme, *18ème Siècle et Directoire*, Éditions Presse Française, Paris, 1913, pp.263–4.

38 *Illustrated London News*, 29 November 1913.

39 See Coignard, op. cit., pp.93ff for the account, largely culled from the Paris paper *Le Temps*.

40 Cited in Donatella Dell'Aquilano, 'D'Annunzio e il

leonardismo fin de siècle', in *Critica Letteraria*, Vol.26, No.3/ 100, 1998, pp.576–7.

41 See account in *Chroniques des arts*, 20 December 1913.

42 Robert Vaucher, 'La Joconde à Rome', in *l'Illustration*, 27 December 1913, p.523.

43 S.R. (Salomon Reinach), 'La "Joconde" au Louvre', in *Revue archéologique*, Vol.22, 1913, p.409.

44 Coignard, op. cit., pp.131–2.

45 Originally in *Le Matin*, 1 January 1914; reprinted in Colette, *Contes des mille et un matins*, Flammarion, Paris, 1970, pp.125–6.

46 Lucie Mazauric, *Le Louvre en voyage 1939–1945: ou Ma vie de château*, Plon, Paris, 1978, p.23.

47 Coignard, op. cit. p.101.

48 Ibid., p.110.

49 See, for instance, *Figaro* and *Stampa Sera* of 29 March 1961, and *The Times*, 30 March 1961; typically, an essay by Robert Mengin underlining Poggi's integrity and valour during the war was entitled 'Giovanni Poggi: l'Homme qui sauva la Joconde', *Revue des deux Mondes*, March 1963, pp.100–10.

50 *Comoedia Illustré*, 5 January 1914, Vol.6, No.7.

51 *Chansons sur la Joconde*, December 1913 (in Bibliothèque Nationale, Paris).

52 See collections of the Louvre (folder Inv 779), Jean Margat, Museo Virtuale Leonardo da Vinci, Vinci; also Enrico Sturani, op. cit.

53 Huysmans, *À Rebours*, op. cit., p.143.

54 Unsigned editorial, 'La Gioconda', in *Saturday Review*, 26 December 1913, pp.770–1.

55 Roberto Longhi, 'Le due Lise', originally in *La Voce*, Vol.6, No.1, 1914, pp.21–5; reprinted in *Edizioni delle opere complete di Roberto Longhi: Vol.1, Scritti giovanili*, Sansoni, Florence, 1956, pp.129–32. Longhi criticised Leonardo again in 1916 (p.298) and 1917 (pp.378–9).

56 Bernard Berenson, *The Study and Criticism of Italian Art*, 3rd series, Bell and Sons Ltd, London, 1916, pp.1–4.

57 Ibid., p.13; see p.23 for Berenson's dismissal of Leonardo's *chiaroscuro* and *contrapposto* as 'mere contrivances'.

58 T.S. Eliot, *The Sacred Wood: Essays on Poetry and Criticism*, Methuen, London, 1920, p.91. For an alternative interpretation linking Eliot's views of Mona Lisa and Gertrude see Jacqueline Rose, 'Hamlet – the *Mona Lisa* of Literature', in *Critical Quarterly*, Vol.28, Nos 1–2, Spring–Summer 1986, pp.35–49.

59 W. Somerset Maugham, *Christmas Holiday*, op. cit., p.213.

60 Here I disagree with, for instance, Vincent Pomarède's view; see his *La Joconde*, Prat/ Europa, Paris, 1988, p.86.

61 Baedeker, *Paris et ses environs*, Paris and Leipzig, 1914, p.119.

62 Baedeker, *Paris et ses environs*, Paris and Leipzig, 1924, p.120.

63 See *Larousse universel*, Paris, 1922, p.1241.

64 See *Le Figaro*, 13 February 1979.

65 Emmanuel Bourcier, *Comment j'ai retrouvé la Joconde*, Henry Étienne, Paris, 1926, p.7.

66 L. Roger-Milès, *Léonard de Vinci*

et les Jocondes, Floury, Paris, 1923, p.106.

CHAPTER EIGHT

1 As explained by André Doderet in his introduction to Gabriele D'Annunzio, *Portrait de Loÿse Baccaris*, Éditions du Sagittaire de Simon Kra, Paris, 1925, p.15.
2 Ibid., pp.31–2.
3 Donatella Dell'Aquilano, '*D'Annunzio e il leonardismo fin de siècle*', op. cit., p.575.
4 De Santi, op. cit., p.75.
5 Gabriele D'Annunzio, 'L'uomo che rubò la Gioconda', Mondadori, Milan, n.d. but 1950.
6 Frey and Pommerechne, op. cit., p.104.
7 This was aired by P.G. Konody and reported in the *New York Times*, 15 February 1914.
8 John R. Eyre, *Monograph on Leonardo da Vinci's 'Mona Lisa'*, Grevel and Co., London and Scribner's, New York, 1915; see p.46 for the claim that it is the better one.
9 Henry F. Pulitzer, *Where is the Mona Lisa?*, The Pulitzer Press, London, n.d. but probably 1967.
10 Ibid., p.9.
11 Georges Pierquin, *Du Mouron pour la Joconde*, Plon, Paris, 1985, p.124.
12 Information on this and other claims in Louvre folder Inv 779.
13 The full story is in Boris Lossky, 'Nouvelles connaissances et considérations au sujet du tableau léonardesque dit "La Colombine" ', in *Bulletin de l'Association Léonard de Vinci*, No.5, October 1965, pp.41–9; Lossky finds the Russian thesis interesting though not convincing. The Hermitage published the original eighty-four-page monograph in 1963 with the title *Kolombina*.
14 This is not to be confused with the so-called 'Richmond *Mona Lisa*', now at the Virginia Museum of Fine Arts, which resembles the *Colombina* of the Hermitage.
15 See, for instance, the Italian daily *Il Momento*, 27 October 1946, 'Dubbi sull'autenticità della Gioconda del Louvre', in Louvre folder Inv 779.
16 Coignard, op. cit., p.141.
17 Seymour Reit, *The Day they Stole the Mona Lisa*, Robert Hale, London, 1981, p.11; two books had already recycled the Decker story: Douglas and Eleanor Rigby's *Lock, Stock and Barrel*, Lippincott, Philadelphia, 1944, and Lawrence Jeppson's *The Fabulous Frauds*, Weybright and Talley, New York, 1970.
18 Robert Noah, *The Man who Stole the Mona Lisa*, St Martin's Press, New York, 1998.
19 Martin Page, *The Man who Stole the Mona Lisa*, John Curley, South Yarmouth, Massachusetts, 1984.
20 Ibid., p.22.
21 Wolf Mankowitz, *Gioconda*, Allen and Unwin, London, 1988, p.4.
22 Ibid., p.70.
23 Ibid., p.116.
24 Stephen Rabley, *Marcel and the Mona Lisa*, Longman, Harlow, 1991.
25 Chris Greenhalgh, *Stealing the Mona Lisa*, Bloodaxe Books, Newcastle, 1994, pp.11–12.
26 Ramsey Montgomery, *The Mona*

Lisa is Missing!, Bantam Books, New York, 1988.

27 Boris Bergman, *Un Tatami pour Mona Lisa*, Le Castor Astral, Bordeaux, 1999, p.158.

28 Laurent Charnin, *La Joconde assassinée*, Axel Noel, Paris, 1991, p.54.

29 Ibid., p.133.

30 Michel Noir, *l'Otage*, Calmann Levy, Paris, 1998.

31 F. Walthéry et Mittéï, *Natacha: l'Hôtesse et Monna Lisa*, Editions Jean Dupuis, Paris, 1979.

32 See Jean Margat, 'Petit traité de Jocondologie', in the special issue of *Bizarre*, May 1959.

33 Cyriel Verleyen, *The Theft of the Mona Lisa*, Chambers, Edinburgh, 1976.

34 It was published with the much longer *Who Goes Here?*, Victor Gollancz, London, 1988.

35 Ibid., pp.245–7.

36 Filippo Tommaso Marinetti, 'Manifesto del Futurismo', in *I futuristi*, ed. Francesco Grisi, Newton, Rome, 1994, pp.28–9.

37 Irina Costache, ' "Mona Lisa" and the Futurists', in *Achademia Leonardi Vinci*, No.111, Vol.3, 1990, p.104.

38 See *Comoedia illustré*, No.8, 15 April 1909, p.235.

39 Ardengo Soffici, *Giornale di bordo*, Vallecchi, Florence, 1921, p.147, entry of 13 July 1915.

40 Elza Adamovicz, *Surrealist Collage in Text and Image: Dissecting the Exquisite Corpse*, Cambridge University Press, 1998, p.75.

41 Ibid., p.160.

42 Daniel Grojnowski, 'Hydropathes and Company', in Phillip Dennis Cate and Mary Shaw (eds), *The Spirit of*
Montmartre: Cabarets, Humor, and the Avant-Garde, 1875–1905 (exhibition catalogue), State University of New Jersey, Rutgers, 1996, pp.104–5; the picture is also used on the cover of the volume.

43 See 'Les Expositions burlesques à Bruxelles de 1870 à 1914', in *Bulletin Bruxelles*, 1988, Louvre folder Inv 779.

44 Hans Belting, 'Le Fétiche de l'art au XX siècle: Le Cas de la Joconde', in *Diogène*, No.183, July–September 1998, p.91.

45 The point about transubstantiation is made by Pierre Bourdieu in *The Field of Cultural Production*, Polity Press, Cambridge, 1988, p.259.

46 Anne d'Harnoncourt and Kyanston McShine (eds), *Marcel Duchamp*, MOMA and the Philadelphia Museum of Art, New York, 1973, p.16.

47 T.H. Robsjohn-Gibbins, *Mona Lisa's Mustache*, Alfred A. Knopf, New York, 1948, pp.178, 189.

48 Pierre Cabanne, *Entretiens avec Marcel Duchamp*, Paris, 1967, republished in 1997 as *Duchamp & Co.*, Terrail, Paris, 1997, p.122.

49 For an analysis of the sexual aspects of *L.H.O.O.Q.*, see Jack J. Spector, 'Duchamp's Androgynous Leonardo: "*Queue*" and "*Cul*" in *L.H.O.O.Q.*', in *Source: Notes in the History of Art*, Vol.11, No.1, Fall 1990, pp.31–5; see also Antoinette LaFarge, 'The Bearded Lady and the Shaven Man: Mona Lisa, Meet Mona/ Leo', in *Leonardo*, Vol.29, No.5, 1996, pp.379–83.

50 Clark, 'Mona Lisa', in *Burlington Magazine*, op. cit., p.150.

51 Jean Glavany, *La Joconde et Platini*, Liana Levy, Paris, 1985.

52 Salvador Dali, 'Why they Attack the *Mona Lisa*', originally printed 1963, reprinted in *ArtNews*, Vol.91, No.9, 1992, p.166.

53 André Gide, *Les Faux-Monnayeurs*, in *Romans*, Gallimard–Pléiade, Paris, 1958, p.1229.

54 Cabanne, op. cit., pp.122–32.

55 Cited in Werner Schmalenbach, *Fernand Léger*, Édition Cercle d'Art, Paris, 1977, p.130.

56 Fernand Léger, 'Le Nouveau réalisme continue' (1936), in *Fonctions de la peinture*, ed. Sylvie Forestier, Gallimard Folio, Paris, 1996, p.198. On the connection between art and politics in Léger see Sarah Wilson, 'Fernand Léger, Art and Politics 1935–1955', in *Fernand Léger: The Later Years*, Whitechapel Art Gallery, London, 1987, pp.55–75.

57 Léger, *Fonctions de la peinture*, op. cit., p.282.

58 Ibid., pp.173–4.

59 I have used the French translation: Nazim Hikmet, *La Joconde et Si-ya-Ou*, Éditeurs Français Réunis, Paris, 1978.

60 Ba Jin, 'Mona Lisa', trans. Simon Johnstone, in *Chinese Literature* 1987, pp.33–7.

61 Severi, op. cit., p.103.

62 Raymond Souplex, *Autour de la Joconde*, Les Meilleures Scènes, Paris, n.d. but 1933.

63 See *Theatre Arts*, Vol.35, No.5, May 1951, where the play version is published.

64 Georges Spitzmuller, *Les Amours de François Ier et de la Joconde*, Fayard, Paris, 1920.

65 Ibid., pp.47, 121.

66 Ibid., p.245.

67 Michelet, op. cit., p.83.

68 Ortega y Gasset, 'La Gioconda', originally in the Buenos Aires paper *La Prensa*, 15 October 1911; reprinted in *Obras Completas*, Vol. 1, Alianza Editorial, Madrid, 1983, pp.553–9. The quotation is on pp.555–6.

69 In the illustrated weekly *La Semaine*, 4 November 1943. See also the memoirs of Lucie Mazauric, who accompanied the paintings, *Le Louvre en voyage*, op. cit. On one occasion she took the *Mona Lisa* into her bedroom because the place allotted to it was too humid. Was Raphael left out in the cold?

CHAPTER NINE

1 Laurie Schneider and Jack D. Flam, 'Visual Convention, Simile and Metaphor in the *Mona Lisa*', in *Storia dell'arte*, No.29, 1977, p.15n.

2 See folder 'Attentat', in Louvre folder Inv 779.

3 Salvador Dali, 'Why they Attack the *Mona Lisa*', op. cit.

4 In France, Villegas's act received a lengthy report in *Paris-Match*, 9 February 1957 and a full commentary in *Le Figaro littéraire*, 5 January 1957.

5 Information obtained from 'The Official Teenage Mutant Ninja Turtle Web Site', © 2000, Mirage Studios.

6 Eduard Gufeld, *My Life in Chess: The Search for La*

Gioconda, International Chess Enterprises, Seattle, 1994; the game is described on p.89.

7 James Haskins (with Kathleen Benson), *Nat King Cole*, Stein and Day, New York, 1984, p.115.

8 See Big Al Pavlow, *Hot Charts 1950*, Music House Publishing, Providence, Rhode Island, 1951, which charts the top singles of the year.

9 'Mona Lisa, fille étrange que veut dire ton sourire si troublent? Mona Lisa, Mona Lisa, mon belle ange, ces mystères attire à toi tous les amants. Malgré moi mon amour à toi s'abbandone ... Dans un beau jardin parmis les fleurs une fille au doux sourire, affollent tous les coeurs, mais elle vit sans amour.' ('Mona Lisa, strange girl, what is the meaning of your disturbing smile? Mona Lisa, Mona Lisa, my beautiful angel, these mysteries attract to you all those in love. In spite of myself my love to you I surrender ... In a pretty garden, among the flowers, a young woman has a smile so sweet to set all hearts on fire, but she lives without love.')

10 See the screenplay: Neil Jordan and David Leland, *Mona Lisa*, Faber and Faber, London, 1986; the speech is on p.57.

11 'Visions of Johanna' (1966), in Bob Dylan, *Writings and Drawings*, Alfred A. Knopf, New York, 1973, p.207.

12 D.H. Lawrence, *The Lovely Lady*, Martin Secker, London, 1932, pp.11–12.

13 Stella Gibbons, *Westwood, or*

The Gentle Powers, Longman, London, 1946, p.39.

14 Lawrence Durrell, *Justine*, Faber and Faber, London, 1957, p.111.

15 Mary McCarthy, *The Group*, Penguin, Harmondsworth, 1964, pp.16–17.

16 Jean Paul Sartre, *Words*, trans. Irene Clephane, Penguin Books, Harmondsworth, 1967, p.29 (originally *Les Mots*, Gallimard, Paris, 1964, p.31).

17 Serge Raffalovich and H.M. Mons, *La Joconde: Le Roman d'amour de Léonard de Vinci et de Mona Lisa*, Fasquelle, Paris, 1935, pp.55–6.

18 Guy Fau, *Le Sourire de la Joconde*, Librairie des Champs-Elysées, Paris, 1961, pp.8, 16, 82.

19 San-Antonio, *Passez-moi la Joconde*, Fleuve Noir, Paris, 1954.

20 Daniel Odier, *Gioconda*, Fayard, Paris, 1984, p.13.

21 Albert Boissière, *La Joconde aux enchères*, Fayard, Paris, 1929, p.17.

22 Jocelyne Zacharezuk, *l'Escapade de Mona Lisa*, Castor Poche Flammarion, Paris, 1994.

23 Catherine Ternaux, *Le Secret de la Joconde*, Grasset–Jeunesse, Paris, 1997.

24 Pat Hutchins, *The Mona Lisa Mystery*, The Bodley Head, London, 1981.

25 James Mayhew, *Katie and the Mona Lisa*, Orchard Books, London, 1998.

26 Jamila Gavin, 'Mona', in Michael Morpurgo (ed.), *Muck 'n' Magic*, Egmont, London, 2001.

27 E.L. Konigsburg, *The Second Mrs Gioconda*, Macmillan, London, 1976 (originally Atheneum Publishers, New York, 1975), p.137.

28 Pierre La Mure, *The Private Life*

of *Mona Lisa*, Collins, London, 1976.

29 Dominique Radrizzani, 'La Joconde fantôme vue de l'orchestre: Mona Lisa dans la bande dessinée', in *Mona Lisa: Un certain sourire . . . : Anthologie d'une obsession*, Université de Lausanne, 1992, p.57.

30 Joseph McAleer, *Passion's Fortune: The Story of Mills and Boon*, Oxford University Press, 1999, p.283.

31 Georgina Hardy, *Aimez-vous la Joconde?*, Collection Turquoise, Presses de la Cité, Paris, 1981.

32 For those unfamiliar with Gibson's work see Miryam Glazer, ' "What is Within Now Seen Without": Romanticism, Neuroromanticism, and the Death of the Imagination in William Gibson's Fictive World', in *Journal of Popular Culture*, Vol.23, Winter 1989, pp.155–64; and David G. Mead, 'Technological Transfiguration in William Gibson's Sprawl Novels', in *Extrapolation*, Vol.32, No.4, 1991, pp.350–60.

33 William Gibson, *Mona Lisa Overdrive*, HarperCollins, London, 2000, pp.246, 181.

CHAPTER TEN

1 On Malraux, French cultural policy and the *Mona Lisa* see Herman Lebovics, *Mona Lisa's Escort: André Malraux and the Reinvention of French Culture*, Cornell University Press, Ithaca and London, 1999.

2 The account by Nicole Hervé Alphand, wife of the then French Ambassador to Washington, suggests that Malraux's answer had not been premeditated; see her 'Malraux, chevalier servant de la Joconde', in *Revue des deux mondes*, May 1976, pp.325–30.

3 See interview in *Le Figaro*, 8 December 1962.

4 See, among many others, *Paris-Match*, 22 December 1962.

5 See, among others, *Paris-Presse l'Intransigeant*, 15 December 1962; *Le Figaro*, 20 December 1963; and the long photo-report in the Italian *Epoca*, 'Leonardo la Gioconda', 26 January 1964.

6 This, and much else, is engagingly related by Lebovics, op. cit., p.10.

7 See *New Yorker*, 9 February 1963.

8 Malraux, *Le Miroir des limbes*, op. cit., p.622.

9 *Time*, 18 January 1963.

10 See Elmer Belt's letter to the *Bulletin de l'Association Léonard de Vinci*, No.5, October 1965, pp.51–2.

11 Rachid Amirou, *Imaginaire du tourisme culturel*, PUF, Paris, 2000, p.104.

12 Mary McCarthy, 'Living with Beautiful Things', in *Occasional Prose*, Harcourt Brace Jovanovich, New York, 1985, pp.113–14.

13 Communication of the Agence télégraphique bulgare, 27 November 1979, and *Troud*, the daily newspaper of the Bulgarian trade unions, 24 November 1979.

14 See the editorial 'La Joconde au pays du sourire', in *Connaissance des arts*, April 1974, p.7.

15 *Connaissance des arts*, November 1972, p.11.

16 Data from the Louvre, *Les Publics du musée du Louvre en 1999: Synthèse*, Observatoire permanent des publics, April 2000, and *Rapport d'activité du musée du Louvre 1999*, pp.31–3.

17 Reproduced in *Washington Post*, 22 March 1992.

18 Art Buchwald, 'Getting Through the Louvre with the Best', *Los Angeles Times*, 25 June 1974.

19 See *Le Monde*, 20–21 April 1974, and *Le Figaro*, 18 April 1974.

20 See Germain Bazin, *The Museum Age*, op. cit., p.277.

21 See McCarthy, 'Living with Beautiful Things', op. cit., p.101.

22 *France-Soir*, 15 January 1963.

23 Robert Guillain, 'La Joc arrive à Tokyo', *Le Monde*, 18 April 1974.

24 See text of speech in the French Ministry of Cultural Affairs, *Bulletin d'information*, No.34, 1 May 1974.

25 Mark Mazower, *Dark Continent: Europe's Twentieth Century*, Alfred A. Knopf, New York, 1999, pp.305–6.

26 J. Christopher Holloway, *The Business of Tourism*, Longman, London, 1998, p.33.

27 Ibid., p.41.

28 Amirou, op. cit., p.37.

29 Data in *Les Visiteurs du Louvre*, Service Culturel du Louvre, April 1999.

30 Letter dated 23 August 1978, in Louvre folder Inv 779.

31 The poem gives its name to the entire collection; see Rosario Castellanos, *Looking at the Mona Lisa*, trans. Maureen Ahern, Rivelin/Ecuatorial, London and Bradford, 1981.

32 Solange Zak, 'Les Randonnées de Mona Lisa', in *Bulletin de l'Association Léonard de Vinci*, No.16, March 1978, p.36.

33 Warhol returned several times to the *Mona Lisa*, with *Four Mona Lisas* and *Double Mona Lisa* in 1963, *63 White Mona Lisas* (1979), *Four White on White Mona Lisas* (1980) and *Two Golden Mona Lisas* (1980).

34 Reproduced in *Copier Créer*, op. cit.

35 Many of these were shown at the important 1978 German exhibition of *Mona Lisa* derivations: *Mona Lisa im 20. Jahrhundert*, Wilhelm-Lehmbruck-Museum der Stad Duisburg, 24 September–3 December 1978, Duisburg, 1978.

36 See Nicholas Treadwell Gallery, *The Mona Lisa Show*, catalogue, n.d. but presumably 1974.

37 Greg Constantine, *Leonardo Visits Los Angeles*, Alfred A. Knopf, New York, 1985.

38 See 'Saatchi Aims to Make Another Sensation', *Independent on Sunday*, 30 January 2000.

39 Catalogue of the exhibition 'Yvaral, Mona Lisa synthétisée: Propositions pour un art digital', Pavillon des Arts, Paris, 14 June–8 September 1985; see also his 'La Joconde est le sésame le plus subtil des portes du rêve', in *Arts*, 24 July 1981.

40 Marie-Thérèse Guichard, 'Les Accros de Mona Lisa', in *Le Point*, No.1236, 25 May 1996.

41 Data supplied by Margat, in Louvre folder Inv 779.

42 Bernard Ceysson, 'Les Dividendes de l'action Mona Lisa', in *Copier Créer*, op. cit., p.343.

43 In *Cousu de fil d'or, Beuys,*

Warhol, Klein, Duchamp, cited in ibid., p.345.

44 Carl Brandon Strehlke, in *Burlington Magazine*, November 1991, pp.780–2; the book was published by Yale University Press.

45 Reported in Robert Baron, 'From Romance to Ritual: Mona Lisa Images for the Modern World', in *Visual Resources*, Vol.15, No.2, 1999, pp.220–1.

46 Ibid., p.233. More examples of Monalisiana can be found on Robert Baron's website: http://www.pipeline.com/rabaron/MONALIST.htm.

47 Cited in Peter Conrad, *Modern Times, Modern Places*, Thames and Hudson, London, 1998, p.587.

48 Fredric Jameson, 'Globalization and Strategy', in *New Left Review*, No.4, July–August 2000, p.53.

49 Conrad, op. cit., p.580.

50 Signe Howell, 'Art and Meaning', in Susan Hiller (ed.), *The Myth of Primitivism: Perspectives on Art*, Routledge, London, 1991, p.228.

51 Cited in Michele H. Bogart, *Advertising, Artists, and the Borders of Art*, University of Chicago Press, 1995, p.211.

52 Mike Dempsey (ed.), *Early Advertising Art from A. & E. Pears Ltd*, Fontana, Glasgow, 1978, pp.3–4.

53 Diana and Geoffrey Hindley, *Advertising in Victorian England 1837–1901*, Wayland, London, 1972, p.44.

54 Roland Marchand, *Advertising the American Dream: Making Way for Modernity*, University of California Press, Berkeley, Los Angeles and London, 1985, p.153.

55 Georges Roque, *Ceci n'est pas un Magritte*, Flammarion, Paris, 1983, p.105.

56 See appendix in Sturani, op. cit.

57 Reported in *La Tribune de Genève*, 13 September 1996.

58 Louvre folder Inv 779, collection D. Schneider; much of the rest has been collected by Jean Margat and deposited at the Louvre. Other examples, mainly American, can be found on Robert Baron's impressive website, op. cit.

59 Two Louvre boxes labelled 'Objets divers'.

60 Mary Rose Storey, *Mona Lisas*, Harry N. Abrams Inc., New York, 1980, p.92.

61 It was founded in May 1987 by Jean Margat.

62 See *Quatre-vingts ans de Jocondiration: La Joconde dans les caricatures et les dessins satiriques*, February 1994, by Les amis de Mona Lisa. I have supplemented these findings with the Margat archives at the Louvre, Inv 779.

63 *Corriere della Sera*, 16 October 1994.

64 See Cummings's cartoon in the *Daily Express*, 24 February 1965.

65 Many of these photomontages can be found in Folder Dérivation III, Louvre folder Inv 779.

66 See, among others, *The American Philatelist*, June 1998.

67 *Horizon*, No.3, Vol.18, 1976.

68 The photo, taken by Béatrice André-Salvin in September 1995, is in Louvre folder Inv 779.

69 *Independent*, 2 September 1997, front-page picture.

70 Baron, op. cit., p.217.

71 See *Hello!* magazine, 9 June 1999.

72 Cited in *Achademia Leonardi Vinci*, Vol.3, 1990, p.106.

73 See report in *Figaro-Magazine*, 4 April 1981; 'Musées: Les Guardiens racontent', in *Le Republicain Lorrain*, 16 August 1981; later reports in *Le Parisien*, 6–7 February 1988: 'Il lache son entreprise pour garder "La Joconde" pendant dix ans'.

74 Michel Nuridsany, 'Orlan: Métamorphoses et mystifications', in *Le Figaro*, 9 November 1990.

75 It is now in Louvre folder Inv 779.

76 Maurice Vieuille, 'Léonard et la Joconde', op. cit., pp.263–4.

77 A photograph of the X-ray is in a folder marked 'Donnée essentielle' in Louvre folder Inv 779.

78 Georges Isarlo, 'Léonard de Vinci', in *Combat*, 26 March 1952.

79 Georges Isarlo, *Les Indépendants dans la peinture ancienne*, Bibliothèque des arts, Paris, 1956. See J.-P. Crespelle, 'La Joconde était un homme', in *France-Soir*, 25 May 1956, *Combat*, 26 May 1956, and the Vienna *Welt im Montag*, 18 October 1954.

80 Lillian Schwarz, 'Leonardo's Mona Lisa', in *Art and Antiques*, January 1987.

81 *Gazette des beaux-arts*, May–June 1987.

82 *Le Figaro*, 13 October 1993; see also *Gazette des beaux-arts*, December 1993, and the magazine *VSD*, 7–13 October 1993, for a full report.

83 See the paper by Steve Seitz and Chuck Dyer on www.cs.wisc.edu/computer-vision/projects/interp/vmorph.html.

84 John Brealey, 'Art Analysis: Probing Beneath the Image', in *IEEE Spectrum*, January 1986, p.66. The discovery was widely reported – see, for instance, *La Stampa*, 17 January 1991: 'Monna Lisa dipinta due volte'.

85 Reported in a number of newspapers, including *Le Point*, 30 May 1992.

86 Margat, 'Petit traité de Jocondologie', op. cit.

87 Jean Suyeux, 'Souvenirs et témoignages', in *Les 100 sourires de Monna Lisa* (exhibition catalogue), 29 January–26 March 2000, Tokyo Metropolitan Museum, p.242.

88 This piece of news was picked up by virtually the entire Italian press: see for example *Il Secolo XIX* of Genoa and *Il Giornale del Mattino di Firenze* on 15 September 1957, and *L'Ora* of Palermo on 21 September.

89 See report in *l'Humanité*, 13 February 1992.

90 See picture in *Le Parisien*, 13 December 1995.

91 Report in *Paris-Presse*, 5 November 1957.

92 You find it! I am not footnoting this one.

93 'Effetto del mal di denti e della sordità l'enigmatico sorriso della Gioconda', in *Il lavoro nuovo*, 11 August 1955.

94 Kenneth D. Keele, 'The Genesis of Mona Lisa', in *Journal of the History of Medicine and Allied Sciences*, Vol.14, No.2, April 1959, p.137.

95 Ibid., p.138.

96 Ibid., p.159.

97 Article in *Clinique*, 15 October 1962, reported in *Connaissance des arts*, March 1963.

98 *Ugeskriftet*, No.137, 1975, pp.1048–52, in Louvre folder Inv 779.

99 Ibid., pp.1668–9.

100 Kedal Adour, 'Mona Lisa Syndrome: Solving the Enigma of the Gioconda Smile', in *Annals of Otology, Rhinology and Laryngology*, Vol.98, No.3, 1989, pp.196–9.

101 Julien Caumer, 'La Joconde est-elle idiote?', in *l'Événement*, 31 October 1991; see also *Le Figaro*, 26 April 1991.

102 Joseph E. Borkowski, 'Mona Lisa: The Enigma of the Smile', in *Journal of Forensic Sciences*, November 1992, pp.1706–11.

103 See *Guardian*, 1 September 1999: 'Neurotic and a Teeth Gnasher: Mona Lisa is Exposed'.

104 See Colin Jones, 'Pulling Teeth in Eighteenth-Century Paris', in *Past and Present*, February 2000, p.123.

105 See Robert Baron's website, op. cit.

BIBLIOGRAPHY

ARCHIVAL MATERIAL AND DOCUMENTATION

Louvre, Service d'étude et documentation du départment des peintures, folders marked Inv 779 in the five cabinet drawers marked 'Joconde', and in addition the twenty-two red boxes containing mostly newspaper files, photographs and assorted *Mona Lisa* objects and derivations (including the material supplied by Jean Margat and other collectors)

Nielsen-CRA survey directed by Renato Mannheimer, Istituto per gli Studi sulla Pubblica Opinione, Milan, 11–13 February 2000

NEWSPAPERS AND MAGAZINES

Action française
The American Philatelist
Atlantic Monthly
Le Cabinet de l'amateur
Combat
Comoedia illustré
Connaissance des arts
Corriere della Sera
Le Cri de Paris
Daily Express
Epoca
l'Évenement
Excelsior
Le Figaro
Le Figaro littéraire
Le Figaro-Magazine
France-Soir

Gazette des beaux-arts
Il Giornale del Mattino
Il Giornale dell'Emilia
Grande revue
Guardian
Hamburger Abendblatt
Hello!
l'Humanité
Illustrated London News
l'Illustration
Independent
Independent on Sunday
Le Journal des arts
Il lavoro nuovo
Il Momento
Le Monde
New Yorker
Nuances
l'Ora
Paris-Match
Paris-Presse
Le Parisien
Le Petit Parisien
Le Point
Le Republicain Lorrain
Saturday Review
Il Secolo XIX
La Semaine
La Stampa
Stampa Sera
Time
The Times
La Tribune de Genève
VSD
Washington Post
Welt am Montag

Bibliography

WEBSITES CONSULTED

www.arkonet.fr/vivamonalisa/
www.cs.wisc.edu/computer-vision/projects/interp/vmorph.html
www.epinions.com
www.italica.rai
www.monalisamania.com
www.ninjaturtles.com
www.pipeline.com/rabaron/MONALIST.htm

BOOKS AND ARTICLES

Adamovicz, Elza, *Surrealist Collage in Text and Image: Dissecting the Exquisite Corpse*, Cambridge University Press, 1998

Adour, Kedai, 'Mona Lisa Syndrome: Solving the Enigma of the Gioconda Smile', in *Annals of Otology, Rhinology and Laryngology*, 1989, Vol.98, No.3

Alanic, Mathilde, *La romance de la Joconde*, Plon, Paris, 1908

Albert, Pierre, 'La presse française de 1871 à 1940', in Claude Bellanger et al., *Histoire générale de la presse française*, Vol.3, PUF, Paris, 1972

Alphand, Nicole Hervé, 'Malraux, chevalier servant de la Joconde', in *Revue des deux mondes*, May 1976

Altick, Richard D., *The English Common Reader*, University of Chicago Press, 1957

Amirou, Rachid, *Imaginaire du tourisme culturel*, PUF, Paris, 2000

Amis de Mona Lisa (Les), *Quatre-vingts ans de Jocondiration: La Joconde dans les caricatures et les dessins satiriques*, February 1994

Angrand, Pierre, 'L'État mécène: Période autoritaire du Second Empire (1851–1860)', in *Gazette des beaux-arts*, Vol.110, Nos.1192–3, May–June 1968

Apollinaire, Guillaume, *Chroniques d'art 1902–1918*, Gallimard, Paris, 1993

Arasse, Daniel, *Le détail: Pour une histoire rapprochée de la peinture*, Champs-Flammarion, Paris, 1996

Arasse, Daniel, *Leonardo da Vinci: The Rhythm of the World*, trans., Konecky and Konecky, New York, 1997

Aubert, Maurice, *Souvenirs du salon de 1859*, Tardieu, Paris, 1859

Ba Jin, 'Mona Lisa', in *Chinese Literature*, 1987

Baedeker, Karl, *Paris and its Environs: Handbook for Travellers*, London, 1878

Baedeker, Karl, *Paris and its Environs*, Leipzig, 1900

Baedeker, Karl, *Paris et ses environs*, Leipzig, 1911

Baedeker, Karl, *Paris et ses environs*, Paris and Leipzig, 1914

Baedeker, Karl, *Paris et ses environs*, Paris and Leipzig, 1924

Barbey d'Aurevilly, Jules, *Les Diaboliques*, Gallimard, Paris, 1973

Barolsky, Paul, '*Mona Lisa* Explained', in *Sources: Notes in the History of Art*, Vol.13, No.2, 1994

Baron, Robert, 'From Romance to Ritual: Mona Lisa Images for the Modern World', in *Visual Resources*, Vol.15, No.2, 1999

Barrès, Maurice, *L'oeuvre de Maurice Barrès*, Plon, Paris, 1965

Batkin, Leonid M., *Leonardo da Vinci*, trans. Gabriele Mazzitelli, Laterza, Bari-Rome, 1988

Baudelaire, Charles, *Les Fleurs du mal*, Paris, 1857 (enlarged 1861, 1868)

Baudelaire, Charles, *L'Art romantique*, GF-Flammarion, Paris, 1968

Baudelaire, Charles, *Fusées: Mon coeur mis à nu: La Belgique déshabillée*, Gallimard, Paris, 1986

Baudelaire in English, ed. Carol Clark and Robert Sykes, Penguin, Harmondsworth, 1997.

Bayer, Raymon, *Léonard de Vinci: La Grâce*, Félix Alcan, Paris, 1933

Bazin, Germain, *Trésors de la peinture au Louvre*, Éditions Somogy, Paris, 1962

Bazin, Germain, *La peinture au Louvre*, Éditions Somogy, Paris, 1966

Bazin, Germain, *The Museum Age*, trans. Jane van Nuis Cahill, Desoeer, Brussels, 1967

Béguin, Sylvie, 'La Joconde: Ombres et lumières', in *Journal des chefs-d'oeuvre de l'art*, No.3, 1963

Béguin, Sylvie, 'Un illustre sourire', in *Vraiment faux*, Fondation Cartier, Jouy-en-Josas, 1988

Béguin, Sylvie, 'La Joconde et le démon', in *Connaissance des arts*, No.475, 1991

Belt, Elmer, 'Letter', in *Bulletin de l'Association Léonard de Vinci*, No.5, October 1965

Belting, Hans, 'Le fétiche de l'art au XX siècle: Le cas de la Joconde', in *Diogène*, No.183, July–September 1998

Benfey, Christopher, 'Tea with Okakura', in *New York Review of Books*, 25 May 2000

Berenson, Bernard, *The Study and Criticism of Italian Art*, 3rd series, Bell and Sons Ltd, London, 1916

Bergman, Boris, *Un Tatami pour Mona Lisa*, Le Castor Astral, Bordeaux, 1999

Bernini, Paolo, 'Women Under the Gaze: A Renaissance Genealogy', in *Art History*, Vol.21, No.4, December 1998

Blackbourn, David, *The Fontana History of Germany: 1780–1918, The Long Nineteenth Century*, Fontana Press, London, 1997

Blamires, Alcuin (ed.), *Woman Defamed and Woman Defended: An Anthology of Medieval Texts*, Clarendon Press, Oxford, 1992

Blanc, Charles, 'La Joconde de Léonard de Vinci gravée par Calamatta', in *Gazette des beaux-arts*, 1 February 1859

Boas, George, 'The *Mona Lisa* in the History of Taste', in *Journal of the History of Ideas*, Vol.1, No.2, April 1940

Bogart, Michele H., *Advertising, Artists, and the Borders of Art*, University of Chicago Press, 1995

Boissière, Albert, *La Joconde aux enchères*, Fayard, Paris, 1929

Bonnamen, René, *La Question de la Joconde: Problème Vinciens*, Imprimerie Legendre, Lyon, 1908

Borin, Françoise, 'Judging by Images', in Natalie Zemon Davis and Arlette Farge (eds), *A History of Women: Renaissance and Enlightenment Paradoxes*, The Belknap Press of Harvard University Press, Cambridge, Massachusetts, 1993

Borkowski, Joseph E., 'Mona Lisa: The Enigma of the Smile', in *Journal of Forensic Sciences*, Vol.37, No.6, November 1992

Bourcier, Emmanuel, *Comment j'ai retrouvé la Joconde*, Henry Étienne, Paris, 1926

Bourdieu, Pierre, *The Field of Cultural Production*, Polity Press, Cambridge, 1988

Bourges, Élémir, *Le Crépuscule des Dieux*, Christian Pirot, Saint-Cyr-sur-Loire, 1987

Boyle, Nicholas, *Goethe: The Poet and the Age: Vol.1, The Poetry of Desire*, Oxford University Press, 1991

Bramly, Serge, *Léonard de Vinci*, Lattès, Paris, 1988

Brealey, John, 'Art Analysis: Probing Beneath the Image', in *IEEE Spectrum*, January 1986

Bresc, Geneviève, *Mémoires du Louvre*, Gallimard and RMN, Paris, 1989

Brewer, E. Cobham, *The Dictionary of Phrase and Fable*, Cassell and Co., London, new and enlarged edition 1894

Brion, Marcel, *Léonard de Vinci*, Albin Michel, Paris, 1952

Brizio, Anna Maria, Maria Vittoria Brugnoli and André Chastel, *Leonardo the Artist*, Hutchinson, London, 1981

Brookner, Anita, *The Genius of the Future: Essays in French Art Criticism*, Cornell University Press, Ithaca, New York, 1971

Brown, David Alan, 'Leonardo and the Idealized Portrait in Milan', in *Arte Lombarda*, no.67, 1983–84

Brown, David Alan, *The Young Correggio and his Leonardesque Sources*, Garland, New York, 1981

Brunoli, Maria Vittoria, 'The Sculptor', in Anna Maria Brizio, Maria Vittoria Brugnoli and André Chastel, *Leonardo the Artist*, Hutchinson, London, 1981

Buchwald, Art, 'Getting Through the Louvre with the Best', in *Los Angeles Times*, 25 June 1974

Bullen, Barrie, 'Walter Pater's *Renaissance* and Leonardo da Vinci's Reputation in the Nineteenth Century', in *Modern Language Review*, Vol.74, 1979

Bullen, J.B., *The Myth of the Renaissance in Nineteenth-Century Writing*, Clarendon Press, Oxford, 1994

Burckhardt, Jacob, *The Civilization of the Renaissance in Italy*, Phaidon Press, London, 1960

Cabanne, Pierre, *Entretiens avec Marcel Duchamp*, Paris, 1967; republished as *Duchamp & Co.*, Terrail, Paris, 1997

Cantarel-Besson, Yveline, *Notes et documents No.2*, RMN, Paris, 1992

Carpenter, Richard B., 'The Mythical Nature of Leonardo da Vinci's "Mona Lisa"', in *Sewanee Review*, Vol.71, No.3, July–September 1963

Castellanos, Rosario, *Looking at the Mona Lisa*, trans. Maureen Ahern, Rivelin/Ecuatorial, London and Bradford, 1981

Castiglione, Baldassare, *Il cortegiano*, Mondadori, Milan, 1991; English trans., *The Book of the Courtier*, Penguin, Harmondsworth, 1967

Catalogue raisonné des oeuvres de Léonard de Vinci au Musée du Louvre et dans les collections françaises, in *Homage à Léonard de Vinci*, Musée du Louvre édition MN, Paris, 1952

Ceppa, Leonardo, 'Freud e il sorriso della Gioconda', in *Belfagor*, Vol.44, No.5, 1989

Ceysson, Bernard, 'Les Dividendes de l'action Mona Lisa', in *Copier Créer*

Chansons sur la Joconde, December 1913 (Bibliothèque Nationale, Paris)

Charnin, Laurent, *La Joconde assassinée*, Axel Noel, Paris, 1991

Chastel, André, 'Un tableau difficile', in *Vraiment faux*, Fondation Cartier pour l'art contemporain, Jouy-en-Josas, 1988

Chastel, André, *Un Cardinale del Rinascimento in viaggio per l'Europa*, Laterza, Bari-Rome, 1995; trans. of *Le Cardinal Louis d'Aragon: Un voyageur princier de la Renaissance*, Fayard, Paris, 1986

Chesterton, G.K., *The Victorian Age in Literature*, Thornton Butterworth, London, 1938

Chroniques des arts, 20 December 1913

Ciardi, Roberto Paolo and Carlo Sisi (eds), 'Leonardo illustrato: genio e morigeratezza', in *L'immagine di Leonardo: Testimonianze figurative dal XVI al XIX secolo*, Giunti, Florence, 1997; including Giovanna Damiani's 'La biografia illustrata' and Federico Tognoli's 'Leonardo: maschera e volto'

Clark, Kenneth, 'Introduction' to Walter Pater, *The Renaissance*, Collins, London, 1961

Clark, Kenneth, 'Mona Lisa', in *Burlington Magazine*, Vol.115, No.840, March 1973

Clark, Kenneth, *Another Part of the Wood*, Hodder and Stoughton, London, 1976

Clark, Kenneth, *Leonardo Da Vinci*, Penguin Books, Harmondsworth, 1993

Clément, Charles, *Michel-Ange, Léonard de Vinci, Raphael*, Michel Lévy Frères, Paris, 1861

Coignard, Jérôme, *On a volé la Joconde*, Adam Biro, June 1990

Colette, *Contes des mille et un matins*, Flammarion, Paris, 1970

Conrad, Peter, *Modern Times, Modern Places*, Thames and Hudson, London, 1998

Constantine, Greg, *Leonardo Visits Los Angeles*, Alfred A. Knopf, New York, 1985

Copier Créer: De Turner à Picasso: 300 oeuvres inspirées par les maîtres du Louvre (exhibition catalogue), Réunion des Musées Nationaux, Paris, 1993

Coppier, André-Charles, 'La "Joconde" est-elle le portrait de "Mona Lisa"?', in *Les Arts*, No.145, January 1914

Coran, Charles, *Les Poésies de Charles Coran*, Vol.1, Le Puy, 1895

Costache, Irina, '"Mona Lisa" and the Futurists', in *Achademia Leonardo Vinci*, No.111, Vol.3, 1990

Couret, B., 'Il y a 500 ans naissait l'ouvrier de l'intelligence Léonard de Vinci', in *Avant-garde*, 14 May 1952

Courthope, W.J., 'Modern Culture', in *Quarterly Review*, No.137, October 1874

Cox-Rearick, Janet, *Chefs-d'oeuvre de la Renaissance: La collection de François Ier*, Albin Michel, Paris, 1995

Cusin, Jean-Pierre, 'Autour de la Joconde' and other essays, in *Copier Créer*, op. cit.

Dacier, E., *Catalogue de la vente Gaignat (1769)*, Paris, 1921

Dali, Salvador, 'Why they Attack the "Mona Lisa"', in *ArtNews*, Vol.91, No.9, 1992

Dalma, Giovanni, 'Tendenze tanatiche in Leonardo: Saggio su di un aspetto della sua personalità', in *Nevrasse*, Vol.50

D'Annunzio, Gabriele, *Portrait de Loÿse Baccaris*, Éditions du Sagittaire de Simon Kra, Paris, 1925

D'Annunzio, Gabriele, *L'uomo che rubò la "Gioconda"*, Mondadori, Milan, n.d. but 1950

D'Annunzio, Gabriele, *L'Isottèo: La Chimera*, Mondadori, Milan, 1996

Danto, Ginger, 'Taking Mona Lisa's Temperature', in *ARTnews*, September 1991

David-Weill, Natalie, *Rêve de pierre: La Quête de la femme chez Théophile Gautier*, Librairie Droz, Geneva, 1989

Davis, Anthony, *Magazine Journalism Today*, Heinemann, London, 1988

de Bassano, Jérôme, 'Le mythe de la Joconde', in *Bulletin de l'Association Léonard de Vinci*, No.16, March 1978

de Beatis, Antonio, *The Travel Journal of Antonio de Beatis: Germany, Switzerland, the Low Countries, France and Italy, 1517–1518*, introduction by John R. Hale, The Hakluyt Society, London, 1979

de Flandreysy, Jeanne, *Femmes et déesses*, Société d'éditions littéraires et artistiques, Paris, 1903

de Lavergnée, A. Brejon, *l'Inventaire de Le Brun de 1683: La collection des tableaux de Louis XIV*, Éditions de la réunion des musées nationaux, Paris, 1987

Delacroix, Eugène, *Journal 1822–1863*, Plon, Paris, 1980

Dell'Aquilano, Donatella, 'D'Annunzio e il leonardismo fin de siècle', in *Critica Letteraria*, Vol.26, No.3/100, 1998

Dempsey, Mike (ed.), *Early Advertising Art from A. & E. Pears Ltd*, Fontana, Glasgow, 1978

de Ris, Clément, 'Musée du Louvre', in *l'Artiste*, 15 January 1849

De Santi, Pier Marco, 'La Gioconda rubata "Tu non saprai giammai perché sorrido" ', in *Achademia Leonardo Vinci*, No.111, 1990

d'Hangest, Germain, *Walter Pater: l'Homme et l'oeuvre*, Vol.1, Didier, Paris, 1961

d'Harnoncourt, Anne and Kyanston McShine (eds), *Marcel*

Duchamp, MOMA and the Philadelphia Museum of Art, New York, 1973

Dickens, Charles, *Pictures from Italy*, Penguin, Harmondsworth, 1998

Diderot and D'Alembert, *Enclycopédie*, Vol.9, Cramer, Geneva, 1772

Dijkstra, Bram, *Idols of Perversity: Fantasies of Feminine Evil in Fin-de-siècle Culture*, Oxford University Press, 1986

Du Camp, Maxime, *Théophile Gautier*, Hachette, Paris, 1890

Dumesnil, Alfred, *l'Art italien*, Giraud, Paris, 1854

Dupuy, Marie-Anne, 'Les Copistes à l'oeuvre', in *Copier Créer*, op. cit.

Durrell, Lawrence, *Justine*, Faber and Faber, London, 1957

Dylan, Bob, *Writings and Drawings*, Alfred A. Knopf, New York, 1973

Eco, Umberto, *Il pendolo di Foucault*, Bompiani, Milan, 1988

Eco, Umberto, *Opera aperta: Forma e indeterminazione nelle poetiche contemporanee*, Bompiani, Milan, 1995

Eliot, George, *The George Eliot Letters*, Vol.5, ed. Gordon S. Haight, Yale University Press, New Haven, 1954–55

Eliot, George, 'Brothers in Opinion: Edgar Quinet and Jules Michelet', in *Selected Essays, Poems and Other Writings*, Penguin, Harmondsworth, 1990

Eliot, T.S., *The Sacred Wood: Essays on Poetry and Criticism*, Methuen, London, 1920

Ellmann, Richard, *Oscar Wilde*, Hamish Hamilton, London, 1987

Enciclopedia italiana, Treccani, Rome, 1933, Vol.XX, entry for 'Leonardo'

Engelberg, Edward, *The Vast Design: Patterns in W.B. Yeats's Aesthetic*, Catholic University of America Press, Washington DC, 1988

Eyre, John R., *Monograph on Leonardo da Vinci's "Mona Lisa"*, Grevel and Co., London and Scribner's, New York, 1915

Fau, Guy, *Le Sourire de la Joconde*, Librairie des Champs-Elysées, Paris, 1961

Fehl, Philip, 'In Praise of Imitation: Leonardo and his Followers', in *Gazette des beaux-arts*, Vol.137, Nos.1518–19, July–August 1995

Filipczak, Z. Zaremba, 'New Light on Mona Lisa: Leonardo's Optical Knowledge and his Choice of Lighting', in *Art Bulletin*, Vol.59, No.4, December 1977

Flaubert, Gustave, *La Tentation de saint Antoine*, Flammarion, Paris, 1967

Flaubert, Gustave, *Mémoires d'un fou: Novembre et autres textes de jeunesse*, Flammarion, Paris, 1991

Fleury, Marie-Antoinette, *Documents du Minutier Central concernant les peintres les sculpteurs et les graveurs au XVIIe siècle (1600–1650)*, Vol.1, Paris, 1969

Focillon, Henri, 'Les Graveurs de la Joconde', in *Revue de l'art ancient et moderne*, Vol.30, 1911

Focillon, Henri, 'La Joconde et ses interpretes', *Technique et sentiment: Études sur l'art moderne*, Henri Laurens, Paris, 1931

Forster, E.M., *A Room with a View*, Penguin, Harmondsworth, 1979

Foucart, Jacques, 'Louis Dimier et la Pratique de l'histoire de l'art, d'aprés sa chronique de l'Action Française (1910–1913)', in *Gazette des beaux-arts*, Vol.141, No.1562, March 1999

Fox, Celina, 'The Development of Social Reportage in English Periodical Illustration During the 1840s and Early 1850s', in *Past and Present*, No.74, February 1977

Freedman, Luba, 'Raphael's Perception of the *Mona Lisa*', in *Gazette des beaux-arts*, Vol.131, No.1450, November 1989

Freud, Sigmund, 'Leonardo da Vinci', in *Art and Literature*, Vol.14 of Pelican Freud Library, Penguin, Harmondsworth, 1990

Frey, Bruno S. and Werner W. Pommerechne, *Muses and Markets: Explorations in the Economics of the Arts*, Blackwell, Oxford, 1989

Gamble, Cynthia J., 'A l'ombre de la vierge dorée de la cathédrale d'Amiens: Ruskin et l'imaginaire proustien', in *Gazette des beaux-arts*, May–June 1995

Gasset, Ortega y, 'La Gioconda', originally in *La Prensa* of 15 October 1911; reprinted in *Obras Completas*, Vol. 1, Alianza Editorial, Madrid, 1983

Gautier, Théophile, *Salon de 1847*, Hetzel, Paris, 1847

Gautier, Théophile, *Les Beaux arts en Europe*, Vol.1, Michel Lévy, Paris, 1855

Gautier, Théophile, 'Les caricatures de Léonard de Vinci', in *l'Artiste*, 12 April 1857

Gautier, Théophile, *Les Dieux et les demi-dieux de la peinture*, Morizot, Paris, 1864

Gautier, Théophile, *Tableaux de siège, Paris 1870–1871*, Charpentier, Paris, 1871

Gautier, Théophile, *Voyage en Italie*, Charpentier, Paris, 1875

Gautier, Théophile, *Guide de l'amateur au musée du Louvre*, Charpentier, Paris, 1882

Gautier, Théophile, *Mademoiselle de Maupin*, GF-Flammarion, Paris, 1966

Gautier, Théophile, *Spirite*, Nizet, Paris, 1970

Gautier, Théophile, *Emaux et camées*, Gallimard, Paris, 1981

Gautier, Théophile, *Récits fantastique*, GF-Flammarion, Paris, 1981

Gautier, Théophile, *Exposition de 1859*, ed. Wolfgang Drost and Ulrike Henninges, Carl Winter Universitätsverlag, Heidelberg, 1992

Gautier, Théophile, *Correspondance générale, Vol.X: 1868–1869*, ed. Claudine Lacoste-Veysseyre, Librairie Droz, Geneva-Paris, 1996

Gautier, Théophile, *Le Roman de la momie*, Livre de Poche, Paris, 1997

Gavin, Jamila, 'Mona', in Michael Morpurgo (ed.), *Muck 'n' Magic*, Egmont, London, 2001

Gay, Peter, *Freud: A Life for our Time*, Macmillan, London, 1989

Gay, Peter, *The Naked Heart*, Vol.4 of *The Bourgeois Experience: Victoria to Freud*, HarperCollins, London, 1996

Gibbons, Stella, *Westwood or The Gentle Powers*, Longman, London, 1946

Gibbs-Smith, Charles H., *Aviation: An Historical Survey from its Origins to the End of World War II*, HMSO, London, 1985

Gibson, William, *Mona Lisa Overdrive*, HarperCollins, London, 2000

Gide, André, *Les Faux-Monnayeurs*, in *Romans*, Gallimard-Pléiade, Paris, 1958

Gille, Bertrand, *Les Ingénieurs de la Renaissance*, Seuil Points, Paris, 1978

Glavany, Jean, *La Joconde et Platini*, Liana Levy, Paris, 1985

Glazer, Miryam, ' "What is Within now Seen Without": Romanticism, Neuroromanticism, and the Death of the Imagination in William Gibson's Fictive World', in *Journal of Popular Culture*, Vol.23, Winter 1989

Goethe, J.W., *Italian Journey*, trans. W.H. Auden and Elizabeth Mayer, Penguin, Harmondsworth, 1970

Gombrich, Ernst, *New Light on Old Masters: Studies in the Art of the Renaissance*, University of Chicago Press, 1986

Gombrich, Ernst, *The Story of Art*, Phaidon, London, 1989

Gombrich, Ernst, 'Portrait of the Artist as a Paradox', in *New York Review of Books*, 20 January 2000

Goncourt, Edmond et Jules de, *Journal: 1851–1863*, Vol.1, Fasquelle et Flammarion, Paris, 1956

Granatella, Laura, ' "La Gioconda" dannunziana: creazione fatale', in *Otto/Novecento*, Vol.12, Nos.3–4, 1988

Greenhalgh, Chris, *Stealing the Mona Lisa*, Bloodaxe Books, Newcastle, 1994

Grieco, Sara F. Matthews, 'The Body, Appearance, and Sexuality', in Natalie Zemon Davis and Arlette Farge (eds), *A History of Women: Renaissance and Enlightenment Paradoxes*, The Belknap Press of Harvard University Press, Cambridge, Massachusetts, 1993

Grojnowski, Daniel, 'Hydropathes and Company', in Phillip Dennis Cate and Mary Shaw (eds), *The Spirit of Montmartre:*

Cabarets, Humor, and the Avant-Garde, 1875–1905, State University of New Jersey, Rutgers, 1996

Gruyer, François-Anatole, *Voyage autour du salon carré au musée du Louvre*, Paris, 1891

Gufeld, Eduard, *My Life in Chess: The Search for La Gioconda*, International Chess Enterprises, Seattle, 1994

Hardy, Georgina, *Aimez-vous la Joconde?*, Presses de la Cité, Paris, 1981

Hart, Ivor B., *The World of Leonardo da Vinci, Man of Science, Engineer and Dreamer of Flight*, Viking Press, New York, 1961

Haskins, James (with Kathleen Benson), *Nat King Cole*, Stein and Day, New York, 1984

Hauser, Arnold, *The Social History of Art: Vol.2, Renaissance, Mannerism, Baroque*, Routledge, London, 1999

Higonnet, Anne, 'Immagini di donne', in Geneviève Fraisse and Michelle Perrot (eds), *Storia delle donne: L'Ottocento*, Laterza, Roma-Bari, 1998

Hikmet, Nazim, *La Joconde et Si-ya-Ou*, Éditeurs Français Réunis, Paris, 1978

Hilton, Tim, *John Ruskin: The Later Years*, Yale University Press, New Haven and London, 2000

Hindley, Diana and Geoffrey, *Advertising in Victorian England 1837–1901*, Wayland, London, 1972

Holloway, J. Christopher, *The Business of Tourism*, Longman, London, 1998

Hope, Charles, 'In Lorenzo's Garden', in *New York Review of Books*, 24 June 1999

Hope, Charles, 'A Wind from the West', in *New York Review of Books*, 2 December 1999

Hours, Magdeleine, 'Radiographie des tableaux de Léonard de Vinci', in *Revue des arts*, No.4, 1952

Houssaye, Arsène, *Histoire de Léonard de Vinci*, Didier et cie, Paris, 1869

Howell, Signe, 'Art and Meaning', in Susan Hiller (ed.), *The Myth of Primitivism: Perspectives on Art*, Routledge, London, 1991

Bibliography

Hufton, Olwen, *The Prospect Before Her: A History of Women in Western Europe, Vol.1: 1500–1800*, HarperCollins, London, 1995

Hutchins, Pat, *The Mona Lisa Mystery*, The Bodley Head, London, 1981

Huysmans, Joris-Karl, *À Rebours*, GF-Flammarion, Paris, 1978

Inman, Billie Andrew, *Walter Pater's Reading: A Bibliography of his Library Borrowings and Literary References, 1858–1873*, Garland Publishing, New York and London, 1981

Isarlo, Georges, 'Léonard de Vinci', in *Combat*, 26 March 1952

Isarlo, Georges, *Les Indépendants dans la peinture ancienne*, Bibliothèque des arts, Paris, 1956

James, Henry, *The Madonna of the Future and Other Tales*, Macmillan, London, 1880

James, Henry, *The Ambassadors*, Penguin, Harmondsworth, 1994

Jameson, Fredric, 'Globalization and Strategy', in *New Left Review*, No.4, July–August 2000

Jardine, Lisa, *Worldly Goods: A New History of the Renaissance*, Macmillan, London and Basingstoke, 1997

Jaspers, Karl, *Leonardo, Descartes, Max Weber: Three Essays*, Routledge and Kegan Paul, London, 1965

Jeffreys, Mark, 'The *Mona Lisa* and the Symbol of Ideas: Pater's Leda as Mother to Yeats's Helen', in *Colby Quarterly*, Vol.29, No.1, 1993

Jones, Colin, 'Pulling Teeth in Eighteenth-Century Paris', in *Past and Present*, No.166, February 2000

Jones, Russell M., 'American Painters in Paris: The Rate of Exchange 1825–48', in *Apollo*, February 1992

Jordan, Neil and David Leland, *Mona Lisa* (screenplay), Faber and Faber, London, 1986

Joyce, James, *The Critical Writings of James Joyce*, ed. Ellsworth Mason and Richard Ellmann, Faber and Faber, London, 1959

Joyce, James, *A Portrait of the Artist as a Young Man*, Viking, New York, 1969

Keele, Kenneth D., 'The Genesis of Mona Lisa', in *Journal of the History of Medicine and Allied Sciences*, Vol.14, No.2, April 1959

Kemp, Martin, *Leonardo da Vinci: The Marvellous Works of Nature and Man*, Dent, London, 1981

Kenner, Hugh, 'O, an Impossible Person', in Mary T. Reynolds, *James Joyce: A Collection of Critical Essays*, Prentice Hall, Englewood Cliffs, New Jersey, 1993

Konigsburg, E.L., *The Second Mrs Gioconda*, Macmillan, London, 1976

Kris, Ernst and Otto Kurz, *Legend, Myth, and Magic in the Image of the Artist*, Yale University Press, New Haven and London, 1979

La Mure, Pierre, *The Private Life of Mona Lisa*, Collins, London, 1976

LaFarge, Antoinette, 'The Bearded Lady and the Shaven Man: Mona Lisa, meet Mona/Leo', in *Leonardo*, Vol.29, No.5, 1996

Lagrange, Léon, 'Du Rang des femmes dans les arts', in *Gazette des beaux-arts*, 1 October 1860

Larousse Universel, Paris, 1922

Larrington, Carolyne, *Women and Writing in Medieval Europe*, Routledge, London, 1995

l'Art et la pensée de Léonard de Vinci, Communications du Congrés International du Val de Loire (7–12 Juillet 1952), Etudes d'Art Nos.8, 9, 10, Paris-Alger, 1953–54

Lasselle, Bruno, *Le Triomphe de l'édition: Histoire du Livre*, Vol.1, Gallimard, Paris, 1998

Lawrence, D.H., *The Lovely Lady*, Martin Secker, London, 1932

Lebègue, Raymond, 'Les Artistes italiens de la Renaissance et les écrivains français du temps', in *l'Art et la pensée de Léonard de Vinci*, op. cit.

Lebovics, Herman, *Mona Lisa's Escort: André Malraux and the Reinvention of French Culture*, Cornell University Press, Ithaca and London, 1999

Lee, Vernon, *Supernatural Tales*, Peter Owen, London, 1987

Léger, Fernand, 'Le nouveau réalisme continue' (1936), in *Fonctions de la peinture*, ed. Sylvie Forestier, Gallimard Folio, Paris, 1996

Leonardo da Vinci, *Leonardo on Painting*, ed. Martin Kemp, Yale University Press, New Haven and London, 1989

Leonardo da Vinci, *L'uomo e la natura*, introduction by Mario De Micheli, Feltrinelli, Milan, 1991

Longhi, Roberto, 'Le due Lise', in *Edizioni delle opere complete di Roberto Longhi: Vol.1, Scritti giovanili*, Sansoni, Florence, 1956

Lorrain, Jean, *Trés Russe*, Hubert Julia, Rouen, 1986

Lossky, Boris, 'Nouvelles connaissances et considérations au sujet du tableau léonardesque di "La Colombine"', in *Bulletin de l'Association Léonard de Vinci*, No.5, October 1965

Louis, Dimier, 'La "Joconde" volée', in *l'Action Française*, 26 August 1911

Louvre, *Les visiteurs du Louvre*, Service Culturel du Louvre, April 1999

Louvre, *Rapport d'activité du musée du Louvre 1999*

Louvre, *Les Publics du musée du Louvre en 1999: Synthèse*, Observatoire permanent des Publics, April 2000

McAleer, Joseph, *Passion's Fortune: The Story of Mills & Boon*, Oxford University Press, 1999

McCarthy, Mary, *The Group*, Penguin, Harmondsworth, 1964

McCarthy, Mary, *Occasional Prose*, Harcourt Brace Jovanovich, New York, 1985

McClelland, Andrew, 'The Musée du Louvre as a Revolutionary Metaphor During the Terror', in *Art Bullettin*, Vol.70, No.2, June 1988

Mackworth, Cecily, *Guillaume Apollinaire and the Cubist Life*, John Murray, London, 1961

Maiorino, Giancarlo, *Leonardo da Vinci: The Daedalian Mythmaker*, Penn State Press, State College Pennsylvania, 1992

Mallarmé, Stéphane, *Correspondance: Vol.1, 1862–1871*, Gallimard, Paris, 1959

Malraux, André, *Les Voix du silence*, La Galerie de la Pléiade, Paris, 1951

Malraux, André, *Le Miroir des limbes*, in *Oeuvres complètes*, Vol.3, Gallimard Pléiade, Paris, 1996

Mankowitz, Wolf, *Gioconda*, Allen and Unwin, London, 1988

Marchand, Roland, *Advertising the American Dream: Making Way for Modernity*, University of California Press, Berkeley, Los Angeles and London, 1985

Marcy, Pierre, *Guide populaire dans les musées du Louvre*, Librairie du Petit Journal, Paris, 1867

Margat, Jean, 'Petit traité de Jocondologie', in the special issue of the magazine *Bizarre*, May 1959, Nos 11–12

Marinetti, Filippo Tommaso, 'Manifesto del Futurismo', in *I futuristi*, ed. Francesco Grisi, Newton, Rome 1994

Marinoni, Augusto, 'La Bicyclette', in Ladislao Reti (ed.), *Léonard de Vinci: l'Humaniste, l'artiste, l'inventeur*, Laffont, Paris, 1974

Maugham, W. Somerset, *Christmas Holiday*, Heinemann, London, 1939

Maugham, W. Somerset, *Of Human Bondage*, Heinemann, London, 1961

Mayhew, James, *Katie and the Mona Lisa*, Orchard Books, London, 1998

Mazauric, Lucie, *Le Louvre en voyage 1939–1945: ou Ma vie de château*, Plon, Paris, 1978

Mazower, Mark, *Dark Continent: Europe's Twentieth Century*, Alfred A. Knopf, New York, 1999

Mead, David G., 'Technological Transfiguration in William Gibson's Sprawl Novels', in *Extrapolation*, Vol.32, No.4, 1991

Mengin, Robert, 'Giovanni Poggi: l'Homme qui sauva la Joconde', *Revue des deux mondes*, March 1963

Mereskovskij, Dimitri, *Leonardo da Vinci: La vita del più grande genio di tutti i tempi*, Giunti, Florence, 1998

Michaud, Stéphane, 'Idolatrie rappresentazioni artistiche e letterarie', in Geneviève Fraisse and Michelle Perrot (eds), *Storia delle donne: L'Ottocento*, Laterza, Roma-Bari, 1998

Michelangelo, *Rime*, Mondadori, Milan, 1998

Michelet, Jules, *Journal, Vol.3: 1861–67*, ed. Claude Digeon, Gallimard, Paris, 1976

Michelet, Jules, *Oeuvres complètes, Vol.7: Histoire de la France au seizième siècle: Renaissance et réforme*, Flammarion, Paris, 1976

Migliore, Sandra, *Tra Hermes e Prometeo: Il mito di Leonardo nel decadentismo Europeo*, Leo S. Olschki, Florence, 1994

Mona Lisa im 20. Jahrhundert, Wilhelm-Lehmbruck-Museum der Stad Duisburg, 24 September–3 December 1978, Duisburg, 1978

Monnier, Gérard, *l'Art et ses institutions en France: De la révolution à nos jours*, Folio-Gallimard, Paris, 1995

Montégut, Maurice, *Les Chevauchées de la Joconde*, Olendorff, Paris, 1901

Montgomery, Ramsey, *The Mona Lisa is Missing!*, Bantam Books, New York, 1988

Moulin, Raymonde, 'La Genèse de la rareté artistique', in *Ethnologie française*, Vol. 8, No.2–3, 1978

Müntz, Eugène, *Léonard de Vinci: l'Artiste, le penseur, le savant*, Hachette, Paris, 1899

Nicholas Treadwell Gallery, *The Mona Lisa Show*, catalogue, n.d., presumably 1974

Noah, Robert, *The Man who Stole the Mona Lisa*, St Martin's Press, New York, 1998

Noir, Michel, *L'Otage*, Calmann Levy, Paris, 1998

Odier, Daniel, *Gioconda*, Fayard, Paris, 1984

Oliphant, Margaret, 'Pater's History of the Renaissance', in *Blackwood's Edinburgh Magazine*, November 1873

Oxford Book of Modern Verse 1892–1935, ed. W.B. Yeats, Clarendon Press, Oxford, 1936

Page, Martin, *The Man who Stole the Mona Lisa*, John Curley, South Yarmouth, Massachusetts, 1984

Pater, Walter, *The Renaissance*, Oxford University Press, 1998

Pavlow, Big Al, *Hot Charts 1950*, Music House Publishing, Providence, Rhode Island, 1951

Pedretti, Carlo, 'Storia della Gioconda di Leonardo da Vinci con nuove congetture sulla persona ritratta', in *Bibliothèque d'humanisme et Renaissance*, Vol.18, 1956

Pedretti, Carlo, *Leonardo: A Study in Chronology and Style*, Thames and Hudson, London, 1973

Péladan, Joséphin, 'La Joconde et le saint Jean', in *La Revue hebdomadaire*, No.36, 9 September 1911

Péladan, Joséphin, 'La Joconde: Histoire d'un tableau', in *Les Arts*, No.121, January 1912

Perdrield-Vaissière, J., *Le Sourire de la Joconde*, Librarie de la Plume, Paris, 1902

Pierquin, Georges, *Du Mouron pour la Joconde*, Plon, Paris, 1985

Planche, Gustave, 'Étude sur l'art et la poésie en Italie: Léonard de Vinci', in *Revue des deux mondes*, Vol.20, September 1850

Pomarède, Vincent, *La Joconde*, Prat/Europa, Paris, 1988

Pope-Hennessy, John, 'The Portrait in the Renaissance', The A.W. Mellon Lectures in the Fine Arts, 1963, National Gallery of Art, Washington DC, Bollinger Series XXXV 12, Pantheon Books, New York, 1966

Poulot, Dominique, 'La Visite au musée: Un Loisir édifiant au XIXe siècle', in *Gazette des beaux-arts*, vol.125, no.1372–3, May–June 1983

Praz, Mario, *La carne, la morte e il diavolo nella letteratura romantica*, Sansoni, Florence, 1966

Predetti, Carlo, 'Quella puttana di Leonardo', in *Achademia Leonardi Vinci*, No.9, 1996

Proust, Marcel, 'Ruskin à Notre-Dame d'Amiens', in *Mercure de France*, Vol.34, April–June 1900

Proust, Marcel, 'Aprés la guerre', in *Essais et articles*, Gallimard, Paris, 1971

Proust, Marcel, *Correspondance*, Vol.2, ed. Philip Kolb, Plon, Paris, 1976

Puelli, C., 'Leonardo e il volto della Gioconda', in *Revue des études italiennes*, No.1, January–March 1959

Pulitzer, Henry F., *Where is the Mona Lisa?*, The Pulitzer Press, London, n.d., probably 1967

Purvis, Florence, 'La Femme universelle', in *Impresario: Magazine of the Arts*, July–August 1966

Quinet, Edgar, *Les Révolutions d'Italie*, in his *Oeuvres complètes*, Vol.2, Hachette, Paris, 1904

Rabley, Stephen, *Marcel and the Mona Lisa*, Longman, Harlow, 1991

Radrizzani, Dominique, 'La Joconde fantôme vue de l'orchestre: Mona Lisa dans la bande dessinée', in *Mona Lisa: Un certain sourire . . . Anthologie d'une obsession*, Université de Lausanne, 1992

Raffalovich, Serge and H.M. Mons, *La Joconde: Le Roman d'amour de Léonard de Vinci et de Mona Lisa*, Fasquelle, Paris, 1935

Ramacciotti Donato, Valeria, 'I decadenti e la Gioconda', in *Studi francesi*, Vol.21, Nos 61–2, January–August 1977

Rambaud, Mireille, *Documents du Minutier central concernant l'histoire de l'art (1700–1750)*, Vol.2, Paris, 1971

Reinach, Salomon, 'La Tristesse de Mona Lisa', in *Bulletin des musées de France*, Vol.2, 1909

Reinach, Salomon (signed 'S.R.'), 'La "Joconde" au Louvre', in *Revue archéologique*, Vol.22, 1913

Reit, Seymour, *The Day they Stole the Mona Lisa*, Robert Hale, London, 1981

Renard, Jules, *Journal: 1887–1910*, Gallimard-Pléiade, Paris, 1965

Renouard, Yves, 'Léonard de Vinci et la France', in *Bulletin de l'Association Léonard de Vinci*, No.17, April 1979

Richardson, Joanna, *Théophile Gautier: His Life and Times*, Max Reinhardt, London, 1958

Riede, David G., *Swinburne: A Study of Romantic Mythmaking*, University Press of Virginia, Charlottesville, 1978

Robsjohn-Gibbins, T.H., *Mona Lisa's Mustache*, Alfred A. Knopf, New York, 1948

Roger-Milès, L., *Léonard de Vinci et les Jocondes*, Floury, Paris, 1923

Roque, Georges, *Ceci n'est pas un Magritte*, Flammarion, Paris, 1983

Rose, Jacqueline, '*Hamlet*: The *Mona Lisa* of Literature', in *Critical Quarterly*, Vol.28, Nos 1–2, Spring–Summer 1986

Rousseau, Jean-Jacques, *Confessions*, trans. J.M. Cohen, Penguin, Harmondsworth, 1960

Ruskin, John, *The Cestus of Aglaia* (1865), in *The Complete Works of John Ruskin*, Vol.19, George Allen, London, 1905

Rzepinska, M., 'The "Lady with the Ermine" Revisited', in *Achademia Leonardi Vinci*, Vol.6, 1993

St. John, Bayle, *The Louvre: Or Biography of a Museum*, Chapman and Hall, London, 1850

San-Antonio, *Passez-moi la Joconde*, Fleuve Noir, Paris, 1954

Sand, George, 'La Joconde de Léonard de Vinci gravée par Louis Calamatta', in *La Presse*, 8 December 1858

Sand, George, *Correspondance*, Vol.15, ed. George Lubin, Garnier, Paris, 1981

Sartre, Jean Paul, *Words*, trans. Irene Clephane, Penguin Books, Harmondsworth, 1967 (orig. *Les Mots*, Gallimard, Paris, 1964)

Sauvage, Marcel, *Jules et Edmond de Goncourt: Précurseurs*, Mercure de France, Paris, 1970

Schapiro, Meyer, 'Leonardo and Freud: An Art-Historical Study', in *Journal of the History of Ideas*, Vol.17, No.2, April 1956

Schmalenbach, Werner, *Fernand Léger*, Éditions Cercle d'Art, Paris, 1977

Schneider, Laurie and Jack D. Flam, 'Visual Convention, Simile and Metaphor in the *Mona Lisa*', in *Storia dell'arte*, No.29, 1977

Schofield, Richard, 'Leonardo's Milanese Architecture: Career, Sources and Graphic Techniques', in *Achademia Leonardi Vinci*, Vol.4, 1991

Schuré, Édouard, *Léonard de Vinci*, in *Le Théâtre de l'âme*, Perrin, Paris, 1905

Schwarz, Lillian, 'Leonardo's Mona Lisa', in *Art and Antiques*, January 1987

Séailles, Gabriel, *Léonard de Vinci: l'Artiste et le savant: Essai de biographie psychologique*, Perrin et cie, Paris, 1892

Severi, Rita, 'The Myth of Leonardo in English Decadent Writers', in *Achademia Leonardi Vinci*, Vol.5, 1992

Shaw, Bob, 'The Gioconda Caper', in *Who Goes Here?* Victor Gollancz, London, 1988

Shell, Janice and Grazioso Sironi, 'Salaì and Leonardo's Legacy', in *Burlington Magazine*, February 1991

Shell, Janice, *Léonard de Vinci*, Réunion des musées nationaux, Paris, 1993

Shelley, Percy Bysshe, *Complete Poetical Works*, Oxford University Press, 1970

Smith, Webster, 'Observations on the *Mona Lisa* Landscape', in *Art Bulletin*, Vol.67, No.2, June 1985

Snell, Robert, *Théophile Gautier: A Romantic Critic of the Visual Arts*, Clarendon Press, Oxford, 1982

Soffici, Ardengo, *Giornale di bordo*, Vallecchi, Florence, 1921

Souplex, Raymond, *Autour de la Joconde*, Les Meilleures Scènes, Paris, n.d., but 1933

Spector, Jack J., 'Duchamp's Androgynous Leonardo: "Queue" and "Cul" in *L.H.O.O.Q.*', in *Source: Notes in the History of Art*, Vol.11, No.1, Fall 1990

Spencer, Michael Clifford, *The Art Criticism of Théophile Gautier*, Librairie Droz, Geneva, 1969

Spitzmuller, Georges, *Les Amours de François Ier et de la Joconde*, Fayard, Paris, 1920

Starnazzi, Carlo, 'Leonardo in terra di Arezzo', in *Studi per l'ecologia del Quarternario*, No.17, 1995

Stendhal, *Oeuvres intimes*, Gallimard-Pléiade, Paris, 1955

Stendhal, *Histoire de la peinture en Italie*, Gallimard Folio, Paris, 1996

Stites, Raymond, 'Monna Lisa Monna Bella', in *Parnassus*, January 1946

Storey, Mary Rose, *Mona Lisas*, Harry N. Abrams Inc., New York, 1980

Sturani, Enrico, 'Le gioconde: Ritratti infedeli', essay in appendix to Marcello Vannucci, *Il furto della Gioconda: Vincenzo Peruggia e la sua storia*, Novecento, Palermo, 1993

Suyeux, Jean, 'Le Testament de Léonard', in *Le Gnomon: Revue internationale d'histoire du notariat*, No.88, June–July 1993

Suyeux, Jean, 'Souvenirs et témoignages', in *Les 100 sourires de Monna Lisa* (exhibition catalogue), 29 January to 26 March 2000 at the Tokyo Metropolitan Museum

Swinburne, Algernon, 'Charles Baudelaire', in *Spectator*, 6 September 1862

Swinburne, Algernon, *The Letters of Algernon Charles Swinburne*, Vol.2, ed. Edmund Gosse and Thomas James Wose, Heinemann, London, 1918

Swinburne, Algernon, *Collected Poetical Works*, Vol.1, Heinemann, London, 1935

Swinburne, Algernon, *Letters*, Vol.1, ed. Cecil Y. Lang, Yale University Press, New Haven, Connecticut, 1959–60

Taine, Hippolyte, *Nouveaux essaix de critique et d'histoire*, Hachette, Paris, 1901

Taine, Hippolyte, *Voyage en Italie*, Édition complexe, Brussels, 1990

Tanaka, Hidemichi, 'Leonardo's Isabella d'Este: A New Analysis of the *Monna Lisa* in the Louvre', in *Annali dell'Istituto Giapponese di Cultura in Roma*, No.13, 1976–77

Taylor, John Russell and Brian Brook, *The Art Dealers*, Hodder and Stoughton, London, 1969

Terlinden, Lord, 'Léonard de Vinci dans la gravure flamande', in *l'Art et la pensée de Léonard de Vinci*, Communications du Congrés International du Val de Loire (7–12 Juillet 1952), Études d'Art Nos 8, 9, 10, Paris–Alger, 1953–54

Ternaux, Catherine, *Le Secret de la Joconde*, Grasset-Jeunesse, Paris, 1997

Thomson, C.W., 'Note sur la diffusion de l'Histoire de la peinture en Italie jusqu'en 1833', in *Stendhal Club*, No.15, 15 April 1971

Tintner, Adeline, 'Henry James's Mona Lisa', in *Essays in Literature*, Vol.8, No.1, 1981

Toren, Christina, 'Leonardo's "Last Supper" in Fiji', in Susan Hiller (ed.), *The Myth of Primitivism: Perspectives on Art*, Routledge, London, 1991

Turner, Richard, *Inventing Leonardo: The Anatomy of a Legend*, Macmillan, Basingstoke and London, 1995

Valéry, Paul, *Cahiers*, Gallimard-Pléiade, Paris, 1974

Vasari, Giorgio, *Le Vite de' più eccellenti pittori, scultori e architetti*, Newton, Rome, 1991

Vecce, Carlo, *Leonardo*, Salerno editrice, Rome, 1998

Vecce, Carlo, 'La Gualanda', in *Achademia Leonardi Vinci*, Vol.3, 1990

Venturi, Adolfo, 'La pittura del cinquecento', in *Storia dell'arte italiana*, Vol.IX, Hoepli, Milan, 1925

Verleyen, Cyriel, *The Theft of the Mona Lisa*, Chambers, Edinburgh, 1976

Verne, Jules, *Monna Lisa*, l'Herne, Paris, 1995

Vezzosi, Alessandro, *Leonardo da Vinci: Arte e scienza dell'universo*, Electa/Gallimard, Trieste, 1996

Viatte, Françoise, *Léonard de Vinci: Isabelle d'Este*, Éditions de la RMN, Paris, 1999

Vieuille, Maurice, 'Léonard et la Joconde', in Saint-Helme, *18e siècle et Directoire*, Presse Française, Paris, 1913

Villot, Frédéric (ed.), *Notice des tableaux exposés dans les galeries du Musée Nationale du Louvre*, 1ère partie, Écoles d'Italie, Musées nationaux, Paris, 1849

Walthéry, F. and Mittéï, *Natacha: l'Hôtesse et Monna Lisa*, Edition Jean Dupuis, Paris, 1979

West, Shearer (ed.), *Italian Culture in Northern Europe in the Eighteenth Century*, Cambridge University Press, 1998

White, Hayden, *Metahistory: The Historical Imagination in Nineteenth-Century Europe*, Johns Hopkins University Press, Baltimore, 1975

Wilde, Oscar, *The Works of Oscar Wilde*, Collins, London and Glasgow, 1948

Williams, Raymond, *The Long Revolution*, Harper, New York, 1966

Williams, Raymond, *Culture and Society*, The Hogarth Press, London, 1987

Wilson, Sarah, 'Fernand Léger, Art and Politics 1935–1955', in *Fernand Léger: The Later Years*, Whitechapel Art Gallery, London, 1987

Wilton, Andrew, 'Symbolism in Britain', in *The Age of Rossetti, Burne-Jones and Watts: Symbolism in Britain*, ed. Andrew Wilton and Robert Upstone, Tate Gallery Publishing, London, 1997

Yvaral, 'La Joconde est le sésame le plus subtil des portes du rêve', in *Arts*, 24 July 1981

Yvaral, *Mona Lisa synthétisée: Propositions pour un art digital* (exhibition catalogue), Pavillon des Arts, Paris, 14 June–8 September 1985

Zacharezuk, Jocelyne, *l'Escapade de Mona Lisa*, Castor Poche Flammarion, Paris, 1994

Zak, Solange, 'Les Randonnées de Mona Lisa', in *Bulletin de l'Association Léonard de Vinci*, No.16, March 1978

Zeri, Federico, *Derrière l'image*, Rivages, Paris, 1988

Zischler, Hanns, *Kafka va au cinéma*, trans. Olivier Mannoni, Cahiers du cinéma, Paris, 1996

Zola, Émile, 'Edouard Manet' (1867), in *Oeuvres Complètes*, Vol.12 (*Oeuvres critiques* 3), ed. Henri Mitterrand, Cercle du livre précieux, Paris, 1969

Zola, Émile *l'Assommoir*, Livre de Poche, Paris, 1979

Zöllner, Frank, 'Leonardo's Portrait of Mona Lisa del Giocondo', in *Gazette des beaux-arts*, Vol.135, No.1490, March 1993

Zorn, Christa, 'Aesthetic Intertextuality as Cultural Critique: Vernon Lee Rewrites History through Walter Pater's La "Gioconda"', in *Victorian Newsletter*, No.91, Spring 1997

INDEX

Index

Index

Leonardo da Vinci – *cont.*
Portrait of a Musician 37, 38; *St Anne with Virgin and Child* 12, 16, 26, 34, 55, 84, 120–1, 144, 184, 198–9; *St John* 12, 16, 26, 43, 60, 128, 185; *Self-Portrait* (?) 86; *Treatise on Painting* 13, 66–7; *Virgin of the Rocks* 55, 111, 138
Leonardo scomparso e ritrovato (exhibition, 1988) 25
Leonardo the Musical: A Portrait of Love 231
Lépicié: *Catalogue des tableaux du Roy* 43
Lévy-Dhurmer, Lucien 184
Lewinsky, Monica 266–7
Li'l Abner 209, 239
Livingston, Jay, and Evans, Ray: 'Mona Lisa' 227–9
Lomazzo, Gianpaolo 85
Longhi, Roberto 57
Lorrain, Claude 184
Lorrain, Jean: *Très russe* 160
Louis XII, of France 86
Louis XIII, of France 43
Louis XIV, of France 43
Louis XVI, of France 44
Louis Napoleon 45–6
Louvre, the 9, 10–11, 43–4, 45, 46–50, 51–3, 88, 143–4, 250, 251–2; paintings stolen 196; theft of *Mona Lisa* 175–6, 177, 178, 182–3, 188–9, 190, 205; website 11
Luini, Bernardino 144–5; *Flora* 41
Lyly, John 108

Maccari, Cesare: *Leonardo che ritrae la Gioconda* 85
McCarthy, Mary 246; *The Group* 233
Machiavelli, Niccolò 72, 73
Maglione, Milva 255
Magritte, René 216, 261; *La Joconde* 254
Maigret, Dr Étienne 274
Maillart, Diogène 183
Maiorino, Giancarlo 148
Major, John 266
Malaguzzi-Valeri, Francesco 126
Malevich, Kasimir: *Composition with Mona Lisa* 212–13
Mallarmé, Stéphane 103, 159

Malraux, André 56, 123, 243–4, 245, 247, 267, 278
Manet, Edouard 50; *Le Déjeuner sur l'herbe* 59, 258
Mangan, James Clarence 158
Mankowitz, Wolf: *Gioconda* 207
Mantegna, Andrea: *Mars and Venus* (*Mount Parnassus*) 190
Mao Tse-tung 266
Marchais, Georges 215
Marcy, Pierre: *Guide populaire dans les musées du Louvre* 131–2
Margat, Jean 258, 264; *Treatise of Jocondology* 272
Marinetti, Filippo 212; *The Futurist Manifesto* 211; *Le Roi Bombance* 211
Marriott's Renaissance hotels 264
Marty, André 211
Marzocco, Il 187
Massard, Jean-Baptiste 95
Massenet, Jules 103
Massoni & Moroni 262
Matin, Le 174, 189
Matisse, Henri 50
Maugham, William Somerset: *Christmas Holiday* 149–50, 195; *Of Human Bondage* 150
Mayhew, James: *Katie and the Mona Lisa* 238
Mazauric, Lucie 189
Medici, Francesco de' 82
Medici, Giuliano de' 20, 25, 27; portrait (Raphael) 40
Mekusa, Léon 269
Melzi, Francesco 29; *Portrait of Colombina* 27, 41–2, 204
Memling, Hans 37, 123; *Benedetto di Tommasi Portinari* 37; *Portrait of an Old Woman* 37; *St John and St Magdalen* 55
Ménageot, François-Guillaume 83
Mercier, Michèle 249
Mercure de France 147, 159
Merezhkovsky, Dmitri 24; *The Resurrection of the Gods* 118, 167–8, 170
Mérimée, Prosper: *Carmen* 119
Messimy, Adolphe 177
Metatools 264
Metzinger, Jean: *Contrasts* 212

Index

Index

Index